Citrix XenApp™ Platinum Edition Advanced Concepts: The Official Guide

ABOUT THE AUTHOR

Citrix Product Development Team engages in the design and development of application virtualization technology solutions that enable secure, on-demand access to information and applications.

This book provides a summary of information regarding advanced concepts of the Citrix XenApp Platinum Edition. To further your knowledge, Citrix offers a full curriculum of structured educational opportunities, including instructor-led training through Citrix Authorized Learning Centers, eLearning, and Citrix Certification exams.

For in-depth training on Citrix products, or to prepare to earn your Citrix Certified Administrator (CCA), Citrix Certified Enterprise Administrator (CCEA), or Citrix Certified Integration Architect (CCIA) certification, we recommend that you visit www.citrix.com/edu.

Citrix XenApp™ Platinum Edition Advanced Concepts: The Official Guide

CITRIX PRODUCT DEVELOPMENT TEAM

New York Chicago San Francisco
Lisbon London Madrid Mexico City Milan
New Delhi San Juan Seoul Singapore Sydney Toronto

The McGraw-Hill Companies

Cataloging-in-Publication Data is on file with the Library of Congress

McGraw-Hill books are available at special quantity discounts to use as premiums and sales promotions, or for use in corporate training programs. To contact a special sales representative, please visit the Contact Us page at www.mhprofessional.com.

Citrix XenApp™ Platinum Edition Advanced Concepts: The Official Guide

1234567890 DOC DOC 0198

ISBN 978-0-07-154381-1
MHID 0-07-154381-3

Sponsoring Editor
Wendy Rinaldi

Editorial Supervisor
Jody McKenzie

Project Manager
Aparna Shukla
(International Typesetting and Composition)

Acquisitions Coordinator
Mandy Canales

Technical Editor
Jennifer Lang

Copy Editor
Andy Saff

Proofreader
Divya Kapoor

Indexer
Broccoli Information Management

Production Supervisor
George Anderson

Composition
International Typesetting and Composition

Illustration
International Typesetting and Composition

Art Director, Cover
Jeff Weeks

CONTENTS

Part II

XenApp Platinum Edition: Administration, Maintenance, and Troubleshooting

Part III

Appendices

FOREWORD

The forces of our dynamic world are creating more and more distance between users and applications across technical, physical, and organizational dimensions. No matter how fast computing evolves, it struggles to keep up with the even more dynamic pace of business change in the 21st century—globalization is shifting work to where the talent lives; consolidation is rampant as industries and companies seek to reduce costs; governments are tightening controls on how digital information is used; disruption caused by disasters is increasingly common; and the Echo Boomers, the children of the Baby Boomers, are taking computing to new heights of user freedom and control. As a result, users are becoming more decentralized for greater freedom and workplace flexibility, while applications are heading in the opposite direction—becoming more centralized to achieve lower management costs and greater data security.

Nearly every business process today relies on applications. As information technology (IT) organizations struggle to keep pace with the demands of business, application delivery is a major priority for CIOs around the world. Industry experts agree the time is right to make the move from static application deployment to dynamic application delivery. Citrix offers a new and different approach—Citrix Delivery Center—the first solution on the market that delivers applications and desktops to any user, any time, anywhere from a secure central location.

Citrix Delivery Center's market-leading application delivery technologies enable IT to improve agility dramatically while enabling the best performance and highest security at the lowest cost. Citrix Delivery Center is dynamic infrastructure that transforms the datacenter from a static, production-oriented facility to a dynamic, service-oriented delivery center.

This book is designed to help you plan, deploy, and administer XenApp Platinum Edition, the most complete solution for meeting the needs of application delivery and helping your enterprise to run more cost-efficiently and grow faster. By providing secure, easy, and instant access to information any time from anywhere using any device, XenApp enables your employees and customers to realize the full potential of an application delivery infrastructure. XenApp Platinum Edition represents the most comprehensive application delivery platform available today to enable flexible, mobile, and secure access to even the most widely dispersed enterprises.

Components comprising the XenApp Platinum Edition include the industry standard for application virtualization, Citrix XenApp (the new name of Citrix Presentation Server); the fastest-growing enterprise single sign-on solution, Citrix Password Manager; and a market-leading Secure Sockets Layer (SSL) Virtual Private Network (VPN), the Citrix Access Gateway.

I am very proud of the Citrix Product Development Team for researching, validating, and documenting the contents of this book. I am grateful to them for their expertise and proud to contribute this foreword.

Although a dynamic application delivery infrastructure simplifies the complexity of information systems, successful implementation requires careful planning and skillful administration. That's what this book is all about, and anyone looking to deliver the best end-to-end virtualization solution to work more productively and run their IT departments at a lower cost will benefit from reading it.

— Keith Turnbull, Vice President of World-Wide Product Development
for the Application Virtualization Group for Citrix

ACKNOWLEDGMENTS

We would like to thank the following departments within Citrix Systems, Inc., for their contribution to the content of the book:

- Product Development
- Technical Communication
- Consulting Services
- Technical Support
- System Engineering

A special thanks to all of the test engineers within Product Development for researching, validating, and documenting the content for this book. We would also like to extend our deepest appreciation to Wendy, Jody, Mandy, Aparna, and the rest of the McGraw-Hill team for all the hard work, patience, and dedication that they have provided to ensure the completion of this book.

In addition to Citrix's help, Tim Reeser, Alan Wood, Steve Kaplan, and Andy Jones contributed through their efforts on previous editions.

INTRODUCTION

This edition of the *Advanced Concepts Guide* expands and updates previous editions to focus on Citrix XenApp (the new name for Citrix Presentation Server) 4.5, Platinum Edition. This book is an ongoing effort to provide a comprehensive book encompassing best practices and recommendations for application delivery.

How This Book Differs from *Citrix Access Suite for Windows Server 2003: The Official Guide*

McGraw-Hill's companion book is written for two audiences: business decision makers who evaluate enterprise IT options, and the IT administrators responsible for implementing and maintaining access infrastructure. It covers both the technical and business requirements of implementing a Citrix access platform capable of accommodating thousands of users running their desktop applications from central datacenters. Topics such as Windows Terminal Server 2003, project and organizational management, and various third-party add-on applications are all discussed at length.

This guide is strictly a technical book focused on the planning, configuration, administration, and troubleshooting of Citrix XenApp Platinum Edition. It provides in-depth analyses of three Platinum Edition components: Citrix Presentation Server, Citrix Access Gateway, and Citrix Password Manager. This book is written for experienced IT administrators who want to improve their Citrix environments by incorporating best practices.

How This Book Is Organized

The book is divided into three main parts. Part I covers the concepts, planning, and configuration of XenApp Platinum Edition. It is designed to assist in the pre-deployment of the different components. It contains best practices and explanations of methods used by Citrix engineers in the planning and configuration of these components within different types of environments. Part I also includes a chapter covering security issues and guideline concerns in a Citrix environment, with a focus on security related to the Platinum Edition components.

Part II presents best practices for the administration, maintenance, and troubleshooting of XenApp Platinum Edition. It is designed to assist in the daily administration and maintenance of Platinum Edition components. Part II is targeted to administrators who need to fine-tune their systems as well as troubleshoot issues that arise within the Citrix environment.

Part III comprises the appendices. Appendix A details error messages, including Independent Management Architecture (IMA) error codes and event log warning and error messages intended to help in troubleshooting and resolving problems with XenApp. Appendix B is a table showing all registered Citrix ports. Appendix C outlines the hardware used in the Citrix eLabs for testing XenApp.

We also include Note, Tip, Important, and Caution elements to supply additional detail to the text. A Note is meant to provide information when the general flow of the discussion is concentrating on a different area or is not as detailed as the Note itself. A Tip is a specific way to do or implement something being discussed. An Important is a specific piece of information that is emphasized in order to catch the reader's attention. A Caution is meant to alert the reader to watch out for a potential problem.

When registry entries are discussed, we have abbreviated the keys to save space. For example, HKEY_LOCAL_MACHINE is abbreviated throughout the text to HKLM.

Throughout the book, we include appropriate references to further documentation that can be accessed from http://support.citrix.com.

PART I

An Introduction to Citrix XenApp, Platinum Edition

CHAPTER 1

Introduction to Citrix XenApp, Platinum Edition and Components

Dynamic application delivery is becoming a major priority for CIOs around the world. Users are becoming more decentralized while IT organizations strive to become more centralized to achieve lower management costs and greater data security. Application delivery gives users access to the information required to build business by providing easy, secure, and instant access to enterprise information and applications from anywhere, using any device or connection.

In addition to providing this ubiquitous access, the Citrix Delivery Center utilizes an effective application delivery infrastructure strategy that both simplifies IT complexity and strengthens administrative control. Application delivery is more efficient, secure, and cost-effective. The Citrix Delivery Center offers organizations the easiest and most cost-effective way to provide secure access to enterprise applications and information on demand. The Citrix Delivery Center ensures a consistent user experience anywhere, on any device or connection, while allowing IT staffs to deliver, manage, monitor, and control enterprise resources centrally.

This chapter introduces Citrix XenApp and the components that comprise it: Citrix XenApp, Citrix Access Gateway Advanced Access Control and Citrix Password Manager. It also introduces Citrix NetScaler, which, while not part of XenApp, Platinum Edition, is often simultaneously deployed to enhance the users' access experience by maximizing the performance of their organization's web applications.

CITRIX XENAPP, PLATINUM EDITION

Citrix XenApp, Platinum Edition is an integrated infrastructure for delivering applications and information resources as IT services to any user, regardless of device, connection, or location. Each product component—Citrix XenApp, Citrix Access Gateway (Citrix XenApp SmartAccess,) Citrix Password Manager, and Citrix EdgeSight—adds to the technology portfolio to solve myriad application delivery challenges for an organization.

Although the following is not a comprehensive list, it contains some of the benefits provided by Citrix XenApp, Platinum Edition:

- **Citrix XenApp** XenApp lowers the cost of IT and greatly improves scalability, adaptability, and predictability through application centralization. Citrix XenApp includes Citrix Conferencing Manager. Conferencing Manager provides intuitive application conferencing to eliminate the geographical distance between team members, thus increasing the productivity of meetings and enabling easy collaboration.
- **Citrix Access Gateway** This feature provides a secure, always-on, single point of access to all applications and protocols. SmartAccess (the Advanced Access Control option) manages both what can be accessed and what actions are permitted based on the user's role, location, and Advanced End-Point Analysis. *Advanced End-Point Analysis* automatically reconfigures the level of access as users roam among devices, locations, and connections.

- **Citrix Password Manager** Password Manager centralizes password management with IT for greater control, strengthens application security and simplifies user experience by providing single sign-on access regardless of how or where users connect to their applications. Password Manager lowers help desk costs by enabling users to reset their own Windows password or unlock their account through Citrix Web Interface. Federated logons are now possible to all types of trusted-partner applications (Windows, Web, and host-based), delivered by XenApp and accessed through Web Interface.

Citrix XenApp Editions

Citrix XenApp enables application virtualization using a centralized and secure architecture. XenApp enables IT to deploy and manage applications centrally while providing secure access to these resources for users anywhere, on any device, and on any network.

Citrix XenApp is available in three different editions: Advanced, Enterprise, and Platinum.

Citrix XenApp, Advanced Edition

Citrix XenApp, Advanced Edition, provides server-side application virtualization and the fundamental functionality for centralizing and delivering Windows-based applications in mission-critical environments. Feature highlights include the Web Interface for Citrix XenApp, user shadowing, ActiveSync support, Support for local TWAIN devices, virtual IP support, bidirectional audio, Novell NDS support and client device support.

Citrix XenApp, Enterprise Edition

Citrix XenApp, Enterprise Edition, delivers a wide variety of mission-critical Windows applications using client-side and server-side application virtualization technologies. Enterprise Edition includes all the features of the Advanced Edition and adds additional features required for enterprise management. These extended features include Resource Manager, Installation Manager, a plug-in for Microsoft Operations Manager, and Network Manager.

Citrix XenApp, Platinum Edition

Citrix XenApp, Platinum Edition, is a strategic end-to-end application delivery system that virtualizes all Windows-based applications, both on the client-side and server-side, for all users at all locations, providing the highest performance and highest data security. Platinum Edition includes all the features of Enterprise Edition and adds critical capabilities for application performance monitoring, SSL VPN remote access with SmartAccess control and single sign-on application security.

Table 1-1 is a comparative matrix of the three different editions and enumerates the feature support available with each edition.

	Citrix XenApp, Advanced Edition	Citrix XenApp, Enterprise Edition	Citrix XenApp, Platinum Edition
APPLICATION DELIVERY			
Server-side Application Virtualization	x	x	x
Client-side Application Virtualization		x	x
Application Hub		x	x
ADVANCED APPLICATION COMPATIBILITY			
Isolation 2.0		x	x
Application Isolation Environment		x	x
Virtual IP Support	x	x	x
Support for local TWAIN devices	x	x	x
Support for ActiveSync	x	x	x
Bidirectional Audio	x	x	x
Support for UNIX Applications		x	x
END-USER EXPERIENCE			
EasyCall			x
SpeedScreen™ Progressive Display	x	x	x
SpeedScreen Latency Reduction Manager	x	x	x
SpeedScreen Browser Acceleration	x	x	x
SpeedScreen Multimedia Acceleration	x	x	x
SpeedScreen Flash Acceleration	x	x	x
SpeedScreen Image Acceleration	x	x	x
Compression	x	x	x

Table 1-1. Citrix XenApp Server Features

	Citrix XenApp, Advanced Edition	Citrix XenApp, Enterprise Edition	Citrix XenApp, Platinum Edition
Priority Packet Tagging	x	x	x
Dynamic Session Resizing	x	x	x
Workspace Control	x	x	x
Session Reliability	x	x	x
Auto Client Reconnect	x	x	x
Always-on SSL VPN access			x
Application Publishing	x	x	x
Content Publishing	x	x	x
Content Redirection	x	x	x
Seamless Windows	x	x	x
Desktop Integration via Program Neighborhood Agent	x	x	x
Conferencing Manager	x	x	x
Pass-Through Authentication	x	x	x
Microsoft Client Support	x	x	x
Web Interface for Citrix XenApp	x	x	x
Multi-Lingual User Interface Support for virtualized applications	x	x	x
Multi Language Supporting in Web Interface	x	x	x
Local Resource Mapping	x	x	x
Local Drive Access	x	x	x
Local Printer Access	x	x	x
PRINTING			
Universal Printer Driver 3	x	x	x
MANAGEMENT			
Application Performance Monitoring (Citrix EdgeSight)			x

Table 1-1. Citrix XenApp Server Features *(continued)*

	Citrix XenApp, Advanced Edition	Citrix XenApp, Enterprise Edition	Citrix XenApp, Platinum Edition
Health Assistant		x	x
Configuration Logging	x	x	x
Active Directory Federation Services(ADFS) support	x	x	x
Client Backup URL	x	x	x
Connection Policies	x	x	x
System Monitoring and Reporting via Resource Manager for Citrix XenApp		x	x
Enhanced Management Experience	x	x	x
Extended Shadowing Support	x	x	x
Automatic Client Updates	x	x	x
Directory Support (Microsoft's Active Directory and Novell's eDirectory)	x	x	x
Installation Manager for Citrix XenApp		x	x
Integration with Network Management Consoles		x	x
Delegated Administration	x	x	x
Printer Management	x	x	x
Centralized Management Console	x	x	x
System Monitoring and Analysis		x	x
Report Center		x	x
Remote Server Management	x	x	x
Connection Control	x	x	x
Management Pack for Microsoft Operations Manager (MOM) 2005	x	x	x

Table 1-1. Citrix XenApp Server Features *(continued)*

	Citrix XenApp, Advanced Edition	Citrix XenApp, Enterprise Edition	Citrix XenApp, Platinum Edition
PERFORMANCE AND SCALABILITY			
Enterprise-Class Scalability	x	x	x
Support for Windows Server 2003 x64 Edition	x	x	x
Load throttling	x	x	x
Enterprise Load Balancing	x	x	x
CPU Utilization Management		x	x
Virtual Memory Optimization		x	x
Multiple Farm Support	x	x	x
SECURITY AND COMPLIANCE			
Application User Load	x	x	x
SmartAuditor			x
SmartAccess (Powered by the Citrix Access Gateway)			x
Universal SSL VPN — supports all applications and protocols			x
Integrated endpoint scanning and extensible endpoint analysis			x
Single Sign-On			x
Self-service Password Reset and Account Unlock			x
Hot Desktop			x
Advanced Encryption Standard Support	x	x	x
Trusted Server Configuration	x	x	x
Two-Factor Authentication Support	x	x	x
Smartcard Support(including Common Access Card (CAC))	x	x	x

Table 1-1. Citrix XenApp Server Features *(continued)*

	Citrix XenApp, Advanced Edition	Citrix XenApp, Enterprise Edition	Citrix XenApp, Platinum Edition
Enhanced Smartcard Support	x	x	x
Secure Gateway for Citrix XenApp	x	x	x
TLS/SSL	x	x	x
Novell Directory Services (NDS) Support	x	x	x
HP Protect Tool Support	x	x	x
USER CONNECTIVITY			
Non-Administrator Client Installation	x	x	x
Browser-only SSL VPN access			x
Web Interface for Remote Access	x	x	x
Web Interface for Microsoft SharePoint™	x	x	x
Universal Device Access	x	x	x
Microsoft Remote Desktop Client Support	x	x	x

Table 1-1. Citrix XenApp Server Features *(continued)*

Citrix Conferencing Manager

Presentations and conferencing have evolved from one-way presentation broadcasts and web conferencing to full collaboration and application conferencing. The trend toward "virtual" teams that work together from remote locations and different time zones is expanding because such teams can reduce overhead costs, drive new business, and optimize productivity.

The lack of information and communication systems' flexibility are often obstacles to enabling the on-demand enterprise because remote people cannot securely connect to the business information they need. *Citrix Conferencing Manager* remedies this by adding intuitive application conferencing to XenApp, helping to increase the productivity of meetings and enabling easy collaboration from different geographic locations.

Citrix Conferencing Manager integrates three components: a Microsoft Exchange/Outlook calendar form; a Citrix Conferencing Manager interface that initiates, cancels, and manages the users and applications of the conferences; and the XenApp session shadowing features. These three components form an intuitive interface by which users create and join a collaborative conference session among multiple people. Teams can share application sessions, work together on documents of all kinds, and conduct online training, regardless of the location of individual team members, the access devices, or network connections they're using.

CITRIX ACCESS GATEWAY

Citrix Access Gateway is a universal Secure Sockets Layer (SSL) virtual private network (VPN) appliance that provides a secure, single point of access to all applications and protocols. Access Gateway is deployed in an organization's DMZ and secures all traffic with standards-based SSL. Remote users connect via a web-downloaded and -updated client, enjoying a rich, desk-like experience. Access Gateway delivers an access solution that is both extremely secure and easy to deploy and use.

Citrix Access Gateway makes any enterprise resource available through a single point of access, securely delivered over the Internet using the best features of IPSec and SSL VPNs to standards-based security—without the need to configure client-side software. IT administrators simply enable network resources to be presented through Citrix Access Gateway and then configure access control based on each user's business requirements.

Advanced Access Control

Advanced Access Control is a software option that increases control over how information is accessed and which actions the user can perform, such as print, save, launch, and view.

SmartAccess

The *SmartAccess* feature of Advanced Access Control delivers advanced policy-based control of XenApp applications and individual features, such as print and save.

SmoothRoaming

The *SmoothRoaming* component of Advanced Access Control enables users to move seamlessly between access scenarios and devices, automatically adapting access to the configuration policy settings.

CITRIX PASSWORD MANAGER

Managing passwords can be problematic. Users tend to forget multiple passwords, select easily guessed words for passwords, or store passwords in insecure places. These problems affect employee productivity, increase support costs, and even threaten system security.

Citrix Password Manager provides password security and Single Sign On access to Windows-, web-, proprietary-, and host-based applications running in the Citrix environment. Citrix Password Manager drives down the costs and confusion in managing multiple passwords while improving network security. Users authenticate once and Citrix Password Manager does the rest, monitoring all password-related events and automating end-user tasks, including logon and password changes. Citrix Password Manager simplifies computing for the end user, who has just one secure password to log on everywhere. This, in turn, helps to reduce the cost of supporting password problems and frees IT staff for more strategic projects.

NOTE One large financial institution we worked with used to have 20.4 percent of its help-desk calls related to password issues (this is about 5 percentage points below the average). After mandating that users implement complex passwords, the ratio of help-desk–related password calls fell by half. Why? There were two reasons for this decrease. Some users simply gave up trying to access certain applications. The primary reason, though, was that virtually everyone compromised authentication security by keeping a list of his or her passwords (usually in their upper-right desk drawer or on a sticky note attached to a monitor). Implementing Citrix Password Manager enabled these users to virtually eliminate password-related help-desk requests while significantly improving security.

Citrix Password Manager is comprised of three components:

- **Citrix Password Manager Agent** This 32-bit agent runs on Citrix XenApp or on a local client workstation. The agent acts as an intermediary between users and the applications that require authentication.
- **Citrix Password Manager Console** This centralized management tool is used to configure the central credential store and control the settings and features available to the agent.
- **Central Credential Store** This is the central location where copies of users' credential records and agent settings files are stored. The central credential store is implemented using a shared folder (file synchronization) or Microsoft Active Directory. The agent synchronizes its local store with the central store, enabling users to access and maintain their credentials from any workstation.

Once a user has logged in and authenticated to a directory service, the agent intercepts any future password requests with a query, asking whether the user would like the password manager to manage this password. If the user answers yes, then the password information is stored in the agent's local store and handed back to the client workstation when the workstation queries for that password again. Depending on configurations in Citrix Password Manager Console, the agent's local store can synchronize this new information with a central credential store.

Citrix Password Manager enhances security by centralizing security policies, providing an encrypted file for each user's credentials, and allowing IT administrators to generate automatically passwords that are more difficult to crack. They can also change the passwords more frequently.

CITRIX NETSCALER

NetScaler is a network appliance that optimizes the delivery of mission-critical web applications. NetScaler has a Transmission Control Protocol (TCP) stack built from the ground up that delivers unparalleled performance. It is a reliable integrated platform for load balancing, caching, compression, SSL acceleration, and security. NetScaler puts a great deal of high-performance function into a small integrated package, which is easy both to install and manage.

Load Balancer

NetScaler's base function is a load balancer. Administrators configure their DNS server, so their domain resolves to a virtual server (*vserver*) IP address owned by the NetScaler. Web-browser Hypertext Transfer Protocol Secure (HTTPS) requests arriving at the NetScaler-owned vserver address are decrypted, if necessary, and buffered until a complete, well-formed request is available. This request is examined as a potential attack. The validated requests are then sent to a service on a real server.

NetScaler monitors the health and load-on services. These monitors—as well as rules based on cookies, uniform resource locators (URLs), or user-agent—can determine which service is selected. NetScaler can also rate limit services and prioritize the resulting request queues. In addition, where needed, various persistence options ensure that sessions started with a service will continue with that particular service.

In addition to load-balancing local pools of servers, the Global Server Load Balancing feature enables load balancing across sites.

Application Accelerator

Integrated with the load-balancing functions previously described, NetScaler has several ways of improving response time and scalability. These include SSL offload, compression, caching, and protocol optimizations.

Secure Sockets Layer (SSL)

A Secure Sockets Layer (SSL) GET request can take up to 40 times the central processing unit (CPU) that an unencrypted GET takes. Offloading all the extra work associated with SSL can give back large amounts of capacity to servers.

Compression

Compression helps clients who must use wide area networks (WANs) to reach their servers. By reducing the number of packets that need to be transmitted across a narrow bandwidth, long latency, or error-prone links, compression enables such clients to see better response time. Reducing bandwidth demand can also save IT organizations money spent on increasing bandwidth. NetScaler does Hypertext Transfer Protocol (HTTP) object compression, TCP compression, and differential compression. This last feature reduces transmitted data by divisors of up to 40 by sending only differences from previously sent data.

Caching

NetScaler *caching* can reduce the load on the entire server infrastructure. Data provided by the NetScaler cache do not need processing by a web server, application server, or database server. NetScaler can do Request for Comment (RFC)-compliant caching. These are conservative rules that ensure that no client ever gets stale data. NetScaler also provides a *dynamic caching* feature that lets a customer who knows the application and the way that the enterprise uses the application to exploit this knowledge aggressively to improve performance. Dynamic caching enables the customer to set rules for cacheability that go beyond RFC compliance to allow caching of frequently accessed data that, while technically dynamic, are infrequently changed.

Protocol Optimizations

NetScaler protocol optimizations, such as *Keep-alive* and *FastRamp,* reduce the need for extra waits for unproductive protocol packets to travel over the WAN. *Request Switching* greatly reduces the number of connections a server must manage. *TCP Buffering* can reduce them even more.

Security

NetScaler has many ways of detecting attacks and protecting the continuous operation of applications. Many forms of attack are partial requests that tie up memory resources waiting for the completion of the requests. Because servers see only complete and vetted requests, these attacks end at the NetScaler. NetScaler can filter for malicious content.

Perl Scripts

If someone writes a Perl script to issue valid GET requests against a site, NetScaler can protect the site's operation. It does this by recognizing that such an attack is under way and challenging clients to execute a JavaScript program. Unless the attacker has provided a JavaScript interpreter along with his attack script, he is unable to respond correctly. Correct responders get cookies that entitle their request to go to the head of the line. The *script kiddies,* or would-be hackers, must languish in the tail of the queue.

SSL VPN

NetScaler provides a high-capacity SSL VPN that supports web, client/server, file-system access and terminal access. It supports common two-factor authentication schemes, such as SecureID and Secure Computing. NetScaler can authenticate via an internal or external Lightweight Directory Access Protocol (LDAP) server, as well as external Radius, Terminal Access Controller Access-Control System (TACACS)+ servers. NetScaler controls access to specific applications by administrator-defined policies that can check all relevant security factors. These include execution of policy-driven client checks.

CHAPTER 2

Server Configuration Design and Recommendations

This chapter covers general recommendations for server hardware and operating system (OS) configurations you should consider before deploying Citrix XenApp for Windows.

HARDWARE CONFIGURATIONS

In multiprocessor configurations, Citrix recommends a Redundant Array of Independent Disks (RAID) setup. Hard disks are the most common type of hardware failure. Taking steps to alleviate the impact of a hard disk failure is typically addressed with a RAID 1 (mirroring) and RAID 5 (striped set with distributed parity) configuration based on cost considerations. See the *Citrix Presentation Server 4.5 with Feature Pack 1 Administrator's Guide* for more information regarding available RAID configurations. If RAID is not an option, a fast Serial Attached Small Computer System Interface (SCSI) (SAS) or a SCSI Ultra-320 drive is recommended. Faster hard disks are inherently more responsive and may eliminate or curtail disk bottlenecks.

For quad and eight-way servers, use a solid state disk or install at least two disk controllers: one for OS disk usage and the other to store applications and temporary files. Isolate the OS as much as possible, with no applications installed on its disk controller. Distribute hard-drive access loads as evenly as possible across the disk controllers.

NOTE In general, Citrix has found that dual-processor (dual-core) deployments provide not only overall efficiency, but also a generally lower total cost of ownership. However, each environment varies in terms of situation, supportability, applications, and the like, so the decision relating to the number of processors should be based on specific requirements. For results of Citrix eLabs testing, see the section "Effects of Varying the Number of CPUs of XenApp."

The sizes of the partitions and hard drives are dependent on both the number of users connecting to XenApp and the applications being used on the server. Microsoft Internet Explorer, Microsoft Office, and other applications can cause user profile directory sizes to increase to hundreds of megabytes. Large numbers of user profiles can use gigabytes of disk space on the server. You must have enough disk space for these profiles on the server and retain a sufficient amount of space for temporary files used by the OS to maintain system stability.

NOTE Roaming profiles and permanent user data should be stored on a centralized file server, System Area Network (SAN), or network-attached storage (NAS) that can adequately support the environment. In addition, this storage medium should be logically located near the XenApp servers so that minimal router hops are required and login times are not unnecessarily increased.

Improve Logon Performance—Enabling Disk Write Caching

An improvement may occur in simultaneous logon performance if disk write caching is enabled on the server's RAID controller, if available. A common misconception is that heavy usage of the data store causes logons to be slow. The logon process is not dependent on the data store; logons are dependent on dynamic information and are handled by a data collector in the farm.

Effects of Varying the Number of CPUs of XenApp

The number of users that XenApp can support depends on several factors, including the following:

- The server's hardware specifications
- The applications used (because of the applications' central processing unit [CPU] and memory requirements)
- The amount of user input being processed by the applications
- The maximum desired resource usage on the server (for example, 90 percent CPU usage or 80 percent memory usage)

This section discusses the increase in user capacity when CPUs with multiple cores are added. First, the Citrix benchmarking test for user capacity, known as ICAMark, is described.

Citrix ICAMark

Citrix ICAMark is an internal tool that is based on the Citrix Server Test Kit (CSTK) and used by Citrix Engineering for benchmarking purposes to quantify the optimal number of simulated client sessions that can be connected to a XenApp server with acceptable performance. Extending the number of concurrent simulated users beyond the optimal results causes a decrease in performance and may impact end-user experience.

The test simulates users constantly typing and performing actions in Microsoft Excel, Microsoft Access, and Microsoft PowerPoint. Other applications can utilize more or less memory and CPU than Microsoft Office and therefore could produce different results. Note also that the simulated users in this test are constantly typing into these applications and may be considered more "rigorous" than normal users.

In this test, a step size "number of users" is defined as 10. During the course of the test, after the first 10 users are logged in, ICAMark launches simulated user scripts on all 10 sessions. Each script opens Microsoft PowerPoint and simulates the creation of a presentation, including copies and deletion of slides, font changes, and presentation viewing. Once the PowerPoint phase is complete, PowerPoint is closed and Microsoft Access is opened. The script then simulates the creation of an Access database, including a table, query, and form, with data manipulation. Once the Access phase is complete, a Microsoft Excel spreadsheet is created and data populated into the spreadsheet are used to do a number of calculations and create charts.

Based on how long the scripts take to complete, an ICAMark score is calculated. For this test, a score of 80 has been determined as the optimal load for a server. This means the server has enough additional CPU and memory resources to handle spikes in performance. When the test iteration score drops below 80, additional users added to the server consume more resources, producing lower test scores and slower performance.

Number of CPUs Effect on User Capacity

The benchmark test was performed with the following:

Server:

- Dual quad-core processors (3.0GHz Xeon with 8MB L2 Cache)
- 6x 73GB 2.5 inch SAS 10K RPM
- 64GB RAM
- 16GB page file
- XenApp 4.5
- Microsoft Windows Server 2003 64-bit
- Microsoft Office 2003 Professional

Clients:

- Intel XEON 2.8GHz Processor
- 1GB RAM
- Citrix Program Neighborhood Client version 10.0
- Microsoft Windows Server 2003 32-bit

Tests were performed by keeping the hardware static and disabling processors on the server.

The following results were collected. Figure 2-1 and Table 2-1 show the effects of multiple CPUs on user capacity.

The results conclude that the performance of eight CPU cores enabled and 417 concurrent simulated users is equivalent to the performance of four CPU cores enabled with 323 concurrent simulated users, which is equivalent to the performance of two CPU cores enabled with 202 concurrent simulated users.

Moving from a dual to a quad-core processor system equates to a 60 percent increase in performance, while moving from a quad to an eight-core processor system equates to only a 29 percent increase in performance. In other words, as CPU cores are added to the server, the performance of the OS increases less. As in this scenario, server scalability is not linear with the number of processors and it drops off sharply between four to eight CPU cores.

All tests were run on Windows Server 2003 64-bit. In this scenario, a 32-bit OS is limited by the amount of kernel memory available. Similar testing was conducted using this scenario on a 32-bit operating system. The results showed that the system was unable to

# of CPUs	# of Cores	# of Simulated Users	% Performance Increase
1	2	202	Not applicable
2	4	323	60
2	8	417	29

Table 2-1. User Capacity Benchmark

scale beyond 200 users. This architecture limitation with 32-bit was worked around by using 32-bit and 64-bit applications on a 64-bit OS.

NOTE When sizing XenApp, the number of actual users per server varies based on the applications deployed.

Performance Analysis of Blades versus Standalone Servers

As datacenters grow larger to support thousands of users, datacenter space becomes increasingly expensive. Space, power, and heating, ventilation, and air conditioning (HVAC) all come at a price, prompting many organizations to look for ways to reduce the number of servers and the amount of rack space associated with housing the servers. To this end, Dell, HP, IBM, and others have developed blade servers that support higher

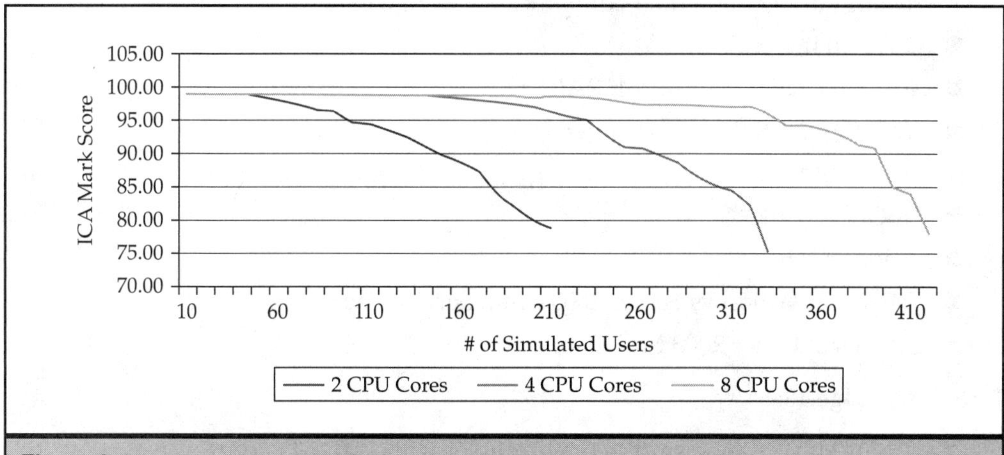

Figure 2-1. User capacity benchmark

Server	Dell PowerEdge 1955	Dell PowerEdge 1855
Results (Simulated Users)	382	167

Table 2-2. Number of Users Supported by the Blade Server and a Standalone Server

density than previous form factors. This density provides tremendous savings in rack space and datacenter space. Using the Single Server Scalability test, designed to quantify the maximum number of client sessions that can be connected to a XenApp with acceptable performance, Table 2-2 shows the number of users supported by a blade server versus a standalone server.

Results

The results of the Single Server Scalability test show that the performance of the Dell PowerEdge 1955 system servicing 382 concurrent users is equivalent to the performance of the Dell PowerEdge 1855 system servicing 167 concurrent users with the variables defined in this test scenario. Extending the number of concurrent users beyond the recommendation in this test environment would result in decreased performance and impact the end-user experience on XenApp. When XenApp is being sized, the number of actual users per server varies based on the applications deployed.

The benchmark test was performed with the following:

Servers:

Dell PowerEdge 1955

- Dual (3.0GHz Xeon dual-core processor 5160 with 2MB L2 cache per core)
- 1333 MHz front-side bus
- 73GB HDD SAS 10K RPM, RAID 1
- Dell SAS 5/iR RAID controller
- 16GB RAM
- 16GB page file
- XenApp 4.5
- Microsoft Windows Server 2003 64-bit Service Pack 1
- Microsoft Office 2003 Professional

Dell PowerEdge 1855

- Dual (3.0GHz Xeon single-core processor with 1MB L2 cache)
- 800 MHz front-side bus

- 36GB HDD U320 SCSI 15K RPM, RAID 1
- Dell PERC 4/IM RAID controller
- 8GB RAM
- 8GB page file
- XenApp 4.5
- Microsoft Windows Server 2003 64-bit Service Pack 1
- Microsoft Office 2003 Professional

Clients:

- Intel XEON 2.8GHz processor
- 1GB RAM
- Citrix Program Neighborhood Client version 9.00.32649
- Microsoft Windows Server 2003 Service Pack 1

Advantages of Windows Server 2003 X64 Edition and Citrix XenApp X64

This section discusses the performance and scalability improvements you may realize when using XenApp for Microsoft Windows Server 2003 x64 Edition. Items discussed include performance improvements in the x64 OS.

Increased Kernel Memory Availability

In 32-bit Windows, memory is limited to the 32-bit address space, thus limiting the amount of virtual memory that can be directly addressed to 4GB (232). This 4GB of addressable memory is divided into two equal parts: 2GB allocated to processes and 2GB allocated to the operating system that is used for the kernel memory, system cache, and drivers.

The /PAE switch in the Boot.ini file can be enabled to increase the physical memory on the server. This switch allows Windows Server 2003 to take advantage of the Physical Address Extensions (PAEs) of x86 processors. Using the /PAE switch can be beneficial when servers are not kernel memory–bound and the published applications use large amounts of memory. The memory enabled with the /PAE switch is allocated to the user space while the kernel is still limited to 2GB. There is also a small kernel memory cost because the operating system needs to track this additional memory in the form of Page Table Entries (PTEs). Note that the /PAE switch requires programmers to use the Address Windows Extensions (AWE) application programming interface (API) to take advantage of the memory.

One of the most obvious advantages of using XenApp x64 with Windows Server 2003 x64 Edition is the increased virtual address space. Windows Server 2003 x64 Edition can address 16TB of virtual memory. This 16TB is divided into equal parts of 8TB of

Physical Memory Limits	**32-Bit**	**64-Bit**
Windows Server 2003, Standard Edition	4GB	32GB
Windows Server 2003, Enterprise Edition	64GB	1TB
Windows Server 2003, Datacenter Edition	64GB	1TB
General Memory Limits	**32-Bit**	**64-Bit**
Total virtual address space (based on a single process)	4GB	16TB
Virtual address space per 32-bit process	2GB*	4GB*
Virtual address space per 64-bit process	Not applicable	8TB
Paged pool	470MB	128GB
Nonpaged pool	256MB	128GB
System PTE	660MB to 900MB	128GB

* Higher if compiled with /LARGEADDRESSAWARE.

Table 2-3. Limitations of Windows Server 2003 Running on a 32-Bit Platform Versus Windows Server 2003 Running on a 64-Bit Platform

virtual address space for applications and 8TB for the operating system. Based on this increase in available user and kernel memory, XenApp can be expected to reach new scalability plateaus without architectural limitations getting in the way. Table 2-3 compares the limitations of Windows Server 2003 running on a 32-bit platform to Windows Server 2003 running on a 64-bit platform.

Server Consolidation by Scaling Up

32-bit Windows servers are limited in their ability to scale up. This limitation is based on the kernel memory constraint. Now that 64-bit has eliminated the kernel memory constraint, XenApp x64 can scale up to unprecedented levels.

The advantages of scaling up with larger, more powerful servers revolve around the lower cost associated with managing fewer servers. Server consolidation leads to cost savings by

- Allowing for fewer administrators to maintain physical servers
- Reducing overhead in managing hotfixes, service packs, and other updates
- Utilizing a smaller footprint in the datacenter, which lowers power and space consumption
- Lowering software costs due to reduced server-based licensing
- Saving on infrastructure costs

For example, a company that needs to support 10,000 users on XenApp would need to purchase and maintain 50 dual- or quad-processor 32-bit servers to service the population, while they would need only 32 quad-processor 64-bit servers.

Compatibility with Existing Applications and Easy Migration from 32-Bit

Windows Server 2003 x64 Edition can execute 64-bit and 32-bit applications. This is accomplished by running 32-bit applications inside the Windows on Windows 64 (WoW64) execution layer. WoW64 isolates 32-bit applications from 64-bit applications while providing interoperability and data exchange through COM and remote procedure calls (RPCs). It also prevents file and registry collisions between 32-bit and 64-bit versions of the same application. 64-bit applications that are written to run natively in Windows Server 2003 x64 Edition have full access to the large virtual memory address space (16TB).

There are some limitations when running 32-bit applications inside WoW64. These include the inability to access directly the operating system's 64-bit dynamic linking libraries (DLLs) and the inability to address the larger memory pool that Windows Server 2003 x64 Edition offers. WoW64 does not support most 16-bit applications and all kernel mode drivers must be 64-bit. From a performance perspective, 32-bit applications running through WoW64 rather than a native 32-bit system can experience a small degradation in performance.

Another important compatibility feature of Windows Server 2003 x64 Edition is the binary compatibility between the AMD64 and Intel EM64T processors that support the x64 extensions. This compatibility allows administrators to purchase the latest hardware on the market and reap the benefits of the faster processor and bus speeds running their 32-bit applications while waiting for their applications to be ported to 64-bit.

Increased Hardware Capability and Performance

A major area of improved efficiency in the 64-bit architecture is the increased number of registers available. All 32-bit x86 processors are limited to eight 32-bit general-purpose registers, eight floating-point registers, and eight Simple Sharing Extensions (SSE)/SSE2 registers. The 64-bit architecture uses twice as many general-purpose registers, each a full 64-bits wide, and doubles the number of 128-bit wide SSE/SSE2 registers to 16.

Another performance improvement with the 64-bit architecture is the gain in overall input/output (I/O) efficiency and throughput. With support for greater physical memory and memory address space, caches can be substantially larger than in 32-bit Windows, enabling the Windows x64 Editions to utilize fully the improved I/O hardware available, such as PCI Express, to improve overall I/O performance. The larger address space allows more I/O to be in progress simultaneously.

OPERATING SYSTEM CONFIGURATIONS

All partitions, especially the system partition, must be in NT File System (NTFS) format to allow security configuration, better performance, and fault tolerance. NTFS also saves disk space usage because NTFS partitions have much smaller and constant cluster sizes;

the minimum size is 4KB. File allocation table (FAT) partitions require much larger cluster sizes as the size of the partition increases, with the minimum being 32KB. More space is wasted on FAT partitions because the file system requires an amount of physical disk space equal to the cluster size of the partition used to store a file, even if the file is smaller than the cluster size. For more information about cluster sizes of FAT and NTFS partitions, see Microsoft Knowledge Base article 140365 or related information.

If possible, install only one network protocol on the server. This practice frees up system resources and reduces network traffic. If multiple protocols are needed, set the bind order so the most commonly used protocol is first.

In Microsoft Windows Server 2003, the Registry Size Limit functionality has been removed. Therefore, there are no longer any limits on the total amount of space that may be consumed by registry data (hives) in paged pool memory or in disk space. Views of the registry files are now mapped in the computer cache address space. Therefore, regardless of the size of the hive, it is not charged for more than 4MB of space.

Performance can be also be increased by properly tuning the page file. For more information about the page file, see Microsoft Knowledge Base article 197379.

Service Packs and Updates

Microsoft, Citrix, and most hardware manufacturers provide patches, service packs, hotfixes, or other updates intended to ensure optimum performance, security, and stability of the systems. It is critical not only to keep up to date, but also to regression-test all updates prior to installing them in a production environment.

NOTE Before installing XenApp, review the online Preinstallation Update Bulletin. The Preinstallation Update Bulletin offers late-breaking information and links to critical updates to server OSs and to Citrix installation files. A link to the bulletin is available on the Installation Checklist accessed through the autorun feature of the installation CDs.

Windows Service Packs

Service packs and hotfixes should be applied uniformly across all servers in the server farm. By ensuring this level of uniformity, you can maintain consistency and reduce troubleshooting time.

XenApp uses Microsoft Jet drivers extensively. The Microsoft Jet Database Engine is used by the local host cache on every XenApp server. It is also used when Resource Management is installed. Citrix recommends installing Microsoft service packs for the Microsoft Jet Database Engine. Older versions contain memory leaks that appear as Independent Management Architecture (IMA) service memory leaks. Apply these service packs and patches before installing XenApp on the servers. See Microsoft Knowledge Base article 239114 or related materials for more information.

You can reduce the amount of memory consumed by the IMA service by changing the maximum buffer size for the Microsoft Jet 4.0 Database Engine.

To change the maximum buffer size, follow these steps:

1. Run regedit.
2. Locate the following registry entry:

   `HKEY_LOCAL_MACHINE\SOFTWARE\Microsoft\Jet\4.0\Engines\Jet 4.0`

3. Double-click the value MaxBufferSize in the right pane.
4. In the DWORD Editor dialog box, enter 0×200 in the Data box. Accept the default radix, Hex, in the Radix box. This sets MaxBufferSize to 512KB.
5. Click OK.

CAUTION Using Registry Editor incorrectly can cause serious problems that can require you to reinstall the OS. Citrix cannot guarantee that problems resulting from incorrect use of Registry Editor can be solved. Use Registry Editor at your own risk. Make sure that you back up the registry before you edit it.

The IMA service consumes less memory if you change the value from 0 to 512KB.

NOTE Installing a new Microsoft Data Access Components (MDAC) or Microsoft Jet Database Engine service pack may reset MaxBufferSize to its default setting. Be sure to check this setting after applying any MDAC or Jet updates.

TEAMING NETWORK INTERFACE CARD CONFIGURATIONS

Previous versions of the Advanced Concepts Guide suggested manually configuring network interface cards (NICs) and switch ports to support full duplex and the highest speed available on both devices. New evidence suggests that NICs and switch ports should be configured to auto for both speed and duplex. See Cisco tech note 10561 for additional information.

Many new servers are procured with two installed NIC ports. These NICs may be configured as follows, as listed in the order of Citrix's recommendation:

- Utilize both NICs and team via switch-assisted load balancing within the same subnet if you are connecting to different blades within a large Layer 3 switch
- Utilize both NICs and team via adaptive load balancing within the same subnet if you are connecting to different blades within a large Layer 3 switch
- Utilize both NICs and configure for failover onto two separate switches
- Utilize one NIC and disable the second
- Utilize both NICs and multihome to two different subnets

Historically, most organizations have used only one NIC in each server. However, if two NIC and switch ports are available, these can be teamed, configured for failover, or multihomed. Of these two options, NIC teaming is considered a Citrix best practice when the switch ports are located on different blades within a large Layer 3 switch (for example, Cisco 6500 series) because this enables both failover and redundancy in addition to higher throughput. Although the Layer 3 switch does represent a single point of failure in this case, the availability of most large Layer 3 switches is in the 99.999 percent range and represents a minimal failure rate. More commonly, an individual blade may fail. If a large Layer 3 switch that supports teaming across blades is unavailable, then a failover configuration is the best option. Although multihoming is a supported practice starting with MetaFrame XP Service Pack 1, NIC teaming is considered the better option in nearly all situations. Multihoming is often configured incorrectly, and security holes could be opened because access control lists configured on the router are bypassed.

If insufficient switch ports or other business decisions make it impossible to team the NICs and switch ports of all XenApp and related servers, it is best to apply this recommendation to the following servers:

- Data store
- Web Interface server(s)
- Secure Gateway server(s)
- Secure Ticket Authority server(s)
- Zone data collector(s)

The following teaming NIC configurations have been tested on XenApp and on an SQL server as the data store. In all cases, Citrix recommends teaming NICs using the Media Access Control (MAC) address, not the Internet Protocol (IP) address. Because the MAC address is at a more basic and lower layer, and is not subject to modification unless the burned-in address (BIA) is modified, this is a more basic and stable configuration. The switch vendor's recommended practice for manually configuring teaming or aggregating of the switch ports should be followed.

Network Fault Tolerance (Failover)

This failover option provides the safety of an additional backup link between the server and the switch. If the primary adapter fails, the secondary adapter takes over with minor interruption in server operations. When tested in Citrix eLabs, failover caused an interruption of less than 0.5 seconds and did not provide any noticeable impact on existing ICA sessions. There is no performance gain with this setting, but fault tolerance is improved.

Transmit Load Balancing (Formerly Adaptive Load Balancing)

This option creates a team of adapters to increase transmission throughput and ensure that all network users experience similar response times. All adapters must be linked to the same network switch. As adapters are added to the server, they are grouped in teams to provide a single virtual adapter with increased transmission bandwidth. For example, a transmit load-balancing team containing two Fast Ethernet adapters configured for full-duplex operation provides an aggregate maximum transmit rate of 200 Mbps and a 100 Mbps receive rate, resulting in a total bandwidth of 300 Mbps. One adapter is configured for transmit and receive, while the others are configured for transmit only. Adapter teams configured for transmit load balancing provide the benefit of network fault tolerance because, if the primary adapter that supports both transmit and receive fails, another adapter then supports this functionality.

Switch-Assisted Load Balancing (Formerly Fast Ether Channel)

Unlike transmit load balancing, you can configure Fast Ether Channel (FEC) to increase both transmitting and receiving channels between the server and switch. For example, an FEC team containing two Fast Ethernet adapters configured for full-duplex operation provides an aggregate maximum transmit rate of 200 Mbps and an aggregate maximum receive rate of 200 Mbps, resulting in a total bandwidth of 400 Mbps. All adapters are configured for transmit and receive, with the load spread roughly equally.

FEC works only with FEC-enabled switches. The FEC software continuously analyzes the load on each adapter and balances network traffic across the adapters as needed. Adapter teams configured for FEC not only provide additional throughput and redundancy, but also provide the benefits of Network Fault Tolerance (NFT). The switch ports should also be manually configured to support this configuration, so autosensed aggregation does not occur. For more information, see Citrix Knowledge Base article CTX434260 and/or contact your hardware vendor.

MULTIHOMING XENAPP

XenApp provides support for multihomed servers. The following section provides the details necessary for implementing XenApp on a server operating with two or more NICs.

Multihoming is commonly used to connect XenApp directly to a database server located in another subnet. This may be advantageous where access to the remote subnet requires crossing several routers that have high latency or other bottlenecks. However, multihoming can create security holes because the normal access medium—for example, the router—is bypassed as well as its security configuration. Multihoming should be carefully considered and security implications should be reviewed.

For example, in the diagram shown in Figure 2-2, if multihoming is not configured properly on the XenApp servers, external users may gain access to the SQL and Oracle database servers by means of the XenApp servers bypassing the router security that has been carefully configured.

CAUTION Multihoming is frequently not configured properly. The steps described in the following section must be followed exactly as specified for multihoming to function correctly and be supported.

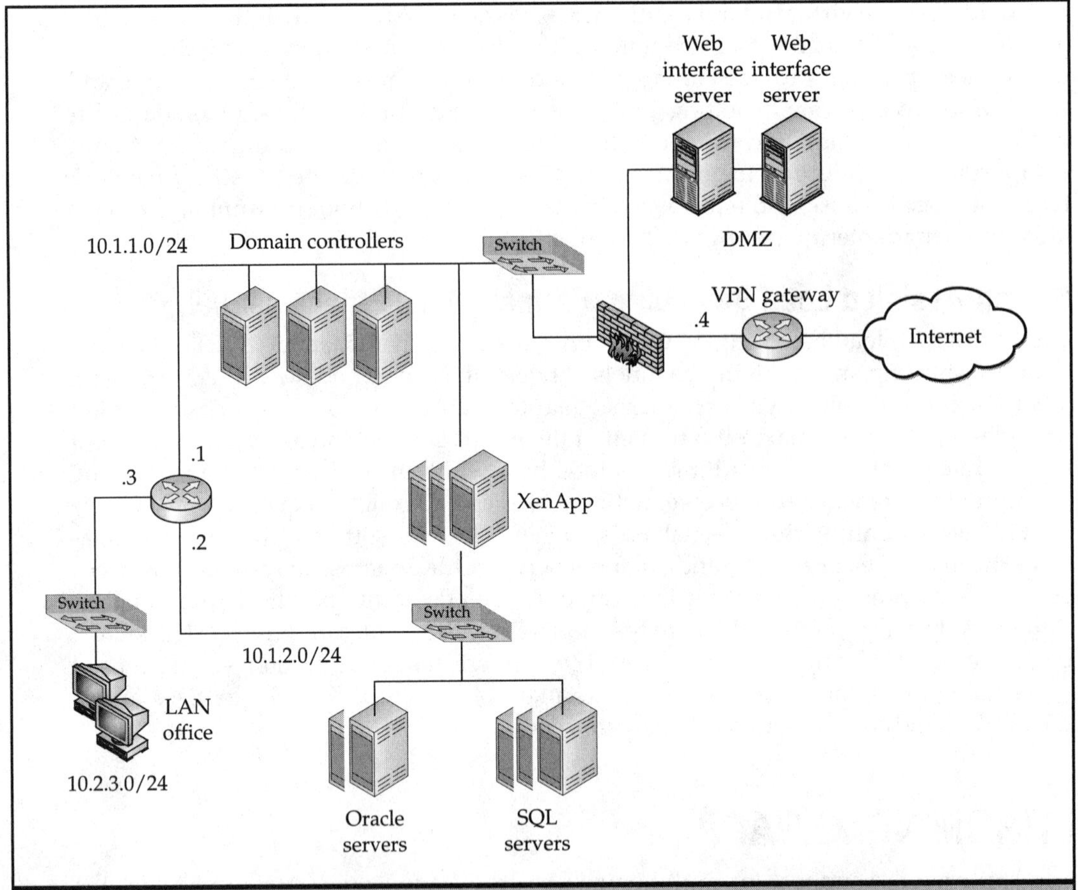

Figure 2-2. Sample environment with multihoming to connect servers to data collectors on different subnets

Previous versions of the Advanced Concepts Guide suggested manually configuring NICs and switch ports to support full duplex and the highest speed available on both devices. New evidence suggests that NICs and switch ports should be configured to auto for both speed and duplex. See Cisco tech note 10561 for additional information.

XenApp multihoming could be used to provide access to two network segments with no direct route to each. However, each network will utilize the same Citrix resources, making the addition of another server farm redundant. Another application of multihoming XenApp would be to separate a network configured as the main corporate backbone dedicated to server-to-server traffic from a second subnet dedicated to ICA Client-to-XenApp traffic. The latter configuration is illustrated in the following figure and is the subject of the remaining example provided in this section.

The recommendation is that multihomed servers running XenApp should not be configured to operate as a router (TCP/IP Forwarding). In addition, XenApp relies on a properly configured local routing table for accurate operation. Because Windows servers automatically build their routing tables, some care must be taken when configuring the network card binding order and default gateway.

Figure 2-3 illustrates two multihomed XenApp servers, each with a connection to the 10.8.1.0/24 and 172.16.1.0/24 subnets. Neither server is configured to route between its two network interfaces.

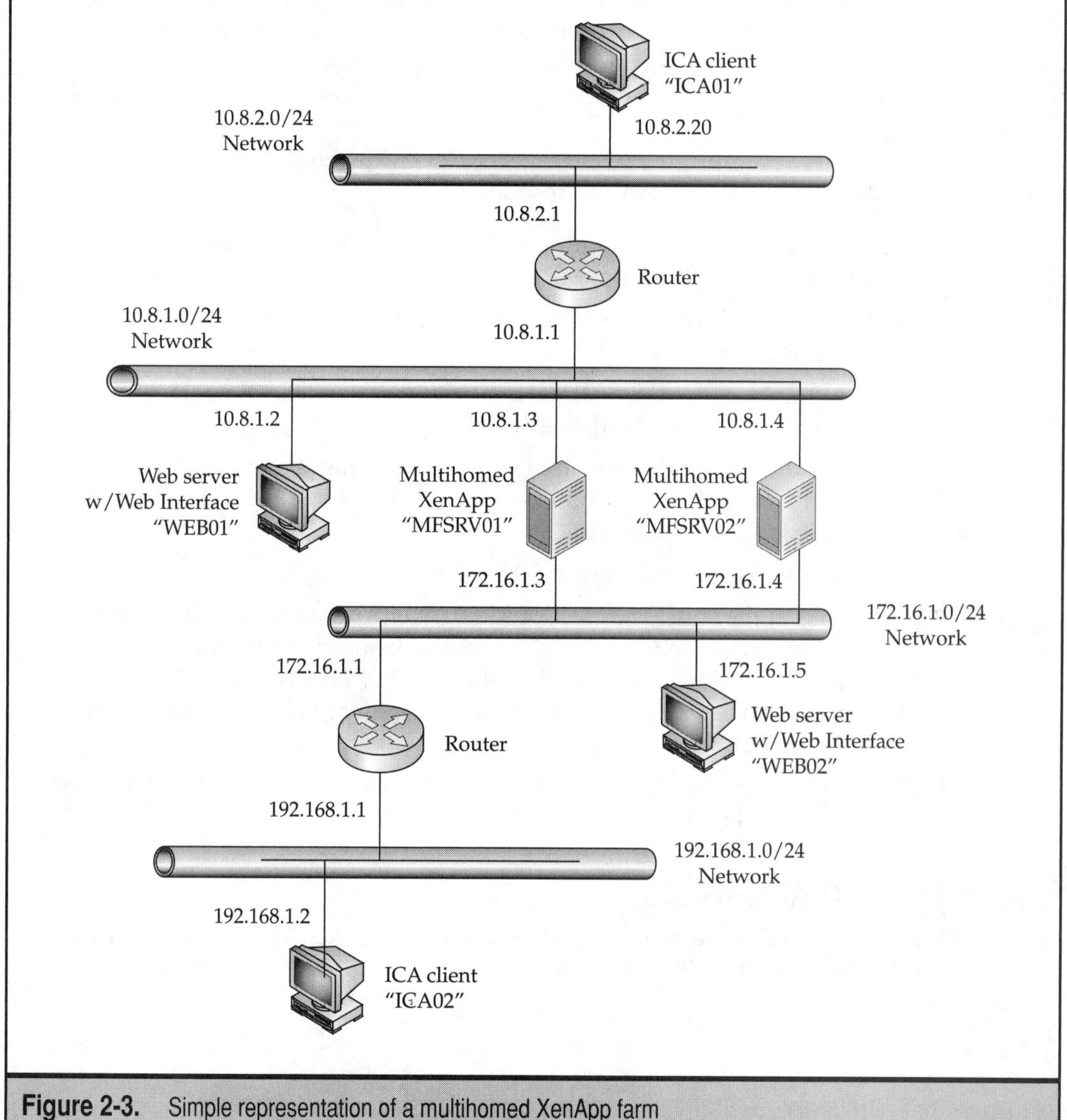

Figure 2-3. Simple representation of a multihomed XenApp farm

ICA clients requesting a server name or published application get a TCP/IP address to a XenApp that contains them. This address is resolved and returned by the XenApp that receives the request. Some types of address resolution requests by ICA clients include the following:

- Find the address of the data collector
- Find the TCP/IP address of a given XenApp name
- Find the TCP/IP address of the least-loaded server for a published application

A XenApp receives an address resolution request from an ICA client and compares the TCP/IP address of the ICA client to its local routing table to determine which network interface to send the appropriate reply to the requesting ICA client. For this reason, the proper functioning of a multihomed XenApp relies heavily on the correct configuration of the routing table.

Continuing with our example, the following steps describe the process from an ICA client request to the XenApp resolution and response:

1. The ICA client with the TCP/IP address 10.8.2.20, ICA01 sends an address resolution request to the XenApp, MFSRV01.
2. MFSRV01 has the TCP/IP address 10.8.1.3. This server also has a second NIC with the TCP/IP address 172.16.1.3.
3. ICA01 is configured with MFSRV01 as its service location. ICA01 contacts MFSRV01 and requests a load-balanced application.
4. The TCP/IP address of the least-loaded server containing the requested published application must be supplied to ICA01. MFSRV01 finds that MFSRV02 is the least-loaded server.
5. MFSRV02 has two TCP/IP addresses, 10.8.1.4 and 172.16.1.4.
6. MFSRV02 looks at the source address of ICA01. XenApp uses its local routing table to determine what network interface should be used to respond to the client. In this case, the NIC configured on the 10.8.2.0/24 network is chosen to send the response to the client. If no corresponding entry is in the local routing table, then the default route is used.
7. MFSRV01 uses the local routing table to respond correctly with the 10.8.1.4 address when referring the client to MFSRV02.

Configuring the Routing Table

You set up a routing table on a multihomed server running XenApp by configuring a single default gateway and adding static routes.

Configuring a Default Gateway

Windows servers automatically build their routing tables by default. For this reason, some care must be taken in the construction of the routing table to allow a multihomed server running XenApp to operate properly. Although Windows servers build multiple default gateways, the network binding order of the NICs in the server determine which default gateway should be utilized. Using our example illustrated previously, we selected the 10.8.1.1 address as our default gateway. The network card operating on the 10.8.1.0/24 network must be moved to the top of the network binding order.

To configure the network binding order, follow these steps:

1. Open Start | Control Panel | Network Connections.
2. Select Advanced | Advanced Settings.
3. Under the section Connections, place the NIC to operate as your default gateway first in the list.

In certain environments, the configuration of the network binding order may not be sufficient for proper XenApp functionality.

An example would be a XenApp with two connections to the Internet, where each provides ICA connectivity for a diverse range of IP subnets. XenApp only uses the default gateway of the first NIC in its network binding order, referenced as Network 1. If the XenApp were to receive a request from a client on Network 2 of its second NIC, which is not the default gateway, and there was no routing table entry for Network 2 in the local routing table of the XenApp, then the response to the client request would be sent through Network 1. This would likely cause the request to fail.

Or, you can remove the additional default gateway configurations from each additional NIC on the server. This is done through the server's TCP/IP configuration. Using servers MFSRV01 and MFSRV02 from the previous example, we select 10.8.1.1 as our default gateway for both servers, and so remove the default gateway setting from the NICs operating on the 172.16.1.0/24 network.

Running the command-line utility IPCONFIG on MFSRV01 shows the following:

```
Windows IP Configuration
Ethernet adapter Local Area Connection #1:
       Connection-specific DNS Suffix  . :
       IP Address. . . . . . . . . . . . : 10.8.1.3
       Subnet Mask . . . . . . . . . . . : 255.255.255.0
       Default Gateway . . . . . . . . . : 10.8.1.1
Ethernet adapter Local Area Connection #2:
       Connection-specific DNS Suffix  . :
       IP Address. . . . . . . . . . . . : 172.16.1.3
       Subnet Mask . . . . . . . . . . . : 255.255.255.0
       Default Gateway . . . . . . . . . :
```

Running IPCONFIG on MFSRV02 generates the following output:

```
Windows IP Configuration
Ethernet adapter Local Area Connection #1:
        Connection-specific DNS Suffix .  :
        IP Address. . . . . . . . . . . . : 10.8.1.4
        Subnet Mask . . . . . . . . . . . : 255.255.255.0
        Default Gateway . . . . . . . . . : 10.8.1.1
Ethernet adapter Local Area Connection #2:
        Connection-specific DNS Suffix .  :
        IP Address. . . . . . . . . . . . : 172.16.1.4
        Subnet Mask . . . . . . . . . . . : 255.255.255.0
        Default Gateway . . . . . . . . . :
```

Adding Static Routes

Defining static, persistent routes is the best way to avoid potential routing conflicts and, depending on your network configuration, this may be the only way to provide ICA connectivity to a multihomed XenApp. Refer to the previous example.

Executing the ROUTE PRINT command from the command prompt on the routing table on MFSRV01 generates the following:

```
===========================================================================
Interface List
0x1 ........................... MS TCP Loopback interface
0x2 ...00 a0 c9 2b f8 dc ...... Intel 8255x-based Integrated Fast Ethernet
0x3 ...00 c0 0d 01 12 f5 ...... Intel(R) PRO Adapter
===========================================================================
===========================================================================
Active Routes:
Network Destination          Netmask         Gateway       Interface    Metric
          0.0.0.0            0.0.0.0        10.8.1.1        10.8.1.3         1
         10.8.1.0      255.255.255.0        10.8.1.3        10.8.1.3         1
         10.8.1.3    255.255.255.255       127.0.0.1       127.0.0.1         1
   10.255.255.255    255.255.255.255        10.8.1.3        10.8.1.3         1
        127.0.0.0          255.0.0.0       127.0.0.1       127.0.0.1         1
       172.16.1.0      255.255.255.0      172.16.1.3      172.16.1.3         1
       172.16.1.3    255.255.255.255       127.0.0.1       127.0.0.1         1
     172.16.1.255    255.255.255.255      172.16.1.3      172.16.1.3         1
        224.0.0.0          224.0.0.0        10.8.1.3        10.8.1.3         1
        224.0.0.0          224.0.0.0      172.16.1.3      172.16.1.3         1
  255.255.255.255    255.255.255.255        10.8.1.3        10.8.1.3         1
   Default Gateway:         10.8.1.1
===========================================================================
Persistent Routes:
None
```

Currently, MFSRV01 is configured with a default gateway using the router at 10.8.1.1. Note that the second client, ICA02, is located on the 192.168.1.0/24 network, which is accessed via the router at 172.16.1.1. For MFSRV01 to have network connectivity and to avoid using the default gateway when responding to requests from ICA02, a static route must be defined for the 192.168.1.0/24 network:

```
ROUTE -p ADD 192.168.1.0 MASK 255.255.255.0 172.16.1.1
```

Executing ROUTE PRINT from a command prompt on MFSRV01 now generates the following:

```
===================================================
Interface List
0x1 ........................... MS TCP Loopback interface
0x2 ...00 a0 c9 2b f8 dc ...... Intel 8255x-based Integrated Fast Ethernet
0x3 ...00 c0 0d 01 12 f5 ...... Intel(R) PRO Adapter
===========================================================================
===========================================================================

Active Routes:
Network Destination          Netmask          Gateway       Interface  Metric
          0.0.0.0            0.0.0.0         10.8.1.1        10.8.1.3       1
         10.8.1.0      255.255.255.0         10.8.1.3        10.8.1.3       1
         10.8.1.3    255.255.255.255        127.0.0.1       127.0.0.1       1
   10.255.255.255    255.255.255.255         10.8.1.3        10.8.1.3       1
        127.0.0.0          255.0.0.0        127.0.0.1       127.0.0.1       1
       172.16.1.0      255.255.255.0       172.16.1.3      172.16.1.3       1
       172.16.1.3    255.255.255.255        127.0.0.1       127.0.0.1       1
     172.16.1.255    255.255.255.255       172.16.1.3      172.16.1.3       1
      192.168.1.0      255.255.255.0       172.16.1.1      172.16.1.3       1
        224.0.0.0          224.0.0.0         10.8.1.3        10.8.1.3       1
        224.0.0.0          224.0.0.0       172.16.1.3      172.16.1.3       1
  255.255.255.255    255.255.255.255         10.8.1.3        10.8.1.3       1
  Default Gateway:          10.8.1.1
===========================================================================
Persistent Routes:
  Network Address          Netmask  Gateway Address  Metric
      192.168.1.0    255.255.255.0       172.16.1.1       1
```

MFSRV02 is handled the same way. When the static routes are set up, both ICA clients can ping both XenApp TCP/IP addresses and the servers can ping the clients.

Each XenApp can now correctly resolve the network interface to which either ICA client is connecting. The TCP/IP addresses that the ICA01 client can receive are 10.8.1.3 and 10.8.1.4. The TCP/IP addresses that the ICA02 client can receive are 172.16.1.3 and 172.16.1.4.

CHAPTER 3

Independent Management Architecture

This chapter discusses Citrix XenApp architecture topics that you must address in the planning and pilot phases before you deploy XenApp in the enterprise. The concepts that you learn about in this section include zones, the server farm's data store, the local host cache, and bandwidth requirements for Independent Management Architecture (IMA) communication in the server farm.

IMA COMPONENTS

Citrix's IMA contains four components: the IMA data store, zone data collectors, local host caches, and the IMA protocol. The *data store* is responsible for keeping information about generally static farm settings, such as published applications, load-balancing parameters, printer options, and security. Farm information that changes regularly, such as the number of connected users or which member servers are currently online, is maintained in an in-memory database on each data collector. Each zone in a farm has its own zone data collector (ZDC), which is responsible for maintaining the operating information for that zone. Data collectors gather their information through communication with the servers in their zone, and then communicate their zone's information to the data collectors in the other zones in the farm. Each server maintains a local database containing a subset of the information in the data store; this local database is referred to as the *local host cache* (LHC). The *IMA protocol* is responsible for communications between XenApp and for communication between servers and the Presentation Server Console.

UNDERSTANDING ZONES

In a XenApp farm, a *zone* is a grouping of XenApp servers that share a common *data collector* (a XenApp that receives information from all the servers in the zone). Zones in a farm serve two purposes: to collect data from member servers in a hierarchical structure and to distribute changes efficiently to all servers in the farm.

All member servers must belong to a zone. By default, the zone name is the subnet ID on which the member server resides. A zone in a XenApp farm elects a ZDC for the zone if a new server joins the zone, if a member server restarts, or if the current ZDC becomes unavailable.

The trade-off of adding more zones is the open link (and, thus, the bandwidth required) to maintain updates between each ZDC, so that all updated data can be propagated throughout the farm. During a zone update, the member server updates the ZDC with the requests and the changed data.

Sizing Zones and Data Collectors

ZDCs are used to keep information within a server farm up to date between member servers and other ZDCs. Every server farm has at least one zone set up by default. The challenge is to design the right number of zones in a farm so that no ZDC becomes overloaded with traffic from its member servers while at the same time limiting the amount of additional load on the ZDCs and bandwidth required by multiple zones. The inter-zone traffic should be both minimized and balanced between ZDCs.

The number of zones needed by a farm is dependent on the topology of the site in which the farm is being deployed, the number of users connecting to the farm, the number of simultaneous user logons, the number of published applications with load evaluators attached, and the length of time that the average user stays logged on to a session (a single daily session or repeated short sessions). The number should be kept to a minimum; the fewer zones a farm has, the more it will scale. The reason is that every time a dynamic event occurs—such as a logon, a logoff, or a disconnect—an update is sent to the ZDC. The ZDC must then forward the update to all other ZDCs in the farm. This consumes both bandwidth and CPU processing because the other ZDCs must keep up with the events in other zones as well as in their own.

Zones should not always be based on subnets. Zones can scale beyond 500 servers, unless other environmental conditions warrant limiting their size. Suppose, for example, that a company has a XenApp farm containing 1000 servers distributed between two distinct datacenters, which each hosting 500 servers. In this case, it would be more desirable to create two separate zones of 500 member servers each. In another scenario, this company plans to expand operations to a small, remote site at another location that would house 10 XenApp servers in the same farm. In this case, it would be optimal for the servers in the new location to join one of the original site's zones. The reason is based on the number of events that would flow across the wide area network (WAN). If the new site was placed in its own zone, the data collector for the new zone would receive replicated events from all the other data collectors in the farm. The number of events (logons, logoffs, and so forth) coming from the other zones would be in the tens of thousands. On the other hand, the number of events generated by the new zone would be in the hundreds. It is optimal not to have to replicate the data collector traffic if this is unnecessary. Therefore, if you consolidate the new site into the one of the original zones, the only traffic flowing across the WAN link would be events sent from the new site's member servers to the original site's ZDC.

ZDC Hardware Configuration

Because the data collectors store all dynamic information in memory, it is important that the ZDC has sufficient random access memory (RAM) to store all the records. For a farm consisting of 1,000 servers and 10,000 users, the data collector consumes approximately 200MB of memory. Memory usage can vary, based on the number of published applications and users in the farm. The central processing unit (CPU) plays an important role in determining the number of resolutions that the data collector can process in conjunction with managing dynamic information. In general, a fast dual processor server with 1GB of memory makes a good ZDC.

It is important that all data collectors in the farm be sized to accommodate the largest zone. Because data collectors must manage the global state of the farm, they require the same processing capability of the other data collectors in the farm, regardless of the size of their particular zone. Likewise, if the data collector needs to be dedicated for one zone, all data collectors in the farm should be dedicated for their own zones.

Traffic from a Member Server to a ZDC

During a zone update, the member server updates the data collector with the requests and the changed data. To approximate the number of bytes sent from a single server to the ZDC during a complete update, use the following formula:

Bytes = 5600 + (200*Con) + (100*$Discon$) + (300*$Apps$)

where

Con = Number of connected sessions
Discon = Number of disconnected sessions
Apps = Number of published applications in the farm

During a zone update, the member server updates the data collector with the requests and the changed data. This amount of traffic is represented by the previous formula. In turn, a small amount of traffic is then sent from the data collector to the member server. This traffic accounts for approximately one-half of the data sent from the member server to the data collector, so for full bandwidth utilization, multiply the number of bytes from the previous formula by 1.5. To approximate the amount of traffic destined for the data collector, multiply the number of bytes from the previous formula by the number of member servers in the zone.

NOTE These numbers are an approximation from data gathered in the Citrix eLabs; actual results may vary.

A *full zone transfer*, the transmission of all of a zone's information, occurs when a ZDC comes online (for example, when it is rebooted or a new ZDC is added) or a new ZDC is elected because of ZDC failure detection. To approximate the amount of data sent between two data collectors during a full zone transfer, use the following formula:

Bytes = 13000 + (300*Con) + (300*$Discon$) + (500*$Apps$)

where

Con = Number of connected sessions
Discon = Number of disconnected sessions
Apps = Number of published applications in the farm

During a zone update, approximately the same amount of data is transmitted between data collectors, so for full bandwidth utilization, be sure to double the bytes from the previous formula. To approximate the amount of traffic across all data collector links, multiply the number of bytes obtained from the previous formula by the number of data collectors minus 1 in the farm.

Traffic Between Zones

Each ZDC has a connection open to all other data collectors in the farm. This connection is used to relay immediately any changes reported by member servers within its own zone to the data collectors of all other zones. Thus, all data collectors are aware of the session information and, for MetaFrame Presentation Server XP with Feature Release 3 and earlier, the server load for every server in the farm. Load sharing between zones is disabled by default in XenApp 4.0 and later. The formula for interzone connections is $N * (N-1)/2$, where N is the number of zones in the farm.

Automatic Farm Tuner

There is a utility included with XenApp called AutoFarmTuner that can assess and adjust the settings discussed in the following two sections, "Configure Data Collectors in Large Zones" and "Data Collector Scalability in Large Farms." AutoFarmTuner is located in the \Support directory on the XenApp installation CD. To use AutoFarm-Tuner, copy the files named AutoFarmTuner.exe and Interop.MetaFrameCOM.dll to the %Systemroot% directory and run AutoFarmTuner.exe from that directory. For additional information about AutoFarmTuner, see Citrix Knowledge Center article CTX108456. Access to CTX108456 requires a My Citrix login.

Configure Data Collectors in Large Zones

The data collector maintains all load and session information for every server in its zone. By default, a single zone supports 512 member servers. If a zone contains more than 512 servers, each ZDC and potential ZDC must have a new registry setting. This new setting controls how many open connections to member servers a data collector can have at one time. Set the registry value higher than the number of servers in the zone to prevent the data collector from constantly destroying and re-creating connections to stay within the limit. This value is configurable by adding the following value to the registry in hex:

```
HKEY_LOCAL_MACHINE\SOFTWARE\Citrix\IMA\Runtime\MaxHostAddress CacheEntries

(DWORD)

Value: 0x200 (default 512 entries)
```

NOTE If you do not have more than 512 servers in a zone, increasing this value does not increase the performance of a zone.

Number of Servers in a Zone

A common misconception is that no more than 100 servers should be placed within a zone. The problem with designing too many zones in a large datacenter deployment is that the presence of multiple zones in a single datacenter can decrease performance of the farm. This decrease results from the ZDCs having to keep up with all the information contained within all other ZDCs in the farm. Each time an event occurs, the ZDC must forward this information to all other ZDCs in the farm. This increases the network consumption and the CPU load on the ZDC as it needs to handle sending and receiving updates for all the events in the farm.

TIP As a starting point, place 300 servers into a single zone, and then monitor the CPU utilization on the ZDC.

Data Collector Scalability in Large Farms

In large farms (800+ servers) containing more than one zone, where the data collectors are heavily utilized performing logon resolutions, a condition could arise causing the data collectors to become overloaded and stop performing resolutions for a short period of time. This state results when all the worker threads on each data collector are processing IMA maintenance items, such as IMA pings, gateway updates, load updates, and so forth. While performing resolutions, these resolutions require the processing of events at the remote data collector, which has no worker threads available to deliver the event.

The following registry setting increases IMA processing bandwidth by increasing the amount of worker threads available to the data collector and shortens the timeout of stale events. Each ZDC and all potential ZDCs must have a new registry setting. These keys need to be created and, as always, use caution when modifying the registry.

```
HKEY_LOCAL_MACHINE\SOFTWARE\Citrix\IMA

WorkQueueThreadCount (DWORD)

Value: 0x00000080 (hex)

IsolationWorkQueueThreadCount (DWORD)

Value: 0x00000080 (hex)

EventTimeout (DWORD)

Value: 0x000007d0 (hex)
```

NOTE This condition occurs only if there are multiple zones and each data collector is processing up to 40 resolutions per second. Setting these registry keys does not improve performance unless this condition exists.

Previous versions of the Advanced Concepts Guide additionally recommended that users create or modify the following registry value:

```
HKEY_LOCAL_MACHINE\SOFTWARE\Citrix\IMA\RUNTIME

GatewayValidationInterval (DWORD)

Value: 0x00007530 (hex)
```

Changing GatewayValidationInterval from the default interval of five minutes is no longer recommended as modifying the interval time may cause an adverse effect in high latency environments. Remove this registry value and restart the IMA service on the ZDCs. Deleting the entry restores the default interval. See Citrix Knowledge Base article CTX111103 for more information.

FUNCTION OF THE DATA STORE IN A CITRIX XENAPP FARM

The data store provides a repository of persistent farm information for all servers to reference. The data store retains information that does not change frequently, including the following:

- Farm configuration information
- Published application configurations
- Server configurations
- Citrix administrator accounts
- Printer configurations

CAUTION Always maintain a backup of the data store database. If you do not have a backup from which to restore, you must re-create the farm if the database is lost. You cannot re-create the database from an existing farm.

Database Format

With the exception of indexes, all information in the data store is in binary format. No meaningful queries can be executed directly against the data store. Neither Citrix administrators nor users should directly query or change information in the data store. Use only IMA-based tools, such as the Presentation Server Console or the Access Management Console, to access the information in the data store.

CAUTION Never directly edit any data in the data store database with IBM DB2, Microsoft SQL Server, or Oracle tools. Directly editing the data with one of these tools corrupts the farm database and causes the farm to become unstable or completely unusable.

Data Store Activity

All servers in the farm query the data store during startup, if it is available. The following registry setting determines whether IMA requires a connection to the data store to start:

```
HKEY_LOCAL_MACHINE\SOFTWARE\Citrix\IMA\Runtime\

PSRequired (DWORD)

Value: 0 or 1
```

If the value is 0, IMA can start without a connection to the data store. If the value is 1, IMA requires a connection to the data store to start. After the first time that the IMA service starts successfully, the value is set to 0.

Data Store and License Server Connectivity

This section addresses the dependencies between XenApp and connectivity to the data store or the license server.

NOTE Effective August 19, 2004, the license server grace period was increased from four days (96 hours) to 30 days. If you obtained your license file before that date, you must reallocate your license files to take advantage of the 30-day grace period. See Citrix Knowledge Base article CTX104782 for more information.

Data Store Connectivity

In MetaFrame XP with Feature Release 3 and earlier versions, if a farm member server is unable to contact the data store for more than 96 consecutive hours, licensing stops functioning on the member server and connections are disabled. Connections to XenApp 3.0 and later are not dependant on connectivity to the data store. After installation, XenApp makes an initial connection to the data store to identify the license server. Provided the XenApp can connect to the license server, or is within the grace period following a loss of connectivity to the license server, a loss of connectivity to the data store does not affect user logins. Although user connections are no longer dependent on a server's ability to connect to the data store, if the farm's member servers are unable to connect to the data store, you will be unable to use the Presentation Server Console or make changes to the farm, such as adding, removing, or modifying the properties of published applications.

License Server Connectivity

User connections to XenApp 3.0 and later are dependent on connectivity to the license server. If a farm member server loses connectivity to the license server, the member server enters into a grace period. During this grace period, logins are not affected, but once the grace period expires, only one administrator logon is granted and all other connections are denied.

Misconception "Data collectors are the only servers that communicate with the data store."

Fact IMA on all the servers must be initialized with the same settings, regardless of the role of the server. Also, when the Presentation Server Console is opened, it connects to a specified XenApp Server. This server's IMA service performs all reads and writes to the data store for the Presentation Server Console. Most changes made through the Presentation Server Console are written to the data store.

CITRIX XENAPP COMMUNICATION BANDWIDTH REQUIREMENTS

The Citrix eLabs used a Microsoft SQL 2005 data store to determine potential bandwidth requirements for normal communication in a XenApp environment. This information can be used to determine potential bandwidth requirements for WAN-based farms.

CAUTION The following results may not hold true for all situations. Recommendations vary based on how much bandwidth other network applications use.

Bandwidth of Server-to-Data Store Communication

The amount of data (in kilobytes) read from the data store during the startup of a XenApp, is approximated by the following formula:

KB Read = 416.8 + (2.04*(*Srvs* -1))

where

Srvs = Number of servers in the farm

Apps = Number of published applications in the farm

The data read from the data store can require higher bandwidth as the farm size increases and certain actions are executed, especially when several servers are started simultaneously. Most network traffic consists of reads from the database. In the case of high-latency or low-bandwidth links, Citrix recommends that the data store be replicated across the link(s) (using the built-in replication tools of the database vendor chosen for your data store—Microsoft SQL, Oracle, or IBM DB2). A replicated data store allows all reads to occur on the network local to XenApp, resulting in improved farm performance.

If performance across the WAN is an issue, and having a replicated database at each site is cost-prohibitive, analyze the WAN links for alternative solutions. The IMA service start time ranges from a few seconds to several minutes. When the amount of data requested from the data store by the IMA service is greater than the size of the pipe between WAN segments, IMA waits for all the data, resulting in a longer startup time.

NOTE A third-party solution can be used to dedicate a certain size pipe for exclusive use by database traffic to avoid network flooding in WAN environments.

When the IMA service takes a long time to start after a restart, an error can display on the console of the server stating that the IMA service could not be started. The event log can have a message stating that the IMA service hung on starting. These errors are benign. The IMA service starts properly after the requests to the data store are serviced.

Event	Data Transmitted (Approximate) (in KB)	Data Received (Approximate) (in KB)
Connect	0.19	0.32
Disconnect	0.51	0.43
Reconnect	0.29	0.30
Logoff	0.31	0.43

Table 3-1. Citrix XenApp 4.5 Sharing Load Information

Bandwidth of Data Collector Communication

To maintain consistent information between zones, data collectors must relay information to all other data collectors in a farm. The tables in this section illustrate the impact on network traffic.

Tables 3-1 and 3-2 list the amount of data transmitted for session-based events. Each time that these events occur, the member server sends data to the zone's data collector, which sends data to all other data collectors in the farm.

Table 3-3 lists the amount of data sent by one data collector to another when operations are performed by the Access Management Console on servers that reside in different zones.

Limit the use of zones to avoid the cost associated with the replication of zone data.

Application Publishing Bandwidth

The bandwidth consumed when you publish an application varies, depending on the number of servers in the server farm. In general, the amount of bandwidth consumed increases 466 bytes for every additional server in the server farm. Starting a new server generates the most amount of traffic to the other data collectors—about 4.56KB worth of traffic to the data collector in a default configuration.

Event	Data Transmitted (Approximate) (in KB)	Data Received (Approximate) (in KB)
Connect	0.07	0.17
Disconnect	0.16	0.21
Reconnect	0.14	0.26
Logoff	0.22	0.43

Table 3-2. Citrix XenApp 4.5 *not* Sharing Load Information

Event	Data Transmitted (Approximate) (in KB)	Data Received (Approximate) (in KB)
Access Management Console server query	0.0	0.0
Application publishing	2.47	1.87
Change of a ZDC	2.19	0.54

Table 3-3. Citrix XenApp 4.5 data collector–to–data collector updates

NOTE You can use a third-party solution to dedicate a pipe for IMA traffic, which uses port 2512 by default, to avoid flooding the network in WAN environments.

Application of IMA Bandwidth Formulas

When a server running XenApp is booted, it must initialize the IMA service during startup and it must also register with the data collector for the zone in which it resides. Figure 3-1 shows the steps for an initial boot of a XenApp farm.

NOTE License communication is not included in this figure.

Communication occurs in the following sequence of events:

1. The IMA service establishes a connection to the data store for the farm. The IMA service then downloads the information it needs to initialize. It also makes sure that the data contained in its LHC are current.
2. After the IMA service is initialized, the member server registers with the data collector for the zone. This is a function of the number of published applications to which the server is contributing.
3. The data collector needs to relay all of the updated information written by the member servers in the zone to *all* other data collectors in the farm to keep them in sync with each other. The data collector–to–data collector updates are a function of the amount of information updated by the member server. The data collectors only replicate the delta, or items that have changed; they do not replicate all their tables every time that an update is sent.

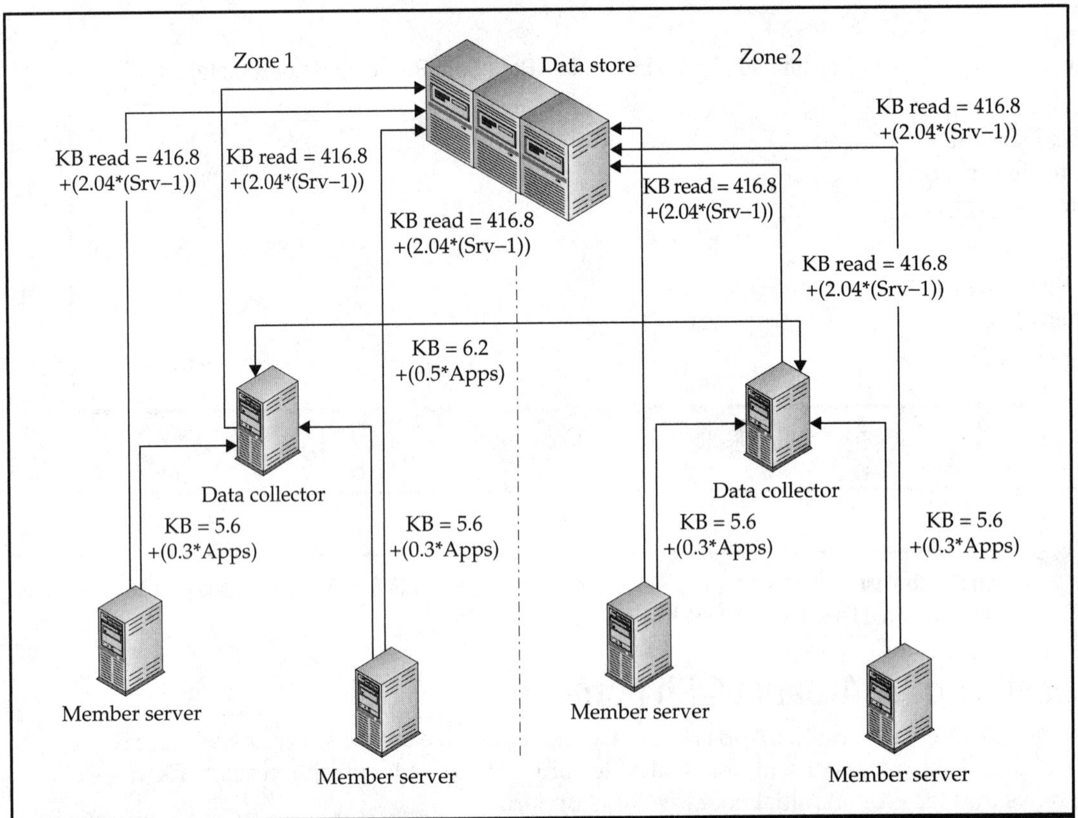

Zone 1
Data store
Zone 2
KB read = 416.8 +(2.04*(Srv–1))
KB read = 416.8 +(2.04*(Srv–1))
KB read = 416.8 +(2.04*(Srv–1))
KB read = 416.8 +(2.04*(Srv–1))
KB read = 416.8 +(2.04*(Srv–1))
KB read = 416.8 +(2.04*(Srv–1))
KB = 6.2 +(0.5*Apps)
Data collector
Data collector
KB = 5.6 +(0.3*Apps)
KB = 5.6 +(0.3*Apps)
KB = 5.6 +(0.3*Apps)
KB = 5.6 +(0.3*Apps)
Member server
Member server
Member server
Member server

Figure 3-1. Initial boot of a Citrix XenApp farm

NOTE In the example in Figure 3-2, there are only two zones, so the data collector must replicate once to the other data collector only the updates it receives from the member servers. If there were three zones, the data collector would have to replicate the same information twice. This causes higher bandwidth consumption and places a higher load on the data collectors in the farm.

Idle Farm Communication

IMA must use a small amount of overhead, even if the farm is idle. Figure 3-2 shows the communication that must take place on a farm after it is initialized. This communication has three primary components: an IMA coherency check between the member server's LHC and the data store, an IMA ping by the ZDC to the member servers in its zone, and an IMA ping to the other ZDCs in the farm.

Event-Based Communication

Most IMA traffic is a result of the generation of events. Figure 3-3 shows an example of a client logon event.

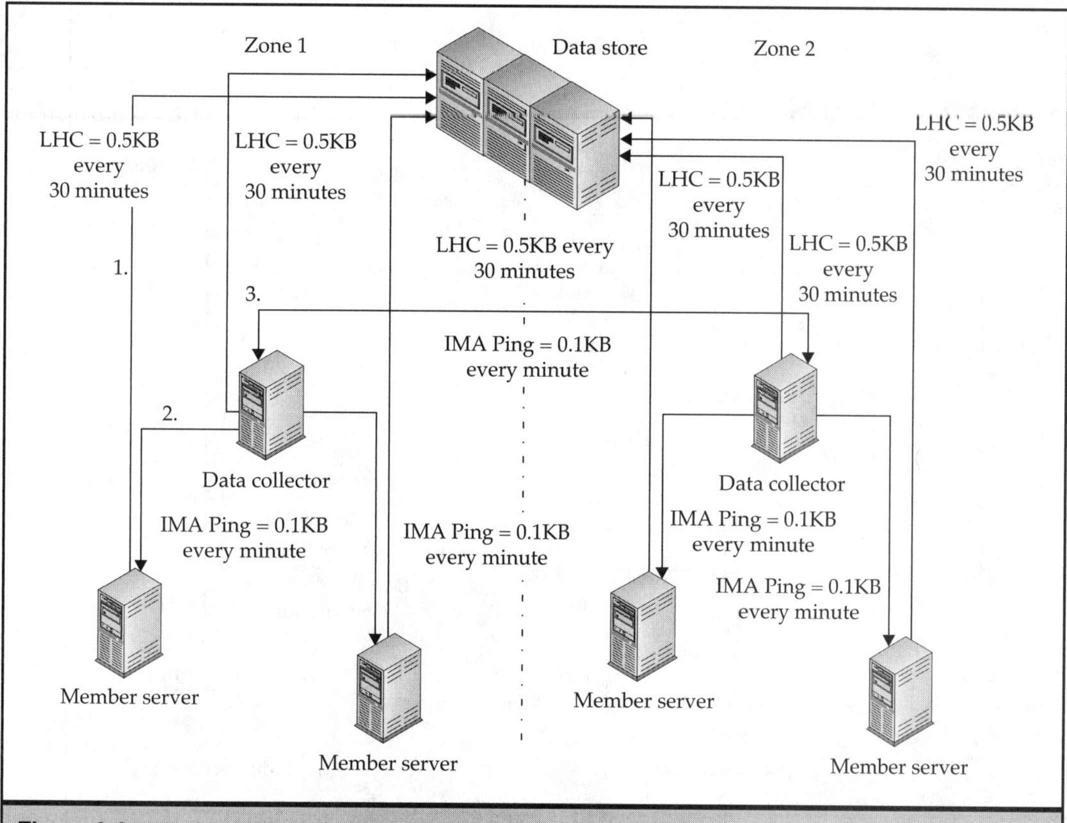

Figure 3-2. Farm replication communication

Most IMA traffic is a result of the generation of events. When a client connects, disconnects, logs off, and so forth, the member server must update information with the data collector in its zone. The data collector in turn must replicate this information to all the other data collectors in the farm. When "Load Share information across zones" is disabled, event-based communication is reduced by approximately 300 bytes. Event-based communication proceeds as follows:

1. The client requests the data collector to resolve the published application to the IP address of the least-loaded servers in the farm.
2. The client then connects to the least-loaded server returned by the data collector.
3. The member server then updates its information to the data collector for its zone.
4. The data collector then forwards this information to all the other data collectors in the farm.

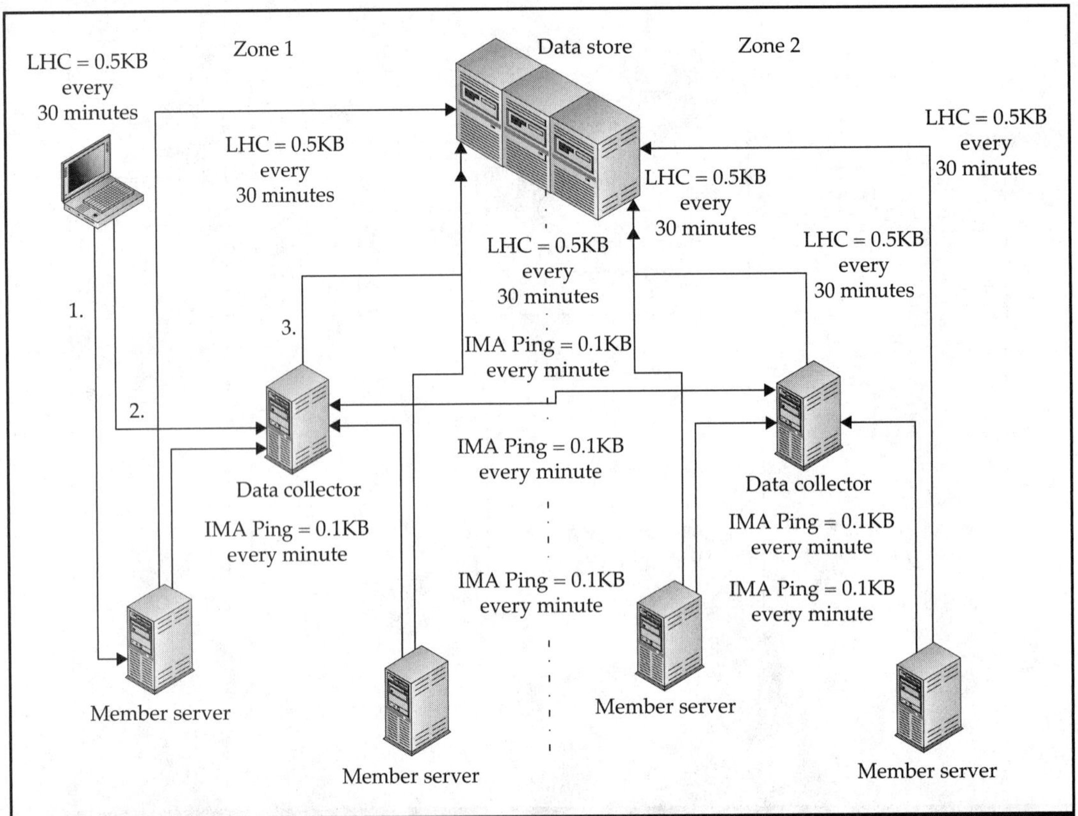

Figure 3-3. Example of a client logon event

NOTE In the client logon event example shown in Figure 3-3, notice that the data store has no communication. Connections are independent of the data store and can occur when the data store is unavailable. Connection performance is not affected by a busy data store.

New Data Collector Election

When a communication failure occurs between a member server and the data collector for its zone or between data collectors, the election process is initiated. This is true whether network problems prevent communications to the network, whether the existing data collector for the zone is shut down gracefully, or whether it has an unplanned failure for some reason (that is, if a RAID controller fails, causing the server to display a blue screen). Figure 3-4 shows an example of this communication.

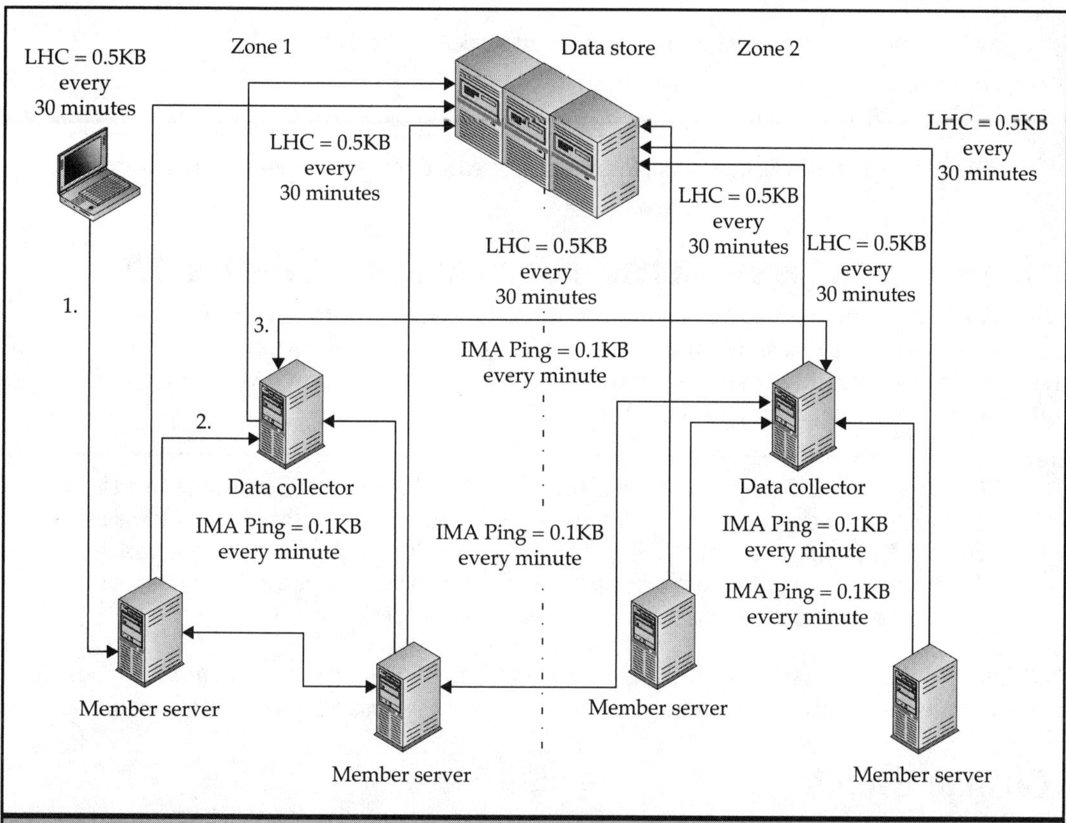

Figure 3-4. Communication example for farm after new data collector is elected

The process follows this sequence:

1. The existing data collector for Zone 1 has an unplanned failure—that is, a RAID controller fails, causing the server to display a blue screen. If the server is shut down gracefully, it triggers the election process before going down.
2. The servers in the zone recognize that the data collector has gone down and start the election process. In this example, the backup data collector is elected as the new data collector for the zone. Note that the "backup" data collector contains no replica information but instead follows the best practice of assigning election priorities to control which server is to become elected as the new data collector.
3. The member servers in the zone then send all their information to the new data collector for the zone. This information is a function of how many sessions, disconnected sessions, and applications each server has.
4. In turn, the new data collector replicates this information to all other data collectors in the farm.

NOTE The data collector election process is not dependent on the data store.

NOTE If the data collector goes down, sessions connected to other servers in the farm are unaffected.

Citrix Presentation Server Console Communication Bandwidth

When the Presentation Server Console is launched, it gathers information from several different sources. It pulls static information, such as the server list, from the data store, dynamic data session information from the data collector, and Resource Manager–specific information from the farm metric server.

TIP When using the Presentation Server Console or Access Management Console to monitor a farm at a remote site, bandwidth across the WAN can be conserved by publishing the Access Management Console or Presentation Server Console application on a remote server and connecting to it using an ICA client locally or by connecting to a remote server's console and executing the Presentation Server Console (in an effort to reduce the number of published applications).

Table 3-4 illustrates bandwidth consumption to the data store when various actions are performed using the Presentation Server Console or Access Management Console.

LHC Change Events

When configuration changes are modified in the Presentation Server Console, the changes are propagated across the farm using directory change notification broadcasts. These broadcasts take place when a change is made that is under 64KB. In XenApp 3.0 and earlier, the broadcast would occur if the change was under 10KB. These broadcasts help to minimize WAN traffic and alleviate contention on the data store. The propagation of the change notification is not guaranteed. If a server misses a change notification, it picks up the change the next time that it does an LHC coherency check.

NOTE Almost all IMA changes are under 64KB.

Figure 3-5 shows a communications example of LHC change events.

Misconception "If a data collector goes down, there is a single point of failure."

Fact The data collector election process is triggered automatically without administrative intervention. Existing users, as well as incoming ones, are unaffected by the election process, as a new data collector is elected almost instantaneously. Data collector elections are not dependent on the data store.

Action	Data Transmitted (in KB)	Data Received (in KB)
Access Management Console discovery (single server)	43.12	162.80
Open Presentation Server Console	21.53	89.24
Server enumeration (one server, Access Management Console refresh)	1.54	24.33
Server details (one server, Access Management Console refresh)	2.0	35.022
Application enumeration (one application)	.87	16.92
Application query	.87	16.87
Publication of a Resource Manager application	19.10	40.80
Change in a farm metric server	4.73	9.29
Any Resource Manager report on the local server	1.75	4.25

Table 3-4. Citrix XenApp 4.5

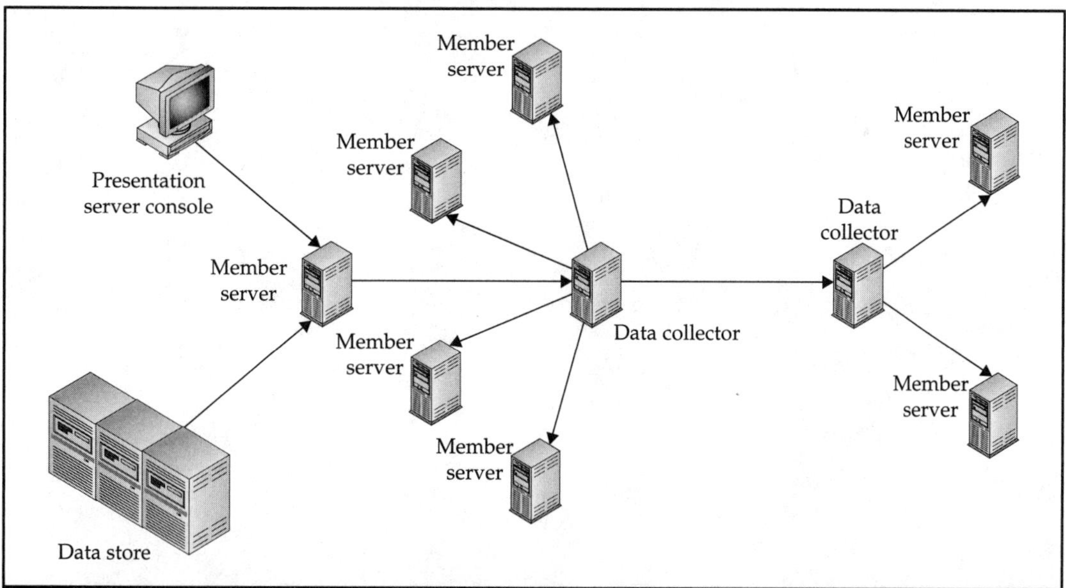

Figure 3-5. LHC change events communication example

The process for handling LHC changes is as follows:

1. The administrator makes a change in the Presentation Server Console affecting all the servers in the farm.
2. The server to which the Presentation Server Console is connected updates its LHC and writes the change to the data store.
3. The member server then forwards the change to the data collector for the zone in which it resides. The data collector updates its LHC.
4. The data collector, in turn, forwards the change to all the member servers in its zone and all other data collectors in the farm. All servers update their LHCs with the change.
5. The data collectors in the other zones, in turn, forward the update to all the member servers in their zones and they subsequently update their LHCs.

CHAPTER 4

Data Store Design and Recommendations

This chapter covers requirements, guidelines and considerations to take into account when planning and deploying your XenApp data store. Topics include hardware and sizing guidelines, network optimizations, database replication and supported databases.

DATA STORE CPU GUIDELINES

When selecting the hardware to host the data store, consider the following variables:

- Number of objects in the farm, including servers, applications, and so forth
- Frequency of events, such as adding or removing servers
- Maximum number of servers starting the Independent Management Architecture (IMA) service simultaneously

Because each of these variables has a bearing on the type of hardware used to host the data store, the individual issues are discussed in the following sections.

Objects in the Data Store

To select properly the hardware to host a data store, you first need a general understanding about the objects stored in the data store. Nearly every item displayed in the Presentation Server Console and Access Management Console represents one or more entries in the data store, as shown in Table 4-1.

Some objects, such as applications and servers, create multiple entries in the data store. As the number of entries in the data store grows, the time required for IMA to search and retrieve the entries also grows.

As servers are added to the farm, the data store needs to service more requests. Plan the data store hardware platform based on the total number of servers that will eventually be in the farm.

Applications	Administrators	Folders	Installation Manager Groups
Installation manager packages	Servers	Load evaluators	Printers
Printer drivers	Policies	Resource Manager metrics	Isolation environment

Table 4-1. Typical Objects in the Data Store

The Size of Data Store Objects

When you create an object in the Presentation Server Console or Access Management Console, such as publishing an application or adding a Citrix administrator, you create a record for that object in the data store database. In the following table, Citrix eLabs has attempted to calculate the estimated size of objects' records as created in a data store utilizing an SQL 2000, service pack 3 database. Note that the measurements shown in Table 4-2

Database Object	Size (Bytes)
Publish an application (Wordpad.exe, application name "Wordpad")	10,217
Create an application isolation environment object (AIE1)	18,284
Insert an application into an application isolation environment object (aiesetup aie1 rp505enu.exe)	4,422
Publish an application into an application isolation environment (Acrobat5 and AIE 1)	10,387
Create a blank policy named "policy one"	9,326
Configure all rules and assign a policy to a domain users group	1,474
Create a Resource Manager application named "notepad" configured for one server	7,191
Import a network printer server with one printer	2,206
Add one printer—"HP laserJet 8100 PS"	3,218
Add Resource Manager metric for one server (Citrix XenApp/data store bytes written per second)	1,242
Add one domain administrator as a Citrix administrator	1,745
Add one user group as a Citrix administrator	1,751
Configure Installation Manager properties (account, path)	1,661
Add a package	6,190
Create a package group named "Group1" that contains one package	4,202
Create a server group for Installation Manager (Server Group 1) with one server	1,135
Add a server folder named "Server Folder" with permissions copied	1,190
Add an application folder named "App folder"	1,191
Create a load evaluator with one evaluation rule (server user load)	1,791
Join a server to the farm	46,986

Table 4-2. Data Store Object/Action and Typical Size

should be considered only as guidelines because the sizes of an object's entries in the data store depend on many factors, such as the name of an object and its configurations.

NOTE In Citrix XenApp 4.5, the Configuration Logging feature has been introduced to track the changes administrators make to the farm. The feature has no effects on the above data object's sizes.

Data Store Hardware Guidelines

As with any client/server database application, the CPU power and speed of the database server can improve the response time of an application. XenApp is no different. In a XenApp environment, you can improve the response time of the following events by increasing the processing power of the data store:

- Starting the IMA service on multiple servers simultaneously
- Adding a server to the farm
- Removing a server from the farm

The response time of other farm events, such as starting the IMA service on a single server, re-creating the local host cache, or replicating printer drivers to all farm servers, is more closely related to the farm size than to the response time of the data store.

Testing shows that adding processors to the data store can dramatically improve response time when multiple simultaneous queries are being executed. If the environment has large groups of servers coming online frequently, the additional processors can service the requests faster.

However, with serial events, such as installing or removing a farm server, the additional processors show lower performance gains. To improve the processing time for these types of events, increase the processor speed of the data store hardware platform.

Data Store Network Optimizations

You can configure the data store in several different ways to increase the performance and throughput of the database server. In large farms with powerful database servers, the network can become the performance bottleneck when reading information from the data store during startup. This is particularly true when the database server hosts various resource-intensive databases. As with XenApp, Citrix recommends that you use a teaming network interface card (NIC) solution, such as switch-assisted load balancing, to improve the available bandwidth of the server hosting the data store. To find out if the network is the bottleneck, monitor the CPU usage on the data store. If the CPU utilization is not at 100 percent while the IMA service is starting and it is still in the process of starting, the network can be the bottleneck. If the CPU utilization is at or near 100 percent, it is likely that additional processor(s) may be needed.

Data store connectivity testing was performed in the Citrix eLabs on a 100 Mbps switched local area network (LAN). This testing was also repeated in a Gigabit Ethernet environment. Two NICs that were teamed via switch-assisted load balancing—that is,

400 Mbps throughput—provided ample throughput without the additional cost associated with gigabit NICs, cables, and switch ports. However, in large environments, gigabit connectivity may be beneficial.

Data Store Guidelines

The general guidelines for choosing a data store are listed in Table 4-3 and are also found in the *Citrix Presentation Server Administrator's Guide.*

The following are general recommendations for the server farm's data store:

- Microsoft Access and Microsoft SQL Server 2005 Express Edition SP1 are suitable for all small and many medium-sized environments.
- Microsoft SQL Server, Oracle, and IBM DB2 are suitable for any size environment and are especially recommended for all large and enterprise environments.

The following is a list of things to consider when choosing a data store for a farm:

- Microsoft Access and Microsoft SQL Server 2005 Express Edition SP1 are best used for centralized farms.
- Microsoft Access and Microsoft SQL Server 2005 Express Edition SP1 support only indirect mode for all servers other than the host server and, therefore, have slower performance than a direct mode data store in large farm implementations.
- Database replication is not supported with Microsoft Access.
- For Microsoft SQL Server 2005 Express Edition SP1 replication information, visit www.microsoft.com/sql/techinfo/development/2000/msde2000.asp.
- Use databases that support replication when deploying large farms across a wide area network (WAN). You can obtain considerable performance advantage by distributing the load over multiple database servers.
- In the Citrix eLabs, Microsoft SQL Server, Oracle, and IBM DB2 perform similarly with large farms. Oracle Real Application Clusters (RAC) includes the added advantage of load balancing incoming requests between the servers.

	Small	Medium	Large	Enterprise
Servers	1–50	25–100	50–100	100 or more
Named users	<150	<3,000	<5,000	>3,000
Applications	<100	<100	<500	<2,000

Table 4-3. Data Store Selection Guidelines

Using Replicated Data Store Databases

Having a single data store is recommended where appropriate, but in some situations, a replicated data store can improve farm performance. This section covers the concerns and situations that arise from using replicated database technology.

High-Latency WAN Concerns

High-latency links without the use of replicated databases can create situations where the data store is locked for extended periods of time while performing maintenance from remote sites. This means that the IMA service may start after extended periods of time and some normal operations may fail when performed from the remote site.

TIP Performing farm maintenance using the Presentation Server Console or Access Management Console from a remote site that has high latency is not recommended. For better performance, run the console as a published application.

In a high-latency situation, the following conditions apply:

- Data store writes take longer to complete and, for a period of time, block all additional writes from local or remote sites.
- Data store reads will probably not adversely affect local connections, but the remote site can experience slower performance.

Replicated Database Issues

Using replicated databases to speed performance may be justified. The farm servers perform many more reads from the data store, than writes to the data store. Most reads occur during startup, when each server populates its local host cache.

In a LAN environment, using replicated databases can speed the startup time of the IMA service and improve the responsiveness of the servers in large farms.

In a WAN environment, the configuration of the data store is important. Because XenApp is read-intensive, place replicas of the data store at sites where a considerable number of servers reside. This practice minimizes reads across the WAN link. Limit the use of replicated databases to situations where the remote site has enough XenApp servers to justify the cost of placing a replicated copy of the database at the site.

TIP Database replication consumes bandwidth. The database server software configuration, not XenApp, controls the frequency of database updates.

THE DATA STORE REQUIREMENTS

Citrix is committed to ensuring that our products function with the latest Microsoft, Oracle, and IBM databases and clients. Citrix will supply best efforts to ensure compatibility with upcoming database releases. New versions of supported databases (SQL,

Oracle, or DB2) released after our products have been released should work. However, Citrix recommends creating a test environment to ensure there are no unforeseen issues related to changes made to the new version or update of the third-party product. Individuals wishing to use the new release with current Citrix products should perform their own testing before using the platform. Citrix does not support any BETA versions of third-party products.

Table 4-4 lists the versions and releases of third-party databases tested during the development of XenApp. For updated database support information see Citrix Knowledge Center article CTX114501.

CAUTION Oracle client 8.1.5 is not supported. This client must be upgraded to 8.1.55 prior to installation. Oracle clients 8.1.5-7,8.0.6,7.3.4 have been validated but are no longer supported since Oracle no longer supports these versions.

Additional considerations for Microsoft Access, Microsoft SQL Server, Oracle, and IBM DB2 as data stores for XenApp are listed below. Although XenApp uses ODBC for connectivity, other ODBC-compliant databases are not supported with XenApp.

Using Microsoft Access

All servers connect indirectly and maintain connections to the host server:

- By default, the server that hosts the database is also its zone's data collector.
- Tuning the Jet Database Engine with registry settings can improve performance for large farms. Consult the Microsoft documentation about performance tuning for the Jet Database Engine. Back up both the registry and the Mf20.mdb file before changing the tuning parameters.
- Use dsmaint backup to perform an online backup of the data store. This can be scripted easily in a batch file.
- Back up the data store before using the Presentation Server Console or Access Management Console to change the data store. Scheduling a daily backup is sufficient in most cases.

Using Microsoft SQL Server

The practices outlined in this section suggest the best practices for using Microsoft SQL Server as the data store. This is not intended as a substitute for the Microsoft SQL Server documentation. Read all of the Microsoft SQL Server documentation prior to installing Microsoft SQL Server. These instructions do not refer to Microsoft SQL Express. See the Administrator's Guide for information about using Microsoft SQL Express as the data store.

Database Version	Database Operating System	Microsoft Data Access Components (MDAC) on XenAPP	Microsoft Access version on XenApp	Client version on XenApp
Microsoft Access	Windows Server 2003 Service Pack 1 (SP1)	2.8	SP8 (4.0.8015.0) + latest security fix	N/A
Microsoft Access	Windows Server 2003 64-bit	2.8	SP8 (4.0.8015.0) + latest security fix	N/A
SQL Express	Windows Server 2003 SP1	2.8	SP8 (4.0.8015.0) + latest security fix	N/A
SQL Express	Windows Server 2003 64-bit	2.8	SP8 (4.0.8015.0) + latest security fix	N/A
SQL 2000 SP3a (or SP4 when available)	Windows Server 2003 SP1	2.8	SP8 (4.0.8015.0) + latest security fix	N/A
SQL 2005	Windows Server 2003 SP1	2.8	SP8 (4.0.8015.0) + latest security fix	N/A
SQL 2005	Windows 2003 64-bit	2.8	SP8 (4.0.8015.0) + latest security fix	N/A
IBM DB2 Enterprise 8.2	Windows Server 2003 SP1	N/A	N/A	IBM DB2 8.2
IBM DB2 Universal Database (UDB) 8.2	Windows Server 2003 64-bit	N/A	N/A	IBM DB2 UDB 8.2
Oracle Enterprise 9.2.0.1	Windows Server 2003 SP1	N/A	N/A	Oracle 9.2.0.1
Oracle Enterprise 9.2.0.1	Solaris SPARC 32	N/A	N/A	Oracle 9.2.0.1
Oracle Enterprise 10.2.0.1.0	Windows Server 2003 SP1	N/A	N/A	Oracle 10.2.0.1.0
Oracle Enterprise 10.2.0.1.0	Windows Server 2003 64-bit	N/A	N/A	Oracle 10.2.0.1.0

Table 4-4. List of Tested and Supported Third-Party Databases

Server Configuration

- When using Microsoft SQL Server in a replicated environment, be sure to use the same user account on each Microsoft SQL Server for the data store.
- Each XenApp farm requires a dedicated database. However, multiple databases can run on a single Microsoft SQL Server. Do not install the XenApp farm in an SQL database that is shared with any other client/server applications.
- Follow Microsoft recommendations for configuring database and transaction logs for recovery.
- Whenever a change is made using the Presentation Server Console or Access Management Console, back up the database. Scheduling a daily backup is sufficient in most cases.
- Disable Hyper-Threading. Tests have shown an increase in performance in administrative actions (IMA start time, Presentation Server Console) when Hyper-Threading is disabled on the SQL server acting as the farm data store. The decrease in performance with Hyper-Threading enabled results when two or more threads do the same type of action (input/output [I/O], calculations, and so forth) on the same physical processor. Note that this recommendation applies to the data store only; although XenApp does realize a benefit from Hyper-Threading, as always, this depends on the types of applications published on those servers. Refer to your server vendor for specific details on disabling Hyper-Threading.

SQL TempDB Considerations

When you are using SQL server as a data store, XenApp operations can cause the tempdb to grow larger than its default size. Although the tempdb database's *Autogrow* feature is set by default in SQL Server 7.0 and 2000, the automatic growth of the tempdb can result in performance degradation. Citrix recommends that you permanently set the tempdb to a reasonable size initially.

The tempdb database is re-created every time that SQL Server starts. By default, the tempdb has a data file of 8.0MB and log file of 0.5MB. By having the tempdb file set to the "typical" size when SQL Server is restarted (and when it is re-created from scratch to the size you set), you can eliminate the overhead from the tempdb growing.

Citrix recommends the following regarding the usage of tempDB in a XenApp farm:

- Permanently change the tempdb database file's initialization size. Set the tempdb data file size according to the size of your farm. Citrix recommends reserving 0.75MB to 1.25MB of space in a tempdb data file for each XenApp server in the farm. For example, in a 100-server farm, Citrix recommends permanently setting the tempdb data file size from 75MB to 125MB and the tempdb log file size to half the data file size. You can accomplish this by using the Enterprise Manager or ALTER DATABSE ... MODIFY FILE command. Even after the SQL server restarts, the tempdb keeps the size you set.

- Set the auto growth increment of the tempdb in terms of file size rather than percentage. For a farm consisting of fewer than 100 servers, set the increment to 50MB for the data file and 25MB for the log file. For a farm consisting of more than 100 servers, set the increment to 100MB for the data file and 50MB for the log file.
- If possible, put the tempdb on its own physical disk, preferably a Redundant Array of Independent Disks (RAID) 0 array or other disk subsystem.
- In SQL server 7.0, make sure the "truncate log on checkpoint database" option is set for tempdb. When this database option is set, the tempdb log will be truncated each time that the checkpoint process is run. To truncate the transaction log on SQL 2000, create a maintenance plan or follow the next recommendation.
- In SQL Server 2000, make sure that the Recovery mode of the tempdb is set to simple. Under this Recovery mode, the tempdb log file automatically truncates when an SQL server checkpoint event occurs.
- If the tempdb transaction log file grows too large before the checkpoint process occurs, you can issue a BACKUP LOG tempdb WITH TRUNCATE_ONLY to truncate the tempdb transaction log manually.

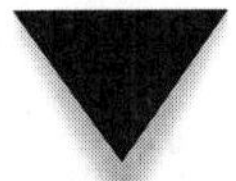

NOTE If the tempdb data file has been expended or has used all the disk space, certain XenApp operations will fail. You can add more data files to the tempdb using either SQL Server Enterprise Manager or the ALTER DATABASE ... ADD FILE command to add more files to the tempdb. The recommendation is to use the previous methods to add more files to the tempdb at installation to prevent the tempdb from being used up.

Using Oracle

The practices outlined in this section are suggested implementations for the Oracle data store. They are not intended to be a substitute for the Oracle documentation. Read all of the Oracle documentation prior to installing Oracle. Guidelines given here can be used on Oracle 7, Oracle 8, Oracle 8*i*, Oracle 9*i*, and Oracle 10*g*, except as noted otherwise.

Failover

Oracle enables administrators to maintain a standby database for quick disaster recovery. A *standby database* maintains a copy of the production database in a permanent state of recovery. If a disaster occurs in the production database, you can open the standby database with a minimum amount of recovery.

Keep in mind the following important facts concerning Oracle failover:

- The standby database must run on the same version of the kernel that is on the production system.
- Standby databases fail only one way. They cannot fail back.

- If a database fails, use dsmaint config to reconfigure XenApp to point to the standby database.
- Citrix recommends the use of a standby database for XenApp farms. See the Oracle documentation for instructions on setting up a standby database.

Using Oracle as a Distributed Database

To reduce the load on a single Oracle database server, use Oracle Synchronous Multi-Master Replication to distribute the database load over multiple Oracle database servers. Install and distribute the farm servers evenly across these databases.

XenApp requires data coherency across multiple databases. Therefore, Synchronous Multi-Master Replication is required for writes to the multiple databases.

Using Oracle as a distributed database solution requires the following:

- All participating databases must be running Oracle Enterprise Versions.
- All clients (XenApp direct servers) must be SQL*Net Version 2 or Net8.
- Install the farm database first on the master definition site and then configure the Multi-Master Replication.
- Replicate all the table objects contained in the data store user's schema and any indexes that are used for performance purposes. Do not replicate the index created automatically by the Oracle server while creating Primary Key Constraint and Unique Constraint.

Citrix recommends that you consult the Oracle documentation when setting up replication:

- The documentation for Oracle9*i* is at the following web address:

  http://www.oracle.com/technology/documentation/oracle9i.html
- The documentation for Oracle10*g* is at the following web address:

  http://www.oracle.com/technology/documentation/database10g.html

Using IBM DB2

XenApp supports IBM DB2 Universal Database Enterprise Edition Version 7.2 for Windows 2000 with FixPak 5 or greater, as well as Version 8.1 for Windows 2000 with FixPak 4 or greater.

Install the IBM DB2 run-time client and apply the latest FixPak on each XenApp that will directly access the database server.

If you have multiple XenApp farms, create a separate database/tablespace for each farm's data store. Restart the system after you install the IBM DB2 run-time client and the FixPak and before you install XenApp. In some cases, you may also need to restart the system after you install the run-time client and before you install the FixPak. See the IBM DB2 documentation for more information.

NOTE XenApp uses the data type of binary large object (BLOB) to store information in an IBM DB2 database. IBM DB2 does not support the use of BLOB data types in an updatable replication scenario. Therefore, if your server farm needs to have updatable replicas, use Microsoft SQL Server or Oracle for the farm's data store instead of IBM DB2.

Depending on the size of your server farm, you may need to modify the following options in IBM DB2 Control Center:

- **appheapsz, app_ctl_heap_sz, maxlocks** You may need to modify these options if you have a large server farm (50 or more servers) that is relatively active.
- **Maxappls** This setting must be greater than the number of servers in the farm, or the servers will fail to connect (the default is 40).
- **avg_appls** This setting should be equal to the number of servers in the farm.
- **logfilsiz, logprimary, logsecond** You may need to adjust these settings upward if you move the farm from another database.

Citrix recommends using a separate database with a dedicated tablespace for the XenApp farm's data store.

LARGE FARM DATABASE MAINTENANCE

In a XenApp environment all farm-wide configuration information is stored in the data store. The main operations IMA service performs on the data store are mostly queries. To speed up the query performance many table indexes are created on the IMA databases tables.

From time to time the IMA service needs to make changes to the IMA database; for example, during the application publishing process, policy editing process, etc. Over time these data update operations will cause the indexes to become fragmented and less organized than they were when they were first created. There will be more page splits, a greater number of pages with less data on them, and consequently, there will be more I/O required to satisfy each query.

As the data and index become increasingly fragmented, the IMA service query performance will be degraded. This will impact IMA service startup time, Access Management Console discovery time and Local Host Cache update time, to name a few. In order to improve the IMA service query performance, some database maintenance operations need to be performed on the data store.

The following steps walk through the actions that can be performed on SQL server 2000 as an example. For similar procedures on Oracle, DB2 and SQL server 2005, consult the documentation for those databases.

1. From Enterprise Manager start the Database Maintenance wizard. Click Next.
2. On the next window, select your data store, click Next.

3. Select reorganize the data and index page, click Next.
4. On the Specify database backup plan window, make sure the check box is cleared, click Next.
5. Accept the default options for the following wizard windows. Name the maintenance plan and click Finish.

It is also possible to include the above index reorganization as part of a regular database maintenance plan that includes a data store backup.

REPLICATING AN SQL SERVER 2000 DATABASE

This section outlines the steps necessary to replicate with SQL Server 2000. To replicate an SQL Server 2000 database, use SQL Enterprise Manager. Begin by creating a new database on the SQL server to be used as the source for all replicas that you create. Be sure that the account that you use to create the database has db_owner permissions and is the same one that you use on the replicated database.

Before setting up replication, ensure the following:

- Ideally, the Windows installations should be clean, fresh (from CD) installations instead of images. If images of Windows are used, make sure that they do not come from the same image, but from different ones for each server. If your Windows installations come from the same image, then replication will not work.
- Do not mix Windows 2000 with Windows 2003. The Distributed Transaction Coordinator service operates differently in Windows 2003 than it does in Windows 2000. If you mix the operating systems (OSs), replication will fail.
- For Windows 2003 Server, verify that both Publisher and Subscriber SQL servers are in the same domain. If they are not, review Microsoft Article 817064.
- Install SQL Server on the servers designated for the data stores.
- Verify that the Microsoft Distributed Transaction Coordinator is installed on the servers designated for the data stores.

Setting Up the SQL Server Data Store for Distribution

Perform these steps for both servers:

1. From the Start menu, start the Services Manager.
2. From Services Manager, set up the same domain log on account for the following services (the local system account does not work):
   - SQLServerAgent
   - MSSQLServer
   - MSDTC (Distributed Transaction Coordinator on Windows 2000)

NOTE If you are configuring SQL replication on a Windows 2003 server, verify that the MSDTC service is using the Network Services security account (this account uses a blank password).

The following describes the general tasks for successfully replicating an SQL Server database. Each task is explained in more detail in the following sections.

1. Establish the distributor server.
2. Set the distributor properties.
3. Publish the source database.
4. Push the published database out to subscribers.

Step 1: Establish the Distributor Server

Complete the following steps to define the server that will act as the distributor. MS SQL 2000 servers acting as Publisher, Distributor, and Subscriber need to be in the same NT/AD domain and the SQL services should be started under the same account.

1. Open Enterprise Manager on the server on which the source database is located.
2. Right-click the Replication folder and select Configure Publishing | Subscribers | Distribution Wizard.
3. On the Select Distributor page, select the current server to act as the distributor.
4. Keep the default Snapshot folder.
5. On the Customize the Configuration page, choose the option No and use the default settings.
6. Click Finish.

Step 2: Set the Distributor Properties

Complete the following steps to set the distributor properties:

1. Right-click the Replication Monitor folder and choose Distributor Properties.
2. On the Publication Databases tab, check the Trans box next to the database you want to replicate, as shown in Figure 4-1.

Step 3: Publish the Source Database

Complete the following steps to publish the database that you want to replicate:

1. Right-click the database name and go to New | Publication to start the Create Publication Wizard.
2. Click Show advanced options in this wizard, and then click Next.
3. On the Choose Publication Database screen, select the database you want to replicate, and then click Next.

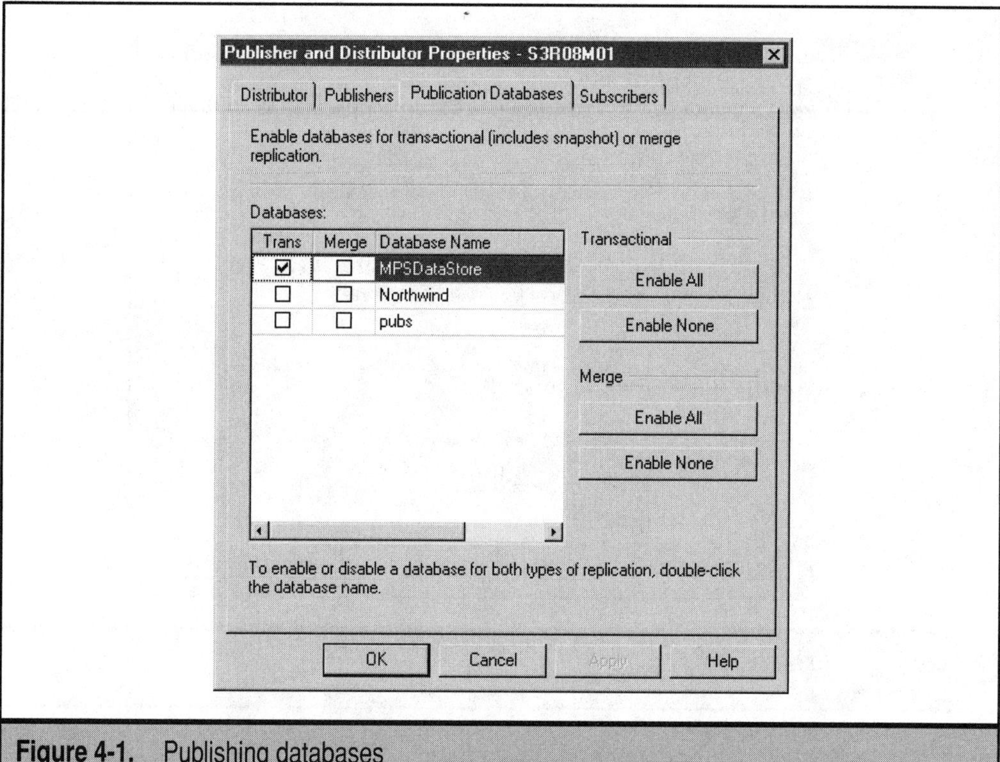

Figure 4-1. Publishing databases

4. On the Select Publication Type page, choose Transactional publication.
5. On the Updatable Subscriptions page, select the Immediate updating option, as shown in Figure 4-2.
6. On the Specify Subscriber Types page, select the Servers running SQL Server 2000 option.
7. On the Specify Articles page, shown in Figure 4-3, select both Show and Publish for the tables object type on the left side of the page. Do not publish stored procedures to the replicated databases. Then follow these steps:
   - Click Next on the Article Issues page.
   - Name the publication.
   - On the Customize the Properties of the Publication page, choose No, create the publication as specified.
   - Click Finish to complete the wizard. The publication is displayed in the Publications folder, as shown in Figure 4-4.

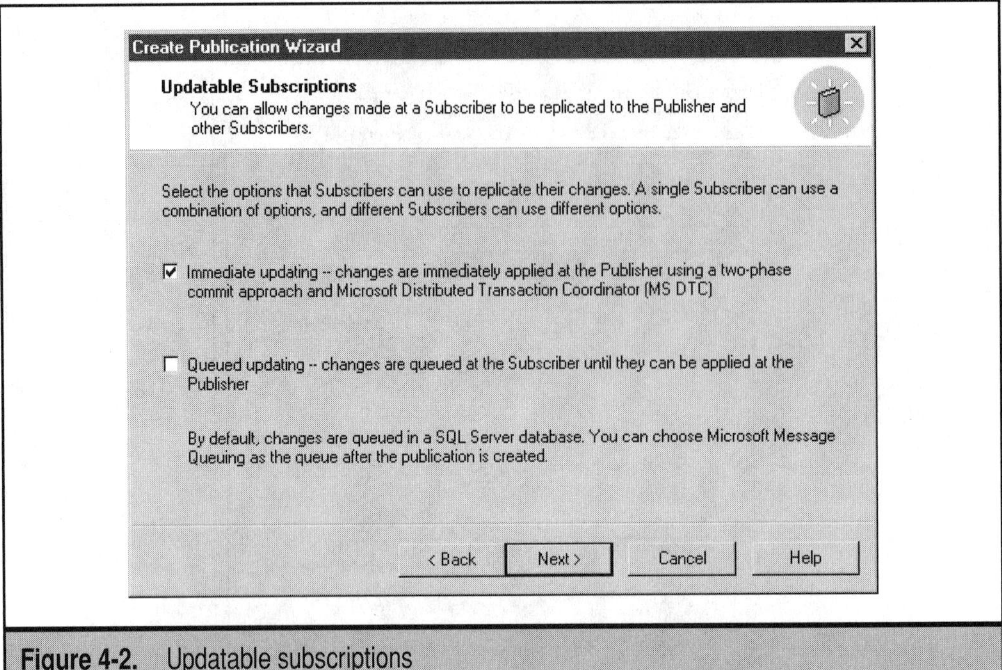

Figure 4-2. Updatable subscriptions

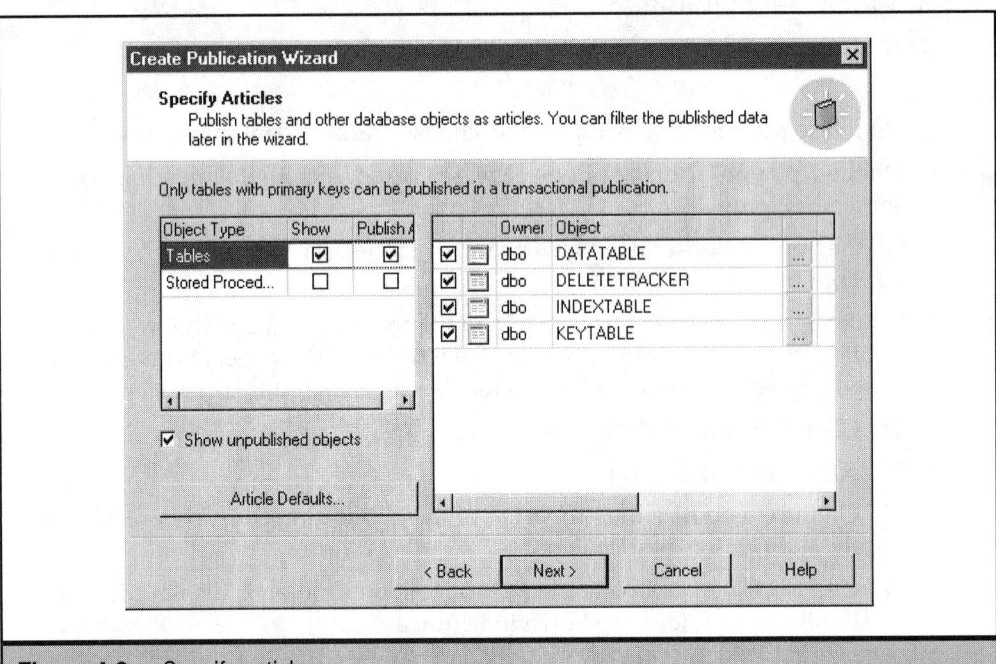

Figure 4-3. Specify articles

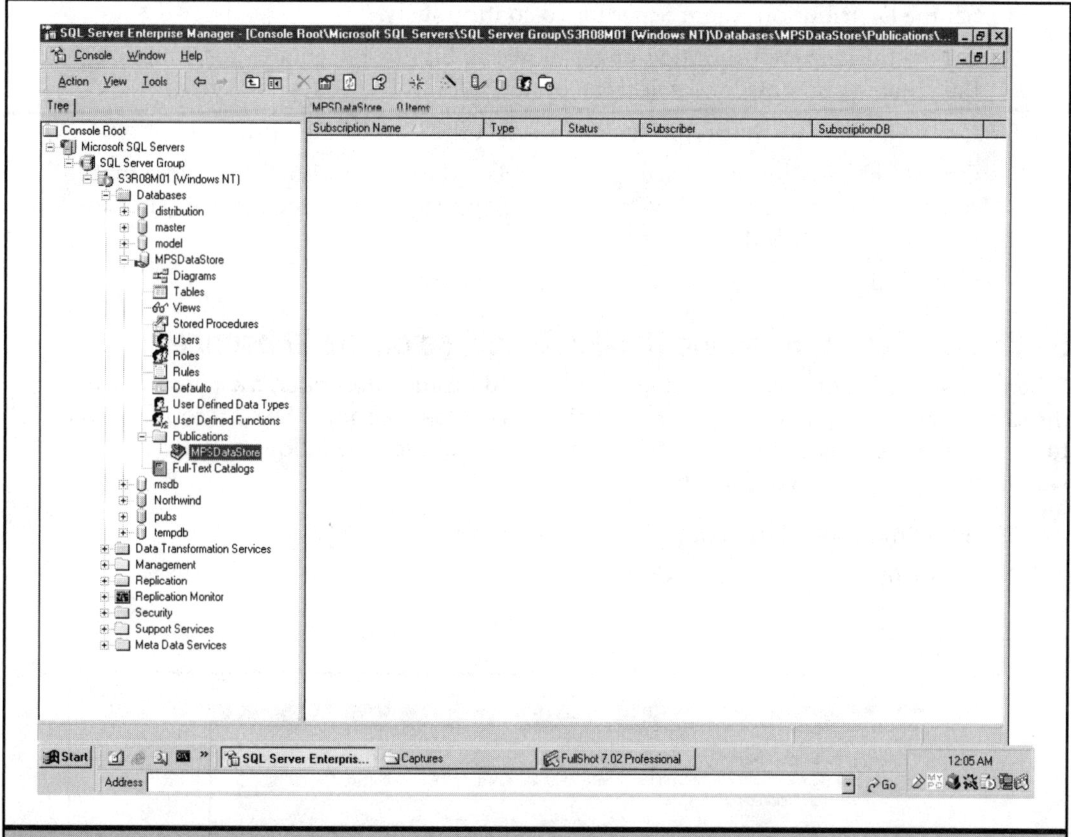

Figure 4-4. Publications folder

Step 4: Push the Published Database to Subscribers

Complete the following steps to push the publication to subscribers:

1. Right-click the published database in the Publications folder and choose Push new subscription to start the Push Subscription Wizard.
2. Click Show advanced options in this wizard and then click Next.
3. On the Choose Subscribers page, select the subscribers for the published database.
4. On the next page, choose the destination database to which you want to replicate the source database.
5. On the Set Distribution Agent Location page, choose to run the agent at the distributor.

6. Set the Distribution Agent Schedule to continuously.
7. On the Initialize Subscription page, shown in Figure 4-5, choose Yes, initialize the schema and data, and select the option to Start the Snapshot Agent.
8. On the Updatable Subscriptions page, select the Immediate updating option.

   On the Start Required Services page, displayed in Figure 4-6, the services that must be running are listed. Verify that the applicable required services are running on the distributor server.
9. Click Finish on the next screen to complete the wizard.

Setting the Password on the Replica Database on the Subscriber

When the subscription (replica) database is created on the subscriber, the password for the sa account is not passed for security reasons. The password for the sa account needs to be manually set on the subscriber for the replica database. The following steps are one way to change the password for the sa account:

1. Select the subscription database on the Subscriber.
2. Select Tools | SQL Query Analyzer.

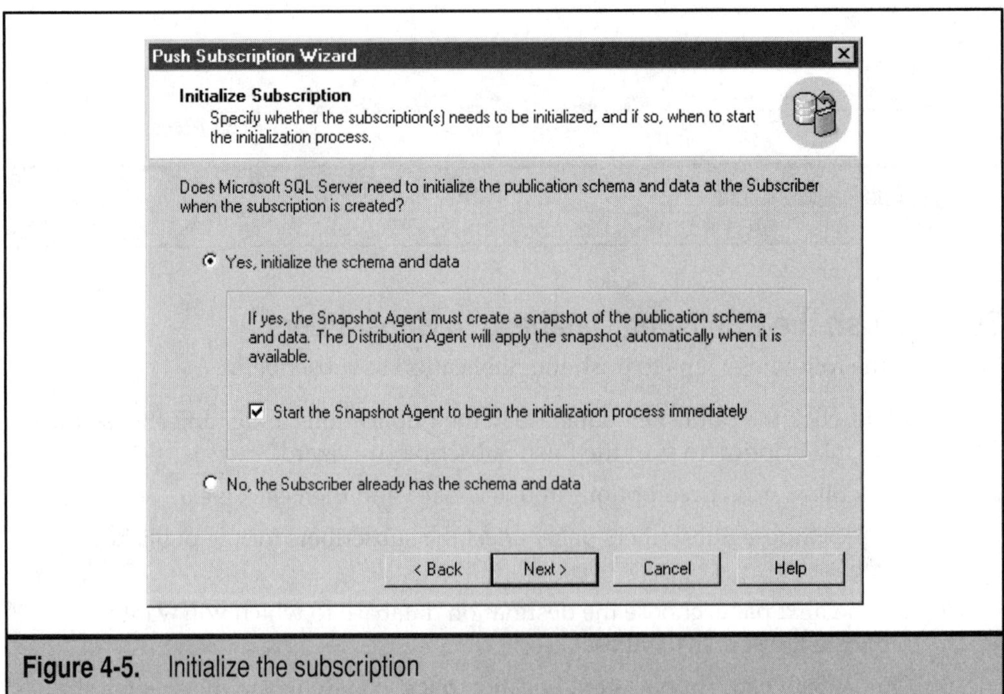

Figure 4-5. Initialize the subscription

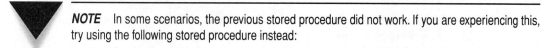

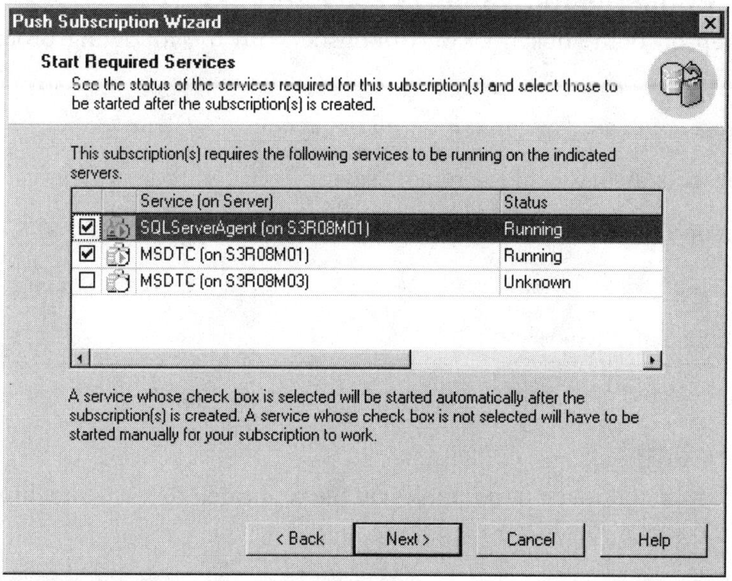

Figure 4-6. Start required services

3. In the SQL Query Analyzer window, type and run the following stored procedure:

```
sp_link_publication '<Distributor>', '<Database>',
'<Publication>', 0, 'SA',
'<Pwd>'
```

where:

Distributor = The name of the distributor server
Database = The name of the published database on the distributor
Publication = The name of the publication that is to be linked
Pwd = The password for the SA account on the distributor

NOTE In some scenarios, the previous stored procedure did not work. If you are experiencing this, try using the following stored procedure instead:

```
sp_link_publication 'publisher', 'database', 'publication', 0, 'sa',
'password', 'distributor'
```

Additional Concerns for Windows 2003 Servers

As a final step on both subscriber and publisher, run the following procedure using Query Analyzer:

```
exec sp_serveroption 'myServer', 'data access', 'true'
```

where myServer is the name of the remote server.

Example run on Publisher:

```
exec sp_serveroption 'SubscriberServer', 'data access', 'true'
```

Example run on Subscriber:

```
exec sp_serveroption 'PublisherServer', 'data access', 'true'
```

Troubleshooting

Make sure that the following seven tables on the replicated database are listed:

- DATATABLE
- INDEXTABLE
- KEYTABLE
- MSreplication_objects
- MSreplication_subscriptions
- MSsubscription_agents
- MSsubscription_properties

If all tables are not listed, delete the replication setup and begin again. The dtproperties table appears if you used the Database Diagram Wizard in Enterprise Manager.

If you are installing XenApp for the first time, select the server hosting the replicated database when prompted.

If you have a server in the server farm that you want to connect to the new database, create a new DSN file on the XenApp and point it to the replicated SQL Server database. You can then use the dsmaint config command to point the IMA Service to the new database.

Multisubscriber Replication

Special consideration must be taken when configuring a multisubscriber model (one publisher and two or more subscribers) for the XenApp database.

By default, Microsoft SQL Server leaves foreign-key referential-integrity constraints intact at the subscriber databases. XenApp uses a two-phase commit between the subscriber and the publisher, so these relationships are not necessary because integrity is maintained at the master/publisher. After a subscriber commits a transaction at the master/publisher, the publisher pushes the changes out to all remaining subscribers. However, the referential integrity constraints on the remaining subscribers prevent the transactions from completing correctly.

When this occurs, you see errors similar to the following:

```
"DELETE statement conflicted with COLUMN REFERENCE constraint
'FK__DATATABLE__nodei__35BCFE0A'. The conflict occurred in database
'CTXIMA', table 'DATATABLE', column 'nodeid'. The row was not found at
the Subscriber when applying the replicated command."
```

To prevent the foreign-key relationships from blocking the replicated transaction, perform the following steps on all of the subscriber servers, as well as the distribution server:

1. In Enterprise Manager, select the XenApp database.
2. Click on Tables.
3. Right-click DATATABLE in right pane and select Design Table from the Context menu.
4. Click the Manage Relationships button.
5. Verify the Enforce Relationship for Replication check box is marked for the relationship that starts with FK__DATATABLE__nodei.
6. Save the changes to DATATABLE.
7. Repeat steps 3 through 6 for INDEXTABLE and the foreign-key relationship that starts with FK__INDEXTABL__nodei.
8. Verify that the foreign-key relationships under KEYTABLE do not have the Enforce relationship for replication box checked.
9. Repeat steps 1 through 8 at each subscriber database.

Promoting a Subscriber to a Publisher

Microsoft SQL Server 2000 has no predefined procedure for promoting a subscriber to a publisher. The recommended method is to stop all replication between the old publisher and all the subscribers and then reestablish subscriptions between the new publisher and the remaining subscribers. These steps also work if the desire is simply to break replication and use the old subscriber as a master instead of a replica.

After discontinuing all replication activities for the XenApp database, perform the following steps on the promoted subscriber *before* reestablishing replication with the former subscribers:

1. Reestablish the autoincrementing functionality of the KEYTABLE *nodeid* field.
   a. In Enterprise Manager, select the XenApp database.
   b. Click on Tables.
   c. Right-click KEYTABLE in the right pane and select Design Table from the Context menu.

   d. Select the *nodeid* field.
   e. From the Columns tab on the bottom panel:
      1) Delete any default value.
      2) Set Identity to a value of Yes.
      3) Set Identity Seed to a value of 1.
      4) Set Identity Increment to a value of 1.
   f. Save the changes made to KEYTABLE.
2. Reestablish the autoincrementing functionality of the DATATABLE *dummyid* field.
   a. In Enterprise Manager, select the XenApp database.
   b. Click on Tables.
   c. Right-click DATATABLE in the right pane and select Context | Design Table.
   d. Select the *dummyid* field.
   e. From the Columns tab on the bottom panel:
      1) Delete any default value.
      2) Set Identity to a value of Yes.
      3) Set Identity Seed to a value of 1.
      4) Set Identity Increment to a value of 1.
   f. Save the changes made to DATATABLE.
3. Reestablish the autoincrementing functionality of the INDEXTABLE *dummyid* field.
   a. In Enterprise Manager, select the XenApp database.
   b. Click on Tables.
   c. Right-click DATATABLE in the right pane and select Context | Design Table.
   d. Select the *dummyid* field.
   e. From the Columns tab on the bottom panel:
      1) Delete any default value.
      2) Set Identity to a value of Yes.
      3) Set Identity Seed to a value of 1.
      4) Set Identity Increment to a value of 1.
   f. Save the changes made to DATATABLE.
4. Reestablish the enforcement of Foreign Key Relationships if in a Multisubscriber scenario.
   a. In Enterprise Manager, select the XenApp database.
   b. Click on Tables.

c. Right-click DATATABLE in the right pane and select Context | Design Table.
d. Click the Manage Relationships button.
e. Verify the Enforce Relationship for Replication check box is marked for the relationship that starts with FK__DATATABLE__nodei.
f. Save the changes to DATATABLE.
g. Repeat steps c through f for INDEXTABLE and the foreign key relationship that starts with FK__INDEXTABL__nodei.

After completing the previous steps, reboot all the SQL servers and the promoted subscriber should be a functional master. The remaining subscribers, if any, may have replication reestablished. At this point, the old publisher/master is no longer functional in that role. If replication is to be reestablished with the old publisher, it must be configured as a subscriber.

Oracle Replication on Oracle 9*i* and 10*g*

Oracle replication involves two types: Basic and Advanced. *Basic replication* provides an elementary means to replicate data between databases. Basic replication is always one-way. *Advanced replication* is available only in the Enterprise Edition of Oracle and provides more complex replication solutions, such as:

- Updatable Materialized views
- Writeable Materialized views
- Multi-Master replication
- Procedural replication

XenApp requires and supports only the Oracle Advanced Replication feature. In particular, XenApp supports Synchronous Multi-Master Replication. Oracle Synchronous Multi-Master Replication can be set up using Oracle Enterprise Manager or the Replication Management application programming interface (API). Citrix recommends using the Replication Management API to set up the Oracle Synchronous Multi-Master Replication.

All the databases involved in the Oracle Synchronous Multi-Master Replications are called *master sites*. For the purpose of this illustration of using the Replication Management API to set up the Synchronous Multi-Master Replication, two databases are used: One is called east.citrix.com and the other is called west.citrix.com. In this example, objects are replicated from east.citrix.com to west.citrix.com.

The general steps for setting up the Oracle Synchronous Multi-Master Replication in Oracle database versions 9*i* and 10*g* are the following:

1. Configure the initialization parameters.
2. Set up master sites.
3. Create necessary schemas on both master sites.
4. Create the master group.
5. Start replication.

Step 1: Configuring the Initialization Parameter

For Oracle replication to work, certain Oracle server initialization parameters must be set. Table 4-6 gives a list of initialization parameters that must be configured for the Oracle Synchronous Multi-Master Replication to work. These parameters must be configured on all the databases involved in the Synchronous Multi-Master Replication.

These parameters need to be set up at both master sites that participated in the Synchronous Multi-Master Replications. You can use the Oracle Server Enterprise Manager to change these parameters or you can use the ALTER SYSTEM command to change these parameters. After you change the initialization parameter, you need to restart your Oracle server to have the initialization parameter take effect.

Step 2: Setting Up Master Sites

Before you set up the master sites, configure your network and Oracle Net so both databases can communicate with each other. The following section illustrates how to set up master sites using the Oracle Management API.

Parameter Name	Default Value	Recommended Value
Global_names	FALSE	It is required to set global_names to TRUE in each database to be involved in Multi-Master Replication.
Job_queue_processes	0	This parameter must be set to the value of at least 1. Citrix recommends 3 + 1 per additional master site.
Open_links	4	Open_links defines the number of concurrent database links that are required to a given database. This parameter needs to be configured for an initial setting of 4 + 2 additional links for each master site.
Processes	Derived from the value of the parameter parallel_max_servers	Add at least 12 to the current value.
Shared_pool_size	OS-dependent	Add 80 *M* for Multi-Master Replication.

Table 4-5. Oracle Initialization Parameters

Complete the following steps to set up the East.citrix.com master site:

1. Connect as SYSTEM at a master site at east.citrix.com:

```
CONNECT SYS/citrix@east.citrix.com as sysdba
```

2. Create the replication administrator at east.citrix.com. The replication administrator must be granted the necessary privileges to create and manage a replication environment. Also, the replication administrator must be created at each database that participates in the replication environment.

```
CREATE USER repadmin IDENTIFIED BY repadmin;
```

3. Grant privileges to the replication administrator at east.citrix.com:

```
BEGIN
DBMS_REPCAT_ADMIN.GRANT_ADMIN_ANY_SCHEMA (
    username => 'repadmin');
END;
/
GRANT COMMENT ANY TABLE TO repadmin;
GRANT LOCK ANY TABLE TO repadmin;
```

The following statement gives repadmin the capability to connect to the Replication Management tool if later on you want to monitor the Multi-Master Replication using the Replication Management tool:

```
GRANT SELECT ANY DICTIONARY TO repadmin;
```

4. Register the propagator at east.citrix.com. The propagator is responsible for propagating the deferred transaction queue to other master sites:

```
BEGIN
DBMS_DEFER_SYS.REGISTER_PROPAGATOR (
    username => 'repadmin');
END;
/
```

5. Register the receiver at east.citrix.com. The receiver receives the propagated deferred transactions sent by the propagator from other master sites.

```
BEGIN
DBMS_REPCAT_ADMIN.REGISTER_USER_REPGROUP (
    username => 'repadmin',
    privilege_type => 'receiver',
    list_of_gnames => NULL);
END;
/
```

6. Schedule purge at master site east.citrix.com. To keep the size of the deferred transaction queue in check, you should purge successfully completed deferred transactions. The SCHEDULE_PURGE procedure automates the purge process for you. You must execute this procedure as the replication administrator.

```
CONNECT repadmin/repadmin@east.citrix.com
BEGIN
DBMS_DEFER_SYS.SCHEDULE_PURGE (
    next_date => SYSDATE,
    interval => 'SYSDATE + 1/24',
    delay_seconds => 0);
END;
/
```

Complete the following steps to set up the west.citrix.com master site:

1. Connect as SYSTEM at a master site at west.citrix.com:

```
CONNECT sys/citrix@west.citrix.com as sysdba
```

2. Create the replication administrator at west.citrix.com. The replication administrator must be granted the necessary privileges to create and manage a replication environment. Also, the replication administrator must be created at each database that participates in the replication environment:

```
Create user REPADMIN identified by REPADMIN;
```

3. Grant privileges to the replication administrator at west.citrix.com:

```
BEGIN
DBMS_REPCAT_ADMIN.GRANT_ADMIN_ANY_SCHEMA (
    username => 'repadmin');
END;
/
GRANT COMMENT ANY TABLE TO repadmin;
GRANT LOCK ANY TABLE TO repadmin;
```

The following statement enables repadmin to connect to the Replication Management tool and then grants SELECT ANY DICTIONARY to repadmin:

```
GRANT SELECT ANY DICTIONARY TO repadmin;
```

4. Register the propagator at west.citrix.com. The propagator is responsible for propagating the deferred transaction queue to other master sites.

```
BEGIN
DBMS_DEFER_SYS.REGISTER_PROPAGATOR (
    username => 'repadmin');
END;
/
```

5. Register the receiver at west.citrix.com. The receiver receives the propagated deferred transactions sent by the propagator from other master sites.

```
BEGIN
DBMS_REPCAT_ADMIN.REGISTER_USER_REPGROUP (
    username => 'repadmin',
    privilege_type => 'receiver',
    list_of_gnames => NULL);
END;
/
```

6. Schedule purge at master site west.citrix.com. To keep the size of the deferred transaction queue in check, you should purge successfully completed deferred transactions. The SCHEDULE_PURGE procedure automates the purge process for you. You must execute this procedure as the replication administrator.

```
CONNECT repadmin/repadmin@west.citrix.com
BEGIN
DBMS_DEFER_SYS.SCHEDULE_PURGE (
    next_date => SYSDATE,
    interval => 'SYSDATE + 1/24',
    delay_seconds => 0);
END;
/
```

Complete the following steps to create database links between the master sites.

1. Create database links between master sites. The database links provide the necessary distributed mechanisms to allow the different replication sites to replicate data among themselves. Before you create any private database links, you must create the public database links that each private database link will use. You then must create a database link between all replication administrators at each of the master sites that you have set up.

```
CONNECT sys/citrix@east.citrix.com as sysdba
CREATE PUBLIC DATABASE LINK west.citrix.com USING 'west.citrix
.com';
CONNECT repadmin/repadmin@east.citrix.com
CREATE DATABASE LINK west.citrix.com CONNECT TO repadmin
IDENTIFIED BY repadmin;
CONNECT sys/citrix@west.citrix.com as sysdba
CREATE PUBLIC DATABASE LINK east.citrix.com USING 'east.citrix
.com';
CONNECT repadmin/repadmin@west.citrix.com
CREATE DATABASE LINK east.citrix.com CONNECT TO repadmin
IDENTIFIED BY repadmin;
```

Step 3: Creating Necessary Schemas on Both Master Sites

Before you create the master group, make sure that you have the tablespaces and users created on both master sites. The user names—that is, schema names—should be identical on both databases participating in Oracle Synchronous Multi-Master Replication. Citrix also recommends creating identical tablespace names on both databases for easy management. If you already installed XenApp using one of your Oracle databases as the data store, you just need to create the tablespace and user on the other database, which will be used as the second master site.

If you have not yet installed XenApp, at least one XenApp server must be installed using the east.citrix.com database as its data store. Refer to the *Citrix Presentation Server Administrator's Guide* for instructions to install XenApp using Oracle 9*i* or Oracle 10*g* as the data store.

Step 4: Creating a Master Group

In this example, you create the CPS_REP master group and replicate the objects that are used by XenApp. The schema used by XenApp is called MPS. Complete the following steps to create the CPS_REP master group:

1. Create the master group. Use the CREATE_MASTER_REPGROUP procedure to define a new master group. When you add an object to your master group or perform other replication administrative tasks, you reference the master group name defined during this step. The replication administrator must complete this step.

```
CONNECT repadmin/repadmin@east.citrix.com
BEGIN
  DBMS_REPCAT.CREATE_MASTER_REPGROUP(
     gname => 'CPS_REP',
     qualifier => '',
     group_comment => '') ;
END;
/
```

2. Add objects to the master group. First, use the CREATE_MASTER_REPOBJECT procedure to add the database tables used by XenApp to the master group:

```
BEGIN
  DBMS_REPCAT.CREATE_MASTER_REPOBJECT(
     gname => 'CPS_REP',
     type => 'TABLE',
     oname => 'deletetracker',
     sname => 'MPS',
     copy_rows => TRUE,
```

```
      use_existing_object => TRUE);
END;
/
BEGIN
  DBMS_REPCAT.CREATE_MASTER_REPOBJECT(
      gname => 'CPS_REP',
      type => 'TABLE',
      oname => 'indextable',
      sname => 'MPS',
      copy_rows => TRUE,
      use_existing_object => TRUE);
END;
/
BEGIN
  DBMS_REPCAT.CREATE_MASTER_REPOBJECT(
      gname => 'CPS_REP',
      type => 'TABLE',
      oname => 'keytable',
      sname => 'MPS',
      copy_rows => TRUE,
      use_existing_object => TRUE);
END;
/
BEGIN
  DBMS_REPCAT.CREATE_MASTER_REPOBJECT(
      gname => 'CPS_REP',
      type => 'TABLE',
      oname => 'seqtab',
      sname => 'MPS',
      copy_rows => TRUE,
      use_existing_object => TRUE);
END;
/
```

3. Add the following index to the master group:

```
BEGIN
  DBMS_REPCAT.CREATE_MASTER_REPOBJECT(
      gname => 'CPS_REP',
      type => 'INDEX',
      oname => 'indexind',
      sname => 'MPS',
      copy_rows => TRUE,
      use_existing_object => TRUE);
END;
/
```

```
BEGIN
  DBMS_REPCAT.CREATE_MASTER_REPOBJECT(
     gname => 'CPS_REP',
     type => 'INDEX',
     oname => 'indexind2',
     sname => 'MPS',
     copy_rows => TRUE,
     use_existing_object => TRUE);
END;
/
BEGIN
  DBMS_REPCAT.CREATE_MASTER_REPOBJECT(
     gname => 'CPS_REP',
     type => 'INDEX',
     oname => 'readbycontextid',
     sname => 'MPS',
     copy_rows => TRUE,
     use_existing_object => TRUE);
END;
/
BEGIN
  DBMS_REPCAT.CREATE_MASTER_REPOBJECT(
     gname => 'CPS_REP',
     type => 'INDEX',
     oname => 'readbyname',
     sname => 'MPS',
     copy_rows => TRUE,
     use_existing_object => TRUE);
END;
/

BEGIN
  DBMS_REPCAT.CREATE_MASTER_REPOBJECT(
     gname => 'CPS_REP',
     type => 'INDEX',
     oname => 'readbyuid',
     sname => 'MPS',
     copy_rows => TRUE,
     use_existing_object => TRUE);
END;
/
```

4. Add additional master sites. After you define your master group at the master definition site (the site where the master group was created becomes the master

definition site by default), you can define the other sites that will participate in the replication environment. The use_existing_objects parameter in the ADD_MASTER_DATABASE procedure is set to FALSE because the schema used by XenApp does not exist at the other master site, west.citrix.com.

```
BEGIN
  DBMS_REPCAT.ADD_MASTER_DATABASE (
     gname => 'CPS_REP',
     master => 'west.citrix.com',
     use_existing_objects => FALSE,
     copy_rows => TRUE,
     propagation_mode => 'SYNCHRONOUS');
END;
/
```

You should wait until west.citrix.com appears in the DBA_REPSITES view before continuing. Execute the following SELECT statement in another SQL*Plus session to make sure that west.citrix.com has appeared:

```
SELECT DBLINK FROM DBA_REPSITES WHERE GNAME = 'CPS_REP';
```

5. Generate replication support:

```
BEGIN
  DBMS_REPCAT.GENERATE_REPLICATION_SUPPORT(
     sname => 'MPS',
     oname => 'deletetracker',
     type => 'TABLE',
     min_communication => TRUE,
     generate_80_compatible => FALSE);
END;
/

BEGIN
  DBMS_REPCAT.GENERATE_REPLICATION_SUPPORT(
     sname => 'MPS',
     oname => 'indextable',
     type => 'TABLE',
     min_communication => TRUE,
     generate_80_compatible => FALSE);
END;
/
BEGIN
  DBMS_REPCAT.GENERATE_REPLICATION_SUPPORT(
     sname => 'MPS',
```

```
        oname => 'keytable',
        type => 'TABLE',
        min_communication => TRUE,
        generate_80_compatible => FALSE);
END;
/
BEGIN
  DBMS_REPCAT.GENERATE_REPLICATION_SUPPORT(
        sname => 'MPS',
        oname => 'seqtab',
        type => 'TABLE',
        min_communication => TRUE,
        generate_80_compatible => FALSE);
END;
/
```

Step 5: Starting Replication

After creating your master group, adding replication objects, generating replication support, and adding additional master databases, you need to start replication activity.

Before resuming replication activity, you must verify for all four tables replication support for objects. Execute the following SELECT statement against DBA_REPOBEJCT view to verify that the value Generation_Status column is shown as Generated for the four tables:

```
SELECT ONAME, GENERATION_STATUS FROM DBA_REPOBJECT WHERE GNAME =
'CPS_REP' AND
TYPE='TABLE';
```

You also need to make sure that the DBA_REPCATLOG view is empty before resuming master activity. Execute the following SELECT statement to monitor your DBA_REPCATLOG view:

```
SELECT COUNT(*) FROM DBA_REPCATLOG WHERE GNAME = 'CPS_REP';
```

You can use the RESUME_MASTER_ACTIVITY procedure to "turn on" replication for the specified master group:

```
BEGIN
DBMS_REPCAT.RESUME_MASTER_ACTIVITY (
gname => 'CPS_REP');
END;
/
```

IMPLEMENTING THE DATA STORE IN A STORAGE AREA NETWORK

Storage Area Network (SAN) is a dedicated high-speed network. It is separate and distinct from the LAN that provides shared storage through an external disk storage pool. The SAN is a back-end network that carries only I/O traffic between servers and a disk storage pool, while the front-end network—the LAN—carries e-mail, file, print, and web traffic.

Fibre Channel Technology

Some early Small Computer System Interface (SCSI) implementations have a distance limitation of 6 feet and can support only seven devices. These implementations use a parallel bus with multiple lines running in parallel.

Although some SAN configurations utilize this implementation, the most commonly used SCSI technology for SAN implementations is Fibre Channel (FC). FC is the standard for bidirectional communications implementing serial SCSI through a single cable connecting servers, storage systems, workstations, hubs, and switches. It features high-performance serial interconnections.

FC has the following capabilities:

- Bidirectional data transfer rates up to 200 Mbps
- Support for up to 126 devices on a single host adapter
- Communications up to 20km (approximately 12 miles)

FC implementations can use either of the following networking technologies:

- **Fibre Channel Arbitrated Loop (FC-AL)** FC-AL networks use shared media technology similar to Fibre Distributed Data Interface (FDDI) or Token Ring. Each network node has one or more ports that allow external communication; FC-AL creates logical point-to-point connections between ports.
- **Fibre Channel Fabric (FC-SW)** Fabric networks use switched network technology similar to switched Ethernet. A fabric switch divides messages into packets containing data and a destination address, and then transmits the packets individually to the receiving node, which reassembles the message. Fabric switches can cascade, allowing a SAN to support thousands of nodes.

Hardware Components

SANs typically include the following hardware components:

- **Host I/O bus** The current I/O bus standard is Peripheral Component Interface (PCI). Older standards include Industry Standard Architecture (ISA) and Extended Industry Standard Architecture (EISA).

- **Host bus adapter** The host bus adapter (HBA) is the interface from the server to the host I/O bus. The HBA is similar in function to a NIC, but it is more complex. HBA functions include the following:
  - Converting signals passed between the LAN and the SAN's serial SCSI
  - Initializing the server onto a FC-AL network or providing a Fabric network logon
  - Scanning the FC-AL or Fabric network, and then attempting to initialize all connected devices in the same way that parallel SCSI scans for logical devices at system startup.
- **Cabling** FC cables include lines for transmitting and for receiving. Because of the shape, you cannot install them incorrectly.
- **SAN networking equipment** Many similarities exist between a SAN and other networks, such as a LAN. The basic network components are the same: hubs, switches, bridges, and routers.
- **Storage devices and subsystems** A *storage subsystem* is a collection of devices that share a power distribution, packaging, or management system, such as tape libraries or RAID disk drives.

SAN Tape Backup Support

SANs provide easy, on-the-fly tape backup strategies. Tape backups are much quicker and consume fewer resources, because all of the disk access occurs on the SAN's fiber network, and not on the LAN. This allows the data store to be backed up easily even while it is in use.

Cluster Failover Support

The data store is an integral part of the XenApp farm architecture. In large enterprise environments, it is important to have the database available all the time. For maximum availability, the data store should be in a clustered database environment with a SAN backbone.

Hardware redundancy allows the SAN to recover from most component failures. Additional software, such as Oracle 9*i* Real Application Cluster or SQL Server 2000 utilizing Microsoft Clustering Services (MSCS), allows for the failover in a catastrophic software failure and in Oracle's case, performance improvements.

NOTE Software such as Compaq's SANWorks is required to manage database clusters in certain hardware configurations.

MSCS makes it possible to send the XenApp farm data store to a functioning server in the event of a catastrophic server failure. MSCS is available on Windows 2000 Advanced Server and DataCenter as well as Windows Server 2003 Enterprise and DataCenter editions.

MSCS monitors the health of standard applications and services and automatically recovers mission-critical data and applications from many common types of failures. A graphical management console enables you to monitor the status of all resources in the cluster and to manage workloads accordingly. In addition, Windows 2000 Server and Windows Server 2003 integrate middleware and load-balancing services that distribute network traffic evenly across the clustered servers.

Redundancy and recovery can be built into each major component of the data store. Deploying the following technologies can eliminate single points of failure from the data store:

- Microsoft Cluster Service
- Redundant hardware
- Software monitoring and management tools.

The basic SAN configuration shown in Figure 4-7 includes each clustered server with dual HBAs cabled to separate FC-AL switches. A system with this redundancy can continue running when any component in this configuration fails.

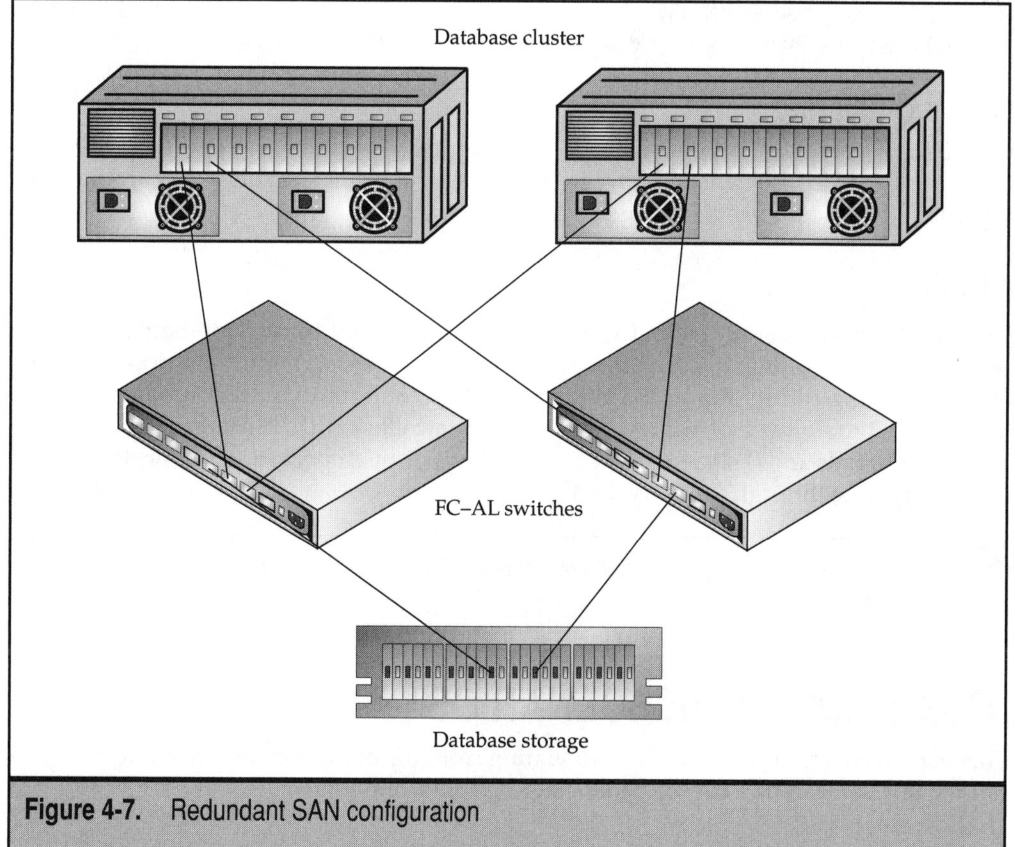

Figure 4-7. Redundant SAN configuration

SAN architecture is, by definition, reliable. It provides redundant systems in all aspects of the configuration with multiple paths to the network. Windows 2000 Advanced Server allows two nodes to be clustered. Windows 2000 DataCenter allows four clustered nodes.

If a software or hardware failure occurs on the owner of the cluster node, XenApp servers lose their IMA connection to the database. When the servers sense that the connection has been dropped, the farm goes into a two-minute wait period. The servers then attempt to reconnect to the database. If IMA cannot immediately reconnect to the data store, it retries, indefinitely, every two minutes. The XenApp servers automatically reconnect to the database, which has the same IP address, once it fails over to the other node of the cluster.

SQL Clustering

SQL clustering does not mean that both databases are active and load balanced. With SQL clustering, the only supported clustering method allows one server to handle all the requests while the other server simply stands by waiting for the other machine to fail. This is referred to as *active/passive clustering*.

NOTE For increased security, when installing XenApp in a farm using a clustered SQL Server, Windows NT authentication should be used for connecting IMA to the database.

Oracle Clustering

Oracle RAC does allow true active/active clustering. As database requests are sent via ODBC, they are load-balanced between the nodes of the cluster. This configuration provides both fault tolerance and increased performance.

SAN Tuning

In addition to increasing reliability, you can tune the SAN to provide better database performance. In testing at the Citrix eLabs, the data store is mainly used as a repository for reading configuration information. In this configuration, the number of reads far exceeds the number of writes. The Array Controller on the SAN can be tuned for 100 percent reads and 0 percent writes. This allows optimal performance for data access to the data store through the SAN.

NOTE Having the SAN tuned to 100 percent reads and 0 percent writes still allows servers to write to the data store.

SPECIAL DATA STORE SCENARIOS

This section covers situations where deviating from the default installation and configuration may be desired or can be beneficial to an environment.

Using Indirect Mode to Access the Data Store

Microsoft SQL Server, Oracle, or IBM DB2 can be used in indirect mode to reduce the number of database connections. This practice is not recommended for use in large farms because it creates a single point of failure at the server hosting the indirect connections.

CAUTION Although this configuration is possible, it is not a recommended architecture for a farm. Using Microsoft SQL Server, Oracle, or IBM DB2 in indirect mode creates a bottleneck and can cause performance issues.

To prevent a single point of failure for the entire farm, install a core set of direct servers and then point groups of member servers to each of the core direct servers. This process provides better performance than sharing a single server for all queries.

Using XenApp in indirect mode does not reduce the number of queries made to the third-party database. Instead, it channels them through a single ODBC connection.

To use indirect mode with a third-party database, follow these steps:

1. Install the first server into the server farm in direct mode and configure it to point properly to the third-party database.
2. You can install subsequent servers in indirect mode by specifying the direct server from step 1.
3. When prompted for the account permissions, specify the user name and password of the Citrix administrator created in step 1.

Dedicating a Host Server in an Indirect Mode Server Farm

When an Access or Microsoft SQL Server 2005 Express Edition SP1 data store resides on XenApp, the data store has only one direct server connection. The other servers in this indirect mode server farm access the data store through this host server. The host server, acting as a single point of access, can potentially be a performance bottleneck. The host server can have further demands on its resources if it is also handling ICA connections.

When the host server has a full user load, the following problems can occur:

- Delays when using the Presentation Server Console to configure applications
- Longer Presentation Server Console refresh times
- Longer IMA start times for member servers because the data store server is splitting processor time between users and the IMA service

For these reasons, configure the host server to have a lighter user load than the other member servers of the server farm. The exact tuning of this is dependent on the applications being used and the usual load on the servers.

Make user load on the host server one-half to two-thirds of the load on member servers. If the farm is using load balancing, tune the parameters so that the host server is sent less user traffic than the other servers. If servers are restarted often, you must factor in longer start times. In larger XenApp environments running in indirect mode, dedicating the host server to handle data store requests exclusively can be necessary.

NOTE If the same server is used as the zone data collector, the recommendations for dedicating a server as a zone data collector take precedence over the recommendations in this section. However, you can achieve better performance by using separate machines for the data collector and direct server in a large farm.

CHAPTER 5

Citrix XenApp Deployment

This section contains deployment recommendations for Citrix XenApp. Citrix recommends installing XenApp on a Windows 2003 member server, not a Domain Controller. The server must have Terminal Server installed in Application mode. In fact, Service Pack 2005.04 for MetaFrame Presentation Server 3.0 and XenApp 4.0 cannot be installed on a Domain Controller. See Citrix Knowledge Base article CTX106529 for more details.

Domain Controllers replicate the Active Directory database and other data and also provide user authentication. They thus have heavy network and processing requirements. More importantly, the security holes that may be opened by allowing users to access applications loaded onto a Domain Controller should be carefully considered.

Additionally, the servers with XenApp installed should not provide any additional services, such as Dynamic Host Configuration Protocol (DHCP), Domain Name System (DNS), and Windows Internet Name Service (WINS). These services not only require additional server resources that reduce user performance, but also utilize network resources to respond to frequent client requests and updates. All available server resources should be available to support XenApp and associated applications.

XenApp setup is compiled into a Windows Installer installation package. A component of Windows 2003 that manages the installation and removal of applications, Windows Installer applies a set of centrally defined setup rules during the installation process that define the configuration of the application. For more information about Windows Installer technology and the Windows Installer service, see the Windows 2003 online help or the Microsoft web site. For more information about working with the XenApp Windows Installer package, see the *Citrix Presentation Server Administrator's Guide.*

NOTE When upgrading a farm using Microsoft Access as the data store, always upgrade the host server first. Otherwise, installation will fail. For additional important considerations during upgrade installations, see the *Citrix Presentation Server Administrator's Guide.*

UPDATES FOR CITRIX XENAPP

The updates for XenApp 4.5 are summarized in the Installation Checklist and the Preinstallation Update Bulletin.

Installation Checklist

After inserting the installation CD and before installing the product, Citrix recommends reading the Installation Checklist. You can view the Installation Checklist by selecting View installation checklist on the XenApp Setup window that appears after you insert your CD. It outlines the following, among other items:

- Downloading and installing critical updates before you install the product
- Meeting system requirements
- Installing and configuring the Citrix Access Suite licensing

- Remapping server drive letters
- Installing XenApp
- Downloading and installing critical updates after you install the product

The focus of this section is on installing the required Preinstallation Updates, and the Critical Installation and Postinstallation Updates, which may be required to install or run the product properly.

Preinstallation Update Bulletin

The Preinstallation Update Bulletin offers late-breaking information and links to critical updates to server operating systems (OSs) and to Citrix installation files. These updates may be required to install or run the product and should be applied prior to installation. Information regarding the required updates can be found on the Preinstallation Update Bulletin. A link to the bulletin is available on the Installation Checklist. The bulletin is divided into three sections, described in the following subsections.

Preinstallation Updates

Follow the instructions in step 1 of the bulletin to download and install the updates to Microsoft OS components required to install or run the product. Links to both the Microsoft Knowledge Base articles and a patch for download are provided. Read the Knowledge Base articles for detailed descriptions of the updates.

Installation Updates

Follow the instructions in step 2 of the bulletin to download and apply critical updates to Citrix installation packages. After downloading and executing the update package, the Critical Update Wizard can guide you through the process of applying the update to the Citrix components. The Critical Update Wizard creates a modified administrative image of the original CD-ROM of XenApp on your hard drive. You need to use the modified administrative image containing the critical installation updates instead of the original CD-ROM to install XenApp.

Postinstallation Updates and the Critical Updates Web Page

Follow the instructions in step 3 of the bulletin to download and install critical postinstallation hotfixes. The instructions in step 3 of the bulletin direct you to the Critical Updates web page, where the hotfixes can be downloaded. You should visit this web page frequently, on an ongoing basis, to determine whether Citrix has recently released any critical hotfixes.

Remapping Server Drives

If you intend to change the server's drive letters to enable users to retain their original drive letters on client devices, do so before installing XenApp or prior to upgrading to XenApp. If you change server drive letters after installing or upgrading, you must do so before you install any applications. To change the server's drive letters, you can use the XenApp CD's Autorun feature, selecting the Remap Drives option from the Product Installations screen.

NOTE If you are upgrading from an earlier release, the Remap Drives option is not available from Autorun. Your existing drive mapping is preserved for the upgrade. To modify the existing drive mapping, run the DriveRemap utility (driveremap.exe) located in the root folder of the XenApp CD. Typically, you should *never* remap the drives as part of an upgrade.

When running driveremap.exe with no parameters, the drive letter choices in the pull-down list may be grayed out. This happens because the program is unable to perform some aspect of remapping the existing drive letters. Some possible reasons include the following:

- Noncontiguous drive letters, for example, *C, D, X*. The mapped drive letters are spread over the interval [a...z] and no reasonable interval shifting can be performed. Shifting *C* to *M* is a shift of 10. Drive letter *X* would not be able to shift 10 letters and wrap around the alphabet. Even network drives are taken into account. To work around this, change the drive letters to *C:*, *D:*, *E:*, and then rerun the utility.
- At the command prompt, if you silently remap to a letter that is in use, such as a mapped network drive, nothing will happen. The process just returns to the prompt. To see whether mappings take place, launch Windows Explorer.
- XenApp drive remapping is not supported on Windows 2003 dynamic disks.

For more detailed information, refer to Citrix Knowledge Base article CTX950520.

NOTE Driveremap.exe does not remap hidden (administrative) shares listed in the registry. For example, if you install Trend ServerProtect on Windows Server 2003 and view the registry value: HKEY_LOCAL_MACHINE\SOFTWARE\TrendMicro\ServerProtect\CurrentVersion\UncHomeDirectory, the value will be similar to: \\%computername%\c$\Program Files\Trend\SProtect. If you remap the server drive at this point, the previous registry value is not modified.

RAPID DEPLOYMENT OF CITRIX XENAPP

Having a means of quickly building or rebuilding XenApp ensures that users are impacted for the minimum period of time if an unplanned failure were to occur. Optimally, an automated process provides the fastest and most efficient means of building or rebuilding a server. This section covers practices regarding rapid deployment of XenApp in the enterprise environment, including server cloning, unattended installations, and simultaneous installations. For further information regarding unattended installations, refer to the *Citrix Presentation Server Administrator's Guide*.

Blades in a Citrix XenApp Environment

The introduction of blade servers has been an ideal fit for XenApp. With server sprawl and increasing datacenter costs, the most-asked question has been shifting from "How many users can I get on a box?" to "How many users can I get per square foot?" Blade servers in the 2P market are traditionally twice as dense as 1U dual servers (pizza boxes). This means 84 servers can now be placed into a single 42U rack.

Most of the major server hardware vendors have introduced blade servers. These servers offer a wide range of options, depending on the vendor, from Storage Area Network (SAN) connectivity to storage blades, to unique imaging solutions.

Blades and Imaging

Most blade servers ship with some form of imaging software. Each of these imaging solutions offers image capture and deployment to servers. A base image can be installed on a single machine, which is stored on the image server and can then be deployed to all other like servers in your data center.

You can image the base OS and then have the imaging software perform an unattended install of XenApp using an answer file, or you can image the system with XenApp already installed.

NOTE If the XenApp is to have remapped drives, then running DriveRemap after the imaging process is complete is best because of incompatibilities with some third-party imaging solutions.

Scripting Configuration after Imaging

If a cloned version of XenApp is deployed, a few steps must first be performed to allow XenApp to function properly.

Most imaging software suites enable the administrator to define scripts to be run on the server after imaging completes. XenApp include a utility called Apputil, a command-line utility that adds a server to the Configured Servers list of a published application. If the application does not exist on the server, then Apputil can also be used to deploy the application using an Installation Manager package.

With this utility, the administrator can script various different configurations of a XenApp installation, depending on the application silo in which it resides. Once the machine has finished imaging, the script executes and the Installation Manager package is deployed to the server.

For more information regarding this utility, please refer to the *Citrix Presentation Server Administrator's Guide.*

The MFCOM software development kit (SDK) also allows for the scripting of other configuration options through most kinds of scripting languages. Through the MFCOM SDK, new applications can be published; the data collector preference level can be set, load evaluators applied, and so forth. This allows XenApp configuration tweaks to be applied on the fly as well. Refer to the MFCOM SDK documentation for scripting usage.

Rip and Replace

In the event of a hardware failure, blades present the opportunity simply to pull out the one experiencing the failure and to replace it with a new server blade. XenApp can then be imaged back down to the new blade. If the blade server assumes the same name, then it continues to function in the capacity as the previous XenApp that had the same name.

NOTE For servers that were previously hosting an indirect data store, the data store needs to be migrated using the dsmaint command. Refer to the *Citrix Presentation Server Administrator's Guide* for instructions.

Server Cloning

A few manual steps are required for cloning XenApp. These steps vary, depending on the type of data store used for the farm, and are described in the following sections. XenApp is compatible with server cloning, but cloning software can sometimes cause the OS or its add-ons to function incorrectly after being cloned. When using server cloning, it is important to clone one server and test its operation before deploying the rest of the farm.

CAUTION Do not attempt to image a server with a Secure Sockets Layer (SSL) certificate installed because SSL certificates are unique to the hardware.

Precloning Considerations

Zone settings are not retained when a server is cloned. When the IMA service on the cloned server starts for the first time, XenApp joins the default zone. The name of the default zone is the ID of the subnet on which the cloned server resides. When deploying images to servers on multiple subnets, assign zone information for each server after the imaging process completes.

Prior to changing the Security ID (SID) on the machine used to access the Presentation Server Console, add one of the following as a Citrix administrator with read-write privileges:

- A domain administrator
- The Local Administrators group
- A local administrator from a machine where the SID is not being changed

CAUTION Do not attempt to use drive image software to restore an image of XenApp with remapped drives. Remapped drives partially revert to the original configuration on the deployed server, rendering the server unusable. Servers with remapped drives may be duplicated using a hardware solution, such as Compaq Smart Array controllers with RAID1 drive mirroring. Also, some drive imaging software, such as Symantec Ghost, provides configuration settings to *preserve* the remapped drives, letters, and signatures. Consult your drive imaging software's documentation to determine whether it supports these features.

You must do the following before re-imaging a server that is already a member of a XenApp farm:

1. From the Access Management Console, remove the list of servers configured to host any applications.
2. Remove the server from the server farm by uninstalling XenApp.
3. If the server entry still exists in the Access Management Console or Presentation Server Console server list, right-click and manually remove the server name from the server list.
4. Apply the system image and add the server to the server farm.

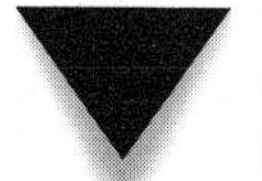

NOTE If a server is not removed from a XenApp farm before a new system image is applied to it, performance problems can result. The Presentation Server Console or Access Management Console can display invalid data if the server is added back to the same server farm. This is because the old server's host record in the data store is applied to the newly imaged server.

If cloning is not an option, such as when you are configuring a server with remapped drives, consider creating custom unattended installation scripts for both the OS and applications, including XenApp.

Rapid Deployment with Microsoft Access or Microsoft SQL Server 2005 Express Edition SP1

Manually install the first server in the new XenApp farm that will host the data store. You can image the second server in the farm for the deployment of additional servers.

To image a server for rapid deployment with Access or Microsoft SQL Server 2005 Express Edition SP1, follow these steps:

1. Follow all necessary steps from the *Citrix Presentation Server Administrator's Guide* to install the first XenApp into the farm.
2. Install a second server into the farm with an indirect connection to the data store created on the first server.
3. With the second server successfully installed and restarted, log on to the console of the second server as a local or domain administrator.
4. On the second server, delete the Wfcname.ini file, if it exists, from the root drive of the server.
5. Stop the IMA service using the Services Control Panel. Set the startup type to Manual.
6. If the Enterprise Edition components are installed, see the "Cloning on XenApp, Enterprise Edition System," section.
7. Take the image of the second server and then restart the second server.
8. Deploy the image obtained in step 7.

NOTE It is important that some type of SID generation utility be executed when deploying Windows 2003 images.

To set up the server and verify that it is added, follow these steps:

1. Set the SID of the server with the SID generator of choice.
2. Rename the new server with a unique name.
3. Manually start the IMA service and set the service to start automatically.
4. Verify that the server was successfully added to the farm by executing qfarm at the command prompt. The newly imaged server appears in the list of servers.
5. Modify the following registry values:

- `HKEY_LOCAL_MACHINE\SOFTWARE\Citrix\IMA change value ServerHost to newservername`
- `HKEY_CLASSES_ROOT\AppID\{BBBF5400-E091-11D8-AD76-005056C00008} change value RunAs to newservername\Ctx_SmaUser`

NOTE This subkey may be alphanumerically different—you may need to search for Ctx_SmaUser to find the correct subkey.

6. Reboot the server.

Rapid Deployment with Microsoft SQL Server, Oracle, or IBM DB2 When using Microsoft SQL Server, Oracle, or IBM DB2 for the server farm data store, you can image the first server in the farm and use it to deploy all other servers.

To image a server for rapid deployment with SQL Server, Oracle, or IBM DB2, follow these steps:

1. Follow the steps from the *Citrix Presentation Server Administrator's Guide* for installing the first XenApp into the farm.
2. When the server is successfully restarted, log on to the console as a local or domain administrator.
3. Delete the Wfcname.ini file, if it exists, from the root drive of the server.
4. Save the changes to the DSN file.
5. Stop the IMA service and set the startup option to Manual.
6. If the Enterprise Edition components are installed, see the "Cloning on XenApp, Enterprise Edition System," section.
7. Take the image of the server, and then restart the server.
8. Deploy the image obtained.

NOTE It is important that some type of SID generation utility be executed when deploying Windows 2003.

To set up the server and verify that it is added, follow these steps:

1. Set the SID of the server with the SID generator of choice.
2. Rename the new server with a unique name.
3. Manually start the IMA service and set the service to start automatically.
4. Verify that the server was successfully added to the farm by executing qfarm at a command prompt on any server in the farm. The newly imaged server appears in the list of servers.

Cloning on XenApp, Enterprise Edition Systems If Resource Manager is installed, re-create the Resource Manager local database (RMLocalDatabase) prior to making an image of the server. To re-create the RMLocalDatabase, delete %Program Files%\Citrix\Citrix Resource Manager\LocalDB\RMLocalDatabase.*. The next time that the IMA service is started, it will automatically re-create the database.

Simultaneous Installations

Citrix recommends that no more than 30 servers be simultaneously installed if you are using a high-powered server for your data store (that is, a current generation dual-CPU database server or above). For older database servers, no more than 10 servers should be installed at the same time. During installation, servers must write configurations to the same indexes in the data store. The more servers installed at once, the greater the probability of creating deadlocks on the database server.

NOTE Deadlocks occur when one server times out while waiting to write to a piece of data that is locked by another server. In this event, the IMA service simply retries after a short interval.

When installing servers to a new zone, it is recommended that you initially install a single server into the new zone. XenApp sets the first server in a zone as the most-preferred data collector. This avoids problems with new servers in the zone becoming the zone data collector during installation. After installation is completed, you can change the data collector election preference by using the Presentation Server Console.

INSTALLATION OF ADMINISTRATIVE TOOLS

This section covers installation scenarios for the Presentation Server Console.

To Skip Installation of the Citrix Presentation Server Console

Use the following command to skip the installation of the Presentation Server Console during XenApp installation:

```
msiexec /i mps.msi CTX_ADDLOCAL=all REINSTALL=CTX_MF_CMC
```

NOTE CTX_MF_CMC must be in uppercase.

To Install or Upgrade the Presentation Server Console on Standalone Servers

Follow these steps to install or upgrade the Presentation Server Console on a standalone server:

1. Run Autorun from the XenApp CD.
2. Select Product installations and updates.
3. Select Install management consoles.
4. Accept the license agreement and click Next | Next to select Presentation Server Console.
5. Follow the dialog boxes to finish the installation of the Presentation Server Console.

If the Sun JRE 1_5_0_02 is already installed when you install the Presentation Server Console, logins to the console may fail. When JRE 1.5 is already present, the JRE 1.4.2_06 installer doesn't add a registry key that is needed by the console. You can resolve this problem manually by adding one key and one value to the registry:

1. Create the following registry key:

   ```
   HKEY_LOCAL_MACHINE\Software\JavaSoft\Java Runtime Environment\1.4
   ```

2. Create a string value `JavaHome`.
3. Locate the following key in the registry:

```
HKEY_LOCAL_MACHINE\Software\JavaSoft\Java Runtime Environment\1.4.2_06
```

4. Copy the data from the `JavaHome` value in that key to the `JavaHome` value in the key that you created.

To Install the Access Management Console on Standalone Servers

Follow these steps to install the Access Management Console on a standalone server:

1. Run Autorun from the XenApp CD.
2. Select Product installations and updates.
3. Select Install management consoles.
4. Accept the license agreement and click Next | Next to select Access Suite Console.
5. Follow the dialog boxes to finish the installation of the Access Suite Console.

PROGRAM NEIGHBORHOOD AGENT AS A PASS-THROUGH CLIENT

You can choose to install Program Neighborhood Agent to be used as a pass-through client on the XenApp during XenApp setup. This configuration enables users to connect to the server desktop and use the functionality of the Program Neighborhood Agent.

To install the Program Neighborhood Agent, click the Program Neighborhood Agent component during the component selection of the XenApp installation and select "Will be installed on local hard drive."

Consider the following before installing the Program Neighborhood Agent:

- If you install the Program Neighborhood Agent, you are prompted later during setup to enter the URL of the server running Web Interface. This server hosts the Program Neighborhood Agent configuration file. By default, XenApp attempts to resolve the local host as a server running Web Interface.
- If you are upgrading from a previous release of XenApp, you will not be given an opportunity to set up the Program Neighborhood Agent as a pass-through client.
- If you performed a fresh install and did not choose to install the Program Neighborhood Agent or you performed an upgrade, you can install the Program Neighborhood Agent after the XenApp setup process.

NOTE By default, Program Neighborhood Agent is not selected to be installed during a XenApp installation.

Installation of Program Neighborhood Agent as a Pass-Through Client

This section describes how to install the Program Neighborhood Agent and use it as a pass-through client on XenApp if the Program Neighborhood Agent was not a selected component during the initial XenApp installation:

1. Launch Add/Remove Programs in the Control Panel.
2. Select Change on Citrix MetaFrame Presentation Server for Windows entry name.
3. Select to Modify the Windows Installer packages installed on the system and click Next.
4. Select the Program Neighborhood Agent component, select "Will be installed on local hard drive," and then click Next.
5. Enter the server URL for the Web Interface server or leave as localhost if Web Interface is installed on the same computer as XenApp.
6. Select whether or not to enable Pass Through Authentication and click Next.
7. Verify the component changes and click Finish.

DEPLOYMENT OF THE XENAPP CLIENT FOR 32-BIT WINDOWS

This section outlines best practices, recommendations, and advanced scenarios when dealing with the various XenApp Clients for 32-bit Windows and XenApp. Refer to the respective client administrative guides for additional information.

Dynamic Client Name versus Machine Name

Dynamic Client Name is a feature that is included in client versions 7.00 and later. Prior versions of the client reported only the client name that was statically configured during the installation of the client and stored in the wfcname.ini file. If the Dynamic Client Name feature is not enabled, the client name that is reported to XenApp when connecting to a session is stored in the following registry key:

```
HKLM\Software\Citrix\ICA Client\ClientName
```

When the Dynamic Client Name feature is enabled, the XenApp client calls the Windows function GetComputerName, which gets the computer's NetBIOS name and is then reported to the XenApp.

The ClientName registry value should not be present when the Dynamic Client Name feature is enabled. Dynamic Client Name is initially enabled or disabled during the install process. In the Program Neighborhood client, this can be changed after install by opening Program Neighborhood and setting the Dynamic Client Name check box under Tools | ICA Settings | General. In all other XenApp Clients, including Program Neighborhood Agent, you can enable or disable this feature by deleting or creating the ClientName registry value in:

```
HKLM\Software\Citrix\ICA Client
```

These changes should take effect on all new connections.

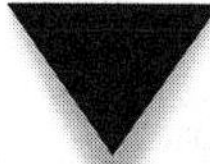

NOTE Earlier releases of XenApp clients (prior to version 7.00) stored the client name in the file C:\wfcname.ini.

CAB-Based Client Packages

Three different CAB packages are available with XenApp:

- **Wfica.cab** This is the full Program Neighborhood client packaged in CAB format (4,331,039 bytes).
- **Wficat.cab** This is the "thick" web client packaged in CAB format (2,425,783 bytes).
- **Wficac.cab** This is the "zero footprint" web client (the new "zero install" client that customers requested) packaged in CAB format (1,507,442 bytes).

There are several benefits to the thin (ActiveX) web clients (wficat.cab and wficac cab), including the following:

- The user doesn't initiate the install. The Internet browser (Internet Explorer or Netscape Navigator) initiates the install on a need-to-download-and-install basis.
- The CAB file package install is fast because it is limited in size.
- The CAB file is expanded into a scratch directory, leaving little or no footprint on the target desktop. Changes made to the locked-down desktop are none or minimal (registration of ActiveX ICA control).

Along with the benefits, there are trade-offs to be made to keep the thin web package small and efficient. Because a smaller footprint means a reduction in size of the client package, certain features from the full-fledged Program Neighborhood or Program Neighborhood Agent are unavailable for the two smaller CAB-based client packages wficat.cab and wficac.cab.

Supported Features

Supported features include wficat.cab and wficac.cab.

Wfica.cab MWfica.cab is the full Program Neighborhood client and all features supported in the Program Neighborhood full-client install are supported by the wfica.cab install.

Wficat.cab The following features are supported by the wficat.cab install: Client engine, Thinwire, Client drive mapping, Licensing, Connection Center, Runtime Manager, Auto-client reconnection, Zero Latency, Font Manager, Client Audio Mapping, Client Printer Mapping, Universal Printer Driver, client COM port mapping, Netscape plug-in, Protocol Driver (128 bit), protocol driver (old compression), smart card support, ActiveX control, ICA Client Object, SSL support, Auto-client update, Name Resolver (TCP/IP), Name Resolver (HTTP), INI files, support dynamic link libraries (DLLs), TCP/IP protocol support, bidirectional audio, session reliability, dynamic session resizing, and login look and feel.

Wficac.cab The following features are supported by the wficac.cab install: Client engine, Thinwire, Client drive mapping, Licensing, Connection Center, Runtime Manager, Auto-client reconnection, Client Printer Mapping, smart card support, ActiveX control, ICA Client Object, SSL support, Name Resolver (TCP/IP), Name Resolver (HTTP), INI files, support DLLs, TCP/IP protocol support, session reliability, dynamic session resizing, and login look and feel.

Features *Not* Supported

The CAB-based client packages wficat.cab and wficac.cab omit support for the following features.

Wficat.cab SpeedScreen Multimedia Acceleration is not supported.

Wficac.cab The following features are not supported: Zero Latency, Font Manager, Client Audio Mapping, universal printer driver, client COM port mapping, Netscape plug-in, Protocol Driver (128 bit), Protocol Driver (old compression), Auto Client update, SpeedScreen Multimedia Acceleration, and bidirectional audio.

Wficac.cab Considerations

The following are some of the known issues and considerations regarding the new CAB file wficac.cab, coupled with any known workarounds.

Upgrade Considerations If one version of the client is already installed on the target machine using any of the following listed packages, the same-version CAB-based web client package will not be downloaded and installed by the Internet Explorer browser:

- Full Program Neighborhood client using Installshield (ICA32.exe)
- Full Program Neighborhood MSI (ica32pkg.msi) install
- Program Neighborhood Agent using Installshield (ICA32a.exe)
- Program Neighborhood Agent MSI (ica32pkg.msi) install
- Thin web client (wficac.cab) install package

For the same version of web client installed on a target machine installed via the thin (wficac.cab) CAB file, users will be unable to install the web client via a thick (wficat .cab) CAB file if a need arises to use more features. The reason for this is that the version numbers on the CAB files remain the same and Internet Explorer will not download and explode the thick (wficat.cab) CAB-based client.

TIP First, the user must uninstall the thin (wficac.cab) CAB-based web client via the Add-Remove applet in the Control Panel and then visit a web page that points the user to the location to download the thick version (wficat.cab) of the web client.

If a lower version of the full web client is installed on the target machine and the user visits a web page that points to a higher version CAB-based web client, Internet Explorer always prompts the user to download and install the latest web client. This leads to multiple client installations on the target machine.

TIP Uninstall the previously installed web client and then visit the web page pointing to a higher-version CAB-based client.

NOTE By installing a smaller-sized CAB client, even if it is a higher version, some features will be lost due to the streamlining of the client.

Limitations and Constraints of Wficac.cab

Any user wanting to use the CAB-based ActiveX Win32 web client needs permissions to download an ActiveX control via Internet Explorer. To register the ActiveX control correctly and to register the .ICA file type extension to support launching of ICA connections outside the browser, the user must have an appropriate level of permissions to be able to create subkeys under the HKEY_CLASSES_ROOT registry hive.

Internet Explorer 4.0 and above is the only supported browser for these versions of the CAB-based client.

Only a limited number of client features, as previously noted, are available in the thin version (wficac.cab) of the CAB-based Win32 ActiveX-based client.

CHAPTER 6

Novell Directory Services Integration

XenApp supports Novell Directory Services (NDS) authentication to XenApp, published applications, and published content. This section explains how to use NDS with XenApp, Web Interface, and the XenApp Client for 32-bit Windows. This section assumes familiarity with NDS and related Novell products. See the Citrix Knowledge Center article CTX108565 and the Novell web site at http://www.novell.com for more information about the Novell products referred to in this chapter.

IMPLEMENTING NDS SUPPORT IN CITRIX XENAPP

XenApp can publish applications, desktops, and content for users managed by NDS or directory services in Windows 2003. However, using XenApp in a network environment that employs multiple directory services requires careful planning.

Read the following sections carefully before installing XenApp in an NDS environment.

Planning Your Deployment of Citrix XenApp for NDS Support

Using XenApp in an NDS environment requires the following tasks in the order they are listed. Each task is explained in detail in this chapter.

1. Decide which servers will host applications and content published for NDS users when XenApp is installed.
2. Install the Novell Client on those servers.
3. Install XenApp.
4. Enable the Dynamic Local User (DLU) policy in ZENworks for Desktops, or make sure the same user accounts and passwords exist in both NDS and Active Directory Services (ADS) domains. You may also enable the SyncedDomainName key on each XenApp with NDS integration. This will not require the ZENworks DLU component requirement. To enable the DLU policy, follow these steps:
   a. Open the Registry Editor on the server running XenApp.
   b. Go to HKEY_LOCAL_MACHINE\SOFTWARE\Citrix and add a new key called NDS.
   c. On the new key, add a new SZ subkey called SyncedDomainName.
   d. Set the value to the NetBIOS name of the domain with which you want to synchronize the user names. It is not required to restart the server or IMA service; users can now synchronize the NetWare users with those of the NT/ADS domain. Both users still need to exist on the NetWare tree and the NT/ADS domain.

5. Enable NDS support in the XenApp farm as follows:
   a. Assign Citrix administrator privileges to NDS objects.
   b. Log on to the Presentation Server Console with NDS credentials.
   c. Publish applications, desktops, or content for NDS users on server running XenApp to which only NDS users will connect.
6. If you are using Web Interface, enable NDS support for Web Interface in the Access Management Console.
7. Instruct end users how to connect to publish applications and content using their NDS credentials. If you are deploying the Program Neighborhood Agent, enable NDS support in the Program Neighborhood Agent.

The sections that follow outline the procedures required to use XenApp in an NDS environment.

Farm Layout and System Requirements

Using XenApp in a network environment that employs multiple directory services requires careful planning. While the farm can contain servers in Windows 2003, domains and servers enabled for NDS, XenApp servers running the Novell Client, and that use Dynamic Local User functionality should be members of a workgroup, and not members of a domain. The Dynamic Local User feature of Novell ZENworks for Desktops must be used in this configuration.

To implement XenApp in an NDS environment, designate application servers to host applications and content published only for NDS users. These servers must run version 4.81 or later of the Novell Client for Windows NT/2000. Figure 6-1 illustrates the required layout of a XenApp farm supporting NDS.

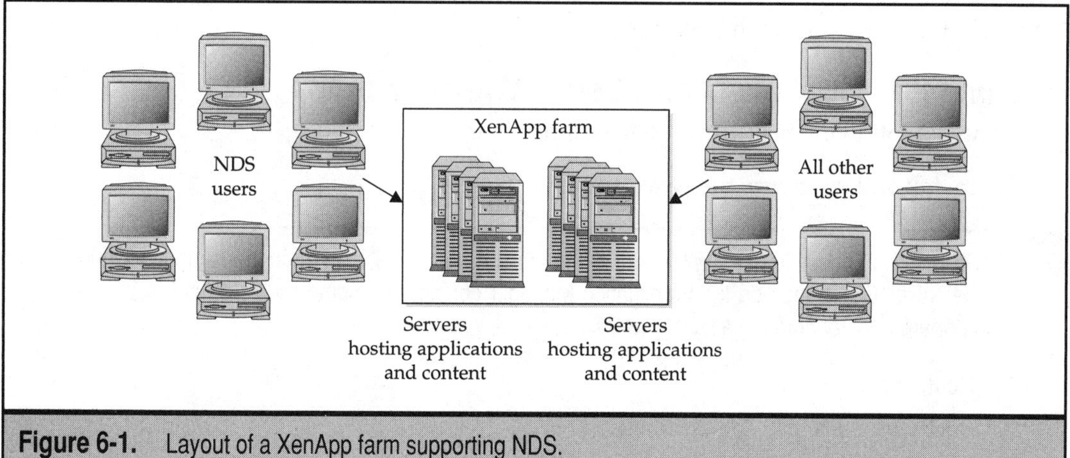

Figure 6-1. Layout of a XenApp farm supporting NDS.

The following software must be installed for XenApp to access NDS successfully.

On the NDS server (a server supporting NDS authentication and responding to NDS queries from clients), the following software is required:

- NDS eDirectory 8.5 for Windows or for Novell NetWare 5 with Support Pack 6 or later, or for Novell NetWare 5.1 with Support Pack 2 or later, or NetWare 6 and later

On XenApp, make sure that the following are installed:

- Novell Client for Windows NT/2000, version 4.81 or later
- MetaFrame XP for Windows, Feature Release 3 or later

If you are using ZENworks' Dynamic Local User function to gain access to Windows, you must install Novell ZENworks for Desktops 3 or later.

If you are not using ZENworks to gain access to Windows, you must have accounts with the same user name and password that exist in both NDS and NT4 or ADS domains.

To synchronize domains, perform either of the following:

- Manually synchronize accounts
- Use third-party software, such as Novell's Account Manager 2.1 for NT or DirXML, that can automatically synchronize accounts between NDS and NT domains

NOTE Internet Protocol (IP) is the only supported protocol for correct interaction between XenApp, NDS, and ZENworks for Desktops.

Installing Required Software

Citrix recommends installing the Novell Client and related service packs on a server before installing XenApp. If the server is already running XenApp, see the section "Installing the Novell Client on a Server with XenApp."

Installing the Novell Client on a Server Without XenApp

Complete the following tasks prior to installing XenApp:

1. Install and configure the Novell Client.

NOTE If you choose to use ZENworks DLU, it may be necessary to perform a custom installation of the Novell Client and add the Workstation Manager component. Some clients do not install this component when performing a typical install.

2. Restart the server.
3. Verify that you can log on to NDS.

If you cannot log on to NDS, you may need to add a Directory Agent (DA) location to the Novell Client. A DA is needed when the NDS server is located on a different subnet. If a DA does not exist, make sure the NDS server and the XenApp are part of the same subnet.

1. To optimize logon and browsing response times, change the order of the network providers using the following steps:
   a. Open Network Connections.
   b. From the Window menu choose Advanced | Advanced Settings. The Advanced Settings dialog box appears.
   c. On the Provider Order tab, adjust the order of the network providers so that Microsoft Windows Network is above NetWare Services.
   d. Click OK to close the Advanced Settings dialog box.
2. To optimize logon time, add the Windows fonts directory located in %SYSTEM-ROOT% to the system-path environment variable.
3. To suppress a XenApp setup program error message that says the FileSysChange parameter is invalid, complete the following steps:
   a. Open the System.ini file located in %SYSTEMROOT%.
   b. In the [386Enh] section of System.ini, set the following value:
   c. FileSysChange=off
   d. Save and close System.ini.

NOTE The appearance of this error message causes unattended setup of XenApp to fail. Make sure the FileSysChange parameter is set to Off before running an unattended installation.

4. Install XenApp. Be sure to activate the appropriate licenses.

Installing the Novell Client on a Server with XenApp

If XenApp is already installed on the server before you install the Novell Client, you must change the Windows registry on the server before *and* after you install the Novell Client. If the Novell Client that you are installing is version 4.9 or later, the following steps are unnecessary because the 4.9 client detects GINA chaining and respects such chaining with Citrix.

If XenApp is already installed on the server, complete the following tasks.

1. Run regedit.
2. Edit the following registry key:

```
HKEY_LOCAL_MACHINE\SOFTWARE\Microsoft\WindowsNT\CurrentVersion\
Winlogon
```

3. Double-click the GinaDLL entry located in the right-hand pane. In the String Editor window that pops up, replace the value Ctxgina.dll with the value Msgina.dll.
4. Install and configure the Novell Client.
5. Do not restart the server when prompted by the Novell Client setup program.
6. Edit the registry entry for GinaDLL, as in step 2. In the String Editor window that appears, replace the value Nwgina.dll with the value Ctxgina.dll.
7. With the key path for Winlogon still selected, choose Edit | Add Value.
8. Type **CTXGINADLL** in the Add Value dialog box. The data type is REG_SZ.
9. Enter **Nwgina.dll** in the String Editor window to assign this value to the new CTXGINADLL entry.
10. Restart the server.

On XenApp servers, Ctxgina.dll is loaded by Winlogon.exe to process the autologon information transmitted by ICA clients. Ctxgina.dll can process autologon credentials in excess of 20 characters. For example, if Ctxgina.dll is not loaded, autologon user names greater than 20 characters are truncated to 20 characters by Termsrv.exe. When Ctxgina.dll acquires the user's autologon credentials, they are passed in their entirety to the installed Gina.dll file to complete the authentication process. In most cases, the installed GINA is Msgina.dll. When the Novell Client is installed, the GINA is Nwgina.dll. The previous steps are required to ensure that Ctxgina is installed on the XenApp. Ctxgina is required for logging on automatically with user names that exceed 20 characters. If the Novell Client that you are installing is version 4.9 or later, the previous steps are unnecessary because the 4.9 client detects GINA chaining and respects such chaining with Citrix.

NOTE If the Novell Client is upgraded after the installation of XenApp, the GINA values are overwritten and it is necessary to reconfigure the registry with the previous steps.

To optimize logon and browsing response times, change the order of the network providers using the following steps:

1. Open Network Connections.
2. From the Window menu choose Advanced | Advanced Settings. The Advanced Settings dialog box appears.
3. On the Provider Order tab, adjust the order of the network providers so that Microsoft Windows Network is above NetWare Services.
4. Click OK to close the Advanced Settings dialog box.

To optimize logon time, add the Windows fonts directory located in %systemroot% to the system-path environment variable.

The system is now ready to set up the Windows account authentication to be used to access Windows 2003 servers.

Windows Account Authentication

When a NetWare Client is running on a Windows 2003 Server, users are required to have two accounts: one for authentication to NDS and one to gain access to Windows.

Two different approaches can give Windows access to users. The first option uses Novell's Dynamic Local User functionality, available in Novell's ZENworks for Desktop product.

The second option is to have the same user name and password in both NDS and ADS domains for each user. This allows integration of XenApp and NDS without the use of Novell's ZENworks.

If you are using XenApp with NDS integration using ZENworks, continue in the following section with "Configuring ZENworks for Desktops Settings for XenApp Support."

If you are using XenApp with NDS integration without ZENworks, skip to the "Configuring NDS Support in Citrix XenApp without ZENworks" section.

Configuring ZENworks for Desktops Settings for XenApp Support

When a Novell Client is running on a Windows 2003 Server, users are normally required to enter separate credentials to log on to Windows and NDS. Enabling the Dynamic Local User policy in ZENworks for Desktops eliminates this need.

The following section explains how to configure the Container Package and User Package in ZENworks for Desktops to eliminate the need to specify two sets of credentials when connecting to XenApp. Configure the Container Package to specify which users (by container) should have the Dynamic Local User policy applied to them. Configure the User Package to specify how the Dynamic Local User policy is applied to those users.

NOTE These settings are configured on the NDS server through ConsoleOne.

Configuring the ZENworks for Desktops Container Package

The Container Package searches for policies located within the tree and then applies them to users who are associated with a particular container. Follow the next example to create a Container Package that searches only the local container for policies applied to users within that container. This sample configuration is useful for small companies.

Perform the following steps for containers that hold user objects that require the Dynamic Local User policy:

1. Select a container that holds user objects.
2. Choose New Object | Policy Package | Container Package.
3. Choose Define Additional Properties and click Finish.
4. On the Policies tab, enable the search policy.
5. In the "search policies up to" field, choose Object Container to search only the container in which the search policy resides.

The other choices are as follows:

- **Root (default)** This option searches the local container and any container in the direct path to the root of the tree. This is not recommended for medium-to-large trees.
- **Partition** This option searches the local container and any container up to the root of the partition. This method works well for large environments, but you need to locate the partition boundaries.
- **Selected Container** This option searches the container between the current container and the root of the tree that you select.

6. Leave the search level at the default setting of 0.
7. Click Apply, and then Close.
8. Click the Associations tab.
9. Choose Add and browse to the container that holds the Container Package that you just created.
10. Click OK, and then Close.

Configuring the ZENworks for Desktops User Package

The User Package in ZENworks for Desktops enables Dynamic Local User functionality for users who are associated with that particular package. Follow the next example to create a User Package that enables the Dynamic Local User functionality.

NOTE If the Container Package, the User Policy Package, and the user are not located in the same container, the User Policy Package that contains the DLU settings will not be applied to the user.

1. Choose the Organizational Unit that holds the Container Package from the previous section.
2. Choose New Object | Policy Package | User Package.
3. Near the end of the Wizard, choose Define Additional Properties, and then click Finish.
4. Choose WinNT-2000 on the Policies tab.
5. Choose Enable Dynamic Local User, and then choose Properties.
6. Choose Dynamic Local User at the top of the page.
7. Choose Manage Existing NT Account (if any). This changes the password and other items to match for a seamless integration.

NOTE Novell recommends that you create a separate Dynamic Local User policy for users who have the user name Administrator if the local administrator account has not been renamed.

8. Choose Use NetWare Credential. This creates a local Microsoft user who has the same name and password as the NDS user. If this is not enabled, the Dynamic Local User feature creates a random user name and password, resulting in a loss of XenApp functionality.
9. Do not enable Volatile User unless you have large profiles and want to conserve disk space.
10. On the Not Member of tab, choose User | Add. Select the users or groups to which the policy will apply. This gives them rights to log on and run XenApp applications.
11. Click Apply, and then OK two times to finish the policy.
12. If XenApp is running on a Windows 2003 server, make sure that you add a Custom Group to the policy. The Custom Group name should be Remote Desktop Users; this is the group that is granted Log On Locally permission to log in remotely through Terminal Services.

Configuring NDS Support in Citrix XenApp without ZENworks

In an environment with a Novell Client running on Windows Server 2003, users are required to enter separate credentials to log on to Windows and NDS. Using synchronized accounts between NDS and ADS domains eliminates this need.

To enable NDS support in XenApp without ZENworks, set the following registry key on all the servers that have the Novell Client installed but are not using ZenWorks For Desktops DLU functionality. Set the Value to the NT or ADS down-level domain name containing the user accounts that match the accounts in NDS.

1. Run regedit.
2. Edit the registry key as follows:

```
HKEY_LOCAL_MACHINE\SOFTWARE\Citrix
```

3. With the key path for Citrix still selected, choose Edit | New Key.
4. Rename the newly created key to NDS.
5. Highlight the new NDS key.
6. With the NDS still selected, choose Edit | New String Value.
7. Type **SyncedDomainName** in the String Value dialog box.
8. Enter the name of the domain that has the same user accounts as NDS in the String Editor window to assign this value to the new SyncedDomainName entry.

NOTE When this registry key is set, ctxgina.dll replaces the NDS tree name passed from the client to the server with the string placed in SyncedDomainName. Ctxgina.dll then passes the credentials on to nwgina.dll. This allows the passed-on user name and password to authenticate to NDS and then the domain specified in the SyncedDomainName.

Enabling NDS Support in the Citrix XenApp Farm

By default, a XenApp farm supports only Microsoft Windows users. Follow the next steps to specify the preferred NDS tree for the farm. XenApp supports only one NDS tree in each farm.

1. Launch the Access Management Console.
2. Right-click the farm node in the left pane of the console and choose Properties.
3. In the Properties dialog box expand the Farm-wide node if necessary, expand the Presentation Server node if necessary and highlight General.
4. Specify the tree name in the NDS Preferred Tree field, and then click OK. To disable NDS support for the farm, erase the value in the NDS Preferred Tree field, and then click OK.

Assigning Citrix Administrator Privileges to NDS Objects

Follow the next steps to assign Citrix administrator privileges to objects in an NDS tree, such as country, organization, organization unit, group, user, or alias:

1. Launch the Access Management Console.
2. Right-click the Administrators node in the left-hand pane and choose New | Add Administrator from the menu that appears.
3. In the Add Citrix Administrator dialog box, click Add and open the NDS tree. Objects in the NDS tree represent container and leaf objects.
4. When prompted to log on to the tree, enter the distinguished name and password of an NDS user.
5. Select the Show Users option to display user and alias objects in this hierarchy.
6. Double-click to open container objects. Select the objects to be granted Citrix administrator privileges. Add at least one NDS user account that has read-write privileges.

NOTE Although it is possible to grant a Citrix administrator access to a context, users within the context or in contexts that are children of the granted context will also be Citrix administrators. Granting such access is not recommended because of the difficulty in managing permissions granted to contexts.

7. Click OK, click Next, then click Next again to assign privileges. Choose View Only, Full Administration, or Custom privileges.
8. Click Finish to close the Add Citrix Administrator dialog box.

CHAPTER 7

Advanced Access Control

This chapter focuses mainly on compatibility with previous implementations of Advanced Access Control, namely Secure Access Manager and Access Gateway Enterprise. Also, content around security of split tunneling and split Domain Name Service (DNS) is considered.

SIMULATING A TRADITIONAL VPN USING CITRIX ACCESS GATEWAY ADVANCED EDITION

Citrix Access Gateway Advanced Edition can easily be configured to use the Secure Access Client as a traditional Virtual Private Network (VPN) client that provides secure access to all internal network resources defined by the administrator.

During VPN configuration, there are both required and optional settings to configure in Advanced Access Control, both of which will be explained in this chapter. If you have an existing VPN solution that you desire to mirror using Advanced Access Control, it will be helpful to document these settings so that you can easily set the same configuration in Advanced Access Control. This chapter assumes that Advanced Access Control has been installed and that the Access Gateway(s) are in Advanced Access Control mode and joined to your Advanced Access Control farm. For details on either of these steps, see the *Citrix Access Gateway with Advanced Access Control Administrator's Guide*.

The required configurations include the following:

- Defining network resources
- Establishing an access policy that grants access to the desired network resources
- Putting in place a connection policy that enables the launching of the Secure Access Client
- Defining the appropriate split tunneling settings

The optional configurations include the following:

- Restricting the access and connection policies by users or groups or filters
- Defining Internet Protocol (IP) pools
- Enabling split DNS

Network Resources

The network resources are used to define which specific subnet ranges, Fully Qualified Domain Names (FQDN), IP addresses, and port/protocol combinations the Secure Access Client is either allowed or denied access to when connected. The administrator can choose to use the preconfigured Entire Network resource, which equates to the network range 0.0.0.0/0.0.0.0 for all ports, or define custom settings using the settings mentioned above.

Using the Entire Network resource provides the quickest and easiest configuration, but also opens the widest network range granting access to the entire network. Administrators should review their network and security requirements to determine whether more granular access is required. If more granular access is required, custom network resources should be defined. For more detail on configuring network resources, see the "Creating Network Resources for VPN Access" section of the *Citrix Access Gateway with Advanced Access Control Administrator's Guide.*

Access Policies

Access policies are used to control which network resources users are allowed and denied access and under which conditions. At least one access policy containing the desired network resources must be configured in order to configure VPN access. The access policy should contain either the Entire Network resource or any custom network resources to which you wish to allow or deny access.

In a situation where you want to explicitly allow and deny access to network resources, separate policies will be needed: one for the allowed resource and one for denied resources.

When custom network resources are defined and used, the Entire Network resource should not be selected because it grants access to the entire network, thereby causing access conflicts with the custom network resources.

NOTE The Entire Network resource cannot be deleted.

For more detail on configuring access policies, see the "Controlling Access through Policies" section of the *Citrix Access Gateway with Advanced Access Control Administrators Guide.*

Connection Policy

Connection policies control the conditions under which the Secure Access Client is launched and the associated settings. The primary setting of concern when configuring VPN access is "Launch the Secure Access Client if access allowed," which controls the launching of the Secure Access Client. At least one connection policy must have this setting enabled. For more information on configuring connection policies, see the "Creating Connection Policies" section of the *Citrix Access Gateway with Advanced Access Control Administrator's Guide.*

SPLIT TUNNELING IN CITRIX ACCESS GATEWAY

Split tunneling enables client devices to communicate with public Internet resources and your corporate network concurrently.

To use split tunneling, you must configure a list of accessible networks so that users can access corporate resources. For example, an accessible network of 0.0.0.0/0.0.0.0 would grant access to the entire network. An accessible network of 10.0.0.0/255.0.0.0 would grant access to only the 10.x.x.x subnet. Your specific network and security requirements will determine which access networks to add. Ensure that any network resources defined earlier fall within the accessible networks range if you are using split tunneling. If this list is not defined, users cannot access any corporate resources regardless of any policies granting access.

Disabling split tunneling maximizes the security of client connections and requires no additional configuration for users to begin accessing corporate resources. When split tunneling is disabled, all network traffic sent by the Secure Access Client is routed through the Access Gateway, including traffic to public Internet Web sites.

For more information on split tunneling, see the "Configuring Split Tunneling" section of the *Citrix Access Gateway with Advanced Access Control Administrator's Guide*.

Optional Configurations

The following are additional optional configurations available for Access Gateway with Advanced Access Control.

Restricting Access and Connection Policies by Users, Groups, or Filters

Both access and connection polices can provide further granular control with the use of filters and user/group access control. Both settings are optional when creating policies and can be changed at any time. For more details on these topics, see the *Citrix Access Gateway with Advanced Access Control Administrator's Guide.*

Using IP Pools

IP pools are optional and can be used to give clients connecting with the Secure Access Client a unique IP address. For this use, a unique IP range should be set aside that does not conflict with any existing DHCP scopes or static IPs in use.

> ***NOTE*** You must reboot an Access Gateway before applying this setting.

For more detail on configuring IP pools, see the "Creating Connection Policies" section of the *Citrix Access Gateway with Advanced Access Control Administrators Guide.*

Enabling Split DNS

Split DNS is an optional setting that allows the failover to a client's local DNS setting should the remote DNS server not be available. By default, Access Gateway checks a user's remote DNS only.

MUTUAL TRUST LIST IN END POINT ANALYSIS

End Point Analysis clients download scan packages from servers that end users have decided to trust. The first time that an end user visits a logon point on a server that is configured for End Point Analysis scans, the user is asked whether he or she wants to trust scan package code from that server. The end user may choose to trust to download packages from a server just once or always to trust that server.

Administrators may also configure End Point Analysis clients to use packages that have already been downloaded from a set of trusted servers. This might be useful in a case where the external users are served by a distinct logon point host in the DMZ but internal connections go through another Advanced Access Control server. A mobile laptop user could connect to both external and internal logon points in such a scenario, and it might be preferable simply to reuse previously downloaded scan packages from one or other servers. The list of such servers is called the *mutual trust list*.

The mutual trust list is controlled via an option in the web.config file in a logon point's physical directory. The list members are specified in the key MutualTrustList and consist of a series of server names separated by spaces. For the "mutual" trust mechanism to work, the administrator should modify the web.config files for the logon points on all the servers in the list.

Here's an example of how this might work. Let's say that the administrator wants users who log in to serverA to trust packages already downloaded from serverB. In the web.config file for one of the logon points on serverA—SampleLogonPoint, for instance––the administrator adds the following:

```
<add key="MutualTrustList" value="serverB"/>
```

Similarly, for a logon point on serverB the administrator changes the web.config to reference serverA:

```
<add key="MutualTrustList" value="serverA"/>
```

Now, when a user logs in to serverA/SampleLogonPoint, his End Point Analysis client records that serverB is trusted. Next time the user logs in to serverB, he may download scan packages that were not downloaded during his initial visit to serverA. Each time that scan package files are downloaded, they are saved to a cache on the endpoint machine. The cache is organized by logon server origin. The mutual trust list for serverB includes serverA and that information is also saved by the End Point Analysis client. When the user returns to a logon point on serverA, and if a new EPA scan package is configured to run for that logon point, which contains a file already downloaded from serverB, then the scan package file is not downloaded from serverA. Instead, it is used from the cached copy for serverB on the endpoint machine.

HTML PREVIEW

By default, Citrix Access Gateway Advanced Edition is configured to support the HTML rendering of Microsoft Word, Excel, Visio, and PowerPoint documents as well as Adobe Acrobat files.

For HTML rendering to occur, Microsoft Office products must be installed on at least one of the Advanced Access Control servers in the farm. Additionally, if the administrator wishes to have PDF document types rendered in HTML, the administrator must also install pdftohtml.exe version 0.36. This executable can be obtained from SourceForge at http://pdftohtml.sourceforge.net/.

The executable should be installed in the C:\Program Files\Citrix\Access Gateway Enterprise\PDF folder. If the administrator wishes to place the executable for PDF conversions outside of the Advanced Access Control install path, he or she should modify a registry key so that Advanced Access Control knows where to find the executable and will activate this type of HTML rendering.

The registry key is located at the following site:

HKLM\software\citrix\msam\activationservice\enginemanager\previewengine
ValueName: PDFConverter
ValueType: string
Default Value: *installpath*\Citrix\Access Gateway Enterprise\PDF\pdftohtml.exe

For HTML-rendered PDF files to illustrate embedded images, the administrator must also install GhostScript version 8.14 or later. Advanced Access Control was tested on version 8.14. You can download GhostScript from http://www.ghostscript.com/. After installing the application, the administrator must add to the server's environmental variables PATH variable the path to the bin directory where the GhostScript executable is located. (A reboot of the server may be necessary at this point.)

Adding Other File Types to Be Associated and Rendered through Existing Rendering Handlers

This section details how to add other file types for rendering by external handlers.

Supported File Type for Each Handler

When a handler is loaded (as determined by the handler list and whether the required component exists), it reports the file type list that can be supported. The handler reads the file type list from registry and, if such a file type list doesn't exist in the registry, a default list is returned.

Table 7-1 indicates the default settings. The registry keys do not exist by default and need to be created to associate additional file types with handlers.

NOTE The registry key values must begin and end with a colon.

Key Name	ROOT\EngineManager\PreviewEngine\caps
Value Names	`MSWORDHANDLER` (Word) `MSVISIOHANDLER` (Visio) `MSPPTHANDLER` (PowerPoint) `PDFHANDLER` (Adobe Acrobat) `MSEXCELHANDLER` (Excel)
Value Type	String
Installation Value	None
Default Value	ExcelHandler `:.xls:.csv:.dbf:.dif:.slk:.wql:.xlt:` PDFHandler `:.pdf:` PowerPntHandler `:.ppt:.pot:.pps:` VisioHandler `:.vsd:.vss:.vst:` WordHandler `:.doc:.ans:.mcw:.rtf:`

Table 7-1. Default File Type Handlers

Step-by-Step Instructions for Modifying an Existing Handler

The following example causes .txt file types to have the preview option available in the choice page and to be rendered as HTML for previewing. This is only an example.

1. Create a registry key named *caps* under the following directory:
   HKLM\software\citrix\msam\activationservice\enginemanager\previewengine
2. Under the new registry key, add the following value:
   - Value Name: MSWORDHANDLER
   - Value Type: String

   Values: `::doc::ans::mcw::rtf::txt:`
3. Stop and start the Citrix Activation Host Service and Citrix Activation Engine Service via the server config console.
4. In the file shares tab of the Navigation user interface (UI), click on a .txt file and notice that Preview is available in the choice page. Select the option and view the text file as rendered HTML.

Key Name	ROOT\EngineManager
Value Name	CacheSize
Value Type	DWORD
Installation Value	None
Default Value	10000

Table 7-2. CacheSize Values

Controlling Cache Behavior

The engine manager service uses the cache to boost performance. The default settings should work well in most cases. The only key that the administrator should modify for this is CacheSize, which by default is set to 10000. If drive space becomes an issue, you should lower this number. The setting should never be less than 2.

In simple terms, the number 10000 refers to the number of folders that appear in C:\Program Files\Citrix\Access Gateway\'ActivationCache before the items begin to overwrite. The order for replacing items is based on the oldest and least-used. So, if the first cached item created is used everyday, it will not be overwritten.

To control the maximum count of cache items, reference Table 7-2 for possible CacheSize values.

MAKING ICA FILE MODIFICATIONS IN ADVANCED ACCESS CONTROL

In Advanced Access Control, ICA file modifications are made by updating two files: ICAFile.xslt and UserPreferences.xslt.

The ICAFile.xslt file is similar to the template.ica file used in Web Interface. This file enables you to make global changes to the parameters generated in an ICA file. ICAFile.xslt is located under \Program Files\Citrix\Access Gateway\Bin\Binders. Any changes to this file should be made on all servers running the Citrix Resource Aggregation Service. After making changes, you must restart the Citrix Resource Aggregation Service for the changes to take effect.

A number of sample modifications are shown next.

Proxy Configuration

Several proxy configurations can be configured by modifying the ICAFile.xslt file. This allows your ICA client to connect to a Citrix Presentation Server through an HTTP or SOCKS proxy server.

```
ProxyType=[VALUES: None, Auto, Socks(Detect Version), SocksV4, SocksV5,
Tunnel, Script]
ProxyHost=[Proxy Address:Proxy Port]
ProxyBypassList=
ProxyAutoConfigURL=[http path to AutoConfig or PAC file]
ProxyUsername=[Proxy/SOCKSv5 Username]
ProxyPassword=[Proxy/SOCKSv5 Password]
ProxyTimeout=[Time in seconds the client waits for initial response
from proxy server]
ProxyUseFQDN=True
```

Auto Client Reconnect

If you want to disable Auto Client Reconnect globally, add the following line:

```
TransportReconnectEnabled=Off
```

Root Certificate for the Java Client

You can use the ICAFile.xslt file to specify a root certificate to be used by the Java ICA client when making ICA connections through Access Gateway. This keeps you from having to package the certificate in a CAB or JAR file. To do this, add the following two lines:

```
SSLNoCACerts=1
SSLCACert0=cert_name.cer
```

If it is a multiple (chain) certificate, you need to modify the following:

```
SSLNoCAcerts=<no. of certs>
SSLCACert0=<sslcert1.cer>
SSLCACert1=<sslcert2.cer>
```

The root certificate must be copied to the Java client directory on the web server.

Remapping Hot Keys

To remap the hot keys, insert the hot-key parameters in the WFClient section of the Icafile .xslt file:

```
ClientName=<xsl:value-of select="ica:ClientName" />
Hotkey1Char=F1
```

```
Hotkey1Shift=Shift
Hotkey2Char=F3
Hotkey2Shift=Shift
Hotkey3Char=F2
Hotkey3Shift=Shift
Hotkey4Char=F1
Hotkey4Shift=Ctrl
Hotkey5Char=F2
Hotkey5Shift=Ctrl
Hotkey6Char=F2
Hotkey6Shift=Alt
Hotkey7Char=plus
Hotkey7Shift=Alt
Hotkey8Char=minus
Hotkey8Shift=Alt
Hotkey9Char=F3
HotKey10Shift=Ctrl
Hotkey10Char=F5
HotKey9Shift=Ctrl
Hotkey11Char=plus
Hotkey11Shift=Ctrl
BrowserRetry=1
BrowserTimeout=20000
HttpBrowserAddress=!
<xsl:apply-templates select="ica:CSGEnabled"/>
```

These are the default hot-key parameters. You can disable them by setting the value to "none," or if any keys affect your application, you can change them to reflect a key that does not conflict with your application.

Customizing Application Launch

The UserPreferences.xslt file can be used to modify launch parameters for specific applications. The UserPreferences.xslt file is located under \Program Files\Citrix\Access Gateway\Bin\Binders. One of the most common modifications is window size. The following listings show two example modifications. The first sets applications to a percent of the screen size:

```
<!--
   This template will set the window type to "Percent" for the named appli-
cation. For all other applications, the above semantics for applying user
preferences are preserved
    -->
    <xsl:template match="ica:WindowType">
      <xsl:choose>
        <xsl:when test="/ica:ICABinding[ica:ApplicationName='Notepad']">
```

```
          <xsl:copy>
            <ica:Percent>100</ica:Percent>
          </xsl:copy>
        </xsl:when>
        <xsl:when test="/ica:ICABinding[ica:ApplicationName='Solitaire']">
          <xsl:copy>
            <ica:Percent>50</ica:Percent>
          </xsl:copy>
        </xsl:when>
        <xsl:otherwise>
          <xsl:call-template name="replace.context.element">
            <xsl:with-param name="replacement"
select="$Transform/Arguments/ica:UserPreferences/
ica:ApplicationSettings/ica:
WindowType"/>
            <xsl:with-param name="allowed"
select="$Transform/Arguments/ApplicationSettingsControl/@WindowType"/>
          </xsl:call-template>
        </xsl:otherwise>
      </xsl:choose>
    </xsl:template>
```

This second example shows how to set an application to a specific window size:

```
<xsl:when test="/ica:ICABinding[ica:ApplicationName='APP01']">
<xsl:copy>
   <ica:Pixels>
      <ica:Width>800</ica:Width>
      <ica:Height>600</ica:Height>
    </ica:Pixels>
   </xsl:copy>
</xsl:when>
```

MANUALLY CHANGE THE LOCATION OF THE ACCESS GATEWAY ENTERPRISE EDITION SERVER WEBSITE

This section describes the steps to change the location of web sites on an Access Gateway Enterprise Edition Server manually.

Step 1: Remove Logon Point Deployments

To remove the logon point deployments, follow these steps:

1. Run the Server Configuration utility by choosing Start | Programs | Citrix | Access Gateway | Server Configuration.

2. Select the configured logon points and remember all whose status is set to "The folder is deployed to the Web site."
3. Remove all deployed logon points.
4. Close the Server Configuration utility.

Step 2: Delete the Remaining IIS Deployments

To delete any remaining ISS deployments, follow this procedure:

1. Run Internet Information Services (IIS) Manager.
2. Delete the following virtual directories from IIS:
   - CitrixAuthService
   - CitrixEPAService
   - CitrixFEI
   - CitrixAccessGatewayConfigService
   - CitrixLogonAgentService
   - CitrixLogonPoint
   - CitrixSessionInit
   - Do not delete aspnet_client, iisstart.htm, or pagerror.gif
3. Delete the physical files for the following virtual directories (do not delete the physical files for WebSiteViewerRoot). The default location is c:\inetpub\wwwroot. Make sure to back up any custom configurations before deleting files.
   - CitrixAuthService
   - CitrixEPAService
   - CitrixFEI
   - CitrixAccessGatewayConfigService
   - CitrixLogonAgentService
   - CitrixLogonPoint
   - CitrixSessionInit

Step 3: Make Registry Modifications

To modify the registry, follow these steps:

1. Run regedit.exe or another registry editing tool.
2. Select the registry key HKLM\Software\Citrix\Msam.
3. Modify the DWORD value of ServerConfigured to 0.
4. Modify the DWORD value of WebServicesConfigured to 0.

Step 4: Redeploy Server

To redeploy the server, follow this procedure:

1. Run Server Configuration (choose Start | Programs | Citrix | Access Gateway | Server Configuration).
2. Select "Join an existing access server farm."
3. Enter all configuration information, including the new web site for deployment.

Step 5: Redeploy Logon Points

To redeploy the logon points, follow this procedure:

1. Run Server Configuration by choosing Start | Programs | Citrix | Access Gateway | Server Configuration.
2. Select the Configured Logon Points task.
3. For each logon point originally deployed on the selected server, select the logon point and click the Deploy button.

THIRD-PARTY FILES IN END POINT ANALYSIS

Third-party vendors can implement End Point Analysis scan packages for Access Gateway with the Advanced Access Control option. Doing so gives customers even more choices for use in the Advanced Access Control policies for configuring filters to grant users access to network resources.

Sometimes vendors ask how they can package additional files in the scan package cabinet (CAB) files. Typically, their implementations require additional data or executable files that perform the examination of the endpoint and then send the results back to the scan package and the End Point Analysis policy system. These files may need to be updated frequently if they include a signature database of viruses or something similar.

Currently, the End Point Analysis scan package format does not provide a means to specify additional files beyond the dispatcher (server-side) and client-side modules. This section presents an alternative approach for storing the additional files in the logon point and then using the vendor's client-side module to download them using an HTTP-style GET.

Caveats

The vendor's client-side module needs to know the URL of the logon point to request the additional files it needs. Two potential problems arise immediately: how to inform the client-side module of this URL, which may be different depending on whether a logon point is accessed internally to the network or externally through Access Gateway; and how to make the additional files visible through Access Gateway.

When a logon point is configured to work with Access Gateway, a copy of certain registered files is made to a cache on Access Gateway. This cache consists of files whose content is static. This performance optimization means that new or updated third-party files copied to the virtual directory of a logon point on an Advanced Access Control server are not automatically replicated to the cache on the Access Gateway. At present, the only way to re-cache the files after a logon point has been configured with Access Gateway is to do so manually in the Advanced Access Control console.

Solution

Allow administrators to enter the URLs to logon points as End Point Analysis scan rule parameters, so logon points can be accessed both internally and externally by client-side modules. Leverage the static content caching feature of Access Gateway to make the third-party files visible externally. Third-party scan package implementers should store their additional files in the logon point directory instead of a separate vendor virtual directory. They should register these files with the Advanced Access Control logon agent service. Any time that updates are made to these files, have the administrator refresh the Access Gateway cache for that logon point.

Creating an End Point Analysis Scan Package Containing Third-Party Files

To create an End Point Analysis scan package that includes third-party files, follow these steps:

1. Create a scan package with client-side and dispatcher modules as usual in Visual Studio using the End Point Analysis Package Wizard.
2. Add a parameter for the logon point URL to the scan package properties:
    a. Open the scan package solution file in Visual Studio.
    b. Navigate to the project node in the solution explorer pane.
    c. Right-click on the node and choose Edit End Point Analysis Package Properties.
    d. Choose the Parameters tab and add a parameter for the URL that the administrator will enter for this scan package.
3. Add a call to a client method and pass the logon point URL as an argument. In the dispatcher, add code similar to this:

```
CComBSTR objectName(L"http://.../ZLTest.cab/1.0/downloadable
/ClientDownload.dll");
CComBSTR methodName(L"DownloadableEntryPoint");
CComPtr<IEPAExpression> exp = NULL;
pEnvironment->CreateExpression(objectName, methodName, &exp);
```

```
CComBSTR URL(L"");
pParameters->get_Value(CComBSTR(L"LogonPointURL"),&URL.m_str);
exp->AddArgument(URL);
pEnvironment->SetEnquiry(MyIdentifier, exp);
```

4. Create another executable that the administrator can run to copy the additional files needed by the scan package to a subdirectory of the logon point. Register these files with the logon agent service. To register the third-party files with the logon agent service, open the web.config file for the CitrixLogonAgentService web service. Add file extensions of the additional files to the StaticFileExtensions key.

Configuring a Test Environment

To configure a test environment for the new configuration, follow these steps:

1. Add internal and external logon points.
2. In the Advanced Access Control console, navigate to the Logon Points node and choose the task "Create logon point."
3. Input a name for the logon point, for example, InternalLogonPoint. Then choose the default values for the rest of the wizard. You see a message that the logon point files have not yet been deployed—that is, they have not been created on the Advanced Access Control server. Ignore that message for now.
4. Go back and choose "Create logon point" again, but this time, name the logon point ExternalLogonPoint and, once more, accept all the defaults in the wizard.
5. Choose Start | All Programs | Citrix | Access Gateway and execute the Server Configuration option. Choose Configured Logon Points on the left. Highlight InternalLogonPoint and choose Deploy. Do the same for ExternalLogonPoint. At this point, verify that virtual directories for both the logon points have been set up in IIS on the Advanced Access Control server.
6. Import the third-party scan package into the Advanced Access Control console.
7. In the Advanced Access Control console, navigate to the End Point Analysis | Miscellaneous node. Choose the "Import scan package" task and import the CAB file for your scan package.

Adding Scan Package Rules for Internal/External Logon Points

To add scan package rules for internal and external logon points, follow this procedure:

1. In the Advanced Access Control console, select the node for the scan package that you just imported.
2. Choose the "Create scan" task.

3. Pick a name for the scan.
4. On the Select Conditions page, choose Logon Point.
5. On the Define Rule page, name the rule InternalLogonPoint Rule.
6. On the Configure Conditions page, select all the operating systems (OSs).
7. On the second Configure Conditions page, select InternalLogonPoint.
8. On the Define Property to Verify page, enter the URL to the subdirectory of your Advanced Access Control logon point virtual directory which contains the third-party files.
9. In the Advanced Access Control console, select the newly created scan package scan node and choose the "Create rule" task. Run through the same steps as before, but this time, call the rule ExternalLogonPoint Rule. In the second Configure Conditions page, select ExternalLogonPoint and, in the Define Property to Verify page, enter the URL to the subdirectory of your Access Gateway server logon point virtual directory which contains the third-party files.

Testing the Internal Logon Point

To test the internal logon point, follow these steps:

1. Copy the additional third-party files to a subdirectory of the internal logon point virtual directory.
2. Log on to Advanced Access Control/InternalLogonPoint and verify that the End Point Analysis scan package functions as expected.

Testing the External Logon Point

To test the external logon point, follow this procedure:

1. Copy the additional third-party files to a subdirectory of the external logon point virtual directory and register the file extensions with the logon agent service.
2. Expose the external logon point through the Access Gateway administration tool.
3. In the Advanced Access Control console, select the ExternalLogonPoint logon point node and choose the "Refresh logon page information" task. This caches the additional files to the Access Gateway server.
4. Log on to Access Gateway/ExternalLogonPoint and verify that the End Point Analysis scan package functions as expected.

CHAPTER 8

Password Manager

In this chapter, we explore Password Manager deployment scenarios, including Installation Manager, Active Directory Group Policy, and other techniques. We also look at several other administrator-related tasks, such as selecting a synchronization solution, performance characteristics, and the scalability of Password Manager.

DEPLOYMENT MODELS AND SCENARIOS

This section details the most common deployment methods for Citrix Password Manager in various scenarios. The methods detailed are the XenApp Installation Management feature, Active Directory Group Policy Objects, and standard file sharing.

Citrix XenApp and Installation Management

You must install the Password Manager agent on all XenApp systems hosting applications that require authentication. The Enterprise version of XenApp has a feature called *Installation Manager* that allows for efficient deployment of Microsoft Installer Service (MSI)–based installs across a XenApp farm. Follow these steps to deploy Password Manager to your XenApp farm quickly:

NOTE Installation Manager deploys the agent MSI in silent mode, so no user interaction is needed for deployment on remote servers.

1. Create the Agent Installation Image MSI file, as detailed in the *Password Manager Administrator's Guide*.
2. Save or copy this MSI to a network share that will be accessible to all the servers in your farm.
3. Open the Presentation Server Console.
4. If Installation Manager was not previously configured with a network account, right-click the Installation Manager node. Select Properties and then enter a valid administrator account that has read access to the previous share and write access to all the servers to which you want to deploy the package.
5. Right-click the Packages node and select "add package."
6. Browse to the location of your saved, previously created, installation-image MSI file.
7. Follow the Installation Manager prompts to deploy the package to all desired servers in the server farm (see the *Citrix Presentation Server Administrator's Guide* for details).

Active Directory Group Policy Objects

Group Policy is a feature available in an Active Directory (AD) domain. You can use a Group Policy to install software on systems within the domain. Detailed information on how to use Group Policy objects can be found on the Microsoft web site. If your server farm is in a pure Active Directory environment, you can use a Group Policy to deploy the Password Manager agent. To create a Group Policy object, follow these steps:

1. Create the desired installation image MSI file as detailed in the *Password Manager Administrator's Guide.*
2. Save or copy this MSI to a network share that will be accessible to all the servers to which you want to deploy the MSI.
3. Create a Group Policy object for the groups of computers or users to which you want to deploy the agent. (Search the Microsoft knowledge base for articles on how to use Group Policy objects, you have many to choose from, depending on your particular environment.)

File Share Deployment

In smaller environments or in certain situations, deployment by file share may be desirable. To deploy by file share, follow these steps:

1. Copy the agent MSI file from the Password Manager install CD (or your installation image MSI file) to a file share location accesible to the machines on which you will deploy.
2. Make sure that MSI 3.0 is already present on your machine.
3. Run the following command:

   ```
   Msiexec /i <path_to_MSI_file_and_its_filename>
   ```

   If you want to suppress rebooting after the install, use the following:

   ```
   Msiexec reboot=suppress /i <path_to_MSI_file_and_its_filename>
   ```

UNDERSTANDING THE LICENSE BEHAVIOR OF CITRIX PASSWORD MANAGER 4.0 AND LATER ON THE CITRIX LICENSING SERVER

Citrix Password Manager requires a license server to distribute and track licenses, as compared to the manual process seen in MetaFrame Password Manager 2.5. An understanding of the technical details of this process enables the administrator to troubleshoot errors quickly and efficiently. This section compares the licensing operation of Password Manager to that of XenApp. It also explores the check-out and check-in process of licenses on the Password Manager server.

Licensing Operation Differences between Citrix Password Manager and Citrix XenApp

The Password Manager licensing operation is similar to the licensing operation used by XenApp. However, their modes of operation have differences:

- **Continuous TCP connection is not used.** Unlike XenApp, Password Manager does not maintain a Transmission Control Protocol (TCP) connection to the license server. TCP connections are established and broken for every individual operation.
- **Heartbeat information is not exchanged between the agent and the license server.** If the communication path between the agent and license server is broken, the agent does not realize the license server is unreachable until it tries to check out, renew, or check in a license.
- **Client software uses a different Macrovision application programming interface (API).** The Password Manager agent uses the Linger API, which is different from the one used by XenApp. The check-in and check-out behavior is also different. If you are trying to interpret the debug log entries on the license server for troubleshooting purposes, you may find that Password Manager log entries are hard to understand at first glance. The next section explains the check-in and check-out behavior (and how to interpret the resulting log entries).

Startup, Check-out, Check-in, Renewal, and Behavior

Password Manager agents require a license server to check out and check in licenses. Password Manager does not function without the presence of a license server. The agent makes a request to the server to check out a license to permit it to operate. After a license is checked out, only that agent can use the license for the duration of the Disconnected mode period, or until the agent checks in the license. One important piece of information to keep in mind is that the agent can only check out licenses and the server can only check in licenses. This process will become clearer with the review of the check-out, renewal, and check-in behavior in the debug log file, found at C:\Program Files\Citrix\Licensing\LS\lmgrd_debug.log.

NOTE For a more in-depth look into licensing, see the Licensing_Guide.pdf in the documentation folder of the Password Manager CD.

Startup Process

When the agent starts up, it checks out a *startup license,* which delivers generic operating parameters to the agent:

```
21:00:50 (CITRIX) TCP_NODELAY enabled
21:00:50 (CITRIX) OUT: "CITRIX" USER15@GENE-VM-2K3 [ec26edf8]
<-Agent checked out startup license
21:00:50 (CITRIX) IN: "CITRIX" USER15@GENE-VM-2K3 [ec26edf8]
<-Agent checked in startup license
21:00:50 (CITRIX) OUT: "MPM_ADV_RC" USER15@GENE-VM-2K3 [ec26edf8]
21:01:05 (CITRIX) OUT: "MPM_ADV_RC" USER15@GENE-VM-2K3 [ec26edf8]
21:01:05 (CITRIX) IN: "MPM_ADV_RC" USER15@GENE-VM-2K3 [ec26edf8]
21:01:40 (CITRIX) IN: "MPM_ADV_RC" USER15@GENE-VM-2K3 [ec26edf8]
```

The agent checks out a startup license and then immediately checks it back in again.

The startup license does not use the Linger API. The OUT: entry represents the license being checked out and the IN: entry represents the license being checked in.

Check-out Process

The agent performs only one type of operation with the license server: check-out. In the following example, a Password Manager agent is started (and receives a license) and is then shut down (and returns the license). Here is what the debug log on the license server shows:

```
21:00:50 (CITRIX) TCP_NODELAY enabled
21:00:50 (CITRIX) OUT: "CITRIX" USER15@GENE-VM-2K3 [ec26edf8]
21:00:50 (CITRIX) IN: "CITRIX" USER15@GENE-VM-2K3 [ec26edf8]
21:00:50 (CITRIX) OUT: "MPM_ADV_RC" USER15@GENE-VM-2K3 [ec26edf8]
<- Agent has checked out a license
21:01:05 (CITRIX) OUT: "MPM_ADV_RC" USER15@GENE-VM-2K3 [ec26edf8]
<- Agent has checked out the license with linger time = 1 second
(Agent intends to return the license)
21:01:05 (CITRIX) IN: "MPM_ADV_RC" USER15@GENE-VM-2K3 [ec26edf8]
21:01:40 (CITRIX) IN: "MPM_ADV_RC" USER15@GENE-VM-2K3 [ec26edf8]
```

The agent has started and has checked out a license. In this example, the agent keeps the licenses, depending on the licensing mode set by the administrator.

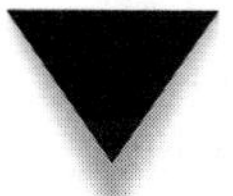

NOTE All OUT: log entries accompany a request from the agent. If you are using a network monitor, you should see communication between the agent and license server at all times that OUT: entries occur.

Check-in Process

To understand the check-in process, see the following debug log entries:

```
21:00:50 (CITRIX) TCP_NODELAY enabled
21:00:50 (CITRIX) OUT: "CITRIX" USER15@GENE-VM-2K3 [ec26edf8]
21:00:50 (CITRIX) IN: "CITRIX" USER15@GENE-VM-2K3 [ec26edf8]
21:00:50 (CITRIX) OUT: "MPM_ADV_RC" USER15@GENE-VM-2K3 [ec26edf8]
21:01:05 (CITRIX) OUT: "MPM_ADV_RC" USER15@GENE-VM-2K3 [ec26edf8]
21:01:05 (CITRIX) IN: "MPM_ADV_RC" USER15@GENE-VM-2K3 [ec26edf8]
<- License server has checked in a license for [ec26edf8].
21:01:40 (CITRIX) IN: "MPM_ADV_RC" USER15@GENE-VM-2K3 [ec26edf8]
<- Linger timer expires, and License server finally checks in the
"last" license for [ec26edf8].
```

This log entry is the result of the agent shutting down and returning the license. Because the agent can perform check-out operations only, the agent needs to check out the same license a second time for only one second, causing the license server to check it back in. This is done by the agent setting a check-out parameter called a linger period to one second, which tells the license server how long to keep the license checked out. At the end of the linger period, the server automatically checks in the license.

Therefore, to return a license, the agent checks *out* a license with a linger time of one second. This, in turn, causes the license server to check in the license a second later:

```
21:01:05 (CITRIX) IN: "MPM_ADV_RC" USER15@GENE-VM-2K3 [ec26edf8]
```

This is the first of two IN: entries that occur. Note that this entry occurs at exactly the same time as the previous OUT: entry. That's because, from the license server's point of view, the previous IN: entry results in two instances of the same licenses [ec26edf8] being checked out. The license server tries to keep only one instance of a license checked out at all times, so it corrects this situation by performing a check-in.

Now only one instance of license with identifier [ec26edf8] is checked out. To release the license fully, another check-in must occur (see the next section).

NOTE Only the license server performs check-ins. Any IN: log entry results from the license server's actions, not from a request from the agent. If you are using a network monitor, you should not expect to see communication between the agent and license server at times that IN: entries occur.

```
21:01:40 (CITRIX) IN: "MPM_ADV_RC" USER15@GENE-VM-2K3 [ec26edf8]
```

Once the Linger timer expires for a particular license, the license is not checked in immediately. Instead, it must wait for a thread of the license server process to wake up and check it in. This thread wakes up every minute, and it may take up to a minute to execute. So it may take up to just under two minutes for a license to be available once again for check-out.

In the previous example, a license was checked in at 21:01:05 with a linger time of one second. Its linger time should have expired at 21:01:06. Finally, at 21:01:40, the license server returned the license to the system. Now no more licenses are checked out with identifier [ec26edf8].

Renewal Process

While an agent is running, it periodically tries to renew its license. There is no renew operation; rather, the agent only attempts to check out the license again using the same linger time.

For example, consider the scenario of a Named User license with a linger time of 21 days. Every six hours, the agent tries to check out a license with a linger time of 21 days.

By having a proper understanding of the technical details of the differences in licensing among the Citrix products and knowledge of the licensing debug log, an administrator can have a valuable tool for troubleshooting. When using the log file, an administrator can see the licensing process to assist in tracking down issues.

NOTE You can clear the log file by restarting the licensing service. To set up the log file to retain the past information, see the Licensing_Guide.pdf.

IDENTITY VERIFICATION QUESTION WITH CITRIX PASSWORD MANAGER

In Citrix Password Manager 4.5, the Multiple-Question Authentication and Identity Verification Question have been replaced with Question-Based Authentication. For more information about Question-Based Authentication, reference "Confirming User Identity Using Question-Based Authentication" in the *Password Manager Administrator's Guide.*

Overview

The *Identity Verification Question*'s primary function is to work as a secondary form of authentication to the agent. The user question is created the first time that a user creates his or her profile.

The first part of the profile setup procedure is to prompt the user to enter his or her Windows domain credentials. After successfully authenticating these credentials, the procedure prompts the user to answer the Identity Verification Question. Whichever Identity Verification Question the user answers (either the custom-created question or the default one) will be the one permanently linked with that user's data.

Whenever the user's Windows domain password is changed, the Password Manager agent asks the Identity Verification Question (to identify the user) and the user needs to provide the answer he or she originally entered during the initial profile setup. In this situation, the user's password storage database is opened and the new Windows domain password will be updated.

Because the Identity Verification Question is stored in the First-Time-User list and it is encrypted, the Identity Verification Question also serves to protect the user's password database from the administrator, who could easily change a user's Windows domain password, but would not know the user's answer to the Identity Verification Question.

Issues

The following issues arise in connection with the Identity Verification Question:

- Each question has its own globally unique identifier (GUID), so if the administrator modifies the Identity Verification Question, the GUID does not change and the user can open his or her database by answering the modified question using his or her old answer. In some cases, this can be misleading and the text of the question should not be modified if users have already answered the question. Refer to the example in the *Password Manager Administrator's Guide.*
- The answer is stored in the user's database with the Question GUID. Once the Identity Verification Question has been answered, the answer can neither be modified nor can the user switch to a different Identity Verification Question and provide a different answer.
- Currently, if the administrator creates a custom Identity Verification Question and then later deletes the FTUlist.ini file from the synchronization point, any users who answered any Identity Verification Question from that file will be unable to unlock their password storage database when their password is changed.
- The default question cannot be edited or deleted.
- On the console, when an administrator creates a custom Identity Verification Question, it cannot be deleted, only disabled. Unfortunately, it still can be overwritten from another console or deleted manually from the file system or Active Directory tree.
- If the administrator wants to delete a user profile, he or she needs to delete all the data from the following points:
  - HKCU\Software\Citrix\MetaFrame Password Manager
  - The folder from C:\Documents and Settings*username*\ApplicationData\Citrix\MetaFrame Password Manager
  - The data from the user's folder under the People folder on the File Synchronization (for file synchronization), or the SSOConfig objects from under the user's object in the Active Directory (for Active Directory synchronization)

Additional Notes

Administrators can use extended characters when creating custom Identity Verification Questions. Users also can use extended characters when answering their Identity Verification Question.

DISABLING THE DEFAULT IDENTITY VERIFICATION QUESTION FOR CITRIX PASSWORD MANAGER

When a user begins using Password Manager for the first time, he or she may be required to define secondary credentials by selecting an Identity Verification Question (also referred to as a User Question in previous versions of Password Manager) and providing an answer to this question. The combination of question and answer is known as the *identity verification phrase*.

In Citrix Password Manager 4.5, users can choose from console-defined questions or the default question. Because the default question does not provide the user with any clue as to what the answer might have been, some administrators see the default question as a source of confusion. Disabling this question enables administrators to customize the user experience further by controlling the set of questions from which the user can choose.

Administrators must be careful with this option as it may prevent existing users from authenticating to the agent. When a user is challenged to answer her Identity Verification Question and the user's chosen question is no longer defined or no longer available, she will be unable to authenticate herself to Password Manager. Because of this, it is important to disable this default question before users begin using the agent. This will ensure that you are not disabling an existing user's Identity Verification Question. If the administrator disables the default question without creating or enabling any custom questions, Password Manager cannot create the user configuration, and Password Manager users must belong to a user configuration.

To disable the default Identity Verification Question, from the Access Management Console, choose User Configuration | *your chosen configuration* | Edit User configuration | Secondary Data Protection. Deselect the check box for "Use identity verification as in previous versions of Password Manager."

FORCING USERS TO COMPLETE THE FIRST-TIME-USE WIZARD

When users first launch the Password Manager agent, they may be presented with the First-Time-Use Wizard if Question-Based Authentication or any of the self-service features are enabled. The wizard prompts users to answer security questions in order to generate the secondary credentials needed to enable these features. If the user does not complete the wizard successfully, the agent will not start and Password Manager will not function.

By default, the user can cancel the First-Time-Use Wizard before completion by clicking the Close button in the upper-right hand corner of the Wizard window. To disable the Close button and force users to complete the First-Time-Use Wizard, add the following registry key value to user workstations where the Password Manager agent is installed:

- **Path** HKLM\Software\Citrix\Metaframe Password Manager\Extensions\SetupManager
- **Key** ForceFTU
- **Type** Dword
- **Value** 0/1

By default, when the registry key is created, it is set to 0—that is, disabled. Set the value to 1 to enable the setting.

HOT DESKTOP HOST EMULATORS SUPPORT

Table 8-1 lists the host emulators supported in the Hot Desktop Environment.

Host Emulator	Version	Executable Name
Attachmate MyExtra!	7.11	extra.exe
IBM Personal Communicator	5.6	pcsfe.exe
NetManage Rumba	7	Rumbawsf.exe
Nexus	4.6	nmt.exe
WRQ Reflections IBM	10.*x*	R8win.exe
ZephyrPC	2002–621	Passport.exe
Ericom PowerTerm Pro	8.8	ptpro.exe
Hummingbird	10	hostex32.exe
Bosanova	6.08	bsmdemul.exe
QWS3270 Plus	3.8	qws3270p.exe
Aviva Scanpak for Terminal Services	9.x	app32d.exe, app52d.exe
Blue Zone Desktop	34	BZMD.exe

Table 8-1. Host Emulators Supported in the Hot Desktop Environment

To configure supported emulators, follow these steps:

1. Create a host-based application definition (see the *Password Manager Administrator's Guide* for details) and add this definition to the desired application group of a user's configuration.
2. Enable support for host emulators from the Password Manager Administrative Console.
   a. Edit the user configuration.
   b. Select the Application Support tab on the left pane.
   c. Select enable support for the terminal emulators' check box.
3. Edit the Process.xml file to launch the defined host emulator as a Hot Desktop user.

NOTE For details about Process.xml, refer to the *Password Manager Administrator's Guide* and "Configuring and Managing a Hot Desktop Environment" in Chapter 15 of this book.

As an example, to launch NetManage Rumba as a Hot Desktop User, you need to edit the ShellExecute entry in the process.xml file as follows:

```
shellexecute_processes
     process
          name rumbawsf.exe/name
     /process
/shellexecute_processes
```

NOTE Executable filenames for supported host emulators are listed in the third column of Table 8-1.

INTEGRATING CITRIX PASSWORD MANAGER WITH A DISTRIBUTED FILE SYSTEM

A Citrix Password Manager file synchronization point can be implemented using Windows 2000 or Windows 2003 distributed file system (DFS). The capabilities to distribute the workload across multiple servers and to provide fault tolerance are among the reasons to consider using DFS as an alternative to a single synchronization point. This section explains the steps to configure DFS for use with Password Manager.

Step 1: Create a Domain DFS Root

The first step to integrate Password Manager with distributed file system (DFS) is to create a domain DFS root. You will not need to do so if your Windows deployment already has one domain DFS root in place. If this is the case, skip to the next section, "Step 2: Prepare the Shares for Citrix Password Manager."

1. Open the mmc snap-in for the Distributed File System, typically located in Start | Programs | Administrative Tools | Distributed File System.
2. Right-click the DFS icon and select the option New DFS root.
3. Click Next.
4. Select "Create a domain DFS root."
5. Click Next.
6. Select the host domain of the DFS root.
7. Click Next.
8. Select the name of the host server for this DFS root.
9. Click Next.
10. Either use an existing share on the server or create a new share to host the DFS tree.
11. Click Next.
12. Type a name for the DFS root.
13. Click Finish.

Step 2: Prepare the Shares for Citrix Password Manager

After creating a domain DFS root, the shares hosting the file synchronization point should be created in the designated servers. The ctxfilesyncprep utility is used to create the directory c:\citrixsync on the C:\ drive and shares it as \\%servername%\citrixsync$, assigning the proper permissions.

1. On two or more Windows 2000/2003 Servers, open a command console.
2. Insert the Password Manager Distribution CD.
3. Type **CD x:**, where *x* is the letter of your CD-ROM, and then press Enter.
4. Type **CD x:\Tools**, and then press Enter.
5. Type **ctxfilesyncprep.exe**, and then press Enter.

Step 3: Create the DFS Link

The third step of the process is creating a DFS link to host the first of the shares created in the previous step. The share name used for the DFS Link is citrixsync$.

1. Open the mmc snap-in for the DFS, typically located in Start | Programs | Administrative Tools | Distributed File System.
2. Right-click the new DFS root and select New DFS Link.

3. In the Link Name Field, write **citrixsync$**.
4. In the Shared Folder, insert the UNC Location (%server1name%\citrixsync$) of the first server hosting the synchronization point.
5. Click OK.

Step 4: Add the Replicas

To have a redundant, fault-tolerant solution, replicas should be added to the synchronization point. The replicas are the additional server shares we created on the other servers.

1. Open the mmc snap-in for the DFS, typically located in Start | Programs | Administrative Tools | Distributed File System.
2. Right-click the DFS link created in the section "Step 3: Create the DFS Link," and select New Replica.
3. In the "Send user to this shared fólder" field, insert the UNC location (%server2name%\citrixsync$) of the server hosting the other synchronization point prepared in the section "Step 2: Prepare the Shares for Citrix Password Manager."
4. Change Replication Policy from Manual Replication to Automatic Replication.
5. Click OK.
6. On the following screen, highlight the first server and Enable Replication.
7. Highlight the second server and Enable Replication.
8. Click OK.
9. Repeat steps 2 through 8 for each of the servers.

Step 5: Connecting to the Share from the Console

Connecting to the DFS Shared Folder and configuring Password Manager to export the configuration to the synchronization point is the final task of the procedure. To connect successfully, the agents and the console must be part of the domain where the DFS was created.

1. Deploy the Password Manager Console on a workstation that is part of the same Active Directory domain.
2. Log on with a user who has administrative rights to the Active Directory domain and select Start | Programs | Citrix | Management Consoles | Access Management Console.
3. Highlight the Password Manager node and select the Configure and run discovery task.
4. Click Next.
5. Select NTFS network share as the central store type.
6. The Shared folder name is \\activedirectorydomainname\DFS\citrixsync$.

Step 6: Distributed File System Replication

Replica Synchronization is managed by the File Replication Service (FRS). FRS operates on Windows Active Directory Domain Controllers and member servers. It is a multithreaded, multimaster replication engine that replicates system policies, login scripts, fault-tolerant DFS root, and child node replicas.

In Active Directory deployments, the Knowledge Consistency Checker (KCC) is responsible for building NT Directory Service (NTDS) connection objects to form a well-connected topology between Domain Controllers in the domain and the forest.

RepAdmin.exe is a utility available in the support.cab archive of the Windows 2000 Servers' installation CD. It can be used to check whether replication is taking place using the default intervals for intersite replication—that is, once every three hours between Domain Controllers in different sites (the minimum is 15 minutes).

FRS replicates whole files in sequential order according to when files are closed, so the entire file will be replicated even if you change only a single byte in the file.

Changes for intersite replication are set using a three second aging cache, so only the last iteration of a file that is constantly modified is sent to the replica members.

Five minutes is the maximum replication value for servers hosting replicas, but this can even be seconds if the server is not overwhelmed.

The following articles can be useful for administrators to set up and tune the FRS: "Description of the FRS Replication Protocol, Notification, and Schedule for DFS Content," at http://support.microsoft.com/default.aspx?scid=kb;en-us;220938&Product=win2000; and "FRS Builds Full-Mesh Replication Topology for Replicated DFS ROOT and Child Replicas," at http://support.microsoft.com/default.aspx?scid=kb;en-us;224512&Product=win2000.

LIMIT THE NUMBER OF DAYS TO KEEP TRACK OF DELETED CREDENTIALS

The "Limit the number of days to keep track of deleted credentials" setting (previously "Days before Delete") is important because it allows the agent to remember what credentials have been deleted. This setting remembers the credentials for the specified amount of time so that the user has the opportunity to synchronize all the Password Manager agents on the other machines. The "Delete user's data folder and registry keys when the agent is shut down" setting (previously "Delete on Shutdown") does not affect this because the data are stored in the Memory Mapped File (MMF) and then synchronized to your synchronization point as the agent is shutting down. Here is an example of what could happen if the agent deleted the credentials without remembering them:

1. The user runs the Password Manager Agent on ComputerA (the user's desktop PC).
2. The user adds credentials for ApplicationA.
3. ApplicationA's credentials are stored in the local MMF and synchronized to the central credential store.

4. The user then runs the agent on ComputerB (for example, the user's laptop PC).
5. The Password Manager agent gets synchronized and ApplicationA gets stored in the local MMF on ComputerB.
6. The user decides to delete ApplicationA's credential and it is removed from the local MMF and the central credential store.
7. Later that day, the user logs back on to ComputerA.
8. The agent on ComputerA synchronizes with the central credential store, which still has ApplicationA's credential stored in its local MMF. It does not see this credential in the central credential store, however, so it adds the ApplicationA credential back.

If users work on only one machine, then the user's local MMF file is stored only on that machine. In theory, the "Limit the number of days to keep track of deleted credentials" setting could be set to 0 without creating any problems in a single-machine scenario. If the scenario is different, however, and the user roams to different machines, has a laptop and a desktop, or uses multiple servers in a XenApp farm, then you should set this value to something higher than 0 (the default is 30 days).

In summary, with "Limit the number of days to keep track of deleted credentials" set to 0, the Password Manager agents would conflict with each other by deleting and re-adding credentials.

USING PROFILES (ROAMING, MANDATORY, AND HYBRID) WITH CITRIX PASSWORD MANAGER

This section discusses best practices concerning user profile issues with Citrix Password Manager. Specifically, local, roaming, mandatory, and hybrid user profiles are discussed here.

Local User Profiles

Local user profiles are stored on the local server to which the user has logged on. Password Manager saves registry information in the HKCU\Software\Citrix\MetaFrame Password Manager hive of the User Registry located at %SystemDrive%\Documents and Settings\%username%\NTUSER.DAT.

Password Manager also saves files in %SystemDrive%\Documents and Settings\%username%\Application Data\Citrix\MetaFrame Password Manager. Windows Vista introduced changes to profiles locations. On Vista, Password Manager will use: %APPDATA%\Roaming\Citrix\MetaFrame Password Manager.

NOTE It is *critical* that Password Manager has Full Control Access to the following files:

Filename	Description
%username%.mmf	User's credential information file with pointers to aelist.ini file
entlist.ini	Application definition file created at enterprise level in the synchronization point or Active Directory
aelist.ini	Application definition file created by merging user's local application definition file (applist.ini) and the Enterprise application definitions (entlist.ini)

Roaming User Profiles

Roaming user profiles are saved in a network share and synchronized to a local server copy each time that the user logs on. Characteristics of a successful roaming profile deployment include high-speed network connectivity, such as a Storage Area Network (SAN) or Network-Attached Storage (NAS). Other common deployments include clustering solutions where the profiles are stored on high-availability servers.

Currently, two issues affect roaming and mandatory profile deployments:

- A single roaming profile can be used only with one file synchronization point. When multiple synchronization points are used, data in the MMF file may get corrupted.
- When roaming profiles are used with multiple concurrent sessions, they share the same back-end MMF file. The end result is that all active sessions share some common session data, such as retry lock counters, last-used data counters, and event log entries.

Mandatory User Profile/Hybrid Profile

Mandatory user profiles are by definition user read-only profiles. Password Manager needs write permission to the profile directory under Application Data. With mandatory profiles, a user may make changes, but the changes are not saved to the profile at logoff. For Password Manager to work correctly in a mandatory profiles environment, the Application Data folder must be redirected.

With Password Manager, the registry changes are written each time that the user logs on and credential information is synchronized with the synchronization point, but the changes are not saved to the profile.

Beginning with Windows 2000, Microsoft provides a mechanism for redirecting the Application Data folder, but using Windows NT4 domain requires login scripts capable of modifying the location of the Application Data folder. You can achieve this by using tools Duch as Kix or VBScript to define a writeable location for the Application Data user folder.

An example using Kix to redirect the Application Data folder during user logon follows:

CAUTION The following sample script is for informational purposes only and should not be used in your environment without previous testing.

```
$LogonServer = "%LOGONSERVER%"
$HKCU = "HKEY_CURRENT_USER"
$ShellFolders_Key =
"$HKCU\Software\Microsoft\Windows\CurrentVersion\Explorer\Shell Folders"
$UserShellFolders_Key =
"$HKCU\Software\Microsoft\Windows\CurrentVersion\Explorer\User Shell Folders"

$UserProfFolder = "$LogonServer\profiles\@userID"
$UserAppData = "$LogonServer\profiles\@userID\Application Data"
$UserDesktop = "$LogonServer\profiles\@userID\Desktop"
$UserFavorites = "$LogonServer\profiles\@userID\Favorites"
$UserPersonal = "X:\My Documents"
$UserRecent = "$LogonServer\profiles\@userID\Recent"

if (exist("$UserAppData") = 0)
     shell '%ComSpec% /c md "$UserAppData"'
endif
if (exist("$UserDesktop") = 0)
     shell '%ComSpec% /c md "$UserDesktop"'
endif

if (exist("$UserRecent") = 0)
     shell '%ComSpec% /c md "$UserRecent"'
endif
if (exist("$UserFavorites") = 0)
     shell '%ComSpec% /c md "$UserFavorites"'
endif
```

The hybrid user profile is another solution for the mandatory profile issue. When the user logs on, the mandatory profile loads, and a custom application loads and unloads user registry hives based on the applications available to the user. The user, as in a mandatory profile scenario, can modify those portions of registry during the session. The big difference from the pure mandatory profile is that changes get saved when the user logs off and they get reloaded when the user logs in again.

When the hybrid profile is used, the following registry keys must be imported and exported as part of the logon and logoff process:

```
HKEY_CURRENT_USER\Software\Citrix\MetaFrame Password
```

Folder Redirection

Folder redirection was introduced as a new feature in the Windows 2000 and Windows 2003 operating systems (OSs). It is implemented using Group Policy objects and Active Directory. Folder redirection uses Group Policies to define a location for folders that are part of the user profile.

Four folders may be redirected using folder redirection:

- My Documents
- Application Data
- Desktop
- Start Menu

Two modes of redirection can be configured using Group Policies: basic redirection and advanced redirection. Both types of redirection are supported with Password Manager. In Windows 2000, the share where application data are stored should be referenced using the user name variable—for example, *servername**sharename*\%*username*%.

Folder redirection is global for the user and it affects all the user's applications; therefore, all applications that use the Application Data folder need to support it.

The following Microsoft articles may be useful in learning more about folder redirection:

- "HOW TO: Dynamically Create Secure Redirected Folders by Using Folder Redirections," http://support.microsoft.com/?kbid=274443
- "Folder Redirection Feature in Windows," http://support.microsoft.com/?kbid=232692
- "Enabling the Administrator to Have Access to Redirected Folders," http://support.microsoft.com/?kbid=288991

Best Practices for Folder Redirection

The following are best practices for folder redirection:

- Use Application Data folder redirection when possible. This practice improves network performance, eliminating the need to copy that data each time a user logs on.
- When troubleshooting a Password Manager agent, always verify that the user logged on has Full Control permission on his or her Application Data folder.

USING REDIRECTED APPLICATION DATA FOLDERS AND CITRIX PASSWORD MANAGER

Many environments utilize the Microsoft Windows Group Policy that enables the redirection of users' Application Data directories to a separate network resource (file server, DFS, and so forth). If Citrix Password Manager is deployed in an environment where a user's application data are redirected, be aware that this will raise some issues that merit consideration.

In each user's Application Data directory, several files are used by Password Manager. Some or all of these files are created when a user goes through his or her "First Time Use" of Password Manager. Here is a basic description of what the files are used for:

- **Applist.ini** This file holds the available applications for which the user does not currently have definitions.
- **Entlist.ini** This file has all the user application definitions.
- **Aelist.ini** This file combines Applist and Entlist. The agent uses this file when working with application definitions.
- **UserName.mmf** This MMF file holds all the admin override data along with the credentials for each application that the user has defined.
- **Ftulist.ini** This file lists the applications available for configuration during the user's First Time Use experience.
- **License.ini** This file holds the user's license information.

If a Group Policy is enforced that redirects the Application Data directory of each user to a separate network resource, then each of the files previously listed is moved from the local profile. The file the user interacts with the most is *UserName*.mmf. This MMF file allocates an address space and links it to a file located on the physical disk. This allocation allows the file to be accessed like a block of memory. Using redirected application data directories may impact the performance of Password Manager. The following are recommended practices when redirecting the Application Data directories of users:

- Do not use "delete on shutdown" with redirected Application Data folders. The "delete on shutdown" option in the Password Manager Console controls whether the user's registry keys and Application Data folder (including encrypted credentials) are deleted when the agent is shut down. Using this option requires a user to re-create each of the files previously listed (from the data located on the synchronization point) each time that the agent is started up again. This can cause a significant delay when the system is using redirected Application Data folders.
- Do not use aggressive synchronization with redirected Application Data folders. The aggressive synchronization option in the Password Manager Console controls whether the agent synchronizes user configuration information

whenever a user launches a recognized application or Logon Manager. Using aggressive synchronization by itself can degrade performance on both the client and server. If you are using this option with redirected application data, folders can cause even slower response times. For specific numbers on using redirected Application Data folders and aggressive synchronization, see the "Agent Response Time" section of the "Citrix Password Manager Performance and Scalability" section later in this chapter.

BEST PRACTICES WITH CITRIX PASSWORD MANAGER AND THE NOVELL CLIENT

The following section is a collection of best-practice recommendations to follow when integrating Citrix Password Manager and the Novell client.

Install the Latest Service Packs

The recommended environment should include installing the latest service packs for the NetWare OS and applying the latest service packs for ZENworks. Reapply the manufacturer's latest network interface card (NIC) drivers (Novell recommends that users always do this, as Support Packs are prone to overwriting NIC drivers).

Novell Client Settings to Enhance Overall Performance

In certain situations with slow responsiveness to XenApp with the Novell client, there are Novell client settings to enhance overall performance. Citrix has tested with the following client32 settings with improved results:

- LIP Start Size = 512 (or try turning off LIP)
- Net Status Busy Timeout = 1
- Burst Mode = on

The recommendation is that the Novell client not be configured with more than two directory agents, as this lengthens the network query time.

Server-Side Settings

On the server side, these settings may also be helpful:

- Set Maximum Concurrent Disk Cache Writes = 300
- Set Maximum Concurrent Directory Cache Writes = 100

Error Messages for Unavailable Services

Occasionally, a Windows 2000 or Windows 2003 server with the Novell 4.9 sp1 client may display a NMASS error after locking the desktop's console. The following error may be displayed when unlocking the console: "Error: NMAS.DLL could not initialize cryptographic services or cryptographic services are not available. (–1497)." A workaround for this error is to disable the NMAS authentication after the install or to remove the NMAS client using Add/Remove Programs.

CITRIX PASSWORD MANAGER AND ENTRUST INTEGRATION

Citrix Password Manager and Entrust Public Key Infrastructure (PKI) can be successfully integrated, deploying Entrust Authority in a Windows 2000 Active Directory Domain, and leveraging Microsoft Lightweight Directory Access Protocol (LDAP) implementation with Entrust certificates. Once the Entrust Authority has been deployed, and the Entrust client has been packaged and configured on a per-user basis, Password Manager can be integrated into the environment. The following versions were used during the testing: Entrust Software Versions 6.01 for the Authority Server and 6.1 SP1 for the Entrust Client Entelligence–Desktop Solutions. The following section guides you through the required steps.

Modify the AD Schema for Entrust

To modify the AD schema for Entrust, follow these steps:

1. On the Domain Controller that holds the Schema Master role, log on with a user who is part of the Domain Administration and Schema Administration groups and extend the schema.
2. Insert the Entrust/PKI CD in the CD-ROM drive, navigate to the \Utilities folder, and run entadconfig.exe to start the Entrust Active Directory Configuration Wizard.
3. Select the Entrust/Authority check box.
4. Select Configure the Active Directory Schema.
5. Create a CA Entry for Entrust/Authority and give it a name.
6. Publish the CA Certificate in the Certification Authorities Container.
7. Create a new domain account or use an existing one.
8. Grant access for Entrust Authority to existing users.
9. Execute the changes and save the log.

Deploy Certification Authority

To deploy Certification Authority (CA), follow this procedure:

1. Deploy the Informix database, which is needed to create the Entrust/Authority database.
2. Make sure, for security reasons, that the server used for Entrust should be different from the Active Directory Domain Controller.
3. Install the Certification Authority after the Informix database.
4. Supply the required licensing information for the Certification Authority, such as serial number, enterprise user limit, and enterprise licensing code.
5. In the screen that appears next, supply the directory node and port. The Using Microsoft Active Directory check box should be selected.
6. In the next screen, enter the fully qualified name of the Domain Controller.
7. Provide the Certification Authority a distinguished name. You can customize the name if the deployment scenario requires that you do so.
8. Confirm the CA name.
9. The Directory Attributes dialog box should be left as LDAP Version 3 with the default transfer mode dimmed.
10. Enter the CA name, using the same name and password specified when you configured AD.
11. On the Advanced Directory Attributes, enter the First Officer DN.
12. Verify the directory information.
13. After a short wait, the ENTDVT Log file dialog box appears and shows Directory Verification completed successfully.
14. The current user's Windows login password is needed to start Entrust Services. This is the login and the password for the Entrust/Authority Service to start when logging in to Entrust/Authority Master Control.
15. Select Yes for the Microsoft Crypto-API–enabled application Interoperability Setup window.
16. On the Entrust Authority Port Configuration, review the default data and make sure that the node name belongs to the server running the Entrust Authority.
17. In the Cryptographic Information dialog box, choose the required parameters for the deployment.
18. Select a lifetime for the CA and complete the CA configuration.

Initialize Certification Authority

The Entrust/PKI Authority must be initialized before it can be used. During the initialization process, the three master users and the first officer should be present.

1. In the Entrust/Authority Master Control Window, choose Log In. A dialog box appears, stating the initialization will take a few minutes.
2. After an Initial Password Entry Dialog Box appears, each of the three users and the First Officer must privately choose, type, and verify their passwords.
3. The next screen communicates that the installation was successful.
4. Log on with one of the Master Users or First Officer Accounts and start the Entrust/Authority Service.

Configure the Client

To configure the client, follow these steps:

1. On the Authority Server, start the Authority/RA Console Administration program and enumerate the users in the Active Directory domain.
2. Open the Properties page of the user you want to add to Entrust Authority.
3. Note the reference number and the authorization code.
4. On a workstation, deploy the Entelligence Desktop Designer and create a deployment package. Deploy the package to the client workstation and change the entrust.ini initialization file to point to the correct Authority and Directory Server.
5. Log on to the client with the user you added to Entrust Authority.
6. Create a new Entrust User Profile. Specify the reference number and the authorization code.
7. Assign the user a password and log on to Entrust.

Deploy the Citrix Password Manager Agent

Deploy the agent and create a new application definition with the console for the Entrust logon:

1. Open the Access Management Console.
2. Select Applications Definitions Node.
3. Select Create Application Definition.
4. Select Create New and set the application type to Windows.
5. Select Start Wizard.

6. Enter Entrust Login as the name.
7. Select Add Form.
8. On the form Identifiers, click the Select button.
9. Select Logon.
10. Right-click the Entrust Icon and select Log In to Entrust.
11. Refresh the Form Wizard and select Entrust Login Form.
12. Define UserID as Combo Box, Password, and OK button.
13. Confirm the default values.
14. Save the application definition.
15. Add the application definition to the user configuration.
16. When a new user needs to log on to Entrust, he or she should right-click the Citrix Password Manager icon and select Logon Using Citrix Password Manager.

NOTE Password Manager does not automatically detect the Logon screen provided by Entrust. This happens because Entrust doesn't use standard calls to the OS and the agent is unable to detect the Logon screen window.

CITRIX PASSWORD MANAGER SCALABILITY AND PERFORMANCE

This chapter covers the performance and scalability characteristics of Citrix Password Manager running with XenApp. All testing was done on XenApp using Windows 2003 Server or Windows 2003x64 Server.

Number of Users per Citrix XenApp

Installing Citrix Password Manager on XenApp can affect the capacity of the server. Capacity is normally discussed in terms of the effective number of users that the server can support.

When installed on XenApp, an instance of Password Manager runs for each client session. For each Password Manager instance, the following processes may be running:

- **ssoshell.exe** This is the primary agent process, which also handles windows applications.
- **ssobho.exe** This process handles web applications.
- **ssomho.exe** This process handles mainframe host emulators.
- **hook64cc.exe (64-bit only)** This process handles 64-bit windows applications.
- **ssobho64cc.exe (64-bit only)** The process handles 64-bit web applications.

In addition, when Password Manager is synchronizing data with the synchronization point, an additional temporary ssoshell.exe process is spawned. This process disappears when the synchronization is complete. All these processes consume server resources that can impact the effective number of users per server.

Single Server Scalability Test

The Single Server Scalability test is designed to quantify—for benchmarking purposes—the optimal number of simulated client sessions that can be connected to XenApp with acceptable performance. Extending the number of concurrent simulated users beyond the acceptable performance recommendation has a result of decreased performance and impacts the end user's experience. The test is made up of three parts: logon, application launch, and sustained user. Password Manager includes only the application launch and sustained user tests. The logon phase of the test was designed to use local users with no passwords. The Password Manager testing requires that the users are part of a domain and have passwords. With these types of users, gathering accurate results is difficult due to the variables experienced when a user logs in to a domain. A score is generated based on the amount of time it takes each user to complete the test script. Note that the simulated users in this test are constantly typing into these applications and may be considered more "rigorous" than normal users. See Figure 8-1 and Figure 8-2 and Tables 8-2 and 8-3.

A baseline test was first run using XenApp without Password Manager. The simulation script simulated user credentials being typed for the password-protected application. The test was then rerun with Password Manager installed on XenApp. The simulation script was modified to allow Password Manager to provide credentials when needed. During the test, mainframe host support was not enabled, so the ssomho.exe process was not running on XenApp.

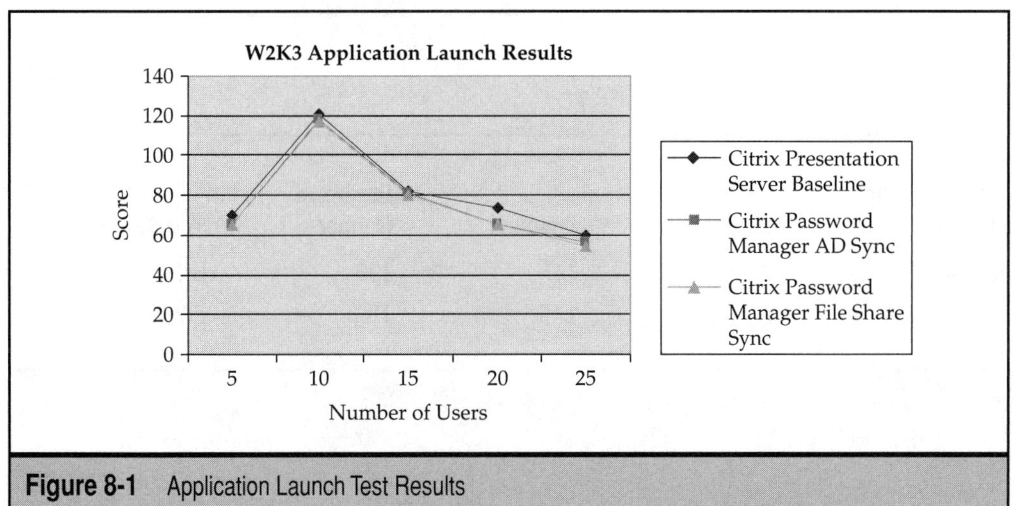

Figure 8-1 Application Launch Test Results

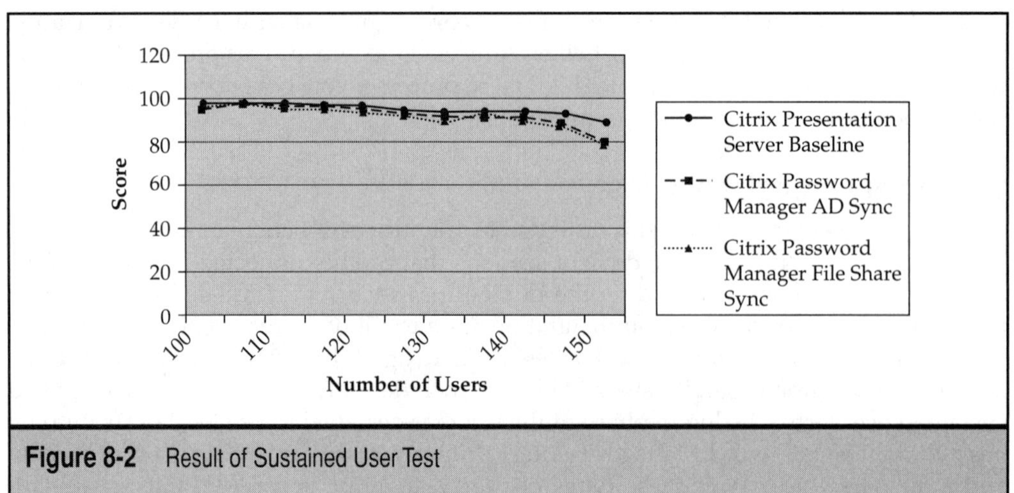

Figure 8-2 Result of Sustained User Test

Synchronization Point Type	Operating System	Baseline	Password Manger	% Difference
File Share	W2K3	29	26	10.34%
Active Directory	W2K3	29	26	10.34%

Table 8-2 Application Launch Test Results

Synchronization Point Type	Operating System	Baseline	Password Manger	% Difference
File Share	W2K3	145	133	8.28%
Active Directory	W2K3	145	133	8.28%

Table 8-3 Sustained User Test Results

The easiest way to determine the server's degradation point is to look at the score column in the test results. For the Application Launch test, a score of 65 was determined as the fail point. For the Sustained user test, a score of 90 was determined as the fail point. This means that the server has enough additional CPU and memory resources to handle spikes in performance and provide a consistent user experience. When the test iteration score drops below the fail points, additional users added to the server consume more resources. This produces lower test scores and slower performance.

On this specific hardware with a specific test (Windows Server 2003, application launch, Active Directory synchronization), extrapolating the results allows for 133 simulated users to be concurrently and constantly running Microsoft Office applications and Citrix Password Manager without significant performance degradation. This is compared to 145 users without Password Manager installed on the server, a 8.28 percent decrease in the total number of users. This decrease is attributed to additional memory resources required by the Citrix Password Manager agent.

Server Hardware Configuration:

- IBM x-Series 335
- Dual Xeon 2.4GHz processors with 512KB L2 cache
- 34GB Ultra 320 Small Computer System Interface (SCSI)
- 3GB random access memory (RAM)
- 4GB page file

Client Hardware Configuration:

- IBM x-Series 335
- Dual Xeon 2.4GHz processors with 512KB L2 cache
- 34GB ultra 320 SCSI
- 1GB RAM
- 3GB page file

Citrix XenApp Software Configuration:

- Windows 2003 Server with Service Pack 2
- Citrix XenApp 4.5 with HRP 1
- Citrix Password Manager 4.6
- Microsoft Office XP—Excel, Access, and PowerPoint

Client Software Configuration:

- Windows 2003 Server with Service Pack 2
- Citrix ICA Program Neighborhood Version 10.100.55836
- 20 ICA sessions existing on each machine

Process	Private Bytes Windows 2003	Private Bytes Windows 2003x64
SSOShell.exe	8.20 MB	10.92 MB
SSOBHO.exe	4.50 MB	6.67 MB
SSOMHO.exe	3.56 MB	*only runs if running an emulator
Hook64cc.exe	n/a	2.95 MB
Ssobho64cc.exe	n/a	2.95 MB
Total	16.26 MB	23.49 MB

Table 8-4 Password Manager Memory Usage Based on Operating System

Citrix Password Manager Memory Usage

Table 8-4 shows the average memory usage observed for each Password Manager process running in a Citrix XenApp client session. These measurements were taken while the processes were idle, but had previously responded to credential requests. These numbers can be used to estimate the amount of additional memory needed for Password Manager.

Credential Synchronization Using NTFS File Share

This section discusses the scalability and performance characteristics related to using an NTFS file share for password synchronization. These include the following:

- Disk space utilization of the file share server
- Network bandwidth utilization between Password Manager agents and the file share server
- Citrix Password Manager agent response times

NOTE Citrix Presentation session login time was not significantly impacted by the Password Manager agent.

The following test bed was used for this phase of testing:

File Server Hardware Configuration:

- Dell Poweredge 1750 (32-bit)
- Dual Xeon 2.8 GHz processors with 512KB L2 cache

- 34 GB Ultra 320 SCSI
- 1GB RAM
- 3GB Page File

- Dell Poweredge 1850 (64-bit)
- Dual Xeon 2.8GHz processors with 512KB L2 cache
- 34GB Ultra 320 SCSI
- 5GB RAM
- 8GB Page File

Citrix XenApp Hardware Configuration:

- Dell Poweredge 1750
- Dual Xeon 2.8GHz processors with 512KB L2 cache
- 34GB Ultra 320 SCSI
- 1GB RAM
- 3GB Page File

- Dell Poweredge 1850 (64-bit)
- Dual Xeon 2.8GHz processors with 512KB L2 cache
- 34GB Ultra 320 SCSI
- 5GB RAM
- 8GB Page File

Client Hardware Configuration:

- Dell Poweredge 1750
- Dual Xeon 2.8GHz processors with 512KB L2 cache
- 34GB Ultra 320 SCSI
- 1GB RAM
- 3GB page file

File Server Software Configuration:

- Windows 2003 with Service Pack 2

Citrix XenApp Software Configuration

- Windows 2003 Server w/SP 2 or Windows 2003x64 Server s/SP 2
- Citrix XenApp 4.5 w/HRP1

- Citrix Password Manager 4.6
- Microsoft Office XP - Excel, Access & PowerPoint

Client Software Configuration

- Windows 2003 Server w/ SP2
- Citrix ICA Program Neighborhood Version 10.100.55836
- 5 ICA sessions exist on each machine

Disk Space Utilization of the File Share Server

With *file share synchronization,* the file share includes a separate directory for each user. Within each user's directory, credential information is stored for each application defined for use with Password Manager. Table 8-5 shows the disk space utilized for a single user with different Password Manager options configured.

Disk Utilization Measurement	Disk usage size (size on disk)	Disk usage per application
First-time user (FTU) w/ Previous Password	4.69 KB (16.0 KB)	0.7 KB (4.0 KB)
FTU w/ Previous Password & 10 apps provisioned	15.2 KB (64.0 KB)	0.7 KB (4.0 KB)
•Disk Usage prior to FTU (only provisioning commands)	14.4 KB (20.0 KB)	n/a
FTU w/ Automatic Key Recovery (AKR)	6.73 KB (24.0 KB)	0.7 KB (4.0 KB)
FTU w/ AKR & 10 apps provisioned	17.2 KB (72.0 KB)	0.7 KB (4.0 KB)
FTU w/ Self-Service Password Reset (SSPR)	7.34 KB (20.0 KB)	0.7 KB (4.0 KB)
FTU w/ SSPR & 10 apps provisioned	17.9 KB (68.0 KB)	0.7 KB (4.0 KB)
FTU w/ AKR & SSPR	9.38 KB (28.0 KB)	0.7 KB (4.0 KB)
FTU w/ AKR & SSPR & 10 apps provisioned	19.9 KB (76.0 KB)	0.7 KB (4.0 KB)

Table 8-5 Disk Utilization of File Share Server Sync Point

With these measurements, the amount of disk space required on a file share server can be calculated with the following formula:

Disk space required = (# of users) * (FTU configuration + (# of defined apps * [user-defined or provisioned apps]))

For example (using XenApp on Windows 2003), 1,000 users who are using Previous Password as their key recovery method, with 20 applications defined via provisioning for each user, would require the following:

- Disk space required = (1,000) * (6.84 + (20 * 0.09))
- Disk space required = 23,840KB or 25MB

Network Bandwidth Utilization among Citrix Password Manager Agents, the File Share Credential Store, and the Citrix Password Manager Server

Different events, such as logging on or changing a password, can trigger synchronization among the Password Manager agent, the central store, or the Password Manager Server. These synchronizations put traffic on the network. The amount of network traffic can differ, depending on some of the following factors:

- Number of application definitions per user
- Whether or not aggressive synchronization is enabled
- Frequency of synchronization events

Network Monitor was used to measure the amount of data in kilobytes passed among the file share credential store, the Password Manager agent, and the Password Manager Server for various synchronization events. Each measurement was taken multiple times to obtain the average value for each event. The users were configured with 10 defined applications divided between Win32 applications and web applications. It is Important to note that, for the most part, application definitions could produce different results (see Table 8-6).

The following list details the various network traffic events that occur for Password Manager–managed applications using a file sync option. These points correlate to data in Tables 8-5 and 8-6.

- **FTU** This is the first-time user-configuration event that takes place when a user logs in for the first time and configures Password Manager.
- **Password Reset** This event happens when a user starts the Self-Service Password Reset feature.
- **Key Recovery** This event occurs after a user's password has been changed by either the domain administrator or the user. Password Manager updates the security keys, so the user can access his or her credentials.

- **Password Reset/Key Recovery** During this process, the user invokes the Self-Service Password Reset feature and changes his or her password. The user then logs in and automatic key recovery takes place.

NOTE In an environment where aggressive synchronization is enabled, every time that an application is launched, a synchronization event takes place. This is comparable to a user using the refresh feature in Logon Manager. Performing synchronizations across a wide area network (WAN) link could cause a bottleneck between the synchronization point and Password Manager agents.

	File Share Credential Store		
Event	**Agent/Sync Point**	**Agent/Service**	**Service/Sync Point**
FTU w/ no applications defined	108.2 KB	0.0 KB	0.0 KB
FTU w/ 10 applications provisioned	241.5 KB	28.1 KB	141.9 KB
FTU (SSPR enabled) w/ no applications defined	112.5 KB	26.4 KB	322.6 KB
FTU (SSPR enabled) w/ 10 applications provisioned	245.5 KB	53.0 KB	465.7 KB
• Password Reset	0.0 KB	50.7 KB	416.8 KB
• Account Unlock	0.0 KB	44.9 KB	433.4 KB
FTU (AKR enabled) w/ no applications defined	161.5 KB	17.5 KB	171.9 KB
FTU (AKR enabled) w/ 10 applications provisioned	243.3 KB	44.1 KB	307.1 KB
• Key Recovery	109.1 KB	16.9 KB	24.7 KB
FTU (AKR & SSPR enabled) w/ no applications defined	114.4 KB	42.4 KB	486.9 KB
FTU (AKR & SSPR enabled) w/ 10 applications provisioned	247.2 KB	68.9 KB	635.2 KB
Post FTU Logon (with no configuration changes)	63.8 KB	0.0 KB	0.0 KB
Refresh from Logon Manager	49.8 KB	0.0 KB	0.0 KB

Table 8-6 Network Traffic for Several Password Manager–Managed Applications

Citrix Password Manager Agent Response Time

The time it takes for Password Manager to recognize a password-protected application and provide its credentials can vary, depending on the user's environment and Password Manager configuration. The following are some factors that may affect response time:

- Network bandwidth availability
- Use of redirected application data folders versus local Windows profiles
- Whether or not aggressive synchronization is enabled
- Citrix XenApp resource availability
- Whether agent synchronization is installed
- Network latency between the synchronization point and the Password Manager agent

Tables 8-7 and 8-8 list agent response times with varying client configurations. All testing was done using a custom Win32 application, a custom web page, Scanpak Aviva

	Results Windows 2003				
Agent Response Time with File Share Synchronization over a LAN	**Windows Application**	**Web Application**	**Terminal Emulator Application**	**Java Application**	**Java Applet**
Single user operating on XenApp with aggressive synchronization disabled & local Windows profile	0.03 sec	0.40 sec	1.98 sec	0.17 sec	0.55 sec
Single user operating on XenApp with aggressive synchronization disabled & Redirected App-Data folders	0.04 sec	0.40 sec	2.05 sec	0.17 sec	0.48 sec
Single user operating on XenApp with aggressive synchronization & local Windows profile	0.49 sec	0.89 sec	2.35 sec	0.63 sec	0.96 sec
Single user operating on XenApp with aggressive synchronization & Redirected App-Data folders	1.20 sec	1.69 sec	3.46 sec	1.44 sec	1.85 sec

Table 8-7 Average Response Time for File Share Sync over LAN Windows 2003 Server

	Results Windows 2003x64				
Agent Response Time with File Share Synchronization over a LAN	**Windows Application**	**Web Application**	**Terminal Emulator Application**	**Java Application**	**Java Applet**
Single user operating on XenApp with synchronization not installed and a local Windows profile	0.02 sec	0.41 sec	N/A	0.17 sec	0.75 sec
Single user operating on XenApp with synchronization not installed and redirected Application Data folders	0.48 sec	0.88 sec	N/A	0.62 sec	1.21 sec
Single user operating on XenApp with aggressive synchronization and a local Windows profile	0.03 sec	0.41 sec	N/A	0.17 sec	0.51 sec
Single user operating on XenApp with aggressive synchronization and redirected Application Data folders	1.28 sec	1.66 sec	N/A	1.33 sec	2.10 sec

Table 8-8 Average Response Time for File Share Sync over LAN Windows Server 2003

Terminal Emulator, a custom Java application, and a custom Java applet running in an ICA session on XenApp. For each configuration, the time between the application loading and the credentials being fully submitted by Password Manager is indicated.

NOTE Response times for Win32, web, Java, and Java applet credential requests were gathered using an automated test tool.

Response times for Terminal Emulator applications were gathered using a stop watch (times may not be accurate due to human error). Mainframe host polling time was set to 700 milliseconds, which may add to response time. The average response times for Windows 2003 Server and Windows Server 2003x64 can be seen in Tables 8-7 and 8-8.

Credential Synchronization Using Microsoft Active Directory

This section discusses the performance and scalability characteristics of using Microsoft Active Directory for credential synchronization. These include the following:

- Active Directory replication network traffic
- Network bandwidth utilization between Password Manager agents and AD Domain Controllers
- Active Directory Domain Controller CPU utilization
- Citrix Password Manager agent response times

In all Active Directory testing, XenApp and the AD synchronization point were in different domains, but in the same forest. The two trusted domains had external non-transitive trust relationships. XenApp session login time was not significantly impacted by the Password Manager agent.

The following test bed was used for this phase of testing:

Active Directory Server Configuration:

- Dell PowerEdge 2650
- Dual Xeon 2.4GHz processors with 512KB L2 cache
- 34GB SCSI HDD
- 1GB RAM
- 4GB page file

Citrix XenApp Hardware Configuration:

- Dell Poweredge 1750
- Dual Xeon 2.8 GHz Processors with 512 KB L2 Cache
- 34 GB Ultra 320 SCSI
- 1 GB RAM
- 3 GB Page File

- Dell Poweredge 1850 (64-bit)
- Dual Xeon 2.8 GHz Processors with 512 KB L2 Cache
- 34 GB Ultra 320 SCSI
- 5 GB RAM
- 8 GB Page File

Client Hardware Configuration:

- Dell Poweredge 1750
- Dual Xeon 2.8 GHz Processors with 512 KB L2 Cache
- 34 GB Ultra 320 SCSI
- 1 GB RAM
- 3 GB Page File

Citrix XenApp Software Configuration

- Windows 2003 Server w/ SP 2 or Windows 2003x64 Server s/ SP 2
- Citrix XenApp 4.5 w/ HRP1
- Citrix Password Manager 4.6
- Microsoft Office XP - Excel, Access & PowerPoint

Client Software Configuration

- Windows 2003 Server w/ SP2
- Citrix ICA Program Neighborhood Version 10.100.55836
- 5 ICA sessions exist on each machine

Active Directory Software Configuration:

- Windows 2003 w/ Service Pack 2

Disk Space Utilization of the Active Directory Domain Controller Server

When Active Directory is used as a central data store, user configuration and credential information is stored in the Active Directory database. The file that makes up this database is labeled NTDS.dit. Active Directory allocates space for this file in 2MB blocks of disk space. Table 8-9 shows the average disk space utilized for a single user.

With these measurements, the amount of disk space required on a file share server can be calculated with the following formula:

Disk space required = (# of users) * (FTU configuration + (# of defined apps * [user-defined or provisioned apps]))

For example (running XenApp on Windows 2003), 1,000 users who are using Previous Password as their key recovery method, with 20 applications defined via provisioning for each user, would require the following:

- Disk space required = (1,000) * (4.88 + (20 * 0.95))
- Disk space required = 23,880KB or 24MB

Disk Utilization Measurement	Disk Usage with No Applications Defined (KB)	Disk Usage per Application (KB)
FTU with Previous Password	4.88	0.7
FTU with Previous Password and Provisioning	14.6	0.95
Disk Usage prior to FTU (Only Provisioning Commands)	14.4	0.95
FTU with AKR	5.34	0.7
FTU with AKR and Provisioning	15.0	0.95
FTU with SSPR	7.61	0.7
FTU with SSPR and Provisioning	17.3	0.95
FTU with AKR and SSPR	8.07	0.7
FTU with AKR, SSPR, and Provisioning	17.7	0.95

Table 8-9 Average Disk Space per User for Active Directory Sync Option

Network Bandwidth Utilization among Password Manager Agents, Active Directory Domain Controllers, and Password Manager Servers

Different events, such as logging on or changing a password, can trigger synchronization among the Password Manager agent, the Active Directory, and the Password Manager Server. These synchronizations place traffic on the network. The amount of network traffic between an agent and an Active Directory Domain Controller can vary, depending on some of the following factors:

- Number of application definitions per user
- Whether or not aggressive synchronization is enabled
- Frequency of synchronization events

Network Monitor was used to measure the amount of data passed among an Active Directory Domain Controller, the Password Manager agent, and Password Manager Server for various synchronization events. Each measurement was taken multiple times to obtain the average value for each event. The users were set up with 10 defined applications (seven Windows-based applications and three web-based applications).

Important to note is that application definitions for the most part could produce different results. Also important to note is that the logon measurements include the amount of bandwidth required during a login without Password Manager. In our test environment, the average amount of bandwidth for a user who logs in for the first time was 150.1KB. Each subsequent login averaged approximately 130.1KB (see Table 8-10).

	Active Directory Credential Store		
Event	**Agent/Sync Point**	**Agent/Service**	**Service/Sync Point**
FTU w/ no applications defined	600.5 KB	0.0 KB	0.0 KB
FTU w/ 10 applications provisioned	1191.6 KB	28.0 KB	132.9.0 KB
FTU (SSPR enabled) w/ no applications defined	600.8 KB	26.4 KB	371.3 KB
FTU (SSPR enabled) w/ 10 applications provisioned	1193.1 KB	53.1 KB	508.7 KB
• Password Reset	0.0 KB	50.7 KB	578.3 KB
• Account Unlock	0.0 KB	44.9 KB	582.4 KB
FTU (AKR enabled) w/ no applications defined	625.8 KB	17.5 KB	228.3 KB
FTU (AKR enabled) w/ 10 applications provisioned	1194.9 KB	44.1 KB	351.9 KB
• Key Recovery	61.8 KB	16.9 KB	42.7 KB
FTU (AKR & SSPR enabled) w/ no applications defined	601.9 KB	42.4 KB	620.1 KB
FTU (AKR & SSPR enabled) w/ 10 applications provisioned	1194.8 KB	69.0 KB	724.6 KB
Post FTU Logon (with no configuration changes)	38.5 KB	0.0 KB	0.0 KB
Refresh from Logon Manager	20.6 KB	0.0 KB	0.0 KB

Table 8-10 Network Bandwidth Usage for Password Manager Managed Applications with Active Directory Sync Option

The following list details the various network traffic events that occur for Password Manager–managed applications using an Active Directory sync option. These points correlate with data in Table 8-10.

- **FTU** This is the first-time user configuration event that takes place when a user logs in for the first time and configures Password Manager.
- **Password reset** This event happens when a user starts the Self-Service Password Reset feature.
- **Key recovery** This event occurs after a user's password has been changed by either the domain administrator or the user. Password Manager updates the security keys so the user can access his or her credentials.
- **Password reset/key recovery** During this process, the user invokes the Self-Service Password Reset feature and changes his or her password. The user then logs in and automatic key recovery takes place.

NOTE In an environment where aggressive synchronization is enabled, every time that an application is launched, a synchronization event takes place. This is comparable to a user using the refresh feature. Performing synchronizations across a WAN link could cause a bottle neck between the synchronization point and Password Manager agents.

Agent Response Time

The time that it takes for Password Manager to recognize a password-protected application and provide its credentials can vary depending on the user's environment and Password Manager configuration. The following are some factors that may affect response time:

- Network bandwidth availability
- Use of redirected Application Data folders versus local Windows profiles
- Whether aggressive synchronization is enabled or not
- XenApp resource availability
- Whether agent synchronization is installed
- Network latency between the synchronization point and the Password Manager agent

Tables 8-11 and 8-12 list agent response times with varying client configurations. All testing was done using a custom Win32 application, a custom web page, Scanpak Aviva Terminal Emulator, a custom Java application, and a custom Java applet running in an

Agent Response Time with Active Directory Synchronization over a LAN	Results Windows 2003 Windows Application	Web Application	Terminal Emulator Application	Java Application	Java Applet
Single user operating on XenApp with aggressive synchronization disabled & local Windows profile	0.03 sec	0.40 sec	2.04 sec	0.17 sec	0.44 sec
Single user operating on XenApp with aggressive synchronization disabled & Redirected App-Data folders	0.04 sec	0.41 sec	2.17 sec	0.18 sec	0.53 sec
Single user operating on XenApp with aggressive synchronization & local Windows profile	0.49 sec	0.89 sec	2.64 sec	0.64 sec	0.93 sec
Single user operating on XenApp with aggressive synchronization & Redirected App-Data folders	1.27 sec	1.64 sec	3.41 sec	1.34 sec	1.90 sec

Table 8-11 Average Response Time for Active Directory Sync over a LAN Windows 2003 Server

ICA session on XenApp. For each configuration, the tables indicate the time between the application loading and the credentials being fully submitted by Password Manager.

NOTE Response times for Win32, Web, Java, and Java applet credential requests were gathered using an automated test tool. Response times for Terminal Emulator applications were gathered using a stop watch (times may not be accurate due to human error). Mainframe host polling time was set to 700 milliseconds, which may add to response time.

Agent Response Time with Active Directory Synchronization over a LAN	Results Windows 2003x64				
	Windows Application	Web Application	Terminal Emulator Application	Java Application	Java Applet
Single user operating on XenApp with aggressive synchronization disabled & local Windows profile	0.02 sec	0.41 sec		0.17 sec	0.75 sec
Single user operating on XenApp with aggressive synchronization disabled & Redirected App-Data folders	0.03 sec	0.40 sec		0.18 sec	0.69 sec
Single user operating on XenApp with aggressive synchronization & local Windows profile	0.48 sec	0.87 sec		0.63 sec	1.35 sec
Single user operating on XenApp with aggressive synchronization & Redirected App-Data folders	1.27 sec	1.69 sec		1.37 sec	1.99 sec

Table 8-12 Average Response Time for Active Directory Sync over a LAN Windows 2003 Server

DETERMINING WHICH FILE SHARE SYNCHRONIZATION POINT THE CITRIX PASSWORD MANAGER 4.*X* AGENT WILL USE AS THE CENTRAL CREDENTIAL STORE

The Citrix Password Manager 4.*x* agent uses a defined logical search order to determine which synchronization point it should use. The agent attempts to locate a synchronization point (for example, HKCU, MMF, and so forth) from numerous places. This process differs slightly between servers with XenApp installed and those without it installed. Figures 8-3 and 8-4 outline how the agent locates a synchronization point and how it accepts a synchronization point for use.

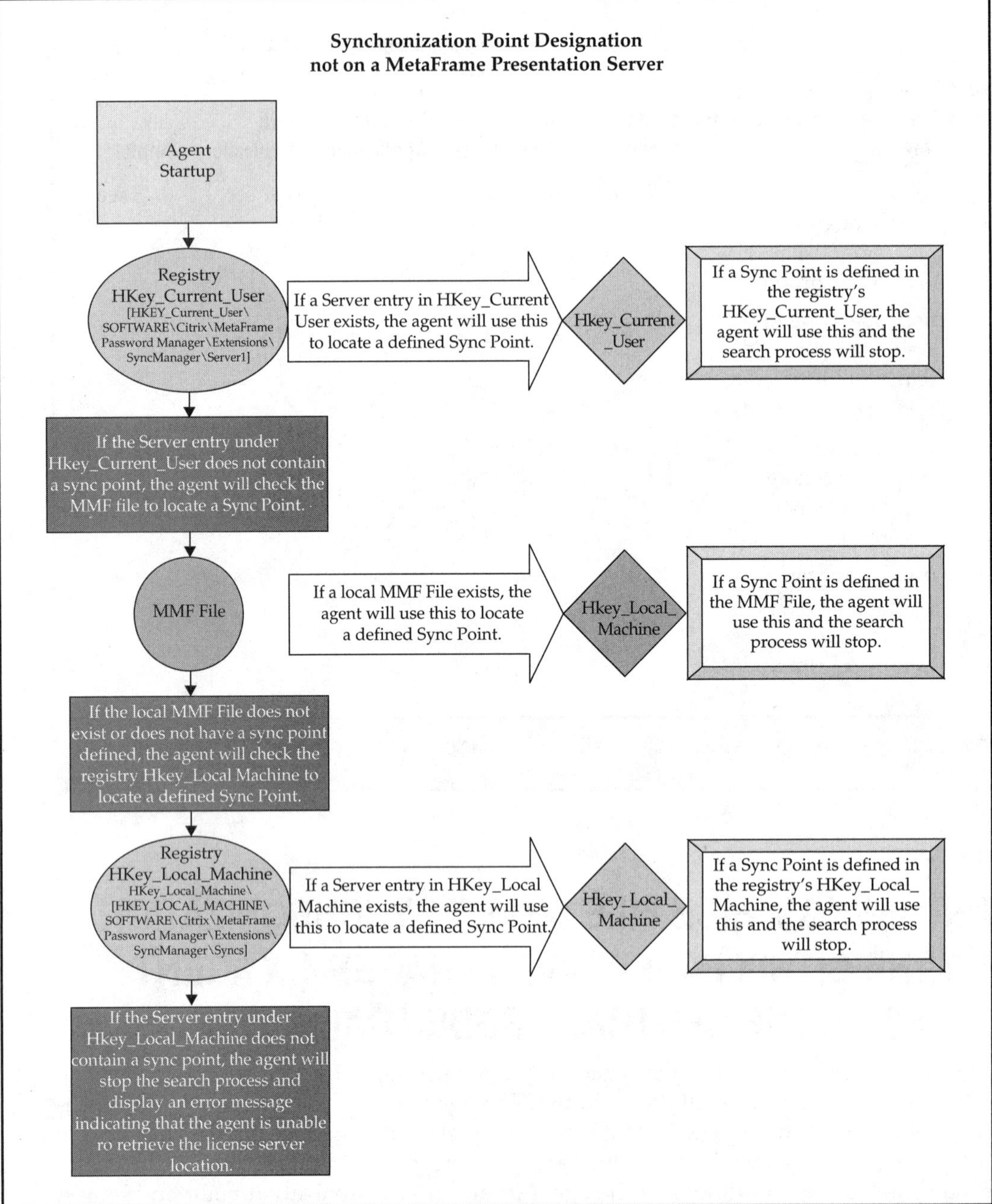
Synchronization Point Designation not on a MetaFrame Presentation Server
Agent Startup
Registry HKey_Current_User [HKEY_Current_User\ SOFTWARE\Citrix\MetaFrame Password Manager\Extensions\ SyncManager\Server1]
If a Server entry in HKey_Current User exists, the agent will use this to locate a defined Sync Point.
Hkey_Current _User
If a Sync Point is defined in the registry's HKey_Current_User, the agent will use this and the search process will stop.
If the Server entry under Hkey_Current_User does not contain a sync point, the agent will check the MMF file to locate a Sync Point.
MMF File
If a local MMF File exists, the agent will use this to locate a defined Sync Point.
Hkey_Local_ Machine
If a Sync Point is defined in the MMF File, the agent will use this and the search process will stop.
If the local MMF File does not exist or does not have a sync point defined, the agent will check the registry Hkey_Local Machine to locate a defined Sync Point.
Registry HKey_Local_Machine HKey_Local_Machine\ [HKEY_LOCAL_MACHINE\ SOFTWARE\Citrix\MetaFrame Password Manager\Extensions\ SyncManager\Syncs]
If a Server entry in HKey_Local Machine exists, the agent will use this to locate a defined Sync Point.
Hkey_Local_ Machine
If a Sync Point is defined in the registry's HKey_Local_ Machine, the agent will use this and the search process will stop.
If the Server entry under Hkey_Local_Machine does not contain a sync point, the agent will stop the search process and display an error message indicating that the agent is unable ro retrieve the license server location.

Figure 8-3 Synchronization point designation not on XenApp

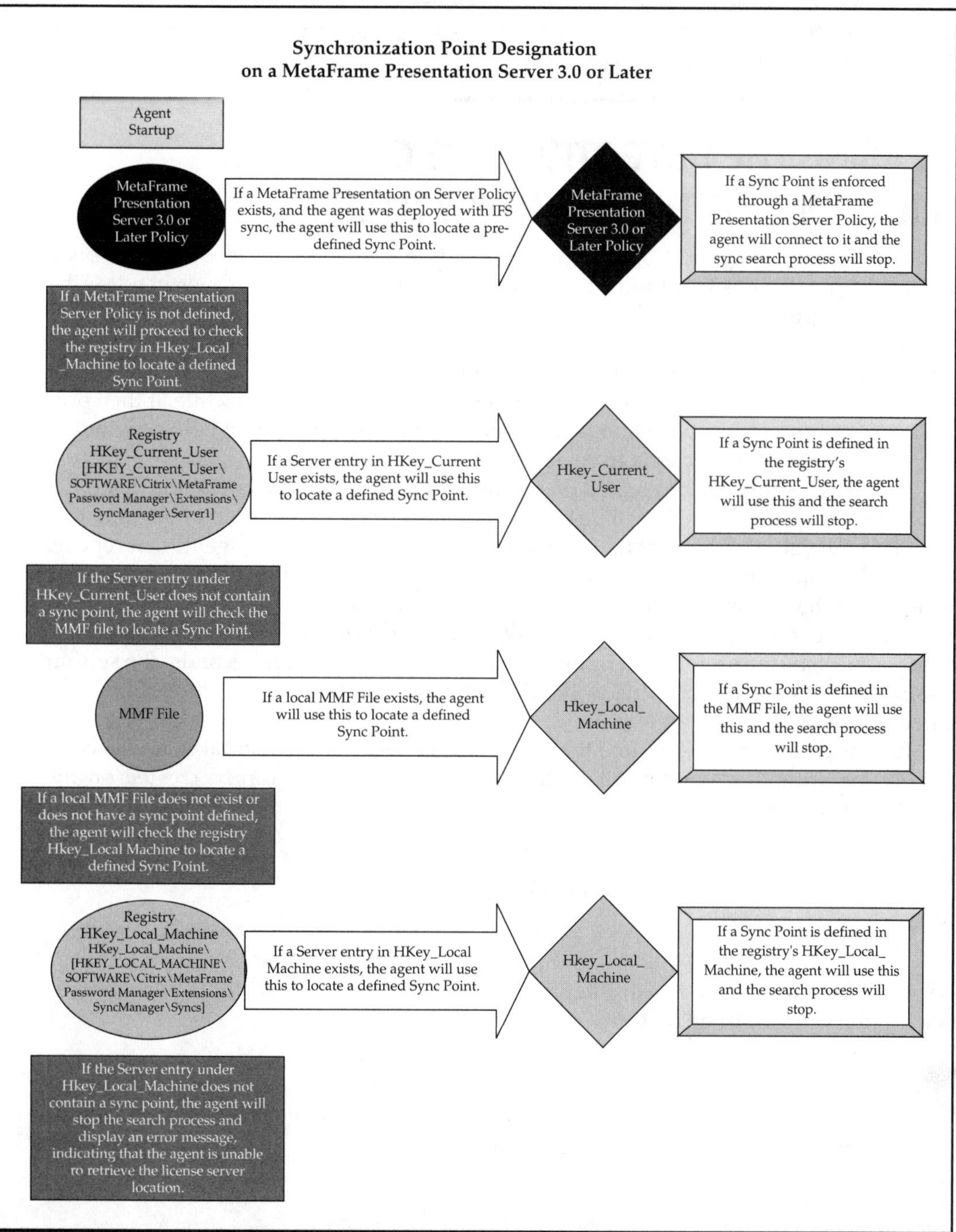
Synchronization Point Designation
on a MetaFrame Presentation Server 3.0 or Later
Agent Startup
MetaFrame Presentation Server 3.0 or Later Policy
If a MetaFrame Presentation on Server Policy exists, and the agent was deployed with IFS sync, the agent will use this to locate a pre-defined Sync Point.
MetaFrame Presentation Server 3.0 or Later Policy
If a Sync Point is enforced through a MetaFrame Presentation Server Policy, the agent will connect to it and the sync search process will stop.
If a MetaFrame Presentation Server Policy is not defined, the agent will proceed to check the registry in Hkey_Local_Machine to locate a defined Sync Point.
Registry HKey_Current_User [HKEY_Current_User\ SOFTWARE\Citrix\MetaFrame Password Manager\Extensions\ SyncManager\Server1]
If a Server entry in HKey_Current User exists, the agent will use this to locate a defined Sync Point.
Hkey_Current_User
If a Sync Point is defined in the registry's HKey_Current_User, the agent will use this and the search process will stop.
If the Server entry under HKey_Current_User does not contain a sync point, the agent will check the MMF file to locate a Sync Point.
MMF File
If a local MMF File exists, the agent will use this to locate a defined Sync Point.
Hkey_Local_Machine
If a Sync Point is defined in the MMF File, the agent will use this and the search process will stop.
If a local MMF File does not exist or does not have a sync point defined, the agent will check the registry Hkey_Local Machine to locate a defined Sync Point.
Registry HKey_Local_Machine HKey_Local_Machine\ [HKEY_LOCAL_MACHINE\ SOFTWARE\Citrix\MetaFrame Password Manager\Extensions\ SyncManager\Syncs]
If a Server entry in HKey_Local Machine exists, the agent will use this to locate a defined Sync Point.
Hkey_Local_Machine
If a Sync Point is defined in the registry's HKey_Local_Machine, the agent will use this and the search process will stop.
If the Server entry under Hkey_Local_Machine does not contain a sync point, the agent will stop the search process and display an error message, indicating that the agent is unable ro retrieve the license server location.

Figure 8-4 Synchronization point designation on XenApp 3.0 or higher

NOTE The Password Manager Policy "Central Credential Store" is applied only at the initialization of each session for which it has been applied.

INCREASING THE DETECTION TIME OF APPLICATIONS WITHOUT WINDOW TITLES

Currently, a defined application with no window title takes a minimum of three seconds to be detected. This is because of the way that Citrix Password Manager handles the detection of applications with no window title.

When the agent detects a window with no title, the agent assumes the window is not initialized completely. The agent then reposts the window detection event every one-half second, up to six times, before determining the window has no window title. It then proceeds to process window detection. This means any defined application with no window title takes at least three seconds to be detected.

A registry setting can be created on the agent workstation to decrease the detection time of such applications. The value allows the repost detection time to be adjusted, based on the value in this setting. With this setting configured, the agent then reposts the application detection event up to the number specified in this registry value. For example, if the administrator prefers to shorten discovery time to two seconds, he or she should set this registry value to four (2 seconds/0.5 second event repost interval). If the administrator prefers to lengthen the discovery time to five seconds, the setting should be configured to a value to 10. The default value of this registry value is 6, or three seconds.

To shorten the amount of time that the Citrix Password Manager takes to detect an application without a window title, the following registry key can be created on the agent workstation:

```
Path:       HKLM\SOFTWARE\CITRIX\Metaframe Password Manager\Shell
Key:        EmptyTitleMaxRepostTime
Type:       Dword
Value:      0/1
```

By default, when the registry key is created, it is set to 0 (disabled). To enable the setting, the value must be set to 1.

NOTE This setting should be customized only when configured Windows applications include those with empty window titles. The agent code uses this registry if it is set in a range between 1 and 20. Otherwise, the agent uses the default value of 6.

CHAPTER 9

Conferencing Manager

The following section describes considerations for integrating Citrix Conferencing Manager, such as Conferencing Manager architecture, sizing of your Conferencing Manager servers, guest user considerations, and users who are members of 200 or more Active Directory groups.

NOTE If you are upgrading Conferencing Manager, note that a direct upgrade from Conferencing Manager 2.0 to version 4.5 is not supported. Refer to the *Citrix Conferencing Manager Administrator's Guide* for more details.

CITRIX CONFERENCING MANAGER ARCHITECTURE AND SCALABILITY

To deploy Conferencing Manager into your existing XenApp environment properly, you must understand how the core components interact and communicate with each other. Conferencing Manager is broken into five components, each of which is necessary to start, join, leave, and end meetings:

- **Conferencing Manager User Interface client** The Conferencing Manager User Interface client is a published application in the XenApp farm. It can be load-balanced like any published application to improve performance. The main function of the Conferencing Manager User Interface client is to allow conference participants access to the conference room.
- **Conference Organizer** The main function of the Conference Organizer is to maintain meeting information for all meeting servers in the farm. This information consists of which meetings have been created, when meetings have started and on what servers, and who is on the attendee lists of those meetings. This information is stored in the registry on the Conference Organizer server. The Conference Organizer is also responsible for load-balancing meetings across your available meeting servers. Only one instance of Conference Organizer is allowed per server farm. It can be installed on a standalone server without XenApp installed, but it must be installed in the same domain where Conference Room and the Conferencing Manager User Interface client are installed.
- **Conference Room** Conference Room is installed as a hidden published application and can be load-balanced like any other published application. Conference Room is invisible to the user, but it is automatically launched via Conference Manger User Interface when a meeting is started or joined. It is the component that provides the actual shadowing session in which the users collaborate during a conference. Note that this published application should not be renamed; otherwise, conferences cannot be started.

- **Conference Room Manager** Conference Room Manager maintains meeting information on a single server. It monitors the attendees and licensing information for the server and is responsible for meeting operations, such as starting, joining, leaving, and ending meetings. Conference Room Manager communicates information with the Conference Organizer service, such as the time when a meeting has started and the attendees who are currently in the meeting.
- **External Conference Service** External Conference Service provides communication to the Conference Organizer from outside a firewall using the HTTP protocol. Requirements are that External Web Service is running on the same server on Conference Organizer and that Microsoft .NET 1.1 is installed.

Citrix Conferencing Manager Communications

When you are deploying Conferencing Manager into your XenApp environment, understanding how Conferencing Manager communicates with its various components is important. This is especially important when deploying over a wide area network (WAN). This section describes which Conferencing Manager components communicate with each other, the protocols they use, and the amount of bandwidth consumed.

It is important to know that when Conferencing Manager is idle—this means no meetings are in progress, and no users are creating and/or joining meetings—no bandwidth is overhead. Figure 9-1 displays the actions that happen when a user launches the Conferencing Manager client, which occur as follows:

1. When a user launches the Conferencing Manager client, it communicates using Remote Procedural Call (RPC) with the Conference Organizer service. This is to retrieve a list of available meetings that the user can join. The amount of bandwidth used during this action is [KB = 11.9 + (1.5 * # of meetings)].
2. The client then communicates to the Exchange server only if there is a valid Outlook profile. This also uses RPC and the amount of bandwidth can be represented by [KB = 2.9 + (24.7 * # of meetings)].
3. The client communicates with the configured Citrix XML service to retrieve its list of available published applications on the XenApp farm. This communication uses the HTTP protocol and the bandwidth is calculated using the following formula [KB = 12.4 + (0.3 * # of meetings)].
4. A user connects to a XenApp farm and launches the Conferencing Manager user-interface Published Application. This communication uses the Independent Computing Architecture (ICA) protocol and is optimized for WAN connections. When the interface is initialized, the communication shown in Figure 9-2 begins.

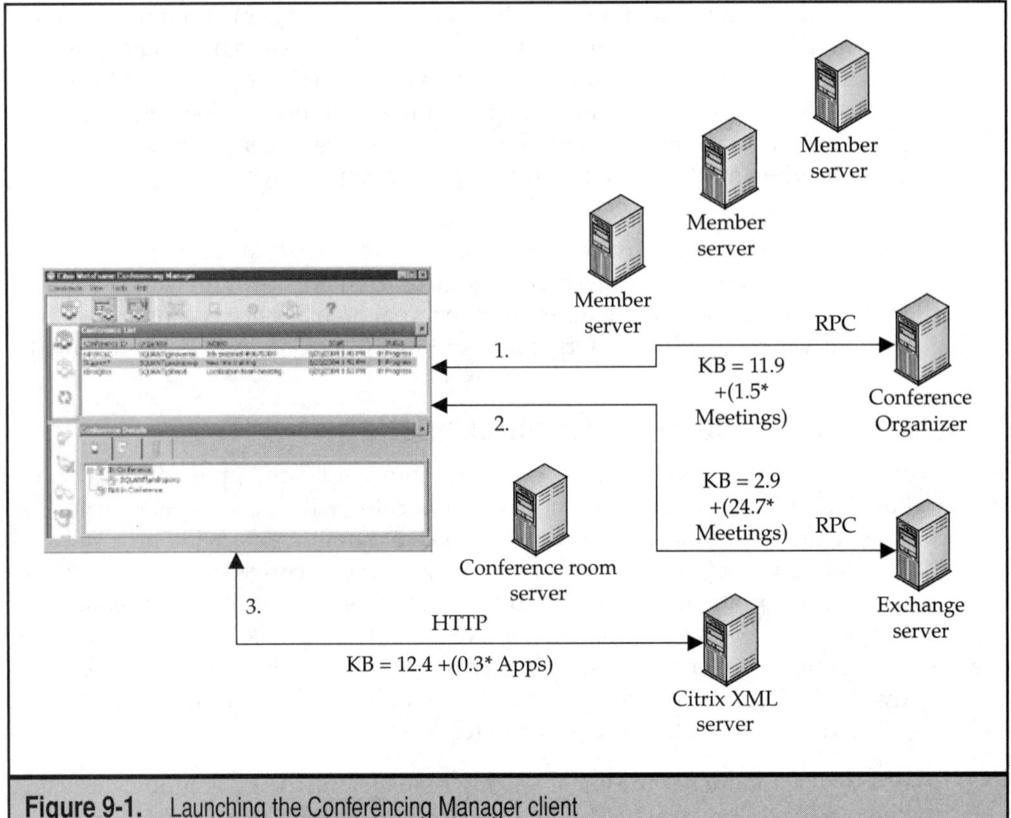

Figure 9-1. Launching the Conferencing Manager client

5. When the user decides to create a meeting, the Citrix Conferencing Manager UI contacts the Conference Organizer and receives an ICA file directing the user to the least-loaded meeting server. When the ICA file is launched, it creates a session on the meeting server and launches the CRoom application.
6. When CRoom initializes, the CRoom Manager communicates to the license server and checks out a license for the meeting host. The bandwidth utilized for a license checkout is 1.3KB per license and uses the Transmission Control Protocol (TCP).
7. The CRoom Manager then communicates to the Conference Organizer that the meeting has started. The meeting is now ready for attendees to join.
8. A user connects to a XenApp farm and launches the Conferencing Manager user interface published application. This communication uses the ICA protocol and is optimized for WAN connections. When the interface is initialized,

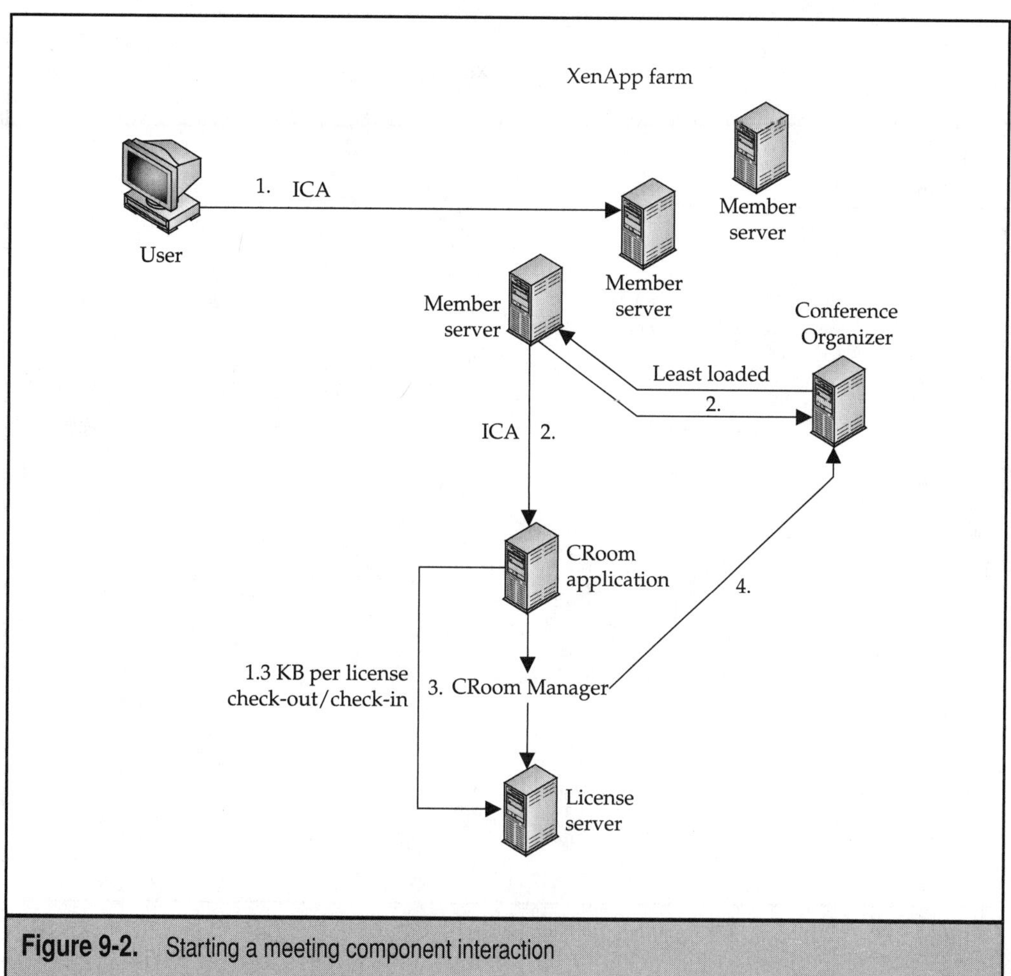

Figure 9-2. Starting a meeting component interaction

the communication shown in Figure 9-3 begins. The user decides to join a meeting displayed in the user interface.

9. When the user decides to join a meeting, the Conferencing Manager UI contacts the Conference Organizer and receives an ICA file directing the user to the meeting server where the conference is hosted. When the ICA file is launched, it creates a session on the meeting server and launches the CRoom application. The CRoom Manager then communicates to the license server and checks out a license for the meeting attendee.
10. After the license acquisition, CRoom shadows the host session and the attendee joins the meeting.
11. The CRoom Manager then communicates to the Conference Organizer that the current attendee has changed.

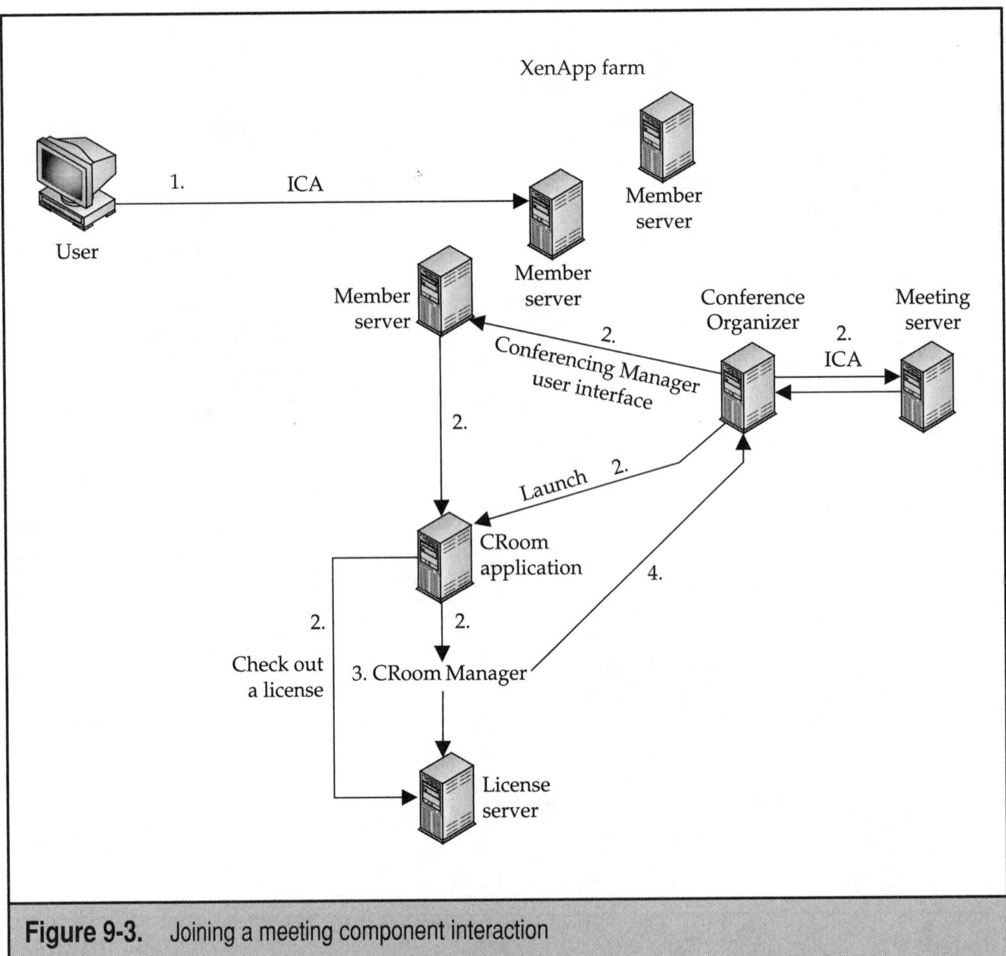

Figure 9-3. Joining a meeting component interaction

Sizing Citrix Conferencing Manager Servers

The number of users that a server can support depends on several factors, including the following:

- The Conferencing Manager server's hardware specifications (processor, memory, disk, and available network bandwidth)
- The applications that are being run (because of the applications' CPU and memory requirements)

- The amount of user input and graphics being processed and displayed by the applications
- The maximum desired resource usage on the server (for example, 90 percent CPU usage or 80 percent memory usage)

This topic discusses how to size a Conference Manager Server, where memory becomes the first performance bottleneck. Also, note that applications that place a heavy load on the processor or consume large amounts of network bandwidth decrease the number of attendees able to join a meeting with acceptable performance. *Acceptable performance* can be described as session latency or how long it takes for all attendees to receive screen updates from the host session. The following scenario describes how to size a Conferencing Manager server that contains all the Conferencing Manager components. The components are as follows:

- Citrix XenApp
- Citrix XML Service
- Conference Organizer Service
- Conference Room Manager Service
- Conference Room Published Application
- Conferencing Manager User Interface

The following formula is used to determine the user capacity for a particular server:

$$\text{\# of users} = \frac{\text{Host Values} = ((\text{Total Memory (Desired Threshold)}) - (\text{SessionMemory} + \text{CRoom} + \text{MCM\_UI} + \text{Apps} + \text{OSOverhead})}{\text{Attendees Values} = (\text{SessionMemory} + \text{CRoom} + \text{MCM\_UI} + \text{CShadow})}$$

where

TotalMemory = The amount of memory available on the server (physical and virtual)

DesiredThreshold = Maximum memory utilization desired

SessionMemory = Memory cost of all the components required for an ICA session (Winlogon.exe, WFShell.exe, Csrss.exe, and SSonSvr.exe). This is the same for both the Host and Attendee sessions. The variable SessionMemory in the numerator refers to the organizer's session memory and the variable Session-Memory in the denominator refers to the attendee's session memory.

MCM_UI = Memory cost of the Citrix MetaFrame Conferencing Manager Client

Apps = Memory cost for applications inside a meeting (Microsoft PowerPoint)

OSOverhead = Memory cost of the operating system (OS) and related services

CRoom = Memory cost of the Conference Room Published Application

CShadow = Memory cost of the CShadow.exe process (attendee only)

Single-Server Example

A Windows Server 2003 Enterprise, with 4GB of physical memory plus 2GB of virtual memory, has 6GB total memory. The desired threshold is 80 percent utilization. The session memory usage is 9.7MB—this includes all the processes associated with an ICA session. The size of the Citrix Conference Manager UI depends on the number of published applications and meetings to which the user has rights and is around 24MB. The PowerPoint application used within the meeting is 10MB and the memory cost of the OS (OSOverhead) is 700MB. The denominator portion of the equation is the attendee's memory usage, which is 54.1MB. This includes all the processes associated with an ICA session, MCM_UI, CRoom, and CShadow (see Figure 9-4).

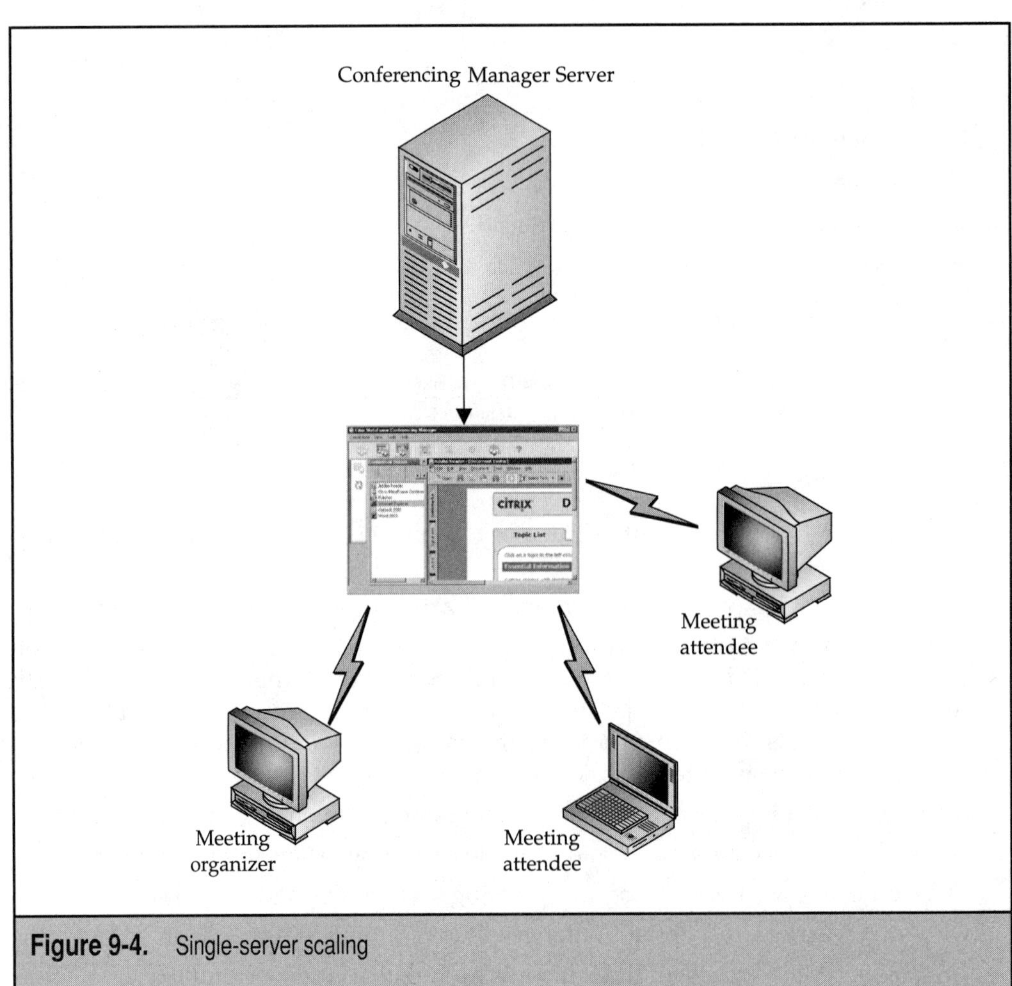

Figure 9-4. Single-server scaling

Multiple-Server Example

Offloading the Citrix Conference Manager UI and applications to other servers running XenApp reduces overall memory utilization. The example in Figure 9-5 load balances the Citrix Conference Manager UI and meeting applications to other MetaFrame servers. This reduces the memory for each attendee by 17MB and the organizer by 21MB.

The multiserver example reaches a limit of 176 users. This formula is accurate up to a certain number of users when based on memory alone. Other considerations, such as OS limitations and latency, prevent scaling this high. Testing in Citrix eLabs shows that a server of this size can adequately support between 90 and 100 users in a multiserver setup. This estimate also depends on the type of applications in use. This is why it is important to size your servers according to your environment before placing them into production.

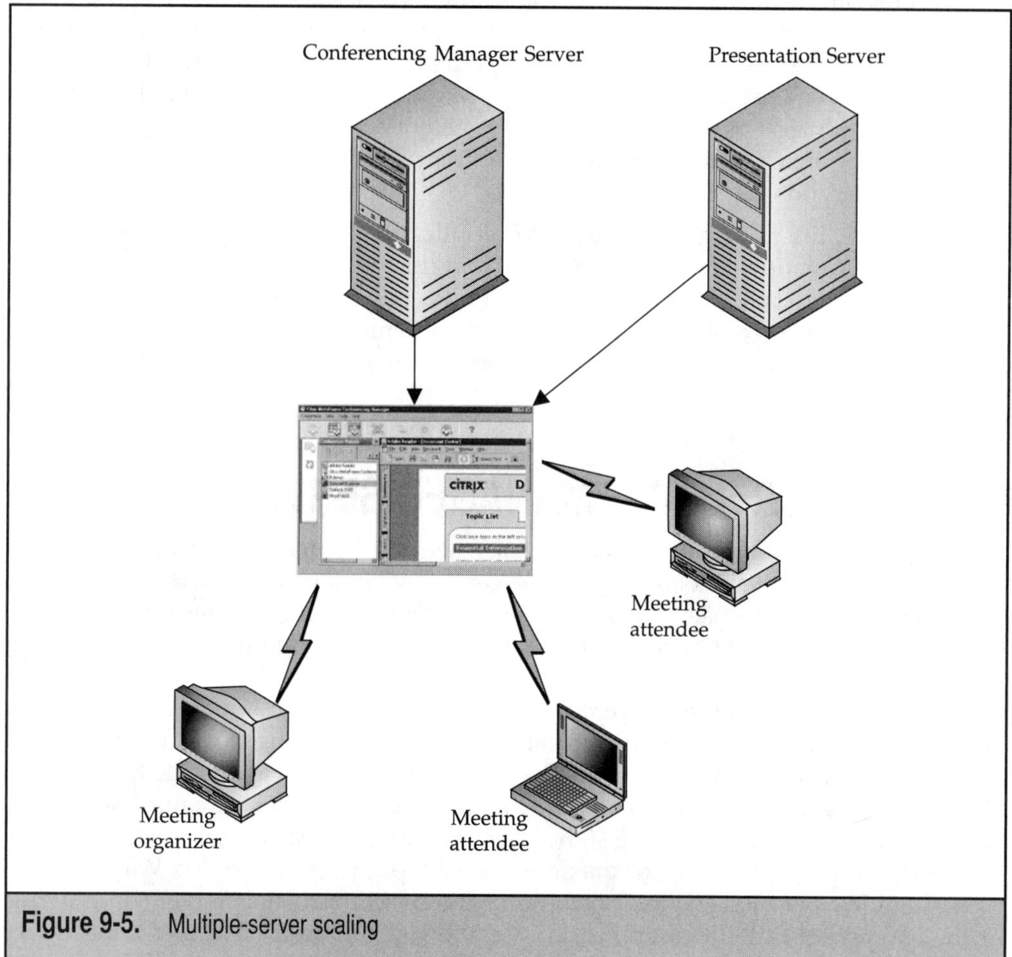

Figure 9-5. Multiple-server scaling

User Experience within a Meeting

When sizing your Conferencing Manager servers, using the memory formula is not enough to determine an accurate value for how many users a server can support. The types of applications in a meeting must also be taken into account. Different applications exhibit different amounts of latency, depending on how much of the screen is changed with every action. *Latency* is defined in this scenario as the time for all attendees in a meeting to receive screen changes. The following lists three types of applications:

- **Documents and spreadsheets** These types of applications, by design, update small portions of the screen. When users collaborate using such applications, they notice small amounts of latency, which is sometimes unnoticeable. These types of meetings can support the most users and the upper end of the memory-formula spectrum.
- **Presentations** These types of applications, by design, update the entire screen when slides are changed. When users collaborate, they notice a degree of latency, depending on the actions performed. Changing the text has little impact, whereas adding pictures and transitions is more intensive. These types of meetings support the middle of the memory-formula spectrum. Typical latency on a meeting viewing a PowerPoint presentation with 60 users is about two seconds per slide.
- **Highly intensive graphic and CAD applications** These types of applications, by design, update the entire screen when changes occur and include complex shapes and colors. When users collaborate, they notice a degree of latency, depending on the actions performed, such as moving and resizing objects. These types of meetings support the lower end of the memory-formula spectrum.

TUNING CONFERENCING MANAGER SERVERS

The largest increase in performance is seen when the Conferencing Manager UI and available applications are load-balanced across the servers in your XenApp farm. This distributes the workload across multiple servers, thus reducing the memory and CPU consumption on the Conferencing Manager server and allowing more users to participate in a meeting.

The administrator can optimize the XenApp Client for 32-bit Windows by disabling any unneeded virtual channels when creating or joining a meeting. For example, if audio and printing are not needed in a conference, the administrator can disable these virtual channels for users connecting to that particular server. These virtual channels would not be initialized during logon, saving some memory and CPU resources.

On the conference server, for maximum-user capacity, all unneeded Windows services should be disabled. Examples would be Internet Information Server (IIS), Alerter, or the Spooler service, if printing is not needed. It is important that any unnecessary processes that exist in every session are disabled. For example, if Microsoft Office is published on the server, processes such as Find Fast, Help Assistant, and the automatic spelling checker should be disabled for each user.

Users Are Members of 200 or More Active Directory Groups

When a user attempts to start a conference, the user cannot see all their published applications or the following error message may appear:

```
An error occurred while processing your request. You do not currently
have access to any published applications. If you continue to receive
this message, contact your MetaFrame Administrator.
```

A possible cause for this error is that the user is a member of 200 or more Active Directory groups.

To enable users to see their published applications, create the following values in the registry:

```
HKEY_LOCAL_MACHINE\SOFTWARE\Citrix\XML Service
Name: MaxRequestSize
Type: DWORD
Data: 0032000
HKEY_LOCAL_MACHINE\SYSTEM\CurrentControlSet\Services\CtxHttp
Name: MaximumIncoming
Type: DWORD
Data: 0032000
```

You can increase the data value to a larger number if the user is a member of more than 200 groups. If the user is a member of more than 200 Active Directory groups, increase the data value by intervals of 4,000 until the error message disappears.

UNINSTALLING CONFERENCING MANAGER

The following section addresses considerations and various methods of uninstalling Conferencing Manager.

NOTE Uninstall Conferencing Manager before uninstalling XenApp.

For an Unattended Uninstall

For an unattended uninstall of Conferencing Manager, run the following from a command line:

```
msiexec /x /q CMCM.msi CTX_ADDLOCAL=CMCM,CR,CO,ECS"
```

where CMCM.msi is the path and name of the Windows Installer package used to install Conferencing Manager.

To Uninstall Using Active Directory Services

An Active Directory Services uninstall is straightforward: Check the box for Uninstall the package when the computer is removed out of the scope of the Group Policy.

To Uninstall Using Installation Manager

Nothing additional needs to be specified; just select Uninstall the package.

TROUBLESHOOTING CONFERENCE MANAGER

This section illustrates some common issues surrounding troubleshooting Conference Manager. Topics discussed include deleted, renamed, or missing Citrix Conference Room Published Applications; failures to start the Conference Room; and problems with the Outlook add-in.

How to Repair the Citrix Conference Room Component If the Published Application "Citrix Conference Room" Is Deleted or Renamed

During the installation of the Citrix Conference Room, a published application is automatically created with the name Citrix Conference Room. This published application is hidden from the browse list of published applications, but it is necessary for the Citrix Conferencing Manager to work properly. If the published application Citrix Conference Room is renamed or deleted for any reason, the Conferencing Manager will no longer work. If the published application is deleted or renamed and someone attempts to create a conference, that user may receive the following error message: "An error occurred while processing your request. Try again. If you continue to receive this message, contact your MetaFrame XP Administrator." You may also see the following event in the server's application event log:

```
Event Type: Error
Event Source: Citrix MetaFrame Conferencing Manager
Event Category: None
Event ID: 1541
Date: 5/5/2007
Time: 2:29:42 PM
User: N/A
Computer: CTXXA3SRV
Description:
The Citrix XML Service returned error code unspecified.
```

To resolve this issue, perform a repair installation of the Citrix Conferencing Manager. The repair can be accomplished through the following steps:

1. Navigate to Start | Settings | Control Panel | Add/Remove Programs.
2. Highlight the program Citrix MetaFrame Conferencing Manager and select Change.
3. On the screen titled Citrix MetaFrame Conferencing Manager Setup–Application Maintenance, select the radio button next to Repair and then select Next.
4. On the next screen, MetaFrame XP Administrator Credentials, select either "Use my current credentials if the current user is a Citrix Administrator" or "Use my MetaFrame XP administrator credentials, if it is necessary to specify another Citrix Administrator's credentials."
5. Enter the appropriate credentials and then select Next.
6. Once you are certain that you have correctly configured all the options, select Next on the Ready to Repair the Application screen.
7. When the repair installation has completed, select Finish.

Error: Citrix Conference Room Failed to Start

When initiating a meeting, you may receive the following error message: "Citrix Conference Room failed to start. The Citrix server is unable to process your request to start this published application at this time. Please try again later. If the problem persists, contact your administrator." This error can occur if the initial published application specified for the meeting and the Conference Room is published on a separate server. To avoid this message, you can increase the amount of time that Conference Room waits before starting the specified initial published application by creating the following registry value:

```
HKEY_LOCAL_MACHINE\ Software\ Citrix\ CMCM
Value: ConferenceDelay (REG_DWORD) : number in milliseconds
```

Initially, configure the delay time to be 5,000 (5 seconds). Increase or decrease this value to avoid the error message and minimize the delay. Adding or modifying this registry value does not require a reboot.

Error When Running InstallAddIn.cmd to Install the Outlook Add-in a DLL

When using InstallAddIn.cmd to install CMCMOL.dll manually on a client machine, you may see the following messages during the execution of the file:

```
C:\>xcopy /y /f CMCMOL.dll "C:\Program Files\Citrix\CMCM\Outlook"
File not found - CMCMOL.dll
```

```
0 File(s) copied
C:\>xcopy /y /f Resources*.txt "C:\Program Files\Citrix\CMCM\Outlook"
File not found - Resources*.txt
0 File(s) copied
```

After executing the file and launching Outlook, you may also notice that you do not see the MetaFrame Conference button on the Outlook menu bar. It may be necessary at the command prompt to change directory locations to the directory that contains InstallAddIn.cmd and its supporting files before running the file. By default, these files are located in the Outlook folder on the Citrix Conferencing Manager CD-ROM.

CHAPTER 10

Security Issues and Guidelines

This chapter covers various security concerns in a Citrix environment. The following guidelines help secure the environment from both server and client perspectives.

SECURING SERVERS

The following section discusses security precautions to consider on all Citrix servers.

Control Physical Access

Restrict physical access to servers to those individuals who are involved with administering the server environment.

Use NT File System (NTFS) Partitions

For maximum security, install XenApp only on NTFS-formatted disk partitions. Installing on NTFS partitions ensures that the local access databases are secured, because the folder %Program Files%\Citrix\Independent Management Architecture is marked so that only SYSTEM and the local Administrators group have full control. Do not change these access control lists (ACLs).

Configuring the Simple Network Management Protocol (SNMP) Service

If you use Network Manager for Citrix Presentation Server or other SNMP management software for monitoring the server only (not remote management), Citrix recommends that the privileges be read-only. If no SNMP consoles are used, remove the SNMP service from the server.

NOTE You must give read create permissions to the SNMP service for administrative tasks, such as logoff and disconnect through Network Manager.

You can configure the SNMP community and designated management consoles to prevent unauthorized access. Configure SNMP agents to accept traps from known SNMP consoles only. For more information about correctly configuring the SNMP agent, see the Windows online help file.

TIP Block incoming SNMP traffic from the Internet by using a firewall that prevents passage of traffic on UDP ports 161 and 162.

Configuring XenApp Administrator Accounts

Limit XenApp Administrator accounts to users who are members of the Windows network Administrators group. This group is presumed to be well controlled and for its users to have administrative access to network resources, including print servers.

To lessen the risk of compromising the domain administrator account, use a global group of limited user accounts to administer XenApp.

To configure administrator accounts using a global group, follow these steps:

1. In the domain where you manage user accounts, create a domain global group named XA Admins.
2. Add the user accounts of people who need XenApp Administrator privileges to the XA Admins global group.
3. Add the XA Admins global group to each XenApp server's local Administrators group.
4. In the Access Management Console, add the XA Admins global group to the list of XenApp Administrators.
5. When a new user account requires XenApp Administrator privileges, add the account to the XA Admins global group.

When setting up XA Admins in an Active Directory domain, use a domain local group for farms within a single Active Directory domain or a universal group for farms that span a forest.

SECURITY CONSIDERATIONS FOR THE DATA STORE

This section outlines Citrix recommendations, which vary for security on the data store depending on the database used for the data store.

In general, users who access XenApp do not require, and should not be granted, any access to the data store.

With direct mode access, all farm servers share a single user account and password for accessing the data store. Select a password that is not easily guessed. Keep the user name and password secure and give it to XenApp Administrators for installation only.

If the user account for direct mode access to the database is changed at a later time, the Independent Management Architecture (IMA) service will fail to start on all XenApp servers configured with that account. To reconfigure the IMA service password, use the dsmaint config command on each affected server. For information about the dsmaint config command, see the *Citrix Presentation Server Administrator's Guide.*

The following subsections discuss additional recommendations for each data store platform.

Microsoft Access

For an Access data store, the default user name is citrix and the password is citrix. If users have access to the data store server, change the password using dsmaint config and keep the information in a safe place.

NOTE Make sure that you back up your data store before using dsmaint config to change the password on your data store.

Microsoft SQL Server

The user account used to access the data store on Microsoft SQL Server has public and db_owner roles on the server and database. SA account credentials are not needed for data store access. Do not use an SA account as it presents an inherent security risk.

If the Microsoft SQL Server is configured for mixed-mode security (you can use either Microsoft SQL Server authentication or Windows NT authentication), it is useful to create a Microsoft SQL Server user for the sole purpose of accessing the data store. Because the Microsoft SQL Server user account would access the data store only, no risk occurs of compromising a Windows domain if the user's password is compromised.

For tighter security, after the initial installation of the database with db_owner permission, you can change the user account's permission to db_reader and db_writer.

NOTE Changing the user account's permission from db_owner might cause installation problems with future service packs or feature releases. Always change the account permission back to db_owner before installing a service pack or feature release.

Oracle

If the data store is hosted on Oracle, give the Oracle user account used for the XenApp farm only connect and resource permissions. SA (system or sys) account permissions are not needed for data store access.

IBM DB2

If the data store is hosted on IBM DB2, give the DB2 user account used for the XenApp farm the following permissions:

- Connect database
- Create tables
- Register functions to execute to database manager's process
- Create schemas implicity

SA (DB2Admin) account permissions are not needed for data store access.

SECURING YOUR NETWORK AGAINST DENIAL OF SERVICE (DoS) ATTACKS

Denial of service (DoS) attacks saturate networks and servers with useless calls for information. Attackers use multiple sites to make distributed attacks on one or more networks, servers, or web sites. Servers subjected to this sort of jamming either crash or become too busy to be of use when a network becomes flooded. Not only is the server compromised for communication, but it also becomes unavailable as a tool for tracing the attacks.

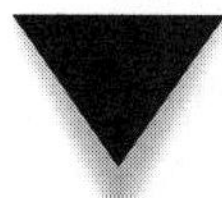

CAUTION Always observe precautions to protect the security and integrity of the registry on XenApp. For information about backing up the registry and other precautions, refer to Microsoft documentation. Editing registry settings, other than those discussed in this chapter, can corrupt your server configuration and is not supported by Citrix.

Microsoft makes recommendations for taking steps and fixing registry settings to make your networks and servers less prone to network DoS attacks. These are found on the Microsoft web site. Perform a keyword search using "Security Considerations for Network Attacks" to see this information. This page suggests changes to the following registry settings to help secure your network against DoS attacks:

- SynAttackProtect
- TcpMaxHalfOpen
- TcpMaxHalfRetried
- Enable PMTUDiscovery
- NoNameReleaseOnDemand
- EnableDeadGWDetect
- KeepAliveTime
- PerformRouterDiscovery
- EnableICMPRedirects

SECURING THE PRESENTATION SERVER CONSOLE

The Presentation Server Console is a Java application that can be run on XenApp, as well as on other servers and workstations. To prevent packet capturing, however, execute the Presentation Server Console only on XenApp or in environments where packet sniffing cannot occur.

To run the management console on a remote server:

1. Make a secure Independent Computing Architecture (ICA) Client connection to XenApp.

2. Launch the Presentation Server Console in the ICA session.
3. In the Log On To Citrix Farm dialog box, select the server on which the ICA session is running.

Ensure that only Citrix administrators have access to the Presentation Server Console. You can set NTFS permissions, so nonadministrators do not have execute permission for the Presentation Server Console executable, Ctxload.exe.

SECURE CLIENT COMMUNICATION

Depending on the environment, several features included with XenApp allow further secure communications between clients and XenApp.

XenApp includes support for ICA encryption, which uses RSA's RC5 encryption, between XenApp and clients. Support for open standards technology was added with the release of MetaFrame XP Feature Release 1. Feature Release 1 added Citrix SSL Relay, which uses standard Secure Sockets Layer (SSL) encryption between XenApp and clients.

MetaFrame XPe and later versions of XenApp include the Secure Gateway. Secure Gateway provides an SSL/TLS Internet gateway between XenApp and clients located on the Internet.

For more information about setting encryption, see the *Secure Gateway for Windows Administrator's Guide*, the *Citrix Presentation Server Administrator's Guide*, and the administrator's guides for the XenApp Client.

SMART CARD DEPLOYMENT

Smart card logon is a strong form of authentication because it uses cryptographically based identification and proof of possession when authenticating a user to a domain. Malicious users who obtain someone's password can use the password to assume that person's identity on the network. Many users choose passwords that they can remember easily, which make passwords inherently weak and open to dictionary attack.

In the case of smart cards, that same malicious person would have to obtain the user's smart card and personal identification number (PIN) to impersonate the user. This combination is obviously more difficult to attack because an additional layer of information is needed to impersonate a user. A further benefit is that smart cards lock after a PIN is entered incorrectly a small number of times in a row (for example, three times). This makes a dictionary attack against a smart card extremely difficult.

Enabling Smart Card Support

The following is a list of the minimum requirements to support smart card use:

- PC/SC software
- Cryptographic service provider (CSP) software
- Smart card reader software drivers

Installing a Smart Card Reader

Smart card readers generally come with instructions on how to connect any necessary cables and software. The following steps can assist you in this process, but the process may differ, depending on the type of card reader and vendor. You can access additional information by referencing the following Microsoft support article: http://www.microsoft.com/technet/prodtechnol/windows2000serv/howto/smrtcard.mspx#EDAA.

To connect a smart card reader, follow these steps:

1. Shut down and turn off your computer.
2. Attach the reader to an available serial port or universal serial bus (USB) port.

NOTE Some vendors require that a USB reader be inserted during the smart card reader device driver installation. Reference the reader's documentation to determine the correct method.

   If your serial reader has a supplementary PS/2 cable/connector, attach your keyboard or mouse connector to it and plug it into your computer's keyboard or mouse port. Many new smart card readers take power from the keyboard or mouse ports because a power supply is not always provided by RS-232 ports and it is both expensive and cumbersome to require a separate power supply.

3. Boot your machine and log on as a user with administrative privileges.

Installing a Smart Card Reader Device Driver

If the smart card reader has been detected and installed, the Welcome to Windows logon screen will acknowledge this. If not, then your smart card reader is not a plug-and-play device. If your smart card reader is not a plug-and-play device, media that contain the appropriate device driver from the vendor of the smart card reader are required.

Configuring a Certificate Authority

A certificate authority (CA) is a service that issues the certificates needed to run a Public Key Infrastructure (PKI). The CA could be an external commercial CA or it could be a CA run by your company. The certificates enable a user to log on using a smart card, send encrypted e-mail, code-sign documents, and more. Because a CA is an important trust point in an organization, most organizations have their own CA.

Microsoft Windows 2000 provides two types of CAs: enterprise and standalone. The policy modules selected during installation determine which CA type is used. Within these classes are two types of CAs: a *root* or a *subordinate*. Typically, you should install an *enterprise CA* if you are issuing certificates to users or computers inside an organization that is part of a Windows 2000 domain. You should install a *standalone CA* if you are issuing certificates to users or computers outside a Windows 2000 domain. An enterprise CA requires that all users requesting certificates have an entry in the Windows 2000 Server Active Directory services, whereas a standalone CA does not. Also, an enterprise CA can issue certificates used to log on to a Windows 2000–based domain, whereas a standalone CA cannot. You can find additional information by referencing Microsoft Knowledge Base support article 231881 (http://support.microsoft.com/default.aspx?scid=kb;EN-US;231881).

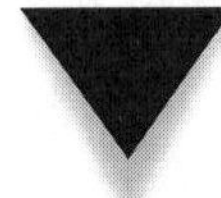

NOTE The configuration steps may vary slightly between Windows 2000 and Windows 2003.

To configure a CA, follow these steps:

1. Click Start | Settings | Control Panel.
2. Double-click Add/Remove Programs.
3. Click Add/Remove Windows Components to start the Windows Components Wizard.
4. Select the Certificate Services check box and click Next.
5. If you intend to use the web components of the Certificate Services, ensure that the IIS check box is selected.
6. The wizard prompts you to specify the type of CA that you want to install. Set up attempts to guess which option is selected to make installation simpler:
   - If no Active Directory is detected, the two enterprise options are disabled.
   - If an Active Directory is detected, the Enterprise root CA option is selected if no CAs are already registered in the Active Directory.
   - If CAs are registered in the Active Directory, the Enterprise subordinate CA option is selected.
7. If you are issuing certificates to entities in your organization or if you need to have seamless integration with the Active Directory or to enable smart card logon, select one of the following enterprise CA options:
   - **Enterprise root CA** This option is appropriate if you do not have any CAs in your directory or if you need a second enterprise root CA. The root CA is registered in the directory, and all computers in your enterprise using that directory automatically trust the root CA. A good security practice is to limit the root CA to issuing certificates to subordinate CAs only, or to issuing only a few special-purpose certificates. Thus, you want to install an enterprise subordinate CA after you finish installing the root CA. However, you can choose only the root CA.
   - **Enterprise subordinate CA** This choice is suitable if you have already installed an enterprise root CA. Typically, you will have multiple enterprise subordinate CAs. Each of these CAs either serves different communities of users or provides different types of certificates. If more than one subordinate exists, it is possible to revoke the subordinate's certificate in case of a disaster and not have to reissue all certificates in the organization.

8. If you are issuing certificates to entities outside your enterprise, and you do not want to use Active Directory or other Windows 2000 PKI features, then you want a standalone CA. Select one of the following:
   - **Standalone CA** Choose this option if you do not already have a standalone CA or if you need a second root for a purpose different than the first.
   - **Standalone subordinate CA** This option is appropriate if the CA will be a member of an existing CA hierarchy. The parent CA in the hierarchy can be a standalone CA, an enterprise CA, or an external commercial CA.
9. If you need to change the default cryptographic settings, select the Advanced Options check box. (Select Advanced Options only if you know how to change cryptographic settings.) Click Next.
10. If you selected Advanced Options, the wizard prompts you to specify the CSP to use. (If you did not select Advanced Options, proceed to step 11.)
11. In this dialog box, you can change the cryptographic settings, such as the CSP, hash algorithm, and other advanced options. In general, you do not need to modify the default settings. Users who need to modify these settings must be familiar with cryptography, Certificate Server, and the CAPI 2.0 architecture.
12. The list of CSPs varies, depending on the software and hardware installed on the server. The key length specifies the length of the public and private key pair. A value of Default key length setting box generates a key pair whose default length is determined by the selected provider. Microsoft recommends you use a long key length, such as 1024 or 2048, for a root CA or an enterprise CA. (A long key length is computationally more expensive and may not be accepted by all hardware devices. For example, some smart cards may not accept certificates issued by a CA that has a 4096 bit key, due to space limitations on the card.)
13. The Use existing keys option enables you to use keys generated previously or to reuse keys from a previously installed CA. When installing a CA, you should almost never reuse keys. The exception to this is when you are restoring a CA after a catastrophic failure. Then you import a set of existing keys and install a new CA that uses those keys. In addition, if you are restoring a CA after a failure, you must select the Use the associated certificate check box. This ensures that the new CA has a certificate identical to the old CA. If you do not check this box, a new certificate is generated that makes the new CA different from the old CA.

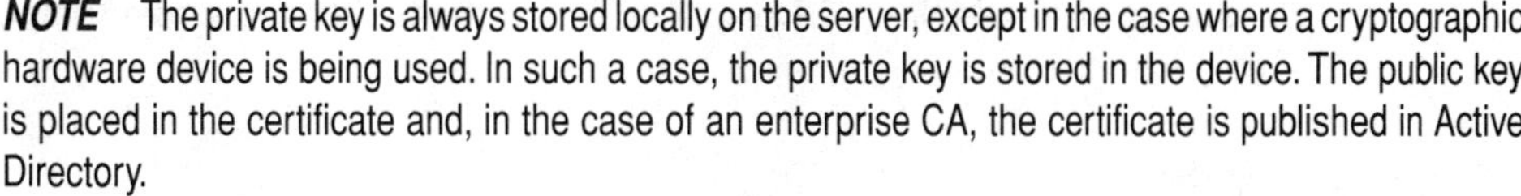

NOTE The private key is always stored locally on the server, except in the case where a cryptographic hardware device is being used. In such a case, the private key is stored in the device. The public key is placed in the certificate and, in the case of an enterprise CA, the certificate is published in Active Directory.

14. The wizard prompts you to supply identifying information appropriate for your site and organization.
15. The CA name (or common name) is critical because it is used to identify the CA object created in the directory. The Valid For time can only be set for a root CA. Set the root CA Valid For time to a reasonable value; the actual duration is a trade-off between security and administrative overhead. Remember that each time a root certificate expires, an administrator has to update all trust relationships and administrative steps need to be taken to move the CA to a new certificate. A time period of two or more years is usually sufficient. When you finish entering the information, click Next.
16. A dialog box defines the locations of the certificate database, configuration information, and the location where the certificate revocation list (CRL) is stored. The enterprise CA always stores its information, including the CRL, in the directory. The recommendation is that you select the Shared Folder check box. This option specifies the location of a folder where configuration information for the CA will be stored. You should make this folder a Universal Naming Convention (UNC) path and have all your CAs point to the same folder. Then the administration tools can use this folder for determining CA configuration if the Active Directory is unavailable. If you have an Active Directory, this folder is optional. If you do not have an Active Directory, this folder is required.
17. If you are installing a CA in the same location as a previously installed CA, the Preserve existing certificate database option is enabled. Check this option if you want your new CA to use this database. Otherwise, the database will be deleted.
18. When you have specified the storage locations for your information, click Next.
19. If Internet Information Server (IIS) is running, a message prompts you to stop the service. Click OK to stop IIS. You must stop IIS to install the web components. If you do not have IIS installed, you will not see this message.
20. If you are installing a subordinate CA, the wizard next prompts you for information about how you will request the certificate.
21. Click Browse to locate an online CA, or select the "Save the request to a file" option if you will be making a request destined for a commercial CA or a CA that is inaccessible from the network. (If you create a file, you must take the file to a CA for processing. The CA provides you with a certificate, which you install using the Microsoft Management Console [MMC] snap-in.) Click Next.
22. If you saved a certificate request to a file, a dialog box called Microsoft Certificate Services displays. Click OK to finish the installation, and then click Finish to close the wizard.

Smart Card Certificate Enrollment

A domain user cannot enroll for a smart card logon (authentication) or smart card user (authentication plus e-mail) certificate unless an SA has granted the user access rights to the Certificate Template stored in Active Directory. This is done because enrollment for a smart card certificate must be a controlled procedure in the same manner that employee badges are controlled for identification and physical access purposes. The recommended method for enrolling users for smart card–based certificates and keys is through the enroll-on-behalf-of station that is integrated with Certificate Services.

When an enterprise CA is installed, the installation includes the enroll-on-behalf-of station. This station lets an administrator act on behalf of a specific user to request and install a smart card logon or smart card user certificate onto the user's smart card. The enrollment station does not provide any card-personalization functions, such as creating a file structure or setting the PIN, because those are card-specific functions and can be performed only using specialized software provided by the smart card manufacturer. You can find additional information by referencing Microsoft Knowledge Base support article 257480 (http://support.microsoft.com/default.aspx?scid=kb;en-us;257480).

To enroll for a smart card logon or smart card user certificate on behalf of a specific user, the administrator must follow this procedure:

1. Launch Microsoft Internet Explorer.
2. To connect to a CA, type **http://machine-name/certsrv** into the Address field of Microsoft Internet Explorer (IE) (where *machine-name* is the name of the computer running the issuing CA).
3. The Microsoft Certificate Services Welcome page appears. Copy the URL address of this page and then click Tools | Internet Options. Select the Security tab, click Trusted Sites, and then click the Sites button. The Trusted Sites window will display; paste the URL in the "Add this web site to the zone" section and uncheck the check box at the bottom, "Requires server verification (HTTPS) for all sites in this zone." Once you have done this, click OK to close the Trusted Sites window, and then click OK again to close the Internet Options windows.

NOTE If this step is not taken, you will receive an error message saying the browser was unable to load an ActiveX control.

4. Select Request a certificate, and then click Next.
5. The Choose Request Type page appears. Select Advanced request, and then click Next.
6. The Advanced Certificate Requests page appears. Select "Request a certificate for a smart card on behalf of another user" using the Smart Card Enrollment Station, and click Next.

7. The first time you use the Smart Card Enrollment Station, a digitally signed Microsoft ActiveX control is downloaded from the CA server to the enrollment station computer. To use the enrollment station, select Yes in the Security Warning dialog box to install the control.
8. The Smart Card Enrollment Station page appears. On this page, you must complete the following before submitting a certificate request on behalf of another user:
   - Select either the Smart Card Logon or Smart Card User Certificate Template.
   - Select a Certification Authority.
   - Select a Cryptographic Service Provider.
   - Select an administrator signing certificate.
   - Select the user to enroll.
   - Complete the first three items by selecting each item from the drop-down list boxes on the Smart Card Enrollment Station page.
9. After selecting the Certificate Template, Certification Authority, and Cryptographic Service Provider, select the administrator signing certificate by clicking Select Certificate. A dialog box appears showing a list of certificates that can be used. Choose only one certificate from the list (if more than one certificate is displayed) and then click OK. Optionally, you can view the certificate by clicking View Certificate. Clicking Cancel results in no certificate being selected.
10. Select the user who is being enrolled for the certificate. Click Select User. Click OK to complete.
11. You are now ready to submit the certificate request. Click Enroll.
12. If the target smart card is not already in the smart card reader, a dialog box appears, prompting you to insert the requested smart card. Once the card is inserted into the smart card reader, click the Retry button.
13. As part of the certificate enrollment procedure, the request must be digitally signed by the private key that corresponds to the public key included in the certificate request. Because the private key is stored on the smart card, the digital signature requires the signer of the request to authenticate the card to ensure that the signer is the owner of the smart card (and, by extension, of the private key). Type in the PIN for the card and then click OK.

Also, the user can change his or her PIN by clicking Change. This opens a new dialog box where the user can input a new alphanumeric PIN. Changing the PIN requires that the user provide the old PIN first to prove ownership of the card. If the CA successfully processes the certificate request, the Smart Card Enrollment Station page informs you that the enrollment is complete and the smart card is ready. You can either view the certificate by clicking View Certificate or specify a new user by clicking New User.

Smart Card Removal Options

You can enable two options for smart card removal. The first option locks the computer when a smart card is removed. The second option logs you off the workstation when you remove a smart card. You can find additional information by referencing Microsoft Knowledge Base support article 227873 (http://support.microsoft.com/default.aspx?scid=kb;en-us;227873).

To enable either of these options, set the data value of the ScRemoveOption value in the following registry key:

```
HKEY_LOCAL_MACHINE\SOFTWARE\Microsoft\Windows NT\CurrentVersion\Winlogon
Value: ScRemoveOption (REG_SZ)
Setting:
0 - No action
1 - Lock workstation
2 - Force logoff
```

Miscellaneous

The following are additional points regarding smart cards:

- Default readers and cards supported by Microsoft are listed in the registry under HKEY_LOCAL_MACHINE\software\Microsoft\Cryptography\Calais.
- Windows 2000, Windows XP, and Windows Server 2003 have native support for some smart card readers. To check whether these operating systems support your reader by default, attach the reader to the client and let the OS detect and install the drivers. After a restart of the system, if there is not an option to log on using the smart card, you must install the vendor's software drivers. Also, Windows 2000 Server, Windows XP, and Windows 2003 Server have default CSPs installed for many Schlumberger and GemPlus smart cards.
- The default PIN for GemPlus GemSAFE (identified by the oval shape of its metal contact) is 1234.
- The default PIN for Schlumberger Cryptoflex (identified by the square shape of its metal contact) is 00000000.
- If a Domain Controller is unavailable, smart card logon fails, even if the user has previously logged on to the computer using a smart card. If the Domain Controller is available, but does not have a valid CRL for the issuing CA, then the logon fails. The error message in each of the previous cases is the same: "The system could not log you on. Your credentials could not be verified."
- Insert the smart card into the smart card reader and enter your PIN. Unlock works the same way as a smart card logon.

AGENT SECURITY FOR CITRIX PASSWORD MANAGER

This section focuses on security concerns for the Citrix Password Manager Agent, otherwise known as the *client-side installation*.

MMF File

The *Username.MMF file* is a binary file that stores the following agent information:

- Agent settings
- Application credentials
- Application credentials that have been deleted from Logon Manager
- Excluded web sites
- Transmit information

The MMF file can be found at the following locations within the Windows user profile:

- **Windows Vista** Users\%Username%\AppData\Roaming\Citrix\MetaFrame Password Manager
- **Windows 2000, Windows 2003, and Windows XP** Documents and Settings\%Username%\ApplicationData\Citrix\MetaFrame Password Manager
- **Windows 2000 and Windows XP—Hot Desktop** Documents and Settings\All Users\Application Data\Citrix\MetaFrame Password Manager\%Username%
- **Windows NT 4** \%SystemRoot%\Profiles\%Username%\Application Data\Citrix\MetaFrame Password Manager

The permissions for the MMF file are

- Administrators—Full Control
- System account—Full Control
- The user—Full Control

The agent updates the synchronization point with the information stored in the MMF file, and vice versa, if Admin/Application overrides are pushed from the console to the synchronization point. If the MMF file is deleted from the user's Windows profile, the agent utilizes the user data cached at the synchronization point to re-create the file. The latest information is always available at the synchronization point because the file cannot be deleted while the agent is running and the agent synchronizes during shutdown.

However, the previous scenario will not be true if the agent is unable to synchronize for prolonged periods of time—for example, if the agent is off the network or synchronization cannot be established. For this reason, the recommendation is that a user back up the file frequently to avoid loss of data. If the user's system were to have a drive failure, the credentials that were added while offline cannot be recovered. Any attempts to manually re-create the file result in the agent not storing new credentials and behaving erratically.

Method of Encryption

The agent uses Triple-DES (Data Encryption Standard) for encryption and the end result can be verified in the following location:

HKEY_CURRENT_USER\Software\Citrix\MetaFrame Password Manager\Shell\CSP

The value should be 6464 (Hex) or 25700 (Decimal).

Delete User's Data Folder and Registry Keys When the Agent Is Shut Down (Previously DeleteOn-Shutdown) as a Security Mechanism

"Delete user's data folder and registry keys when the agent is shut down" (previously DeleteOn-Shutdown) can be used by an administrator to make the agent more secure. When enabled, this setting removes specific files and registry keys from a user's profile and from HKEY_CURRENT_USER.

You should consider enabling "Delete user's data folder and registry keys when the agent is shut down" when a high number of users use the same computer or when physical security concerns exist.

Location of Files

The following paths and registry keys, based on the client operating system, will have content removed when you use the setting "Delete user's data folder and registry keys when the agent is shut down":

- **Windows Vista** Users\%Username%\AppData\Roaming\Citrix\MetaFrame Password Manager
- **Windows 2000, Windows XP Pro, and Windows 2003** Documents and Settings\%Username%\Application Data\Citrix\MetaFrame Password Manager
- **Windows 2000 and Windows XP Pro—Hot Desktop** Documents and Settings\All Users\Application Data\Citrix\MetaFrame Password Manager\%Username%
- **Windows NT 4.0** %SystemRoot%\Profiles\%Username%\Application Data\Citrix\MetaFrame Password Manager

Files removed by the agent during shutdown from the user's profile include the following:

- **AEList.ini** This file consists of merged applist.ini and entlist.ini files. Agents use aelist.ini to identify and respond to credential and password change requests initiated by applications.
- **ENTList.ini** This file contains the application definitions for Windows, web, and host applications.

- **Username.mmf** This is the local storage file used by the agent.
- **Lock Folder** The folder contains a lock file that tracks changes made to the MMF file.
- **FTUList.ini** This file contains the administrator-created questions and bulk-add information.
- **Registry.mmf** This file contains the registry information normally found at HKEY_CURRENT_USER\Software\Citrix\MetaFrame Password Manager. This file is only present on a Hot Desktop–enabled workstation.

Registry keys removed by the agent during shutdown from HKEY_CURRENT_ USER include HKEY_CURRENT_USER\Software\Citrix\MetaFrame Password Manager.

NOTE This is not the case when you are working with a Hot Desktop–enabled workstation.

USING CONSOLE SETTINGS TO SECURE THE AGENT

Additional settings can be used to secure the agent against a walk-away scenario or when using sensitive applications:

- **Force User to Re-Authenticate before Submitting Application Credentials** This application-specific setting instructs the agent to verify the user. When the setting is enabled, the user is required to re-authenticate with the agent before the agent submits credentials to an application. You can use this setting to prevent a third party from using an authenticated agent's configured credentials. You might use this setting, for example, if users have access to confidential applications such as payroll.
- **Time between Agent Re-Authentication Requests** This setting determines how long the user remains authenticated with the agent. By default, the timer is set to eight hours; however, you can set it to a shorter length of time. Doing so forces the user to re-authenticate frequently and makes it more difficult for a third party to access stored credentials. This setting can be found under the Basic Agent Interaction section of the user configuration.

The agent monitors the Windows Screensaver functionality, which is used to trigger a lockdown event. Depending on how the screensaver options are set, the agent will behave differently during the lockdown process:

- **Windows Screensaver with Password Protected Option Enabled** When the screensaver activates, the workstation is placed in a lockdown mode. Unlocking the workstation also unlocks the agent because the agent's GINA monitors the unlocking of the workstation and passes the same credentials to the agent.

▲ **Windows Screensaver with Password Protected Option Disabled** When the screensaver activates, the agent continues to run, but it does not provide credentials to any applications that might run in the background. Any input from the user disables the screensaver and allows the agent, once again, to provide credentials without requiring the user to re-authenticate.

CONFIGURING CITRIX PASSWORD MANAGER ADMINISTRATIVE ACCESS WITHOUT BEING A DOMAIN ADMINISTRATOR

This section discusses the process for delegating administration of a Citrix Password Manager central store to a group or user account that is not a domain administrator. By default, Password Manager installation assumes that the Password Manager administrator is also a domain administrator. When that assumption is not true, this information can be used as a guide to set up the necessary permissions for the Password Manager Administrator account to operate as a delegate.

This section's discussion assumes that you have created a Password Manager Administrator account or Password Manager Administrators group that contains the user accounts with administrative permissions. That user or group is granted permissions to configure, maintain, and manage a Password Manager deployment. Because groups allow for easier management, the Password Manager Administrator user or group is collectively referred to as the Password Manager Administrators group throughout the remainder of this section.

Configuring Access to the Central Store

The central store repository is divided into two areas: the synchronization area and the administrative data area. The *synchronization area* is a location that the agents contact to obtain agent settings and also store their encrypted credentials. By default, the *synchronization location* is secured so only Password Manager administrators and the individual user can access the data. The *administrative data area* is a central location where the console stores the administrative configurations used to create the agent settings for the users, including application definitions, password policies, identity verification, and so forth. By default, the administrative data location is secured to allow only Password Manager administrators access to the folder.

The set of delegation steps depend on where your central store resides. The following describes the configuration and setup for both types of central store hosts (NTFS file share or Microsoft Active Directory).

NTFS File Share

The configuration for access to the central store when using a NTFS File Share is detailed here.

Storage Structure With a file share host, up to three folders are used to store the different areas of the central store repository. These folders are found in the root of the central store share. The synchronization location is kept in a folder called People in the root of the central store share. Under the People folder, each user has his or her own folder with appropriate permissions for reading and writing that user's credential data. The administrators have permissions to add and remove agent settings from the individual user's folders.

The administrative data are kept in a folder called CentralStoreRoot in the root of the central store share. By default, only administrators have permissions to read and write data within the CentralStoreRoot folder.

The domain hierarchy data are kept in a folder named using the NetBIOS name of the domain. This folder is only present when using NT or Active Directory domains for primary authentication with the file share and contains the user configuration settings when they are assigned to organizational units or individual users. The folder contains subfolders that are named using the Security ID (SID) of the Organizational Unit (OU) or user to which the settings should be applied. By default, only administrators have permissions to read and write data within the domain folder. Users have read permissions for this folder, so they can locate the settings that apply to them.

Depending on the type of file share host, the types of permissions granted will be different.

By default, no permissions are allowed to propagate from root share to the child folders CentralStoreRoot and People. However, permissions assigned at the root folder are allowed to propagate to the domain folder. The *CTXFILESYNCPREP tool* automatically grants Full Control to the local Administrators group for both the CentralStoreRoot and People subfolders, and it removes all permissions for authenticated users. No other folders are created by CTXFILESYNCPREP.

The Password Manager agent is responsible for creating all the subfolders inside the People folder and, on creation, sets the permissions of the folder to modify for the Creator/Owner and enables inheritable permissions to propagate from the parent folder.

All remaining folders in the central store repository are created by the Password Manager Console during use, as necessary. The console creates the CentralStoreRoot/AdminConsole folder during discovery and, if an NT or AD domain is used, it creates a folder in the root of the central store share. The console automatically grants the current user modify permissions for every folder created and leaves the propagation flag for inheritance enabled.

Delegation Setup Although local and domain administrators are configured by the Citrix prep tools to have write access to the appropriate folders, any additional accounts need to have permissions explicitly granted to them. For the most part, granting the permissions at the appropriate level allows access to the Password Manager Administrator account. To grant permissions, follow these steps:

1. Run CTXFILESYNCPREP to create the root share and the two subfolders People and CentralStoreRoot. If the folders are already created, proceed to the next step.

2. Grant the Password Manager Administrator account Full Control of the root share folder and both the subfolders inside the shared folder (CentralStoreRoot and People).
3. Log in as a Password Manager administrator and launch the console. This causes all subsequent folders and objects to be created with the appropriate Password Manager administrator permissions automatically.
4. Verify that the appropriate permissions are added to the AdminConsole folder.

Further Delegation You may want to delegate or control permissions further by individually modifying the permissions on the appropriate folders within the file folder hierarchy. Be aware that the access permissions do not take effect until the user logs off and logs back on again and then relaunches the console. In addition, each time that the Password Manager administrator's permissions change, the Password Manager administrator should rerun discovery to refresh the object cache and display only objects to which the user has access. If the Password Manager administrator chooses not to run discovery, the access permissions are still enforced because the Password Manager Console verifies permissions before each read or write from the console.

Active Directory

The configuration for access to the central store when using Active Directory is detailed here.

Schema Preparation The schema preparation tool, CTXSCHEMAPREP.EXE, must still be run by a member of the Schema Administrators group for the target forest. The CTXSCHEMAPREP.EXE tool adds several classes and attributes to the forest schema, allowing Password Manager to store user configuration data and encrypted credential information as objects inside Active Directory.

Domain Preparation The domain preparation tool, CTXDOMAINPREP.EXE, must still be run by a member of the Domain Administrators group for the target domain.

When run without specifying a location, CTXDOMAINPREP affects the entire domain. However, if necessary, the tool can be run on a per-OU basis. To prepare only an individual OU, provide the relative distinguished name of the OU on the command line following the executable name. For example, to apply the permissions to the Users container, use the following command:

```
CTXDOMAINPREP CN=Users
```

Note the full distinguished name (CN=Users, DC=Example, or DC=com) is not used because the tool automatically appends the distinguished name for the domain. If you run this command for more than one OU within the domain, you may receive a message indicating a previous installation was found. This is normal behavior, as the tool expects to create the central store location each time it is executed.

Storage Structure With an Active Directory host for the central store repository, the synchronization and domain hierarchy data are stored in the individual containers for users and organizational units. The administrative data are stored in an application data partition found under the domain root and can be viewed using ADSI Edit (available from www.microsoft.com) by opening the appropriate domain and navigating down the following containers: Program Data, Citrix, MetaFrame Password Manager, and CentralStoreRoot.

For Password Manager Administrator access, the administrator needs the appropriate permissions to the following containers:

- CN=CentralStoreRoot, CN=MetaFrame Password Manager, CN=Citrix, and CN= Program Data
- OU containers to be managed
- User containers to be managed

By default, "Allow inheritable permissions from parent to propagate to this object" is set for all objects in the Program Data, MetaFrame Password Manager, and CentralStore-Root containers. Therefore, any permissions delegated at the root of the Program Data container flow down to the CentralStoreRoot container.

The CTXDOMAINPREP tool assigns Full Control to the Domain Administrators group and System account, restricts authenticated users to read permissions, and allows the Self account to create and delete Citrix SSO objects. For more information on the exact permissions assigned, see the *Password Manager Administrator's Guide*.

NOTE By design, the Domain Administrator account has "Allow inheritable permissions from parent to propagate to this object" disabled. This setting prevents the domain administrator from using Automatic Key Recovery and Self-Service Password Reset functionality.

Delegation Setup All administrators accessing the central store need the same set of permissions. In an environment with multiple administrators, the recommended method is to create a Password Manager Administrators group with permissions for the central store. After creating the Password Manager Administrators group, assign the necessary central store permissions by following these steps:

1. Using ADSI Edit, navigate to the Citrix | Program Data | MetaFrame Password Manager | CentralStoreRoot container.
2. Right-click and choose Context | Properties.
3. Select the Security tab.
4. Click Advanced.
5. Click Add and enter the Password Manager Administrators group in the Name field.

6. Set the Apply Onto field to "This object and all child objects."
7. Select the Allow check box for the following permission:
   - Full
8. Click OK to close the Permission Entry dialog box.
9. Click OK to close the Access Control Setting dialog box.
10. Click OK to close the CentralStoreRoot properties dialog box.
11. Add all user accounts that need to administer Password Manager to the Password Manager Administrators group.

Delegated Permissions For each user account that will be a Password Manager Administrator, you must delegate control of the domain, OUs, or user accounts that the Password Manager Administrators will manage. Remember, if the user account will manage all user accounts or domain-level settings, they need to have control delegated at the root of the domain. To delegate permissions for a user or group account, follow these steps:

1. Using ADSI Edit, navigate to the OU or domain object for the delegated permissions.
2. Right-click the OU or domain name (for domain-level permissions) and select Properties.
3. Select the Security tab.
4. Click Advanced.
5. Click Add and enter the Password Manager Administrator's account in the Name field that will have administrator permissions for this OU or domain, and then click OK.
6. Set the Apply Onto field to "This object and all child objects."
7. Select the Allow check box for each of the following permissions:
   - Create citrix-SSOConfig Objects
   - Delete citrix-SSOConfig Objects
   - Create citrix-SSOLicense Class Objects
   - Delete citrix-SSOLicense Class Objects
8. Click OK.
9. Click Add and enter the Password Manager Administrator's account in the Name field that will have administrator permissions for this OU or domain, and then click OK.
10. Set the **Apply Onto** field to: "**citrix-SSOSecret objects**"
11. Select the **Allow** checkbox for Modify Owner

12. Click **OK**
13. Click **Add** and enter the Password Manager Administrator's account in the **Name** field that will have administrator permissions for this OU or domain and then click **OK**.
14. Set the Apply Onto field to "User objects."
15. Select the Allow check box for Full Control.
16. Click OK.
17. To grant Full Control for the Citrix objects, repeat steps 13 through 15, changing the Apply Onto field from "User objects" to each of the following object types:
    - citrix-SSOConfig objects
    - citrix-SSOSecret objects
18. Click OK to close the Access Control Setting dialog box.
19. Click OK to close the OU Properties dialog box.

NOTE The Active Directory Users & Computers MMC Snap-in does not provide access to all the Citrix class objects. The previous steps need to be completed using ADSI Edit. Also, in testing, it was discovered that the Delegate Control Wizard may not properly assign the correct permissions, so using ADSI Edit is recommended.

Further Delegation You can delegate permissions further by granting granular access to the individual objects within the central store and the individual OUs as necessary. When modifying permissions, remember that the administrators should run discovery to obtain the latest list of objects in the central store along with their associated permissions.

Running the Console

Launching the console as the Password Manager Administrator's account for the first time causes all objects to inherit the permissions from the original CentralStoreRoot folder. When running the console with a delegated administrator, remember that the current user must have access to all the locations and containers where an object is stored or the update will fail. This means that delegated administrators cannot update global objects (such as the Identity Verification Question) unless they have access to all the user accounts and OUs where the global object is used.

CAUTION The Citrix Password Manager Console only checks permissions on the CentralStore object before performing the delete. If the administrative user does not have permissions to delete user objects in the OU, the object is left in the OU and removed from the central store.

Using the ADT as a Password Manager Administrator

The console automatically uses the credentials of the logged-in user for access to Active Directory. The same permissions for the full Access Management Console are also required when accessing the Central Data Store through the Application Definition Tool (ADT). If an application definition is used in deployed Application groups, the Password Manager Administrator needs permissions to write objects to those containers where the application definition is being used.

Configuration of the Password Manager Service

Depending on the modules installed in the Citrix Password Manager Service, you may need to complete different delegation steps. The following discusses each of the modules and the associated changes.

Service Machine

Put the "Password Manager Administors" group in the local administrators group of the machine(s) running the Password Manager Service. This will allow Password Manager Administrators to the administer the service setting, data signing, provisioning, etc.

Data Integrity

When using the Citrix Password Manager Service, you need to grant access to the Password Manager Administrators group to authenticate to the service if the optional Data Integrity Assurance feature is enabled. To grant access for the Password Manager Administrators to sign data settings, complete the following steps:

1. Launch Notepad.
2. Open the httpd.conf file found at %ProgramFiles%\Common Files\Citrix\XTE\conf.
3. Locate the XML section titled Files AuthenticatedWS.asmx.
4. Add another require group statement below the Domain Administrators statement specifying the domain name and the name of the Password Manager Administrators group: require group *DOMAINNAME*\\Password Manager Administrators.
5. Save and close the httpd.conf file.
6. Launch notepad once again, and open the httpd.conf.template file found at %ProgramFiles%\Citrix\MetaFrame Password Manager\Service.
7. Locate the XML section titled **<Files AuthenticatedWS.asmx>**
8. Add another require group statement below the Domain Administrators statement specifying the domain name and the name of the Password Manager Administrators group, like this:

   require group "*DOMAINNAME*\\ Password Manager Administrators"

9. Launch Windows Explorer.
10. Navigate to %ProgramFiles%\Citrix\MetaFrame Password Manager\Service\Certificates.
11. Highlight **both** PrivateKeyCert.cert and PublicKeyCert.cert, right click, and choose **Properties**.

    Navigate to the Security tab, and give Full permissions to the "Password Manager Administrators" group.

CAUTION The ServiceConfigurationTool.exe automatically replaces the httpd.conf file each time that it is used to make changes to the service configuration. Manually complete the previous steps after using the Service Configuration tool to make changes to the Password Manager Service.

Provisioning

When using the Citrix Password Manager Service, you will need to grant access to the Password Manager Administrators group to authenticate to the service if the optional Provisioning Service feature is enabled. To grant access for the Password Manager Administrators to provision credentials, complete the following steps:

1. Launch Notepad.
2. Open the **httpd.conf** file found at %ProgramFiles%\Common Files\Citrix\XTE\conf.
3. Locate the XML section titled **<Files ProvisionSvc.asmx>**.
4. Add another require group statement below the Domain Administrators statement specifying the domain name and the name of the Password Manager Administrators group, like this:

    require group "*DOMAINNAME*\\ Password Manager Administrators "
5. Save and close the httpd.conf file.
6. Launch notepad once again, and open the httpd.conf.template file found at %ProgramFiles%\Citrix\MetaFrame Password Manager\Service.
7. Locate the XML section titled **<Files ProvisionSvc.asmx>**.
8. Add another require group statement below the Domain Administrators statement specifying the domain name and the name of the Password Manager Administrators group, like this:

    require group "*DOMAINNAME*\\CPM Password Manager Administrators"

Automatic Key Recovery

If the deployment includes using the Password Manager Service for Automatic Key Recovery, you need to configure a data proxy account that has access to the central store and all the OUs that contain the Password Manager user accounts. Adding the data proxy account to the Password Manager Administrators group grants access to the central store. You then need to delegate control to the data proxy account at the appropriate domain level, OU level, or shared folder resource by completing the steps in the delegation section for appropriate central store type.

In the file share environment, the data proxy account should have the following permissions:

- Configure the data proxy account to be a regular Domain User.
- Give the user Full Control permissions to the central store as follows:
  - For the CitrixSync$ folder (root), give Full Control for Share permissions to this user.
  - For the CitrixSync folder (root), give Full Control for NTFS permissions to this user.
  - For the CentralStoreRoot, give Full Control for NTFS permissions to this user.
  - The *Domain Name* folder inherits Full Control from the Parent folder, so no changes are needed here.
  - For the People folder, give Full Control for NTFS permissions to this user.

In the Active Directory environment, you grant the data proxy account the appropriate permissions by completing the steps outlined in the previous section "Delegated Permissions" for the data proxy account.

Self-Service Password Reset

If the deployment includes using the Password Manager Service for Self-Service Password Reset, you need to configure a data proxy account that has access to the central store and all the OUs that contain the Password Manager user accounts.

Adding the data proxy account to the Password Manager Administrators group grants access to the central store. You then need to delegate control to the data proxy account at the appropriate domain-level, OU-level, or shared folder resource by completing the steps in the delegation section for appropriate central store type.

In the file share environment, the data proxy account should be a member of the Local Administrator's group on the server hosting the file share. In the Active Directory environment, the data proxy account is granted the appropriate permissions by completing the previously outlined steps in the section "Delegated Permissions" for the data proxy account.

Password Reset Account

For most deployments, the data proxy accounts have Full Control of user objects and can be used as the Password Reset account. However, if you require a separate, more restricted account, you can follow the preceding steps to grant the minimum necessary permissions to the Password Reset Account in Active Directory:

1. Using ADSI Edit, navigate to the OU or domain object for the delegated permissions. (The domain object is recommended for password reset.)
2. Right-click on the OU or domain name (for domain-level permissions) and select Properties.
3. Select the Security tab.
4. Click Advanced.
5. Click Add. Enter the Password Reset account in the Name, and then click OK.
6. Set the Apply Onto field to "User objects."
7. Select the Allow check box for the following permissions:
   - Reset Password
   - Read PwdLastSet
   - Write PwdLastSet
   - Read Lockout Time
   - Write Lockout Time
   - Read ntPwdHistory
   - Write ntPwdHistory
8. Click OK to close the Permissions dialog box.
9. Click OK to close the Access Control Setting dialog box.
10. Click OK to close the OU Properties dialog box.

Use the ServiceConfiguration tool executable to modify the Password Reset account. Remember that if Data Integrity Assurance is enabled, the httpd.conf file needs to be modified again to add the Password Manager Administrators group. When complete, restart the Citrix XTE Service.

Citrix Password Manager Support for Strong Authentication

Table 10-1 shows the smart cards tested with Citrix Password Manager.

BROWSER SECURITY CONSIDERATIONS FOR ADVANCED ACCESS CONTROL

Certain custom web browser security settings can prevent users from accessing Advanced Access Control. Therefore, follow these guidelines to ensure that users can access the appropriate servers within your network.

Vendor	Products	Form Factor	Tested in 4.5	Tested in 4.6	Tested in 4.1	Tested in 4.1 with Ilot Desktop
ActivCard Gold for DOD / CAC - PKI 3.0	Axalto/Schlumberger Card Readers: *Reflex 72 Reader Reflex USB	Smart card	✓			
ActivClient—DOD/CAC PKI 5.0	ActivCard—64KB V1 Readers: *ActivCard Reader V2.0	Smart card	✓	✓		
ActivCard 5.4	ActivCard—64KB V1 Readers: *ActivCard Reader V2.0	Smart card			✓	✓
Alladin	eToken	USB-based tokens	✓			
Axalto/Schlumberger	CyberFlex Version 2 Card Axalto/Schlumberger Readers: *Reflex 72 Reader *Reflex USB	Smart card	✓	✓	✓	✓
Ensure Technologies	XyLoc Enterprise 3.x XyLoc MD 3.*x* Xyloc XC-2	Proximity	✓	•	✓	•
Ensure Technologies	XyLoc Solo 7.*x*	Proximity	✓	•		
Gemplus	GemSAFE Logon Card (8KB, 16KB, 32Kb) Readers: *Gemplus Serial GemPC 410 *GemPC 430 USB *GemPC USB-SL	Smartcard	✓	✓	✓	✓
PassGo	Defender v5	Hardware and software tokens		X		X
Precise100MC	Biometric Fingerprint/ Smart Card Reader	Biometric	✓	X		X
RSA	RSA SecureID for Windows 5.X RSA SecureID for Windows 6.X	Token	✓	X	✓	X
Saflink	SafLink/Safe Solution Enterprise SafRemote Authenticator	Biometric	✓	✓	✓	✓
Secure Computing	SafeWord for Citrix MetaFrame 2.0	Token	✓	X	✓	X

Legend: ✓ = tested by Citrix; X = known issues; • = requires vendor modification.

Table 10-1. Tested Smart Card Solutions for Password Manager

For users to access corporate resources properly through Advanced Access Control, the following browser security settings must be enabled:

- **Cookies** Advanced Access Control uses per-session cookies that are not stored on disk. Therefore, third parties cannot access the cookies. Disallowing per-session cookies prevents connections to Advanced Access Control. Users cannot log on to Advanced Access Control because logging on requires a session cookie.
- **File download** Disabling "File download" prevents the downloading of files from the corporate network, the launching of any seamless ICA session, and access to internal web servers outside the XenApp farm.
- **Scripting** Disabling active scripting makes Advanced Access Control inaccessible. Disabling Java applet scripting prevents users from launching published applications with the client for Java.

  Also note the following security setting tips:
- Change the security settings only for zones that contain resources accessed through Advanced Access Control. If you fully trust the sites on your company's intranet, you can set the Local Intranet zone security level to Low. If you do not fully trust the sites on your intranet, keep the Local Intranet zone set to Medium-Low or Medium.
- Several browser security settings required to access Advanced Access Control servers are disabled under the High security setting. Therefore, the security level for the Local Intranet zone is set to High.
- If you not only want to keep the default security settings, but also customize individual security settings of your Advanced Access Control servers, you can configure each server in the access server farm as a trusted site.
- Configuring servers as trusted sites lets you customize their security settings without affecting the Internet and Local Intranet settings.

NOTE If your access server farm requires SSL, make sure that SSL is required for all sites in the Trusted Site zone.

Customizing Browser Security Settings

Table 10-2 lists additional IE browser security settings required for those deployment scenarios requiring client software. Most of these settings are available from the Security tab of the Internet Options dialog box.

Deployment Scenario	Require Settings
Endpoint Analysis Client	Run ActiveX controls and plug-ins (Enable) Script ActiveX controls marked safe for scripting (Enable) File download (Enable)
Live Edit Client	Run ActiveX controls and plug-ins (Enable) Script ActiveX controls marked safe for scripting (Enable) File download (Enable)
Website Viewer CDA (ActiveX mode)	Run ActiveX controls and plug-ins (Enable)
Web Client	Run ActiveX controls and plug-ins (Enable) Script ActiveX controls marked safe for scripting (Enable) File download (Enable) Do not save encrypted pages to disk (Disable)
Client for Java	Java Permissions (High safety or Custom) If you select Custom, set the following options: Run Unsigned Content (Run in sandbox) Run Signed Content (Prompt or Enable) Do not save encrypted pages to disk (Disable All) Additional Signed Permissions must also be set to Prompt or Enable

Table 10-2. Internet Explorer Browser Required Settings for Specific Deployment Scenarios

PART II

XenApp Platinum Edition: Administration, Maintenance, and Troubleshooting

CHAPTER 11

Application Publishing and Deployment

XenApp provides access flexibility by enabling users to utilize published applications and content redirection within Program Neighborhood, Program Neighborhood Agent, and a web browser. Handling application publishing according to the environment and adopting appropriate techniques can simplify maintenance and improve performance. This chapter contains recommendations for publishing application packages (Microsoft System Installer [MSI] file or Installation Manager's application deployment format [ADF]) with Installation Manager, as well as for application deployment considerations with Installation Manager. This chapter also covers working with both content redirection and enhanced content and publishing in the Web Interface for XenApp 4.5.

PUBLISHING APPLICATIONS

This section contains recommendations for publishing packages (MSI) with Installation Manager, environments of thousands of objects, and content redirection.

MSI Considerations with Installation Manager

The following section outlines MSI considerations during deployment of applications using Installation Management.

When you are applying more than one transform file for the same MSI, each file installs different components but applies them to the same MSI package. The selected components from the transforms do not get deployed, even though the installation job reports success.

Recording Microsoft Patch (MSP) packages is unnecessary. You can browse through Installation Manager and add the *.msp file.

You may uninstall an MSP package from the target server, but you cannot uninstall the patch from the server to which it was deployed. If you need to apply another patch to the application installed on the target server, uninstall the application on the target server first and then redeploy the application and patch.

CAUTION When installing many MSI packages with or without Installation Manager, a memory leak may be detected in msiexec.exe. To avoid this issue, install the latest Windows 2000 service pack delivered by Microsoft.

Force Reinstall Option

When a package is scheduled to deploy to a target server, Installation Manager detects whether the package is already installed. If it detects the application, Installation Manager aborts the new installation and returns an Already Installed status. If you need to overwrite an existing installation, set the Force Reinstall option from the properties screen of the already-installed package. This new installation can be used to fix any previously damaged installations or overwrite the existing application of the same version, with changes.

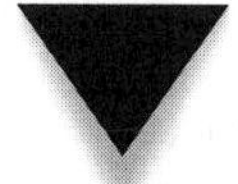

NOTE After you set Force Reinstall to reinstall a package, you cannot use the previous package to uninstall the application from the target server. Uninstall can proceed from only the newly installed package.

After you use Force Reinstall to install the same package, the Installed Packages tab of the target server reports two records for the same package.

Installation Manager Interoperability

Installation Manager, which ships with XenApp, supports packages made using Installation Manager 2.3 shipped with MetaFrame XP Server Feature Release 3, Installation Manager 2.2 shipped with MetaFrame XP Server Feature Release 2, and Installation Manager 2.1 shipped with MetaFrame XP Server Feature Release 1. However, some applications may cause issues with this compatibility. Because of this, Citrix recommends that you re-create the packages using the latest version of Installation Manager. Packages created with earlier versions may have been packaged on servers that did not have the operating system (OS) and other updates that your XenApp farm contains. When recording a package, the source server should have a similar configuration to that of the target servers.

Interaction with Load Manager and Application Publishing

Use the Application Publishing Wizard to add the Installation Manager package to the farm through the Installation Manager node of the Presentation Server Console. The wizard lets you automatically install, publish, and load-balance the applications. Additionally, the command-line utility apputil can be used to add and remove servers from these published packages via scripting, further automating the application installation process. If you use Installation Manager without the wizard, applications are not automatically published or load-balanced. For more information about apputil, see the *Citrix Presentation Server Administrator's Guide.*

NOTE Packages created by earlier versions of Installation Manager may not allow access to this feature.

Uninstall Behavior

By default, a deployed package can only be uninstalled from the original package.

You cannot directly uninstall an ADF package that has a status of Already Installed. Instead, perform another full installation using the Force Reinstall option, which can be used to uninstall the same package. The application can also be uninstalled from target servers locally, without Installation Manager, using Add/Remove Programs.

NOTE If you uninstall from the Already Installed package, the target server will not detect the uninstall and will still report that the MSI package is installed.

Publishing in Domains with Thousands of Objects

XenApp was tested in domains with over 10,000 objects in a single directory services container. A directory services or domain environment that contains a large number of objects, such as Novell Directory Service or Microsoft Active Directory Service, has factors to be considered. Recommendations for this type of environment are as follows:

- Use groups to categorize and easily assign permissions to large numbers of users. An application published to one group of 1,000 users requires XenApp to validate only one object for all 1,000 users. That same application published to 1,000 individual user accounts requires Independent Management Architecture (IMA) to validate 1,000 objects.
- Publish applications with less than 1,000 users or group objects. This practice decreases the application publishing time, because all user and group accounts must be verified. Publishing an application with 10,000 objects may take up to 41 minutes to complete. Although the Presentation Server Console may time out after five minutes, IMA continues to publish the application in the background.
- Use the Add List of Names button instead of scrolling to locate a user when the user's container holds thousands of objects.

Working with the Content Redirection Feature

This section concerns the various scenarios surrounding Content Redirection. Client-to-server, server-to-client, and server-to-server Content Redirection are discussed.

Redirecting Content from Client to Server

When you configure Content Redirection from client to server, users running the Program Neighborhood Agent open all files of the associated type encountered in locally running applications with applications published on the XenApp. You must use the Web Interface to enable users to connect to published applications with the Program Neighborhood Agent.

NOTE Content Redirection from client to server is available only with Citrix XenApp Advanced and Enterprise editions.

The *Program Neighborhood Agent* gets updated properties for published applications from the server running the Web Interface. When you publish an application and associate it with file types, the application's file type association is changed to reference the published application in the client device's Windows registry.

If you have users who run applications such as e-mail programs locally, you can use XenApp's Content Redirection capability with the Program Neighborhood Agent to redirect application launching from client device to XenApp. When a user double-clicks attachments encountered in an e-mail application running locally, the attachment opens in an application published on the XenApp, associated with the corresponding file type, and assigned to the user.

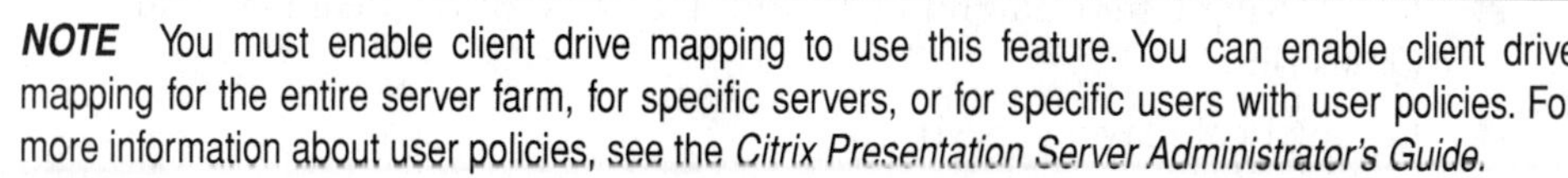

NOTE You must enable client drive mapping to use this feature. You can enable client drive mapping for the entire server farm, for specific servers, or for specific users with user policies. For more information about user policies, see the *Citrix Presentation Server Administrator's Guide.*

If you do not want such redirection to occur for *any* Program Neighborhood Agent users, do not associate the published application with any file types. If you do not want redirection to occur for *specific* Program Neighborhood Agent users, do not assign those users to the published application associated with the file type.

Follow the next procedure to configure Content Redirection from client to server:

1. Determine which of your users connect to published applications using the Program Neighborhood Agent. Content Redirection from client to server applies only to those users connecting with the Program Neighborhood Agent.
2. Verify that client drive mapping is enabled. You can enable client drive mapping for a specific connection using Citrix Connection Configuration or for specific users by creating user policies.
3. Publish applications that you want the Program Neighborhood Agent users to open on XenApp.
4. When you publish the application, associate it with file types on the last page of the Application Publishing Wizard.

Redirecting Content from Server to Client

When you enable Content Redirection from server to client, embedded uniform resource locators (URLs) are intercepted on the XenApp server and sent to the Citrix Client using the ICA Control virtual channel. The user's locally installed browser is used to play the URL. Users cannot disable this feature.

For example, users may frequently access web and multimedia URLs they encounter when running an e-mail program published on XenApp. If you do not enable Content Redirection from server to client, users open these URLs with web browsers or multimedia players present on XenApp.

To free servers from processing these types of requests, you can redirect application launching for supported URLs from XenApp to the local client device.

NOTE If the client device fails to connect to a URL, the URL is redirected back to the server.

The following URL types are opened locally on Windows 32-bit and Linux XenApp Clients when this type of Content Redirection is enabled:

- Hypertext Transfer Protocol (HTTP)
- Secure Hypertext Transfer Protocol (HTTPS)
- Real-Time Streaming Protocol (RTSP) (Real Player and QuickTime)

- RTSP Using User Datagram Protocol (UDP) (RTSPU) (Real Player and QuickTime)
- Legacy Real Player (PNM)
- Microsoft Media Services (MMS) (Microsoft's media format)

NOTE If Content Redirection from server to client is not working for some of the HTTPS links, verify that the client device has an appropriate certificate installed. If the appropriate certificate is not installed, the HTTP ping from the client device to the URL fails and the URL is redirected back to the server. Content Redirection from server to client requires Internet Explorer Version 5.5 with Service Pack 2 or later on systems running Windows 98 or later.

Follow the next procedure to enable Content Redirection from server to client:

1. Determine whether you want Content Redirection from server to client to apply for the entire server farm, for specific XenApp servers, or for specific users only.
2. To apply the behavior to the entire server farm, select the farm in the left pane of Access Management console and from the Action menu, select Modify form properties > Modify all properties. From the Properties list, select Server Default > Presentation Server > Content Redirection. Select the option Content Redirection from Server to Client.
3. To apply the behavior to a specific server, select the server in the left pane of the Access Management console and from the Action menu, select Modify server properties > Modify all properties. From the Properties list, select Presentation Secure > Content Redirection. Select the option Content Redirection from Server to Client.
4. To apply the behavior to specific users, create a user policy and enable the rule Content Redirection from Server to Client. Assign the policy only to those users you want to open supported URL file types on client devices. For more information about user policies, see the *Citrix Presentation Server Administrator's Guide.*

CHAPTER 12

Advanced Multimedia, CPU and Memory Optimization, and Virtual IP Addressing

XenApp provides significant enhancements to an application delivery infrastructure by dramatically improving the speed and subsequent usefulness of multimedia applications. XenApp now also enables TWAIN redirection in addition to many new features around Virtual IP addressing, PDA synchronization, CPU and memory management tools, and multiple monitor support improvements, to name a few. This chapter covers the optimization of SpeedScreen Browser Acceleration, both with Internet Explorer (IE) and with the XenApp Client, including all the previously mentioned improvements.

OPTIMIZING SPEEDSCREEN BROWSER ACCELERATION

This section addresses SpeedScreen Browser Acceleration with Internet Explorer. We will review minimum browser requirements, XenApp Client requirements, and a few registry optimizations.

SpeedScreen Browser Acceleration and Internet Explorer

SpeedScreen Browser Acceleration improves the responsiveness of HTML pages when using Microsoft Outlook, Outlook Express, and IE 5.5 or higher as published applications. With SpeedScreen Browser Acceleration enabled, version 7.0 or later of the XenApp Clients for Win32, and a XenApp connection with a color depth of High Color (16 bit) or greater, the user can scroll the pages and use the Back and Stop buttons immediately while image files download in the background. The following sections provide methods for the MetaFrame administrator to optimize the user's experience further, by controlling the default behavior of SpeedScreen Browser Acceleration through the use of registry value modifications and Independent Computing Architecture (ICA) file settings.

Play Animations in Web Page

When the Play Animations in Web Page feature is enabled, animated GIF images are rendered as animations and SpeedScreen Browser Acceleration support for GIF images is disabled. Citrix recommends disabling this feature. When this feature is disabled, SpeedScreen Browser Acceleration support for GIF images is enabled. The secondary benefit is a further bandwidth reduction due to the absence of animations, which consume significant bandwidth.

XenApp, by default, disables the Play Animations in Web Pages option for all users on the server. The feature is disabled when the user logs in for the first time following the installation of XenApp. If a user subsequently enables the setting, it will not be modified again unless the administrator changes specific values in the registry. For information about the necessary registry changes, see the following section, "Advanced Configuration Information."

You can access this feature by opening IE and selecting Tools | Internet Options | Advanced, or by navigating to Internet Options under the Control Panel.

Advanced Configuration Information

XenApp disables the IE feature Play Animations in Web Pages the first time that a user logs in following the installation of XenApp. This feature is disabled only following the first login.

A registry entry controls the disabling of this feature. The registry value Disable-PlayAnimations is contained in the registry key HKCU\Software\Citrix.

If this value is not present in the registry at login, or is set to the default value of 1, the IE option is automatically disabled for the user. If the value is set to 0, the server does not attempt to disable the feature in the user's session at login, whether or not the feature is currently enabled or disabled in the user's profile.

Administrators may find this information useful when designing logoff scripts. Always having this option disabled at login may be useful, in which case a logoff script can be used to set the registry value to 1.

Configuring SpeedScreen Browser Acceleration on the XenApp Client

There is no Program Neighborhood user interface (UI) control for SpeedScreen Browser Acceleration. SpeedScreen Browser Acceleration settings must be configured in the ICA files. The preferred configuration method is through Web Interface. By default, Speed-Screen Browser Acceleration is enabled on the client for all connections. Note that if either the server or the client has SpeedScreen Browser Acceleration configured to be off, then it will be disabled for that connection.

This section describes the ICA file parameters that can be used to configure Speed-Screen Browser Acceleration. It is divided into two subsections covering basic and advanced settings. Typically, administrators should only need to use the basic settings.

Basic SpeedScreen Browser Acceleration ICA File Settings

The following examples illustrate the basic settings for SpeedScreen Browser Acceleration. You would edit these settings or add them to a standard ICA file.

SpeedScreenBA

- **Usage** SpeedScreenBA=[ON | OFF]
- **Description** Setting SpeedScreenBA=On enables SpeedScreen Browser Acceleration for a connection. Note that the server settings may override SpeedScreenBA=On. Disabling SpeedScreen Browser Acceleration on the server causes this setting to be ignored for a connection. Setting SpeedScreenBA=Off disables SpeedScreen Browser Acceleration for a connection, even if the server setting specifies that SpeedScreen Browser Acceleration is to be enabled.

SpeedScreenBACompressionEnabled

- **Usage** SpeedScreenBACompressionEnabled=[ON | OFF]
- **Description** Setting SpeedScreenBACompressionEnabled=On enables SpeedScreen Browser Acceleration JPEG image compression for a connection. Note that the server settings may override SpeedScreenBACompressionEnabled= On. If the server has disabled JPEG Image compression, then the server setting overrides the client setting. Setting SpeedScreenBACompressionEnabled=Off disables SpeedScreen Browser Acceleration JPEG compression for a connection, even if the server setting specifies that JPEG compression is to be enabled.

Advanced SpeedScreen ICA File Settings

Administrators may utilize the advanced cache file and compression settings of SpeedScreen to optimize SpeedScreen Browser Acceleration for slow connections, servers with limited memory or drive space, or servers with an overabundance of memory or drive space. Usage within the ICA file is as follows:

SpeedScreenBACompressedCacheSize=*value*

SpeedScreenBADecompressedCacheSize=*value*

SpeedScreenBAMaximumCompressionLevel=*value*

SpeedScreenBACompressedCacheSize

- **Usage** SpeedScreenBACompressedCacheSize= *value*
- **Description** SpeedScreen uses a compressed cache to store JPEG and GIF data sent from XenApp. Because these data are cached on the client, pages that are revisited display faster because the server does not retransmit the cached images to the client. The size of the cache determines how long images remain inside the cache and also, generally, the number of images that can fit into the cache. When the cache is filled, images previously added to the cache are removed. The least recently used image is deleted from the cache first. Initially the cache is empty and does not consume memory. As images are added to the cache, the cache grows to accommodate the images. If an image exceeds the maximum compressed cache size, it is not displayed through SpeedScreen.

The *value* parameter is the maximum memory consumption that SpeedScreen uses to store JPEG and GIF image data, measured in kilobytes (KB). The default value for this parameter is 16384KB (16MB). Administrators can use this setting either to limit the maximum memory consumption of the client or to allow higher maximum memory consumption.

Increasing the memory consumption may provide some benefit on slow connections, where the transmission time for images is high. If images remain on the client for a longer duration, then a retransmit of an image is less likely to be necessary.

SpeedScreenBADecompressedCacheSize

- ▼ **Usage** SpeedScreenBADecompressedCacheSize= *value*
- ▲ **Description** SpeedScreen stores the bitmap representations of JPEG and GIF images in a decompressed cache. Because a decompressed cache is used, the JPEG and GIF images do not need to be decompressed each time that they are drawn. Using a decompressed cache provides a significant performance boost when a page is scrolled because a scroll operation results in a number of drawing operations on the same image.

When an image needs to be drawn, it is decompressed and added to the decompressed cache. Images remain in the decompressed cache until more space is required in the cache. Images are deleted from the decompressed cache when the operation of adding a new image could exceed the maximum decompressed cache size. Images can be added and removed from the decompressed cache any number of times while the image is in the compressed cache.

The maximum size of the decompressed cache size determines the maximum dimensions of an image that can be displayed through SpeedScreen. JPEG images require 24bpp (bits per pixel), while GIF images require 8bpp. A larger decompressed cache size allows images with a larger dimension to be displayed. Reducing the size of the decompressed cache reduces the maximum image dimensions that can be displayed.

Images that exceed the maximum decompressed cache size when decompressed are not downloaded to the client at all and are displayed in Legacy mode.

SpeedScreenBAMaximumCompressionLevel

- ▼ **Usage** SpeedScreenBAMaximumCompressionLevel= *value*
- ▲ **Description** The SpeedScreenBAMaximumCompressionLevel ICA file parameter defines the maximum SpeedScreen compression level for a connection. The valid values for this parameter are as follows:

  0 Low compression

  1 Medium compression

  2 High compression

The default value for this parameter is 2 (high compression).

As previously explained, SpeedScreen JPEG image recompression performs a lossy compression on the JPEG images transferred to the client. A higher compression level results in reduced bandwidth consumption, but has the most significant impact on image quality.

The lower of the two compression levels specified on the client and the server is used as the maximum compression level for a connection. Thus, if the client specifies medium compression and the server high, then the maximum compression level used for the connection will be medium compression.

This parameter is ignored if either the client or server indicates that compression is not enabled for a connection.

SPEEDSCREEN BROWSER ACCELERATION LIMITATIONS AND KNOWN ISSUES

This section outlines the known issues and limitations of SpeedScreen Browser Acceleration.

No Support for Transparent GIF Images

SpeedScreen Browser Acceleration does not support transparent GIF images. Transparent GIF images are rendered in Legacy mode.

Images Resized in HTML

The HTML that describes a web page can also specify the width and the height that an image may use. This may be different from the actual width and height of the image. In this case, IE grows or shrinks the image as required to fit it into the size specified in the HTML.

SpeedScreen Browser Acceleration does not support images that are resized using this technique. Images that are resized in HTML are drawn in Legacy mode.

This feature is not the same as the Automatic Image Resizing feature available in IE. *Automatic Image Resizing* refers to the scaling of an image that is larger than the browser display area, so it fits into the display area of the browser.

MEDIA FORMATS SUPPORTED BY SPEEDSCREEN MULTIMEDIA ACCELERATION

This section describes the range of multimedia playback support for SpeedScreen Multimedia Acceleration. Table 12-1 lists a few of the media types that were tested successfully using Windows Media Player 6.4/8.0/9.0 and Real One Player. In general, SpeedScreen Multimedia Acceleration supports all media types that can be decoded by a DirectShow-based codec, regardless of file format. SpeedScreen Multimedia Acceleration is supported when you are connecting from Windows clients.

NOTE Media type differs from the file format. Some examples of file formats are AVI, MPEG, MPG, ASF, WMV, WMA, and MP3.

Media Type (Media Encoding Format)	File Format (File Extension)	Media Player 6.4/8.0/9.0	RealOne Player	QuickTime	DirectShow Based Media Players
DIVX Video	AVI, MPEG,	–	–	X	–
XVID Video	MPG, ASF	–	–	X	–
Microsoft Video 1		–	–	X	–
MPEG-1 Video		–	–	X	–
MPEG-4 Video		–	–	X	–
Indeo Interactive Video		–	–	X	–
MPEG-1 Audio		–	–	X	–
AC3 Audio		–	–	X	–
Fraunhofer MPEG Layer-3 Codec		–	–	X	–
MP3	MP3	_*	X	X	X
WMA	WMA	_*	X	X	X
WMV	WMV	X	X	X	X
Real Media	RM	X	X	X	X
Quick Time	MOV	X	X	X	X

Legend:

_Supported through SpeedScreen Multimedia Acceleration.

X Not supported through SpeedScreen Multimedia Acceleration.

* Supported through SpeedScreen Multimedia Acceleration only when playing through Windows Media Player 9.0. Data are transferred in an uncompressed format.

Table 12-1. File Formats Supported by SpeedScreen Multimedia Acceleration

These file formats can encapsulate various media types, such as those listed in Table 12-1. For example, a single AVI file could contain a DIVX video stream and an AC3 digital audio stream and would need both the DIVX and AC3 DirectShow codecs for proper playback.

NOTE Table 12-1 describes only some of the more popular media types and file formats. As previously stated, in general, SpeedScreen Multimedia Acceleration supports all media types that can be decoded by a DirectShow-based codec, regardless of file format.

Best Practices

The following are best practices regarding multimedia playback:

- Always upgrade the client devices to use the latest version of Microsoft's DirectX software.
- Keep the server's version of Microsoft Windows Media Player upgraded to the latest version/update.
- When publishing audio applications, it is advisable to disable the Windows logon sound event. This is because the Citrix Audio Driver can only be opened one process at a time, and the published application's attempt to open the Citrix Audio Driver could fail because the Windows logon event has exclusive access to the device until the sound has finished playing.
- SpeedScreen Multimedia Acceleration does not support QuickTime, so you should configure SpeedScreen Multimedia Acceleration to use WaveOut instead of DirectSound. This is because Microsoft's DirectSound emulation for Terminal Server is not as efficient as the Citrix audio implementation and is therefore prone to poor performance and degraded audio quality.

SPEEDSCREEN MULTIMEDIA ACCELERATION INI FILE OPTIONS

The following examples illustrate the basic settings for SpeedScreen Multimedia Acceleration.

SpeedScreenMMAVideoEnabled

- **Default Value** TRUE
- **Description** Enable or disable video playback through SpeedScreen Multimedia Acceleration.

SpeedScreenMMAAudioEnabled

- ▼ **Default Value** TRUE
- ▲ **Description** Enable or disable audio playback through SpeedScreen Multimedia Acceleration.

SpeedScreenMMASecondsToBuffer

- ▼ **Default Value** 10
- ▲ **Description** Set the approximate amount of seconds of buffer in the client. Values range from 1–10. The server and client both have this value set, and the connection is set up with the smaller of the values (that is, if the server sets five seconds and the client sets four seconds, then the connection is set up with a four second buffer).

SpeedScreenMMAMaximumBufferSize

- ▼ **Default Value** 30240
- ▲ **Description** Maximum size in kilobytes of the media queue that the client can create. This size is per stream, so the client could create a 30,240KB queue for audio and 30240 queue for video.

SpeedScreenMMAMinBufferThreshHold

- ▼ **Default Value** 10
- ▲ **Description** Set the minimum buffer threshold with a percent value within a range of 5–15. When the data in the media queue reach this value, then the client requests a burst from the server to replenish its media queue.

SpeedScreenMMAMaxBufferThreshHold

- ▼ **Default Value** 90
- ▲ **Description** Set the maximum buffer threshold with a percent value within a range of 85–95. When the data in the media queue reach this value, then the client requests that the server stop sending data until the level of data in the queue levels off.

SpeedScreenMMAPlaybackPercent

- ▼ **Default Value** 35
- ▲ **Description** Set the MMA playback percent value with a range of 25–45. This is the percent of the media queue that needs to be filled before playback on the client end begins.

RECORDING SOUND IN A CITRIX XENAPP SESSION

One of the new features of XenApp 3.0 was the capability to record sound inside an ICA session. This feature was continued with XenApp 4.0 and XenApp 4.5. One of the primary uses for this is for professionals to be able to dictate a recording in one session and then have those data transcribed at a later date. This feature requires a XenApp 3.0 or later and an 8.0 Client or higher.

This process is usually facilitated by third-party software vendors, such as WinScribe, with its Internet Author and Internet Typist software. Usually, software like this is used with Philips SpeechMike devices or similar hardware.

Also, note that playback can take advantage of the new SpeedScreen Multimedia Acceleration when playing MP3 or other such audio. In this case, XenApp doesn't play the data and send WAV data out to the client but instead streams the compressed codec data to the client and enables the client to decompress and play the data.

The settings that control SpeedScreen Multimedia Acceleration are totally separate from the settings that control the recording of audio. A user could use SpeedScreen Multimedia Acceleration for playback and optimize his or her settings for recording without degrading playback quality.

Setting Up for Recording Audio

The following section discusses the configuration required on both XenApp and Client in order to utilize the audio recording features.

Configuring the Server

By default, XenApp doesn't need any configuration to work. This lets you record audio using a standard microphone. However, to use the Philips SpeechMike devices, you must install the drivers on all servers that are to have sessions that will record audio. The recommendation is that you install the Philips drivers before installing XenApp.

Additionally, if you are using WinScribe's software, the Internet Author and/or the Internet Typist programs need to be installed on the servers. Refer to the WinScribe documentation for setup instructions.

Published desktops or published recording applications should be configured to use legacy audio. The client connection's Audio Quality setting should be set to medium or high. Medium is the default and should be satisfactory for most applications. If the Philips SpeechMagic speech-recognition server is used with WinScribe's software, high-quality audio is required for accurate speech-to-text translation. This is because high-quality audio does not use lossy compression on the recorded audio, which can interfere with the accuracy of the speech-recognition algorithms.

You can also use policies to control audio recordings. See the policy documentation in the *Administrator's Guide* for more configuration information.

Configuring the Client

The client must have an audio playback device, such as a soundcard, and an audio recording device, such as a microphone. The Philips SpeechMike devices often serve both purposes. Audio needs to be enabled in the Program Neighborhood, Program Neighborhood Agent, or Web Interface clients, depending on which is used. (SpeechMike works with all of them.) Ensure that either desktop sessions or published audio-recording applications are properly configured to allow sound in the client settings. For most uses, medium audio quality is the recommended setting.

Ensure that the audio-security settings, available from the connection center or via a session's system menu, are configured to allow the recording of audio. These settings work in the same manner as the preexisting file security dialogs.

Using the Philips SpeechMike

Using a Philips SpeechMike should be a relatively straightforward process. Ensure that the drivers for the device are installed correctly on both the client and server. Make sure that the recorder works correctly on the local client. Do this by loading the recorder utility that comes with the drivers. Ensure that audio records and plays back locally.

XenApp supports using the SpeechMike controls and foot pedal devices as well. Before attempting to use them in a session, however, test them locally once again in the Philips recording utility. If everything is working fine locally on a client device, then you should have no problems using the same devices inside an ICA session.

SpeechMike controls may also have to be enabled inside the applications. This is currently true for Internet Author and Internet Typist. See the specific application documentation for details. Additionally, Citrix testing has uncovered problems with configured USB foot pedals in Internet Author and Internet Typist. The recommendation is that if you are using these devices, you should leave the settings for them at their default or at none.

CLIENT AUDIO MAPPING VIRTUAL DRIVER

This section describes the Client Audio Mapping Virtual Driver configuration settings and the best practices when changing these settings in the Module.ini file.

NOTE In client versions10.x and later, Module.ini file modifications should instead be configured in the client's registry in the registry key HKEY_LOCAL_MACHINE\SOFTWARE\Citrix\ICA Client\Engine\Configuration\Advanced\Modules

NumCommandBuffers = 64

- **Description** This setting defines how many commands can be buffered going from server to client.
- **Maximum Limit** 65,000. It is unadvisable to increase this value higher than 64 commands for the best performance of the server and client.

- ▲ **Minimum Limit** 0. Setting this value to 0 affects the performance of the server and client. The client slows down or may not respond to the commands sent by the server. Having the proper buffers defined is necessary because, after executing a command sent by the server, the client looks in the buffer for the next command. Also, if no buffers are in the commands sent to the client, the server might not be stored on the client and executed. The best practice is to set it to 64.

NumDataBuffers = 24

- ▼ **Description** This setting specifies the maximum number of buffers that are dynamically allocated. This is only for version 9.*x* XenApp clients for 32-bit Windows and later. For previous versions of the client connecting to XenApp 4.0 or later, this setting defines how many data buffers are available on the client to store the sound data sent by the server to the client.
- ■ **Maximum Limit** 65,000. It is unadvisable to set this value to the maximum, as this might lead to memory hogging on the client and could eventually result in degrading the performance of the client. The best practice is to set the NumDataBuffers value to 32 for the best performance of the server and the client.
- ▲ **Minimum Limit** 0. If you set this value to 0, no data buffers are available on the client, and the sound data being sent from the server to the client are not stored and eventually will not play. The best practice is to set this value to 32. These 32 buffers are defined to store a maximum of 2,048 bytes of sound data.

MaxDataBufferSize = 2048

- ▼ **Description** This setting defines the size of the data buffer. It also defines how many bytes of sound data can be sent to the client from the server.
- ■ **Maximum Limit** 2048 bytes. Out of 2048 bytes, 10 bytes are reserved for the sound packet header, while the remainder is the actual sound that gets played on the client.
- ▲ **Minimum Limit** 1,000 bytes. The best practice is to set it to 2,048 bytes for the best sound performance on the client.

CommandAckThresh = 1

- ▼ **Description** This setting specifies that the client will wait for one command to be sent by the server before it sends an acknowledgment to the server for all the commands received.
- ▲ **Maximum Limit** The maximum limit depends on the NumCommandBuffers. If NumCommandBuffers is set to 64, then CommandAckThresh should not be set to more than 64, as the client does not acknowledge more than 64 commands. The best practice is to set CommandAckThresh to 1 for the best performance of the client and server.

DataAckThresh = 1

- ▼ **Description** This setting defines that the client will wait for one sound data/packet to be sent by the server before it sends an acknowledgment to the server for all the sound data/packets received.
- ▲ **Maximum Limit** The maximum limit depends on NumDataBuffers. If NumDataBuffers is set to 32, then DataAckThresh should not be set higher than 32, as the client does not acknowledge more than 32 sound data/packets. The best practice is to set DataAckThresh to 1 for the best performance of the client and server.

AckDelayThresh = 50

- ▼ **Description** This setting defines that the client will wait for 50 milliseconds before it sends an acknowledgment to the server for all the commands received from the server.
- ■ **Maximum Limit** 350. AckDelayThresh and CommandAckThresh are not interdependent. Suppose, for example, CommandAckThresh is set to 10 and AckDelayThresh to 350. If 350 milliseconds have not yet passed since the client last sent an acknowledgment, but 10 commands have been sent by the server to the client, the client will still send the acknowledgment. The same holds true if the 350 milliseconds have passed but the server has not sent 10 commands. The client sends the acknowledgment to the server without waiting for 10 commands.
- ▲ **Minimum Limit** 50. Anything less than 50 milliseconds might degrade the performance of the client, as it will start acknowledging to the servers regularly, which will interfere with execution of the commands from the server.

PlaybackDelayThresh = 50

- ▼ **Description** This setting defines that the client will wait for 50 milliseconds before it sends an acknowledgment to the server for all the sound data/packets received from the server.
- ■ **Maximum Limit** 250. PlaybackDelayThresh and DataAckThresh are not interdependent. For example, if DataAckThresh is set to 10 and PlaybackDelayThresh to 250, if 250 milliseconds have passed after the client has sent an acknowledgment, but 10 sound data/packets have not been sent by the server to the client, the client will still send the acknowledgment. The same holds true if the 250 milliseconds have not yet passed, but the server has already sent 10 sound data/packets. The client will send the acknowledgment to the server without waiting for 250 milliseconds.

- **Minimum Limit** 50. Anything less than 50 milliseconds might degrade the performance of the client, as it will send acknowledgments to the servers too often, which will interfere with the playing of the sound data/packets from the server.

PDA SYNCHRONIZATION

XenApp now supports the synchronization of USB-tethered and Microsoft Windows–powered PDAs that use ActiveSync as a synchronization agent. The following section addresses important factors to consider when incorporating this feature into your environment.

Using ActiveSync in an ICA Session

A long-standing obstacle to making ActiveSync available to users via XenApp is that ActiveSync is not a Terminal Services–aware application. Even though ActiveSync is not a multi-user or Terminal Services–aware application, XenApp utilizes the Virtual IP feature, as well as other techniques, to make it compatible with Terminal Services. Although Virtual IP is used to enable PDA synchronization with ActiveSync, no explicit Virtual IP configurations are required by an administrator for PDA synchronization to work properly.

To enable PDA synchronization, follow these steps:

1. Open the properties of a policy in which you want to enable PDA synchronization.
2. Enable the rule Client Devices | Resources | PDA Devices | Turn on automatic virtual COM port mapping.
3. Disable the rule Client Devices | Resources | Ports | Turn off COM ports (or set it to Not Configured).

NOTE Do not plug PDAs into the server console while ICA sessions are connected. If you do so, although PDA users in ICA sessions are isolated from each other, they might have access to the PDA on the server console. In addition, if you then unplug the PDA from the server console, all the PDAs in ICA sessions are disconnected.

Publishing ActiveSync

To make ActiveSync available as a published application properly, it is important to specify WCESMGR.EXE as the application to be launched, not WCESCOMM.EXE. WCESCOMM.EXE is the system tray process. Although both executables can start each other once a PDA is detected, if WCESCOMM.EXE is the only application in a session and no PDA is present at ICA session startup, the ICA session may log off before a user can insert a PDA.

If you connect to a published desktop as any user after ActiveSync has been installed, you may see the ActiveSync icon in the system tray. Also, if you have a PDA plugged into the USB port on the client, ActiveSync may attempt to synchronize to the device. The administrator can do the following to prevent this from occurring:

- Using the System Configuration Utility (MSCONFIG), remove the ActiveSync options from the Startup tab.
- Even if ActiveSync is removed from the startup options, it still runs on the console and re-creates the startup entries the next time it is launched. To prevent ActiveSync from re-creating the startup entries, delete the following registry value:

```
HKCU\Software\Microsoft\Windows\CurrentVersion\Run: H/PC Connection Agent
```

Additional Considerations

The following are additional considerations to keep in mind when using the PDA synchronization feature:

- Symbian operating system (OS)–based and Blackberry PDAs are not supported.
- ActiveSync does not need to be installed on every client.
- A device driver for the PDA must be installed on the local client workstation so that the client's operating system (OS) can recognize the PDA device.
- See Citrix Knowledge Center articles CTX821115 and CTX114161 for more information.

USING ACTIVESYNC 4.0

To use ActiveSync on a 64-bit XenApp, you must install and publish ActiveSync 4.0 in a Citrix Application Isolation Environment (AIE). This involves the following actions:

- Creating an AIE using the Access Management Console
- Creating rules for the AIE
- Installing ActiveSync 4.0 in the AIE
- Publishing ActiveSync 4.0 in the AIE
- Associating other applications outside the AIE to ActiveSync 4.0

To create an AIE using the Presentation Server Console, follow these steps:

1. Launch the Presentation Server Console.
2. Right-click the Isolation Environments node and click New isolation environment.
3. Name the isolation environment and click OK.

To configure the first AIE rule, follow these steps:

1. In the Presentation Server Console, click the Isolation Environments node.
2. In the right pane, right-click the isolation environment that you created and click Properties.
3. In the left pane, click Rules and then click Add.
4. In the Action group box, click Isolate. Then, in the Object group box, click Named Objects.
5. Click Next and then click Add.
6. In the Named field, type **global\AS_ACCEPTANCE_SEMA** and then click OK.
7. Click Add and, in the Named field, type **global\RAPIMgr8a0cc91f-759a-4b35-9906-d7e44ffc4d88**.
8. Click OK and then Next.
9. Click "Per isolation environment" and then click Next.
10. Assign a name or accept the default name, and then click Finish.

To configure the second AIE rule, follow these steps:

1. Click Add.
2. In the Action group box, click Ignore. In the Object group box, click Registry Entries.
3. Click Next, and then click "Some registry entries."
4. Click Add. Then, in the Choose Registry Entry dialog box, from the Hive list, click HKEY_LOCAL_MACHINE.
5. In the Key field, type **Software\Citrix\IMA**. Then click OK.
6. Click Next and then Finish.
7. Click OK to close the dialog box.

To install ActiveSync 4.0 in the AIE, follow these steps:

1. From a command prompt, change the directory to the folder where the ActiveSync 4.0 install program is located.
2. At the command prompt, type **aiesetup** ***isolation environment name ActiveSync 4.0 install program name***. For example, if the isolation environment name is AS-Isolation and the ActiveSync 4.0 installation program name is setup.exe, type the command **aiesetup AS-Isolation setup.exe**.
3. Press Enter. The Microsoft ActiveSync 4.0 Installation dialog box appears.
4. Install ActiveSync 4.0.

5. After the installation is complete, click Finish. Then press Enter and proceed with the application discovery process.
6. When the process is complete, close the window.

To publish ActiveSync 4.0 in the AIE, follow these steps:

1. In the Management Console, right-click the Applications node and then click Publish Application.
2. In the Display Name and Application Description fields, identify the application and click Next.
3. In the Specify What To Publish page, select the Isolate Application check box and click Settings.
4. In the Isolation environment list, click the isolation environment that you created for ActiveSync.
5. Select the "Application was installed into environment" check box.
6. In the "Choose installed application" box, click Microsoft ActiveSync.
7. Click OK and then click Next.
8. Follow the remaining wizard instructions to publish the application and assign users.

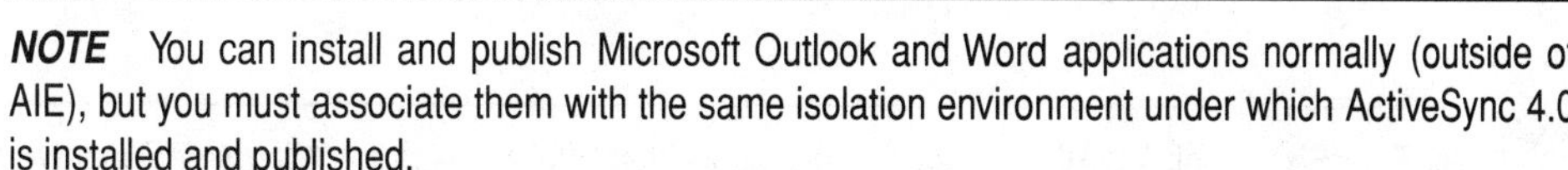

NOTE You can install and publish Microsoft Outlook and Word applications normally (outside of AIE), but you must associate them with the same isolation environment under which ActiveSync 4.0 is installed and published.

To associate published applications that reside outside the ActiveSync AIE, follow these steps:

1. After you install and publish Microsoft Outlook or Word, in the Citrix Management Console, click the Isolation Environments node.
2. Right-click the isolation environment where you installed and published ActiveSync 4.0.
3. Click Properties.
4. In the left pane, click Applications and then click Add.
5. From the list of applications, click the published application (for example, Outlook or Word) and then click OK. The application is associated with the isolation environment that you created for ActiveSync.

Important Notes

Note the following regarding the use of ActiveSync:

- ActiveSync 4.0 is not supported on XenApp for 32-bit servers.
- The PDA Synchronization feature of XenApp for Microsoft Windows Server 2003 x64 Edition does not support the Remote Application Programming Interface (RAPI).
- The PDA Synchronization feature is supported only through ActiveSync 4.0 published application sessions (PDA Synchronization is not supported in a desktop session running an ActiveSync 4.0 application).
- The PDA Synchronization feature is supported only on the Enterprise version of XenApp for Microsoft Windows Server 2003 x64 Edition.
- To enable the Explore functionality of ActiveSync 4.0 on 64-bit platforms, you must add the following Microsoft registry keys to the registry using regedit.exe:

```
[HKEY_LOCAL_MACHINE\SOFTWARE\Wow6432Node\Microsoft\WindowsNT\CurrentVersion\
Terminal Server\Compatibility\Applications\wcescomm]
"Flags"=dword:0x00000408
[HKEY_LOCAL_MACHINE\SOFTWARE\Wow6432Node\Microsoft\WindowsNT\CurrentVersion\
Terminal Server\Compatibility\Applications\wcesmgr]
"Flags"=dword:0x00000408
```

NOTE Sixteen-bit TWAIN drivers are not supported. On XenApp for Microsoft Windows Server 2003 x64 Edition, only 32-bit TWAIN applications are supported.

Sample .reg File

The following is an example of a simple file that can be copied to Notepad and saved as a .reg file to automate enabling these flags on your XenApp:

```
Windows Registry Editor Version 5.00
[HKEY_LOCAL_MACHINE\SOFTWARE\Microsoft\Windows NT\CurrentVersion\Terminal
Server\Compatibility\Applications\Photoshop]
"Flags"=dword:00000408
```

For Citrix XenApp 4.5 for Microsoft Windows Server 2003 x64 Edition, the registry location should be specified as follows:

```
[HKEY_LOCAL_MACHINE\SOFTWARE\Wow6432Node\Microsoft\Windows NT\CurrentVersion\Terminal
Server\Compatibility\Applications\Photoshop]
"Flags"=dword:00000408
```

VIRTUAL IP

Some applications use the machine IP address for addressing, licensing, identification, or other purposes. Therefore, for these applications to function properly in a XenApp environment, a unique IP addresses for each user is required. Other applications may also simply try to bind to a static port; then if multiple attempts are made to launch the application in a multi-user environment, they will fail because the port is already in use.

The Virtual IP feature enables you to assign a static range of IP addresses to a server and have these addresses individually allocated to each session so that configured applications that run within that session appear to have a unique address. Also, applications that depend on communications with localhost (127.0.0.1 by default) can be configured to use a unique address in the localhost range (127.*).

How to Use Virtual IP

To use Virtual IP effectively, it may be helpful to have a better understanding of how the feature is implemented and how it should be configured. First, you need to configure ranges of IP addresses that are excluded from any Dynamic Host Configuration Protocol (DHCP) servers. These ranges should share the same subnets as the assigned IP addresses of the XenApp servers that will be configured for Virtual IP. The pool of IP addresses assigned to the XenApp farm needs to be large enough to include all user sessions on every server to be configured, not just the sessions running the application(s) that require Virtual IP address functionality. These ranges are added to the XenApp farm in the Farm Properties | Virtual IP Addresses page, and the servers that require Virtual IP functionality that share the same subnet as the address range should be added to the range.

At this time, the addresses in the range are divided equally (by default) among the selected servers and assigned. You can then change the number of addresses assigned to each server. The recommendation is that you configure a Load Management Server User Load rule that is equal to or less than the total number of addresses assigned to the server.

How Virtual IP Works

During Independent Management Architecture (IMA) service startup, the Virtual IP address assigner binds the assigned IP addresses to the network interface card (NIC) that matches the same subnet as the virtual addresses. When Virtual IP is enabled on the server, the Virtual IP address allocator will allocate an address from the pool of available addresses, which were assigned by the Virtual IP address assigner, to all new sessions connecting to the server. This allocated address is assigned to the new session and removed from the pool of available addresses. This assigned address can be seen in the Presentation Server Console Servers node in the Sessions tab or via MFCOM (Metaframe COM server) calls. When the session logs off, the allocated address is returned to the available address pool.

Once an address is allocated to a session, any application configured for Virtual IP uses the allocated virtual address rather than the system's primary IP address whenever the following calls are made:

Bind	Closesocket	Connect	WSAConnect	WSAAccept
Getpeername	Getsockname	Sendto	WSASendTo	WSASocketW
Gethostbyname	Gethostbyaddr	Getnameinfo	Getaddrinfo	

Remember, all processes that require this feature must be individually added to the Virtual IP Process list, in the Presentation Server Console Farm Properties' Virtual IP Processes section. Child processes do not automatically inherit this functionality. Processes can be configured with full paths or just the executable name. For security reasons, the recommendation is to use full paths.

The Virtual Loopback functionality is simply either enabled or disabled, and other than specifying which processes use the feature, it does not require any additional configuration. When an application uses the localhost address (127.0.0.1) in a Winsock call, the Virtual Loopback feature simply replaces 127.0.0.1 with 127.*X*.*X*.*X*, where *X*.*X*.*X* is a representation of the session ID + 1. For example, a session ID of 7 would be 127.0.0.8. If the session ID exceeds the fourth octet (more than 255), it rolls over to the next octet (127.0.1.0), all the way to the maximum of 127.255.255.255 (it is highly unlikely to ever get that high).

The Virtual Loopback functionality allows multiple published applications that depend on the localhost interface for interprocess communication to function properly within the session. A good example of such an application is Microsoft ActiveSync. In fact, to provide the PDA Synchronization feature, XenApp utilizes the Virtual IP feature, in addition to other techniques, to create Terminal Services compatibility for ActiveSync.

Binding applications to specific IP addresses is achieved by inserting a filter component between the application and Winsock function calls, so out of all IP addresses allocated to the XenApp, the application sees only the IP address that it is supposed to use. Any attempt by the application to listen (for Transmission Control Protocol [TCP] or User Datagram Protocol [UDP]) is automatically bound to the Virtual IP address (or loopback address) that it is supposed to use. Also, any originating connections opened by the application are originated from the IP address that this particular application or user is supposed to use.

In functions that return an address, such as gethostbyname() and GetAddrInfo(), if the local host's IP address is being requested, Virtual IP looks at the returned IP address and changes it to the session's Virtual IP address. Thus, applications that try to get the local server's IP address through such name functions see only the unique Virtual IP address assigned to that session. This IP address is often used in subsequent socket calls (such as bind or connect).

Often, an application requests to bind to a port for listening on the address 0.0.0.0 (INADDR_ANY, which means all interfaces). When an application does this and uses a static port, you cannot launch more than one instance of the application. The Virtual IP feature also looks for 0.0.0.0 in these types of calls and changes the call to listen on the specific Virtual IP address. This allows more than one application to listen on the same port on the same machine as they are all listening on different addresses. (This is changed only if it's in an ICA session and the Virtual IP feature is turned on.) For example, if two instances of an application running in different sessions both try to bind to all interfaces (0.0.0.0) and a specific port, such as 9000, they would be bound to VIPAddress1:9000 and VIPAddress2:9000. There would no longer be a conflict.

Configuring Virtual IP for Applications

When you are attempting to configure Virtual IP for a particular application, the first step should be to load a tool such as the TCPView tool from Sysinternals (http://technet.microsoft.com/en-us/sysinternals/default.aspx). This tool lists all applications that attempt to bind specific IP addresses and ports. The recommendation is to disable the Resolve Addresses feature so that you see the IP addresses instead of hostnames. Launch the application and take note of which IP addresses and ports are opened by the application. Also, take note of which process names are opening these ports. Any processes that attempt to open either the server's IP address or 0.0.0.0 should be configured in the Virtual IP Process section in Farm Properties. Any processes that attempt to open 127.0.0.1 should be specified in the Virtual Loopback process section in Farm Properties. You may also want to attempt to launch an additional instance of the application to be sure that it does not attempt to open the same IP address(es) on a different port. If that is the case, Virtual IP may be unnecessary for this application.

Client IP Address Feature

If an application is failing only because it requires a unique address strictly for identification or licensing purposes, but does not require a virtual address for actual communication, you may want to explore the Client IP Address feature. This feature hooks only calls that return the host's IP address, such as GetHostByName. This feature should only be used by an application that takes the value in this type of call and sends the value to the server application for identification or licensing.

This feature is currently only enabled by changing several registry settings on the server. To configure this feature, two new registry entries can be added on the server where the application is deployed:

```
HKEY_LOCAL_MACHINE\Software\Citrix\VIP\
UseClientIP: REG_DWORD: 1 (enable) or 0 (disable, default)
HookProcessesClientIP: REG_MULTI_SZ
```

where

UseClientIP = a DWORD value that should be set to either 1 or 0 (enable/disable this feature). The disabled state is the default if the registry value is not present.
HookProcessesClientIP = a multi-string of process names from the application (the executable names) that are to use the Client IP Address feature rather than normal Virtual IP.

Once these values are configured, you must also configure either the Virtual IP processes or the Virtual Loopback processes with the same process names. The reason is that this function creates and manages the following registry entry, which is still required for the ClientIP feature to work:

`HKEY_LOCAL_MACHINE\Software\Citrix\CtxHook\AppInit_Dlls\VIPHook\`*`Processname`*

NOTE The Virtual IP address features (including Virtual Loopback and Client IP Address) function only with applications that load the user32.dll system dynamic library.

CPU UTILIZATION MANAGEMENT

The CPU utilization management feature introduced in XenApp 4.0 ensures that the CPU resources are equitably shared among users. The feature accomplishes this by providing CPU reservation and CPU shares:

- **CPU reservation** A defined percentage of CPU is guaranteed to be available to a user. If all the allocated reservation is not being used, other users or processes can use the available resource as needed.
- **CPU shares** A share is a relative percentage of the CPU time. By default, CPU utilization management allocates eight shares for each user. If two users are logged into a server (and no console session), each of the users gets 50 percent of the CPU. If there are four users with eight shares each, each user receives 25 percent of the CPU time.

NOTE The range for CPU share is 1–64. For CPU reservation, the total cannot be more than 100 percent, which represents the entire CPU resource on the machine.

License Requirement for CPU Utilization

CPU utilization management requires an Enterprise or Platinum Edition license for XenApp.

Changing the Default Values for CPU Utilization via the Registry

By default, each user receives eight CPU shares. A *share* is a relative percentage of CPU time. If two users have eight shares each, they get 50 percent of CPU time. Similarly, if three users have eight shares each, they get one-third of the CPU time each. It is expected that the default values can accommodate most users' needs. However, it is possible to change the default values in the registry. If two users are present and the first user has a need for 16 shares (assuming the user needs more CPU time) and the second user receives eight shares, then the first user gets 66 percent of the CPU time and the second user gets the remaining 33 percent.

Changing the CPU Share Allotment for a User

To change a user's CPU share allotment, follow these steps:

1. Go to HKLM\Software\Citrix\CTXCPU.
2. In the right pane, double-click the "Policy" Multi-String value.
3. In the Edit Multi-String window, you can see the default data for the NT AUTHORITY\SYSTEM context, which is 20000, meaning 20 percent of CPU reservation.
4. Go to the end of the line and press Enter to go to the next line.
5. To set CPU shares for a local user named "u1" on a XenApp server named "Server1," type the following:

   Server1\u1,cpu.shares=16

   Note that 16 is the number of shares you want to assign to a user. This can be any number between 1 and 64.
6. Exit from registry editor to save the settings.
7. Restart the services CTXCPUUtilMgmt User/Session Synchronization and CTXCPUUtilMgmt Resource Management.

Changing the CPU Reservation for Users

To change a user's CPU reservation, follow these steps:

1. Open the registry by choosing Start | Run and typing **regedt32**.
2. Go to HKLM\Software\Citrix\CTXCPU.
3. In the right pane, double-click the Policy Multi-String.
4. In the Edit Multi-String window, you see the default data for the NT AUTHORITY\ SYSTEM context, which is 20000. This represents the desired percentage of reservation multiplied by 1,000, which in this example is 20 percent of CPU reservation.
5. Go to the end of line and press Enter to go to the next line.
6. To set CPU shares for u1, u2, u3, and u4 on XenApp server Server1, type the following:

   Server1\u1,cpu.reservation=20000

   Server1\u2,cpu.reservation=20000

   Server1\u3,cpu.reservation=20000

   Server1\u4,cpu.reservation=20000
7. Exit from registry editor to save the setting.
8. Restart the services CTXCPUUtilMgmt User/Session Synchronization and CTXCPUUtilMgmt Resource Management.

NOTE CPU share/reservation can be assigned only toward individual users, not toward user groups or applications. Also, CPU time sharing within a session is done by the OS, *not* by CPU utilization management.

Services Required for CPU Utilization

The services used for CPU Utilization are CTXCPUUtilMgmt User/Session Synchronization and CTXCPUUtilMgmt Resource Management. In addition to these two services, the Citrix CPU Utilization Mgmt/CPU Rebalancer service is installed on Windows Server 2003 multiprocessor systems.

Citrix CPU Utilization Mgmt/CPU Rebalancer Service

By design, the CPU rebalancer service is installed only on multiprocessor servers running Windows Server 2003. The service is not installed on Windows 2000 Server or servers with only one processor. The CPU Rebalancer service is used to alleviate a Microsoft issue that demonstrates itself under stress environments where a lot of short-lived processes are started and stopped. Because of the impact of this service on performance, the service is set by default to Manual.

The recommendation is to consider starting the CPU Rebalancer service, and setting, the service to Automatic, if your environment is running a lot of short-lived applications that all appear to be running on the same CPU (for example, if you see one CPU is running at 100 percent and another CPU is at 20 percent utilization). The CPU Rebalancer service attempts to correct this by balancing the load equally across processors.

Performance Counters to Monitor CPU Utilization

Five performance counters are available for CPU utilization. The counters are listed under the CTXCPUUtilMgmtUser object on XenApp:

- CPU Entitlement
- CPU Reservations
- CPU Share
- CPU Usage
- Long-Term CPU Usage

NOTE The CPU Utilization management services must be running to add the performance counters to Performance Monitor.

Report Generation for CPU Utilization

You can generate a CPU Utilization report by using the Report Center feature in the Access Suite Console. Generating CPU Utilization reports requires RM Summary Database.

For more information about the CPU Utilization management feature, refer to the Citrix Knowledge Base article CTX106021.

VIRTUAL MEMORY OPTIMIZATION

The Virtual Memory Optimization feature reduces the amount of virtual memory usage by rebasing DLLs to an optimized virtual address to avoid relocation of DLLs. The rebasing of the DLLs prevents any decrease in performance caused by relocating. The rebasing performed by the Virtual Memory Optimization feature modifies a copy of a DLL, so it loads at an optimal base memory address to avoid collisions and relocations.

License Requirement for Virtual Memory Optimization

Virtual Memory Optimization requires an Enterprise or Platinum Edition license for XenApp.

Exclusion List

The following applications are excluded from being rebased by Virtual Memory Optimization:

- Applications that have digitally signed components.
- Applications whose DLLs are protected by Windows Rights Management (WRM). Applications such as Office 2003 do not benefit from this feature because it uses WRM.
- Applications whose executable programmatically checks the DLL after it has been loaded.

The system automatically detects the digitally signed files and the components protected by WRM and excludes them from rebasing. The excluded DLLs and executables can be found in the registry at the following locations:

- HKEY_LOCAL_MACHINE\SOFTWARE\Citrix\SFO\ComponentExclusionList
- HKEY_LOCAL_MACHINE\SOFTWARE\Citrix\SFO\ProcessExclusionList

Services Required for Virtual Memory Optimization

The Citrix Virtual Memory Optimization Service is responsible for the Virtual Memory Optimization feature. The service uses the Windows Task Scheduler to schedule memory optimization.

Scheduling of Memory Optimization

By default, rebasing is scheduled to occur daily at 3 A.M. You can use the options in the Optimization Interval node under Farm Properties in the Access Management Console to change the default scheduling. To access this setting, select the farm in the left pane of the Access Management Console and fram the Action menu, select Modify farm properties > Modify all properties. From the Properties list, select Farm-wide > Memory/cpu > Optimization interval. Also, an alternate user account can be selected to run the scheduled task instead of using the local system account.

Troubleshooting Tips

The following session will provide troubleshooting guidelines for the most common issues around memory optimization.

Using Process Explorer to View Relocated DLLs

Sometimes it becomes difficult to ascertain whether the feature is truly rebasing DLLs or not. You can use Process Explorer from http://technet.microsoft.com/en-us/sysinternals/default.aspx to verify this. The goal of Process Explorer is to reduce the relocation of DLLs for applications. Process Explorer shows the relocated DLLs and, if the feature is working properly, the number of relocated DLLs should be minimal.

To use Process Explorer, follow these steps:

1. Install Process Explorer on all servers running XenApp.
2. Launch Process Explorer. Select the View DLLs button (the fifth button from the left on the toolbar, or press Ctrl-D to view DLLs in a selected process).
3. Choose Options | Configure Highlighting. Check Relocated DLLs and change the highlight color to one that you can easily spot.
4. Once Process Explorer is configured, if a running process (such as Visio32.exe) is selected from the upper panel, the DLLs/components loaded by that process are shown in the lower panel. The relocated DLLs should be highlighted.

Using the Repair.sfo File to View Rebased DLLs and DLLs That Are Pending Rebasing

Repair.sfo is located in Program Files | Citrix | Server Resource Management | Memory Optimization Management | Data and contains the list of DLLs that have been rebased. Repair.sfo also lists the DLLs that are "pending." To troubleshoot Virtual Memory Optimization, you can view this XML file. The file is created by the Citrix Virtual Memory Optimization Service (CtxSFOSvc.exe).

NOTE It takes time to fully rebase all the DLLs for a system. Virtual Memory Optimization is a gradual process. For various reasons—such as files being used—sometimes all the DLLs cannot be optimized in a short period of time, but they are eventually rebased over a longer period of time.

Generating Reports for Memory Optimization

The Report Center in the Access Suite Console contains reporting for virtual memory optimization. The report lists the virtual memory savings received when Virtual Memory Optimization is being used.

Additional Information

For more information about the Virtual Memory Optimization feature, refer to the Citrix Knowledge Base article CTX106023.

MULTIPLE-MONITOR CONFIGURATION SETTINGS AND REFERENCE

This section provides the available configuration settings that can be used to control specific multiple-monitor functionality in a Citrix environment. This includes controlling the interaction and display of specified applications and application windows as well as ICA session behavior.

Under most circumstances, the default settings will suffice for the majority of applications. The additional settings described allow you to have a more granular control over multiple-monitor sessions that may be required with some custom applications and/or in some deployments.

Citrix Multiple-Monitor Background

Enhanced multiple-monitor support was introduced in and requires Hotfix Rollup Pack 1 for Citrix XenApp 4.5 and version 10.100 of the XenApp for Windows Client or later.

Limited support is available for previous versions of Citrix Presentation Server and the Presentation Server for Windows Client. Citrix recommends that if you are planning to use multiple-monitor workstations to connect to published applications, you should upgrade to Citrix XenApp 4.5 Hotfix Rollup Pack 1 or later.

Terminal Services sessions in both Windows 2000 and Windows 2003 do not have support for multiple-monitor clients for either RDP or ICA. A Terminal Services session treats the sum of the client side monitors that the client is connecting with as one large monitor or screen size. For example, if a client is connecting with 2 monitors each set at 1024x768, then the session screen size will be 2048x768.

Citrix Multiple-Monitor Server Configuration Prerequisites

This section outlines some very important server considerations in multiple-monitor deployments.

Session Graphics Memory

When working with multiple-monitor ICA sessions, it is very important to calculate the amount of ICA session graphics required. This is the memory allocated to each session for its graphics data and it is set to the default of 5120 bytes and limited to 8192 bytes in the Access Management Console. It is possible to have a virtual desktop whose session graphics memory is larger than the maximum amount assigned in the Access Management Console. When such an event occurs, either the color depth or resolution will be automatically reduced, based on the settings in the Access Management Console.

Session Graphics Memory Calculation Table

X-Width of the ICA session window
Y- Height of the ICA session window
Z-Color Depth of the ICA session window (1-8 bit, 2-16 bit, 3-24 bit)
M-Session Graphics Memory Required
M=X*Y*Z

For example: for a 1024x768x24 bit session M = 1024*768*3 = 2,359,296 bytes.

Disconnect and Reconnect Session Graphical Memory Calculations

An important consideration when calculating the amount of session display memory required in a deployment, is that users may frequently disconnect and reconnect. During reconnect, twice the usual amount of memory is required, since the server still needs to keep the memory allocated for a disconnected session. Thus, for the above example 1024x768x24 bit session, the amount of graphics memory required during reconnect will be 4,718,592 bytes.

Registry Modification to Allow More Memory for Session Graphics

NOTE Adjusting these parameters on your server may negatively affect the scalability of the server because every session can potentially consume more memory.

The steps outlined below allow specifying more memory for ICA session graphics than available in the Access Management Console. These steps require modifying the XenApp registry. Such adjustments should be performed only if there are specific server needs to raise the session display memory above 8MB.

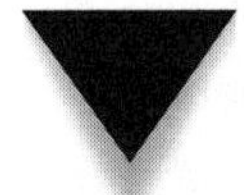

CAUTION Using the Registry Editor incorrectly can cause serious problems that may require you to reinstall your operating system. Citrix cannot guarantee that problems resulting from the incorrect use of the Registry Editor can be solved. Use the Registry Editor at your own risk. Back up the registry before editing it.

1. Launch the Access Management Console and edit the server properties for each server that requires adjustment. Go to the **Display** settings page and deselect **Use farm settings**. Without this step, IMA overrides any change made to thinwire's MaxLVBMem parameter in the registry with the appropriate farm setting.

2. Determine the MaxLVBMem parameter from the maximum session size and depth.

   If X,Y represent the dimensions of bounding rectangle for all monitors, and D is the maximum pixel bit depth, then MaxLVBMem is given by:

   X * Y * D / 8

3. Adjust Window's SessionPoolSize parameter as needed to accommodate increased LVB memory requirements.

   MaxLVBMem should ideally consume no more than 35–40 percent of the system's allocated SessionPoolSize. If more than 40 percent of SessionPoolSize would be consumed, then adjust the SessionPoolSize parameter upward in the system registry and restart the system.

   SessionPoolSize parameter is held in a DWORD value named SessionPoolSize in system registry at HKLM\SYSTEM\CurrentControlSet\Control\Session Manager\Memory Management. It is expressed in megabytes. Microsoft recommends raising this setting in increments of 16MB.

   Default SessionPoolSize for x86 systems is either 16 MB or 32 MB depending upon how much memory with which your system is configured. Default SessionPoolSize for x64 systems is 64 MB.

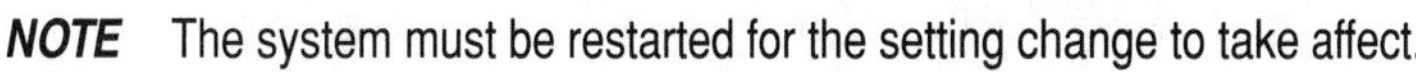

NOTE The system must be restarted for the setting change to take affect.

4. Launch regedit and go to:

   HKLM\SYSTEM\CurrentControlSet\Control\Terminal Server\Wds\icawd\thin16.

5. Edit the value named MaxLVBMem and increase it to the value derived in step 1.

How to Calculate Virtual ICA Session Desktop Size

Graphics axis is calculated from the top left corner of the virtual ICA desktop. That point is considered X=0, Y=0, where X is horizontal and Y is vertical. Graphical location is calculated by adding positive numbers to X and Y and counting down and to the right from 0,0 location. Thus, for 1024x768 monitor, the bottom right corner would be X=1024, Y=768.

The way the ICA multiple-monitor virtual desktop is configured is based on the full rectangle and not on the top left corner of the left-most monitor. Thus the virtual desktop area could be larger than the area covered by the monitors of the client. For example, in Figure 12-1, the top left corner of the virtual desktop is the top left corner of the rectangle made with the three monitors. However, the area inside the virtual desktop where there is no monitor is still addressable, but cannot be shown and is thus considered a gray area.

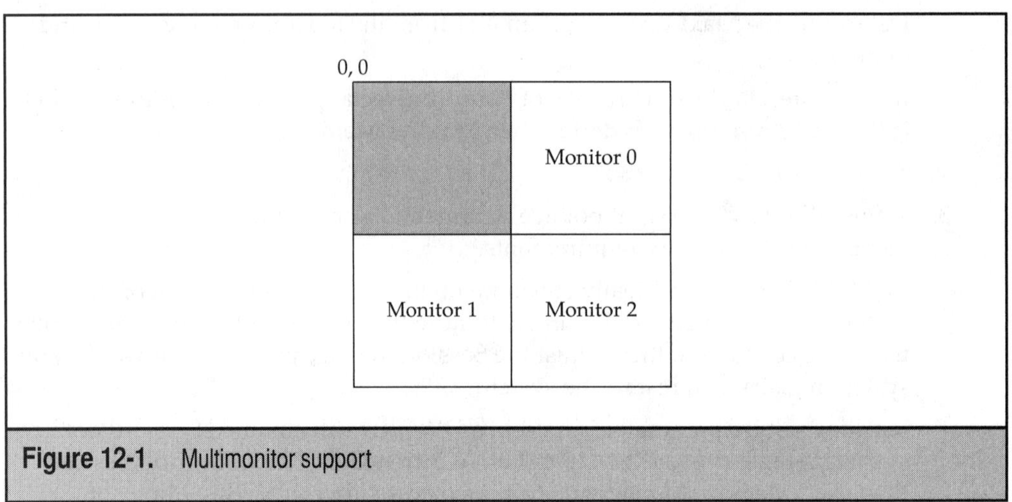

Figure 12-1. Multimonitor support

It is important to include the gray area in calculations of the ICA session size and locations and to calculate ICA session windows to be outside of the gray area.

Figure 12-1 The ICA multiple-monitor virtual desktop is configured based upon the full rectangle and not on the top left corner of the left-most monitor.

Monitor Enumeration

The following section describes the differences between monitor resolution in Windows and an ICA session.

Windows: In Windows, computer monitors are enumerated from left to right, top to bottom. The first monitor is assigned number zero (0), the next number 1 and so forth.

ICA Session: It is important to note that monitor enumeration inside an ICA session is specific to the monitor the session window is on. Thus, for example, if the session window is on Monitor 0 and Monitor 2 of Figure 12-1, then enumeration would be Windows Monitor 0 is session Monitor 0, and Windows Monitor 2 is session Monitor 1. If the session window is on Monitors 1 and Monitor 2, the Session Monitor 0 is Windows Monitor 1, and Session Monitor 1 is Windows Monitor 2.

Example 1 – 4 Monitor configuration: In Figure 12-2 you can see how the coordinates and Windows monitor enumeration would be calculated on a four-monitor configuration. In this example, each client monitor is configured for a resolution of 1024x768. You can see the gray area not covered by any of the monitors and also see coordinates of all monitor

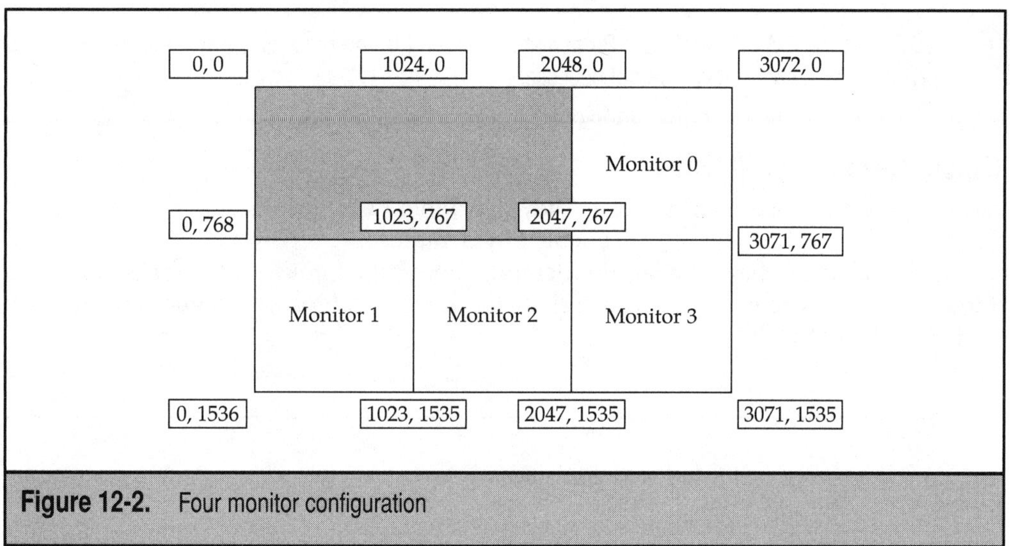

Figure 12-2. Four monitor configuration

corners and thus be able to calculate the position and size of the ICA session window so that it would be able to take advantage of available screen resources.

The range of pixels contained in monitor 0 is from (0,0) to (1023,767) . Note that this is one less than the resolution of the monitor.

Citrix Multiple-Monitor Server Side Registry Settings

Multiple-monitor configuration is performed by setting registry values.

On 32-bit servers the registry key is:

HKLM\Software\Citrix\CtxHook\AppInit_dlls\Multiple Monitor Hook

On 64-bit servers registry key is:

HKLM\Software\Wow6432Node\Citrix\CtxHook\AppInit_dlls\Multiple Monitor Hook

Setting a DWORD named **DefaultHooks** changes the set of hooks used by all applications on the server.

The preferred method to work with problematic applications is to set a DWORD **[ImageName]** that will override the server defaults for a specific application.

NOTE In the DWORD for Citrix Presentation Server 4.0, the brackets [ ] are required. For Citrix XenApp 4.5, the brackets [ ] are not necessary.

Calculating the DWORD

Each hook has an associated value as shown in Table 12-2.

The hooks marked with **, are enabled by default.

To change the behavior from the default, choose the hooks you want enabled and add them together, remember to use decimal mode when entering the value in the registry, or first convert to HEX.

Flag name	Decimal value	Hex value	When to use
**COLORADOHOOKS	1	0x1	This hook is part of the base set of hooks and should not be turned off, unless you wish to disable hooks for an application. It is responsible for correct maximizing/minimizing and clipping of top-level windows.
**SYSTEMMETRICSHOOK	2	0x2	This hook is part of the base set of hooks and should not be turned off, unless you wish to disable hooks for an application. It is responsible for reporting the correct number of client monitors (SM_CMONITORS) within the session. See http://msdn2.microsoft.com/en-us/library/ms724385.aspx for more details.
**GETMONFROMWINDOWHOOK	4	0x4	Use this hook to ensure the MonitorFromWindow API works correctly. Applications use this API to determine which monitor a window resides on. See http://msdn2.microsoft.com/e<a name=n-us/library/ms534601.aspx">http://msdn2.microsoft.com/en-us/library/ms534601.aspx for more details.

Table 12-2 Multiple-Monitor Server Side Registry Settings

Flag name	Decimal value	Hex value	When to use
**GETMONFROMRECTHOOK	8	0x8	Use this hook to ensure that the MonitorFromRect API works correctly. Applications use this API to determine which monitor a specified rectangle (for example, window rectangle) resides on. See http://msdn2.microsoft.com/en-us/library/ms534605.aspx]http://msdn2.microsoft.com/en-us/library/ms534605.aspx for more details.
**GETMONFROMPOINTHOOK	16	0x10	Use this hook to ensure that the MonitorFromPoint API works correctly. Applications use this API to determine which monitor a specified point (for example, window coordinate) resides on. See http://msdn2.microsoft.com/en-us/library/ms534603.aspx for more details.
**GETMONINFOHOOK	32	0x20	Use this hook to ensure that the GetMonitorInfo API returns a correctly populated MONITORINFO structure. Applications usually use this API during monitor enumeration, and use the results to position top-level windows accordingly. See http://msdn2.microsoft.com/en-us/library/ms534599.aspx for more details.
**ENUMDISPMONHOOK	64	0x40	Use this hook to ensure that the EnumDisplayMonitors API enumerates the correct number of client monitors. This hook is usually used in conjuction with GETMONINFOHOOK (see above). Applications that enumerates monitors (for example, PowerPoint in Presenter mode allows you to select which monitor the presentation should be displayed on) should have this hook turned on. See http://msdn2.microsoft.com/en-us/library/ms534809.aspx for more details.

Table 12-2 Multiple-Monitor Server Side Registry Settings (*continued*)

Flag name	Decimal value	Hex value	When to use
ENUMDISPDEVHOOK	128	0x80	Use this hook to ensure that the EnumDisplayDevices API enumerates the correct number of client monitors (devices). The DISPLAY_DEVICE structure will be populated with client monitor information. Some applications use this API to query device specific information (such as device name). See http://msdn2.microsoft.com/en-us/library/ms533226.aspx for more details.
ENUMDISPSETHOOK	256	0x100	Use this hook to ensure that the EnumDisplaySettings API retrieves graphics mode information for each monitor. The DEV_MODE structure will be partially populated with graphics mode information. Some applications use this API in order to determine specific graphics mode capabilities. Applications suffering from drawing/painting issues (for example, client area not painted correctly on resize) should try this hook. See http://msdn2.microsoft.com/en-us/library/ms533265.aspx for more details.
**CREATEDCHOOK	512	0x200	Use this hook to ensure that the CreateDC API correctly creates a device context associated with the primary display, and not individual client monitors (display). Applications use this API to permit drawing to a specified monitor in a desired format (for example, monitors on the same system can have different pixel formats). However, since the session is really a single display, the hook is used to force create device contexts associated with the primary display device. Use this hook if an application suffers from painting issues. See http://msdn2.microsoft.com/en-us/library/ms533246.aspx for more details.

Table 12-2 Multiple-Monitor Server Side Registry Settings (*continued*)

Flag name	Decimal value	Hex value	When to use
**CBTDIALOGHOOK	1024	0x400	This hook is part of the base set of hooks and should not be turned off, unless you wish to disable hooks for an application. It is responsible for correct placing/centering child dialogs (for example, message boxes).
LAUNCHONMONITORHOOK	2048	0x800	This hook attempts to position an application on a particular monitor, on startup. If enabled, the default monitor can be specified by the ICA parameter PreferredLaunchMonitor which accepts a value from 0 .. (n-1) where n is the number of client monitors. The monitors are enumerated in row-major order in other words, top-left to bottom-right. Currently, the Colorado server-side DefaultLaunchMonitor registry value is disabled.
**WINDOWLONGHOOKS	4096	0x1000	This hook is part of the base set of hooks and should not be turned off, unless you wish to disable hooks for an application. It is responsible for catching applications that dynamically subclass windows, and enforcing MMHook's COLORADOHOOKS. See http://msdn2.microsoft.com/en-us/library/ms633584.aspx http://msdn2.microsoft.com/en-us/library/ms633585.aspx http://msdn2.microsoft.com/en-us/library/ms633591.aspx http://msdn2.microsoft.com/en-us/library/ms644898.aspx for more details.
IGNORE_WS_MAXIMIZE_BOX	8192	0x2000	Before sub classing a window (applying COLORADOHOOKS), MMHook examines a window's style to ensure a maximize box is present. This is used as a marker for the maximize window capability, and to ensure MMHook does not subclass windows unnecessarily. If a window can be maximized (for example, from the taskbar), but does not have a maximize button, this check can be turned off by setting this flag.

Table 12-2 Multiple-Monitor Server Side Registry Settings (*continued*)

Flag name	Decimal value	Hex value	When to use
**SUBCLASS_OWNED_WINDOWS	16384	0x4000	MMHook identifies a top-level window as a window that does not have a parent. However, some applications use, as their main window, an owned window. If an application window is maximizing across screens, try turning this flag on as it may be an owned window.
SYSTEMPARAMETERSINFOHOOK	32768	0x8000	Used to return the work-area of the primary monitor. See http://msdn2.microsoft.com/en-us/library/ms724947.aspx, SPI_GETWORKAREA for more details.
FORCEMAXIMIZETOMONITOR	65536	0x10000	Applications that intercept the WM_GETMINMAXINFO notification (see http://msdn2.microsoft.com/en-us/library/ms632626.aspx for more details) can restrict the area a window is maximized to. To override this behavior, set this flag.

Table 12-2 Multiple-Monitor Server Side Registry Settings (*continued*)

Setting a value of zero is the same as disabling MMHook, this can be done for all processes or per application as described above.

CAUTION Do not disable only winlogon.exe - this could cause a reduction in performance as every process tries to find the mapped file that doesn't exist.

Citrix Multiple-Monitor Client Side Settings

The following describes the available Multiple-Monitor client-side settings.

INI and ICA file parameters

Several enhancements were made involving application windows that are created in an ICA session over previous versions of XenApp. Test your application's behavior on Citrix XenApp 4.5 Hotfix Rollup Pack 01 or later, before using the following settings.

Below are the details describing parameters available for configuration of ICA session windows. These parameters can be applied either to saved ICA files or INI files.

NOTE These parameters require setting the parameter **DesiredWinType=16** in the ICA or INI files.

Positioning Parameters: DesiredVPOS and DesiredHPOS

DesiredVPOS specifies the desired vertical coordinates of the top left corner of the ICA session window.

NOTE This number is counted down from top left corner of the virtual desktop (position 0, 0).

DesiredHPos specifies the desired horizontal coordinates of the top left corner of the ICA session window.

NOTE This number is counted from left to right from top left corner of the virtual desktop (position 0, 0).

Resolution Parameters: DesiredVRES and DesiredHRES

DesiredVRES specifies the desired height of the ICA session window, counting down from the **DesiredVPOS** location.

DesiredHRES specifies the desired width of the ICA session window, counting to the right from **DesiredHPOS** location.

Usage Example:

```
[Desktop 2]
DesiredWinType=16
DesiredHPos=2048
DesiredVPos=0
DesiredHRES=1024
DesiredVRES=1536
```

In this configuration, on the 4-monitor client configuration shown in figure 12-2, the ICA session window would start from top left corner of Monitor 0 (top right monitor). The ICA session window would be 1024 wide and 1536 high (1024x1536) and would cover the Windows Monitor 0 and Monitor 3.

Monitor Preference Parameter: PreferredLaunchMonitor

This setting is only recommended for use with problematic applications.

PreferredLaunchMonitor specifies on which of the session monitors should the applications launched inside the ICA session start.

NOTE It does not specify the monitor for the session, but for applications launched **inside** the ICA session.

It is important to note that the monitor enumeration for the [Desktop2] ICA session is different and because it has only two monitors used (Windows Monitor 0 and Windows Monitor 2); these monitors become Session Monitor 0 and Session Monitor 1 accordingly. Session Monitor numbers are used with the PreferredLaunchMonitor parameter.

```
[Desktop 2]
DesiredWinType=16
DesiredHPos=2048
DesiredVPos=0
DesiredHRES=1024
DesiredVRES=1536
PreferredLaunchMonitor=1
```

In this example, applications launched inside the Desktop 2 ICA session window would launch on Windows Monitor 2 which is also Session Monitor 1.

Return to Maximized Parameter: DefaultMaximizedPos

DefaultMaximizedPos parameter specifies the location and window size for an ICA session window that is returned from resized or minimized mode.

Usage example – in this configuration, the minimized or resized ICA session window would always be maximized back to its original size.

NOTE You can specify different location and window sizes, if needed.

DefaultMaximizedPos={2048,0,1024,1536}

Additional Notes

MMHook is loaded into every session because there is only one chance to set hooks into a process (when it starts). As any session can be reconnected from a different client computer with a potentially different monitor layout, there is always the possibility that even though the hooks are not needed immediately they may be needed later in the session's lifespan. This is why the DLL is now active in all sessions.

Some applications perform their own handling of maximize events and startup positioning. It would be very difficult and potentially dangerous to force applications to size themselves the way we think they should in all cases. Therefore, there may be some applications that behave incorrectly regardless of what is configured. The main aim of the new feature is to ALLOW programs access to monitor tables through familiar Windows Application Programming Interfaces (APIs), not to reprogram application behavior in every case.

TWAIN REDIRECTION SUPPORT

XenApp can redirect client-connected TWAIN imaging devices—notably document scanners—from the client to the server, regardless of connection type. This enables users to control client-attached imaging devices from applications that run on the server; the redirection is transparent.

To capture an image, users connect to a server from a client machine that has an imaging device and the associated vendor-supplied TWAIN driver installed locally. When the TWAIN application is run from within this session, the application detects and interacts with the client-side device. The server-based application that is accessed runs in the same way as a client-based application.

Redirection support for TWAIN devices is available in the Advanced and Enterprise Editions of XenApp.

By default, users can use published applications to process data acquired by locally connected TWAIN devices. You can control the redirection of TWAIN devices by enabling the policy rule Configure TWAIN redirection, as follows:

1. Open the properties of a policy in which you want to control TWAIN redirection.
2. Enable the rule Client Devices | Resources | Other | Configure TWAIN redirection.
3. Use the options to allow and disallow TWAIN redirection, as well as to control the level of data compression.

TWAIN Additional Considerations

The following are additional considerations to be aware of when using TWAIN redirection:

- The Imaging/Scanner software must be installed on the XenApp. Examples of supported applications include the following:
  - Microsoft's PictureIT
  - OmniPage
  - PaperPort
  - Photoshop
  - Paint Shop Pro
  - IrFanView

NOTE Sixteen-bit TWAIN drivers are not supported.

- You need scanner software on the client OS that can provide the USB device drivers. If a test utility for the scanner is available, the recommendation is to install the utility on the client workstation to ensure functionality.
- For TWAIN Redirection, some applications are not Terminal Services–aware and look for TWAIN32.DLL in the \WINDOWS directory of the User's profile (that is, C:\Documents and Settings\UserName\WINDOWS, unless the path has otherwise been changed). One resolution is to copy TWAIN32.DLL into the \WINDOWS directory of each user's profile. Referring to Microsoft Knowledge Base article 186499, it is also possible to fix this problem by adding the application to the Terminal Services application compatibility list with the following two flags specified:
  - Windows 32-bit application: 0x00000008
  - Do not substitute user Windows directory: 0x00000400

Sample .REG file

The following is an example of a simple file that can be copied to Notepad and saved as a .reg file to automate the enabling of these flags on XenApp:

```
Windows Registry Editor Version 5.00
[HKEY_LOCAL_MACHINE\SOFTWARE\Microsoft\Windows NT\CurrentVersion\
Terminal Server\Compatibility\Applications\Photoshop]
"Flags"=dword:00000408
```

NOTE You may need to combine these flags with any other compatibility flags needed for the application.

Support for TWAIN Modes of Information Transfer

There are three modes of information transfer:

- Native
- Disk File
- Buffered Memory

Most scanning software works by default in Buffered Memory mode. Disk File transfer is not supported. Native and Buffered Memory modes are supported.

Tested TWAIN Devices

The following is a list of devices used during the testing of the TWAIN Redirection feature. These are not the only supported devices to use with XenApp:

- Canon CanonScan 3200F
- Epson Perfection 3170 Photo – USB
- Hewlett Packard OfficeJet 7130 All-In-One
- Hewlett Packard ScanJet 8290
- Microtek ScanMaker 5950 – USB
- QuickCam Messenger Logitech
- Visioneer OneTouch 9320
- Xerox DocuMate 510

Supported XenApp Clients

Version 9.*x* or later of the XenApp client for 32-bit Windows is required to use this feature.

CHAPTER 13

Printer Management

Since the inception of networking, printing has been a primary concern during the design and implementation phases of building a network. Whether the issue is the quality of the print job, bandwidth needs, performance requirements, paper tray demystification, or simply determining where a print job went, administrators have struggled with providing secure, fast, and simple printing solutions to their users.

Because we covered, in detail, Windows printer management, configuration, troubleshooting, and the use of third-party tools in *Citrix Access Suite for Windows Server 2003: The Official Guide,* we focus in this chapter on the centralized printer management features in the Presentation Server Console. We start with an overview of XenApp print architecture. Print driver replication is discussed at length, along with optimizing printer creation and the Session Printers Policy features.

XENAPP PRINT ARCHITECTURE

Users connecting to a XenApp environment can print to the following types of printers:

- Printers connected to ports on the user's client device on Windows, Windows CE, DOS, Linux, UNIX, or Mac operating system (OS) platforms
- Virtual printers created for tasks such as printing from a PostScript driver to a file on a Windows client device
- Shared printers connected to print servers on a Windows network
- Printers connected directly to servers running XenApp

The printer objects that XenApp clients use can be categorized by connection types. Three kinds of printer connections are in a XenApp farm: client connections, network connections, and local connections. This chapter refers to printers in a XenApp farm as client printers, network printers, or local printers, depending on the type of connection they have in the farm.

Client Printers

Client printers are defined differently, depending on the XenApp client platform:

- On DOS-based and Windows CE client devices, a client printer is physically connected to a port on the client device by a cable.
- On UNIX and Macintosh client devices, a PC or PostScript printer connected to a serial port (or a USB port for newer Macintoshes) is considered a client printer.
- On 32-bit Windows platforms (Windows 9*x*, Windows NT, Windows 2000, and Windows XP), any printer that is set up in Windows is a *client printer* (these printers appear in the Printers folder on the client device). Locally connected printers, printers that are connected on a network, and virtual printers are all considered client printers.

Network Printers

Printers that are connected to print servers and shared on a Windows network are referred to as *network printers*. In Windows network environments, users can set up a network printer on their computers if they have permission to connect to the print server. In a XenApp environment, administrators can import network printers and assign them to users based on group membership. When a network printer is set up for use on an individual Windows computer, the printer is a client printer on the client device.

Local Printers

A *local printer* is created by an administrator on a server running XenApp using the Add Printer Wizard from within the Printers applet in the Control Panel. As with a network printer, print jobs printed to a local printer bypass the client device and can be sent either to a Windows print server or directly to a printer, depending on how the printer has been created on the server. If the printer is added to XenApp with the port pointing to a share such as *printserver**sharename*, the print job is sent to the print server before heading to the printer.

The print queue can be Windows-, NetWare-, or UNIX-based. If the printer is added and the port specifies the actual printer itself (such as an lpr queue to the printer's IP address), XenApp is essentially the print server, and the job is sent directly to the printer. Local printers are not typically utilized in an enterprise XenApp environment because of the need for the Citrix administrator to set up every printer in the environment on each XenApp server. However, local printers can be utilized successfully in smaller XenApp farms (three or fewer servers).

PRINTER DRIVER REPLICATION

Printer driver replication was introduced in XenApp to reduce the management nightmare of ensuring that all XenApp servers in the farm have the required printer drivers for an environment.

Printer driver replication is designed to copy printer driver files and registry settings across the server farm. You can install all required printer drivers on one XenApp in the farm and then replicate the files and registry settings to all other servers in the farm. Management of printer driver replication is performed through the Presentation Server Console. Printer driver replication does not replicate printer properties, such as paper size and print quality.

TIP Printer driver replication can be CPU-intensive on the source server. To improve performance, avoid replicating drivers while the farm is under heavy load, such as when many users are logging on.

Managing the Printer Driver Replication Queue

Each printer driver/server combination creates an item in the printer replication queue. For best performance, this queue should not exceed 1,500 entries in length. To determine the queue size, use the following formula:

QueueSize = *Drivers* * *Servers*

where *Drivers* is the number of printer drivers and *Servers* is the number of servers to which the printer drivers are being replicated.

Using this formula, the queue can include 30 drivers for replication to 50 servers (30 * 50 = 1,500) or three drivers for replication to 500 servers (3 * 500 = 1,500) without exceeding the queue size recommendation.

The replication queue items can be monitored with the qprinter/replica command. For more information on the qprinter command, see the next section, "Qprinter Command."

Qprinter Command

The *qprinter command* is a utility designed to enable administrators to monitor the progress of the printer driver replication queue and import printer name–mapping parameters into the data store. The syntax of the qprinter command is

```
qprinter [/replica]

qprinter [/imprmapping mappingfilename]
```

where *mappingfilename* specifies the full path to the text file containing the printer-mapping parameters to import. The filename cannot have more than 256 characters and cannot contain quotation marks.

Here are the options for the qprinter command:

- **/replica** This option displays all the replication entries queued for distribution, but not yet completed. The /replica switch displays all events in the queue, including broken or failed events.
- **/imprmapping *mappingfilename*** This option imports printer mappings from the file specified by *mappingfilename* into the data store. The file format can be in either the *Wtsprnt.inf* format or the *Wtsuprn.txt* format. The /imprmapping switch allows central administration of all printer name mappings. The file can be imported once from any server in the farm and is available for all servers in the farm. The/imprmapping switch does not process an improperly formatted file and does not return an error when provided with an invalid file format. To verify that the information is correctly imported into the data store, use the Presentation Server Console.

NOTE Only Citrix administrators can execute this command.

XenApp installation first attempts to import the *Wtsuprn.txt* file, followed by the *Wtsprnt .inf* file. If the two files fail to import, no error is returned. Use the /imprmapping switch to import either file manually.

Qprinter is not installed by default. It is in the \support\debug\W2K3 folder on the XenApp Server CD.

TIP You can determine the success or failure of printer driver replication by checking the Application log in Event Viewer on the target servers.

Driver Replication and Performance Issues

The number of printer drivers installed on or replicated to each server in the farm can affect server performance and the IMA service response time. The following sections provide recommendations for minimizing potential performance issues when installing or replicating printer drivers.

Driver Replication and Server Performance

The time required to complete printer driver replications depends on network traffic and server load. The IMA service handles the replication distribution queue.

The printer driver replication subsystem can process an average of 50 entries a minute in a 50-server farm under a light user and network load. A 500-server farm under the same conditions can process an average of 20 entries a minute.

The distribution subsystem monitors the load on the XenApp that is replicating the print drivers while they are distributed across the server farm.

To complete printer driver replication as quickly as possible, Citrix recommends that it be executed during off-peak hours, when higher-priority network traffic is at a minimum.

TIP You can monitor the progress of the replication jobs by running qprinter/replica.

Driver Replication and IMA Performance

The data store holds one record for each printer driver, one record for each farm server, and one record for each printer driver/server combination. The more printer drivers installed on farm servers, the larger the printer driver tables in the data store, and the more time that will be required to query information from the data store at startup. Introducing a large number of printer drivers to XenApp —whether they are manually installed or replicated—slows IMA response time.

The best practice is to limit the number of printer drivers in the farm using the following guidelines:

- Install printer drivers only for printers to be used by XenApp clients in the farm.
- Install printer drivers only on servers that will host users who need access to the printers.

- Install printer drivers that work for multiple printer types if possible.
- Remove unnecessary printer drivers from cloned images.
- In WAN environments where a large number of printer drivers are installed, use a replicated data store if better performance is necessary.
- Use the Citrix Universal Print Driver (UPD) instead of the native Windows drivers if possible.

Using Autoreplication

Each XenApp maintains a list of drivers that it received through autoreplication under HKLM\SOFTWARE\Citrix\IMAPrinter:AutoReplicate. This registry value contains IMA user IDs (UIDs) for each driver configured for autoreplication. During IMA service startup, the IMA service's Printer subsystem checks whether a driver's UID is already present in the registry. If a driver is already registered as being replicated to a server, that driver is not reinstalled, even if the overwrite option is checked.

For "regular" replication (when autoreplication is not selected), when the replication job is started, if overwrite is not selected, the target server is checked to verify whether the server already contains the files necessary to install the driver. If the files exist, the server is told to install the driver. If the driver files are not already available on the target server, they are sent from the source server to the target server and installed. If overwrite is selected, the drivers are always sent from the source server to the targets.

This behavior ensures that every server has the same version of the driver installed.

When an autoreplication job is scheduled, if the driver is not already detected as replicated in the aforementioned registry key, the IMA service attempts to download it during IMA service startup. If several printer replication jobs are destined for a server, the IMA service may take an extended period of time to start. If autoreplication must be used, keep the number of printer drivers to be replicated to a minimum.

OPTIMIZING PRINTER CREATION

Network printer shares that reside on the client system can increase client login times because the printers are created and deleted during each logon and logoff. Using auto-created network printers, instead of client network printer shares, can reduce login times because the connections to the network printers remain persistent. If the network printer is on the XenApp, no other action is required; otherwise, you need to perform the following steps to import the required network print servers into the farm.

To add network printers to a XenApp farm, follow these steps:

1. Open the Presentation Server Console and select the Printer Management node.
2. Right-click Printer Management and select Import Network Print Server.
3. Specify the network print server to import and add any necessary authentication credentials. When the operation finishes, the print server appears on the Network Print Servers tab.

4. Install the printer drivers for your network printers on a Presentation Server in the server farm.
5. Within the Presentation Server Console, expand the Printer Management node, right-click Drivers, and select Auto-Replication to distribute the drivers to all XenApp servers in the farm. This also maintains the replication job in the data store so that these drivers can be added to any new servers added to the farm in the future. Use the guidelines outlined previously in the section "Using Autoreplication" when performing replication.

To allocate network printers to users, follow these steps:

1. Within the Presentation Server Console, expand the Printer Management node.
2. Select the Printers node and then select a printer.
3. Right-click on a printer and select Auto-Creation.
4. Specify a domain and then select the groups and users who need to use the printer.

When a specified user logs on to a XenApp in the farm, the printer becomes available in the user's ICA session as if the printer were installed on the user's client device.

Controlling the Behavior of Autocreated Network Printers

By default, if a client machine's network printers are allowed to be autocreated in a session, during client logon XenApp determines whether it can contact the print server directly. If it determines that it can, then XenApp creates the user's network printer as if the network printer were configured on XenApp. When a print job is sent to this printer, instead of being sent back to the client through the ICA printer virtual channel, the print job is sent directly from XenApp to the print server.

In certain scenarios (such as when the print server is located across the WAN) or if you want to control client printing bandwidth, this can cause performance issues. With previous versions of XenApp, a registry modification was required to control whether network printers were created with a direct connection from the server to the printer or as client printers that print through the ICA client device. With XenApp, you can configure a print job routing policy to control how printing requests to network printers are processed. For more information about using policies, see the *Citrix Presentation Server Administrator's Guide* and the Presentation Server Console online help.

SESSION PRINTERS POLICY

XenApp has incorporated printer connections into the policy engine. This new policy setting lets Citrix administrators create customized printing workspaces based on any policy criteria. The administrator now can define a default printer without having to resort to login scripts.

The New Session Printers Policy

The *session printers policy* feature represents an extension of the current autocreated network printer functionality. By using the policy engine, administrators can now customize a client printer workspace based on criteria such as client name, client IP address, server, user, or group.

The session printers policy enables administrators to designate the following:

- Which network printer(s) to connect within the session
- Whether a particular printer should be the user's default printer
- Whether they will be able to override default values of common printer settings for network printers

These new options extend the flexibility of policies to allow customized printer workspaces to be constructed for specific sites, groups, users, servers, clients, and so forth. These new policy options also add the long sought-after capability to set the default printer explicitly for a user without resorting to login scripts and preserve the printer properties' overrides available with autocreated network printer support.

Creating and Applying Policies for Session Printing

Three aspects are involved in the creation and application of a policy configuration:

- The creation of a policy, its settings, and its resolution
- The way that XenApp determines which settings in a policy to apply
- Policy enforcement

Configuration To create a policy that uses the session printers rule, the administrator first creates a new policy object in the Presentation Server Management Console. The session printers rule is not configured by default. Next the administrator modifies the session printers rule by either enabling or disabling it. If the rule is enabled, the administrator can then modify its settings. After the rule is configured, the administrator can update the policy's filter and priority.

Resolution Resolution of the session printers policy rule occurs when a user creates a new session. Typically for every rule, the policy engine examines each policy in order of priority. For the majority of the policy rules, if the state of the highest priority policy is enabled, then the settings from this policy are used. The policy engine ignores any other rule defined in any of the other lower-priority policies. In contrast to this behavior, the session printers rule can merge with lower priority policies. Such a merger allows for more flexible printer workspace configurations based on different filtering criteria. XenApp reflects the resultant policy into the system registry, including the list of configured printers and the default printer.

Enforcement The enforcement code for printer connections executes during the logon process. XenApp gets the printer connection settings from the registry and then interacts with the IMA printer subsystem to create the printers specified by the policy and possibly override their settings.

Important Considerations

Some situations must be taken into consideration when introducing the new session printers policy into your environment:

- The session printers policy rule merges its properties with lower-priority policies.
- Note that in XenApp, the printer autocreation functionality in the Printer node has been removed from the Presentation Server Console. The session printers policy thus is now the only mechanism for adjusting printer settings on a network printer. Given that the session printers policy is available only as part of XenApp 4.0 and later, you will be unable to administer previous versions of XenApp's printer autocreation settings with the new version of the Presentation Server Console. Instead, use a previous version of the Presentation Server Console to access the autocreate objects.
- Session printers policies do not affect the functionality of older servers. The IMA service continues to hold autoconnect network printer objects and can still create, delete, and manage them separately from session printers policies. The Presentation Server Console UI for this functionality has been removed, so administrators need to use a previous version of the Presentation Server Console to administer autoconnect printer objects for XenApp 3.0 and earlier.

Troubleshooting

The following scenarios may arise when using the new session printers policy rules. At the end of each scenario's description, a possible resolution is provided.

Scenario 1: A New Printer Fails to Autocreate An administrator has created a session printers policy and assigned it to users of the Education Department. The administrator has defined two network printers—Printer1 and Printer2—to users of the Education Department. Now the department gets a new printer named Printer3. The administrator adds Printer3 to the policy, which is assigned to users of the Education Department.

When the users of the Education department login to XenApp through an ICA session, they only see Printer1 and Printer2, but Printer3 is not getting autocreated.

Resolution: The administrator should install the driver for Printer3 on XenApp. If the driver for the network printer is unavailable, the printer will not be autocreated.

Scenario 2: Session Network Printers Are Not Autocreated The administrator has a policy defined to autocreate printers using the Universal Printer Driver only, but the session network printers defined through a session printers policy are not autocreated using the Universal Printer Driver.

Resolution: Session network printers are never autocreated using the Universal Printer Driver; they are always autocreated using the native drivers. In fact, none of the other printer policies affect the session printers policy.

Scenario 3: Users Working in Multiple Groups Want a Different Default Printer An administrator has two session printers policies—Policy1 and Policy2—and these are assigned to users of the Education Department and users of the Support Department, respectively. Policy1 has Printer1 and Printer2 defined to it, and Printer2 is further defined as the default printer. Policy2 has Printer3 and Printer4 defined to it, and Printer4 is defined as the default printer. Two users—User21 and User23—are members of both departments/groups, but they are currently working in the Education Department. When User21 and User23 connect to the server through an ICA session, Printer1, Printer2, Printer3, and Printer4 are all autocreated, but Printer4 is set as the default printer. But, because User21 and User23 are currently working for the Education Department, they want their default printer to be Printer2.

Resolution: Policy2 has been set to a higher priority than Policy1. Set Policy1 to a higher priority than Policy2.

Session Printing Registry Settings

XenApp provides registry settings that can be used to change the behavior of session printing. These settings are used to track the various printing-related settings on a per-session basis.

During login, the actual session settings for printing are derived from a combination of XenApp policies, base Terminal Server defaults, and an optional DefaultPrnFlags value in the XenApp registry. In the absence of a configured policy or modifications to base Terminal Server defaults, default values for all bit flags listed in the following are initially zero. Setting a bit to one enables one of the following documented functions. As you can see from the names, enabling the bit flag is often used to disable or turn off default behavior.

To modify the system default values, follow these steps:

1. Navigate to HKLM\Software\Citrix\Print.
2. Add a REG_DWORD value named DefaultPrnFlags to the registry key.

For some settings, default values (before policy application) are taken from settings managed by the Terminal Server base functionality instead of the DefaultPrnFlags value. All settings with an initial default provided by Terminal Server are highlighted in the following. These defaults apply, unless the CTXPRN_OVERRIDE_TS_DEFAULTS bit is set in the DefaultPrnFLags value.

NOTE Configured and enabled XenApp policy rules always override default settings whether they are read from the registry or provided by Terminal Server. However, policies do not exist for many of these settings as they may either not be of general interest or intended only as a failsafe to disable certain features for troubleshooting.

CTXPRN_OVERRIDE_TS_DEFAULTS (0x00000080)

Windows manages several printing-related session settings, which it derives from group policies, user settings, or the connection type defaults. Unless overridden, we use these settings as intended defaults. Settings that favor a Terminal Server–provided default are highlighted. To override Terminal Server default for any of the identified settings, this flag must be set in the DefaultPrnFlags registry value read from HKLM\Software\Citrix\Print in the system registry. If this flag is not set, then the normal Terminal Server defaults apply.

Client Printer Autocreation Flags

- CTXPRN_CLNTPRN_AUTOCREATE_NONE (0x00000004)
- CTXPRN_CLNTPRN_AUTOCREATE_LOCAL_ONLY (0x00000002)
- CTXPRN_CLNTPRN_AUTOCREATE_DEFAULT_ONLY (0x00000001)

By default, all discovered client printers are autocreated. However, if any of these flags are set, only a subset of discovered client printers will be autocreated. If CTXPRN_CLNTPRN_AUTOCREATE_NONE is set, then none of the discovered client printers are autocreated. If AUTOCREATE_NONE is not set and CTXPRN_CLNTPRN_AUTOCREATE_LOCAL_ONLY is set, then only printers that appear to be local to the client are autocreated. If AUOTCREATE_NONE and AUTOCREATE_LOCAL_ONLY are not set, but CTXPRN_CLNTPRN_AUTOCREATE_DEFAULT_ONLY is set, then only the default client printer will be autocreated.

Default Value Unless overridden, Terminal Server defaults for these settings are used. If the CTXPRN_ OVERRIDE_TS_DEFAULTS flag is set in the DefaultPrnFlags value at HKLM\ Software\Citrix\Print\, then the Terminal Server defaults are ignored and default bit values are taken from this REG_DWORD value.

Overriding the XenApp Policy Rule To override the Presentation Server policy rule, choose Printing | Client Printers | Auto-Creation.

CTXPRN_DISABLE_DIRECT_CONNECT_FOR_CLNTPRNS (0x00200000)

When autocreating a client printer that is a connection to a shared network printer, the system first attempts to establish a direct connection from the server session to the network print server using the login credentials of the server session. Failing this, the printer is still connected as a client printer. If this flag is set, the attempt to establish a direct printer connection from XenApp to the print server is avoided, thereby forcing all client printers to be connected indirectly through the client.

Default Value The default value is zero unless the appropriate bit value is set in the REG_DWORD registry value DefaultPrnFlags at HKLM\Software\Citrix\Print\.

Overriding the XenApp Policy Rule To override the XenApp policy rule, choose Printing | Client Printers | Print Job Routing.

CTXPRN_DONT_SET_DEFAULT_CLIENT_PRINTER (0x00000800)

By default, the system sets the session user's default printer to the client's default printer. If this flag is set, the client's default printer will not be set as the session user's default.

Default Value Unless overridden, the Terminal Server default for this setting is used. If CTXPRN_OVERRIDE_TS_DEFAULTS flag is set in the DefaultPrnFlags value at HKLM\ Software\Citrix\Print\, then the Terminal Server default is ignored and the default bit value is taken from this REG_DWORD value.

Overriding the XenApp Policy Rule To override the XenApp policy rule, choose Printing | Session Printers.

CTXPRN_CREATE_LEGACY_CLIENT_PRINTERS (0x00000010)

By default, the system uses printer names and ports that are qualified by the session ID, so they will be unique to a particular session. If set, this flag causes old-style printer and port names derived only from the client name to be used. Although less secure, this setting is useful for applications that expect the old-style printer names to be used.

Default Value The default value is zero unless the appropriate bit value is set in the REG_DWORD registry value DefaultPrnFlags at HKLM\Software\Citrix\Print\.

Overriding the XenApp Policy Rule To override the XenApp policy rule, choose Printing | Client Printers | Legacy Client Printers.

CTXPRN_AUTO_CREATE_GENERIC_UPD_PRINTER (0x00000020)

The latest 32-bit Windows clients are capable of receiving and displaying print jobs in a viewer application on the client. For such a client, it is possible to create a single generic universal printer within the session that is not bound to any of the underlying client printers. This printer is generic in the sense that it does not know about, or manage, any device-specific settings. As such, it is also more efficient to use because there is no need for capabilities or document settings exchanges with the client when printing. Because creating any additional printer within a session incurs overhead, by default, the creation of the generic UPD printer is turned off. If this flag is set, then the system will autocreate the generic "Citrix UNIVERSAL Printer" in addition to the other printers dictated by other autocreation flags. For customers who do not require special printer capabilities, creating only a single generic UPD printer within the session—instead of one printer for each underlying client printer—can provide scalability savings. To see these savings, they must not only enable this flag but must also use policies to override or assign default autocreation policies.

Default Value The default value is zero unless the appropriate bit value is set in the REG_DWORD registry value DefaultPrnFlags at HKLM\Software\Citrix\Print\.

Overriding the XenApp Policy Rule There is no way to override the XenApp policy rule.

Printer Driver Flags

Printer driver flags include the following:

- CTXPRN_DRIVERS_AVOID_REGULAR_DRIVERS (0x00000100)
- CTXPRN_DRIVERS_NO_UPD_FALLBACK (0x00000200)
- CTXPRN_DRIVERS_ENABLE_UPD (0x00000400)

By default, the system attempts to use standard printer drivers as requested by the client if they are available. If the specific driver is unavailable and the client supports a UPD, then the printer will be autocreated using the universal driver as a fallback. The default behavior is modified by setting any of the following combinations:

- CTXPRN_DRIVERS_AVOID_REGULAR_DRIVERS and CTXPRN_DRIVERS_ENABLE_UPD (use the universal driver only)
- CTXPRN_DRIVERS_NO_UPD_FALLBACK set, others 0 (use model specific drivers only)

Default Value Default values are all zero unless one or more of the appropriate bit values are set in the REG_DWORD registry value DefaultPrnFlags at HKLM\Software\Citrix\Print\.

Overriding the XenApp Policy Rule To override the XenApp policy rule, choose Printing | Drivers | Universal Driver.

CTXPRN_DRIVERS_DISABLE_AUTO_INSTALL (0x00100000)

By default, both the network printer and client printer autocreation processes attempt to install needed drivers from the native set of printer drivers that ships with Windows (for example, Driver.cab/ntprint.inf). If set, this flag disables all such automatic driver installations, implying that all drivers must be preinstalled or replicated to all required XenApp servers.

Default Value The default value is zero unless the appropriate bit value is set in the REG_DWORD registry value DefaultPrnFlags at HKLM\Software\Citrix\Print\.

Overriding the XenApp Policy Rule To override the XenApp policy rule, choose Printing | Drivers | Native Printer Driver Autoinstall.

CTXPRN_NO_UPD_FALLBACK_FOR_DISALLOWED_DRIVER (0x10000000)

When a driver name presented from the client fails the compatibility test (for example, the driver name is present in an exclude list or not present in an allow-only list), assuming UPD fallback is enabled, the normal behavior is to try and create the printer using the UPD. If set, this flag changes the default and avoids UPD creation for printers whose drivers fail the compatibility test.

Default Value The default value is zero unless the appropriate bit value is set in the REG_DWORD registry value DefaultPrnFlags at HKLM\Software\Citrix\Print\.

Overriding the XenApp Policy Rule There is no way to override the XenApp policy rule.

Client Printer Properties Retention Flags

- CTXPRN_DISABLE_CLNTPRN_PROPS_EXCHANGE_WITH_CLIENT (0x00001000)
- CTXPRN_DISABLE_CLNTPRN_PROPS_PROFILE_SAVE_RESTORE (0x00002000)

By default, the system first attempts to save modified printer properties by sending them back to the client (if supported). Failing that, the system tries to save them in the user profile on the server. Setting either flag has the effect of disabling the printer properties save/restore to either (or both) the client exchange and/or the user profile.

Default Value The default value is zero unless the appropriate bit value is set in the REG_DWORD registry value DefaultPrnFlags at HKLM\Software\Citrix\Print\.

Overriding the XenApp Policy Rule To override the XenApp policy rule, choose Printing | Drivers | Printer Properties Retention.

Client Printer Port Management Flags

Client printer port management flags include the following:

- CTXPRN_CREATE_BOTH_STD_AND_LEGACY_CLNTPRN_PORTS (0x01000000)
- CTXPRN_CREATE_PORTS_FOR_AUTOCREATED_CLNTPRNS_ONLY (0x02000000)
- CTXPRN_DONT_DELETE_CLNTPRN_PORTS (0x04000000)

By default, the system creates ports for all discovered client printers during login or reconnects and deletes them at logout. The style of port created depends on the state of the CTXPRN_CREATE_LEGACY_CLIENT_PRINTERS flag. If any of these flags are set, the default port creation and deletion behavior is modified as follows:

- **CTXPRN_CREATE_BOTH_STD_AND_LEGACY_CLNTPRN_PORTS** Instead of creating either legacy style or standard port names, both types of ports are created.
- **CTXPRN_CREATE_PORTS_FOR_AUTOCREATED_CLNTPRNS_ONLY** This setting creates ports only as needed for autocreated printers rather than for every discovered client printer.
- **CTXPRN_DONT_DELETE_CLNTPRN_PORTS** This setting does not delete ports at logout. This works around a Windows 2000 spooler issue (see Microsoft Knowledge Base article 893691) that can trap the spooler service.

However, enabling this setting can lead to substantial port and handle accumulations in the spooler service that eventually require the service to be restarted.

Default Value All default values are zero unless one or more of the appropriate bit values are set in the REG_DWORD registry value DefaultPrnFlags at HKLM\Software\Citrix\Print\.

Overriding the XenApp Policy Rule There is no way to override the XenApp policy rule.

Network Printer Connection Flags

Network printer connection flags include the following:

- CTXPRN_DISABLE_NETWORK_PRINTER_AUTOCONNECT (0x00400000)
- CTXPRN_DISABLE_NETWORK_PRINTER_DISCONNECT (0x00800000)

XenApp policies evaluated at login and reconnect include a special policy rule called Session Printers, which can be used to add and delete network printer connections on behalf of the login user based on various policy criteria. Normally, these network printer connections are added during logins or reconnects and then deleted during logout. The two flags listed previously are failsafes that allow the administrator to disable temporarily all printer connection additions and deletions all at once without having to disable many different policies. Of course, this is mostly useful in certain troubleshooting scenarios. That said, turning off only the disconnection of network printers can improve server scalability at the expense of allowing printer connections made by the Session Printers policy rule to accumulate in user profiles.

Default Value The default values are all zero unless one or more of the appropriate bit values are set in the REG_DWORD registry value DefaultPrnFlags at HKLM\Software\Citrix\Print\.

Overriding the XenApp Policy Rule There is no way to override the XenApp policy rule.

Client-Printer Mapping Disabling Flag

The flag for disabling client-printer mapping is as follows:

- CTXPRN_DISABLE_CLIENT_PRINTER_MAPPING (0x00000008)

By default, the SPL virtual channel is initialized and client-printer mapping is enabled. If set, this flag disables the SPL virtual channel, thereby disabling the client-printer mapping functionality of the system.

Default Value Unless overridden, the Terminal Server default for this setting is used. If the CTXPRN_ OVERRIDE_TS_DEFAULTS flag is set in the DefaultPrnFlags value at HKLM \Software\Citrix\Print\, then the Terminal Server defaults are ignored and the default flag value is taken from this REG_DWORD value.

Overriding the XenApp Policy Rule To override the XenApp policy rule, click Printing | Client Printers | Client Printer Mapping.

CTXPRN_DONT_AUTO_CONNECT_LPTS (0x00000040)

For compatibility reasons, LPT ports discovered on the client are automatically mapped in client sessions. If the remapped LPT port is never used, then there is no good reason to have mapped it. If this flag is set, LPT ports can still be mapped in a client session, but they will not be automatically mapped. Instead, a net use command or the equivalent WNet* API must be used to establish any mapping, just as one would do for a redirected COM port.

Default Value Default values are all zero unless one or more of the appropriate bit values are set in the REG_DWORD registry value DefaultPrnFlags at HKLM\Software\Citrix\Print\.

Overriding the XenApp Policy Rule There is no way to override the XenApp policy rule.

CTXPRN_ADMINS_CAN_MANAGE (0x00004000)

To preclude the possibility of an administrative user inadvertently printing to a printer in someone else's Terminal Services session, the default security descriptor used to autocreate client printers no longer includes any rights for the administrator's group. Only the user executing in the proper session context has rights to the autocreated printers for the session. Administrators may still grant themselves rights to any client printer by taking ownership of the print queue and adding the desired rights. Because this is a cumbersome process, administrators not requiring the level of security provided may opt to set this flag; the system then automatically adds usage rights to all autocreated client printers for members of the administrator's group.

Default Value The default value is zero unless the appropriate bit value is set in the REG_DWORD registry value DefaultPrnFlags at HKLM\Software\Citrix\Print\.

Overriding the XenApp Policy Rule There is no way to override the XenApp policy rule.

CTXPRN_DONT_LOG_AUTOCREATE_FAILURE (0x08000000)

By default, printer autocreation failures cause events to be logged in the event viewer's application log. Even printers created by UPD result in an event because this is one of the few ways that administrators can find out precisely which printer models are in use by the client population. Because this can result in a flood of events in the event viewer, this flag provides the means to avoid generating event log entries for autocreation failures.

Default Value The default value is zero unless the appropriate bit value is set in the REG_DWORD registry value DefaultPrnFlags at HKLM\Software\Citrix\Print\.

Overriding the XenApp Policy Rule There is no way to override the XenApp policy rule.

CHAPTER 14

Farm Maintenance

This chapter covers best practices, recommendations, and maintenance issues that you might encounter while administering a Citrix XenApp farm.

CONSOLIDATING MULTIPLE LICENSE FILES

If you have multiple Citrix license files installed on one license server, you can combine the files into one single file.

NOTE You can only combine license files containing the same hostname value. Consolidating license files from multiple servers or combining Citrix license files with another company's license files is not supported.

If your license files are compatible, you can use any text editor to combine them. The basic concept of creating a single license file is a process of empty text file creation, where you copy appropriate sections into the file, save the file, and then force the Citrix License Server to reread the file. Think of the individual license files as INI files (with multiple sections). Follow this example:

1. Because all license files being combined are from the same hostname server, the following section only needs to occur once at the top of the file. Take this section from your existing license files and paste it into your new "empty" one:

```
# This file is in UTF-8 format.
#
SERVER this_host HOSTNAME=domain
VENDOR CITRIX
USE_SERVER
```

2. Combine all of the following lines from each license file into one contiguous list:

```
INCREMENT MPS_ENT_CCU CITRIX 2004.1027 27-oct-2004 99 \
VENDOR_STRING=;LT=NFR;GP=96;CL=ENT,ADV,STD;SA=0;ODP=0;AP=ADMIN/LOGON/
ALW:NONADMIN/
LOGON/ALW \
DUP_GROUP=V ISSUED=30-Apr-2004 NOTICE="Citrix Systems France" \
SN=OR867:1265 START=30-apr-2004 SIGN="XXXX XXXX XXXX XXXX XXXX \
XXXX XXXX XXXX XXXX XXXX XXXX XXXX XXXX XXXX XXXX XXXX \
XXXX XXXX XXXX XXXX XXXX XXXX XXXX XXXX XXXX XXXX XXXX XXXX \
XXXX "
```

3. Append the CITRIXTERMs at the end of the license file (especially if you have different edition licenses):

```
#[English]
#CITRIXTERM     FEATURE     1.0     MPS_STD_CCU     EN     MetaFrame
                                                           Presentation
Server, Standard Edition|Concurrent User
#CITRIXTERM     FEATURE     1.0     MPS_ADV_CCU     EN     MetaFrame
                                                           Presentation
Server, Advanced Edition|Concurrent User
#CITRIXTERM     FEATURE     1.0     MPS_ENT_CCU     EN     MetaFrame
                                                           Presentation
Server, Enterprise Edition|Concurrent User
#[German]
#CITRIXTERM     FEATURE     1.0     MPS_STD_CCU     DE     MetaFrame
                                                           Presentation
Server, Standard Edition|Gleichzeitige Benutzer
#CITRIXTERM     FEATURE     1.0     MPS_ADV_CCU     DE     MetaFrame
                                                           Presentation
Server, Advanced Edition|Gleichzeitige Benutzer
#CITRIXTERM     FEATURE     1.0     MPS_ENT_CCU     DE     MetaFrame
                                                           Presentation
Server, Enterprise Edition|Gleichzeitige Benutzer
#[French]
#CITRIXTERM     FEATURE     1.0     MPS_STD_CCU     FR     MetaFrame
                                                           Presentation
Server, édition Standard|Utilisateurs simultanés
#CITRIXTERM     FEATURE     1.0     MPS_ADV_CCU     FR     MetaFrame
                                                           Presentation
Server, édition Advanced|Utilisateurs simultanés
#CITRIXTERM     FEATURE     1.0     MPS_ENT_CCU     FR     MetaFrame
                                                           Presentation
Server, édition Enterprise|Utilisateurs simultanés
#[Spanish]
#CITRIXTERM     FEATURE     1.0     MPS_STD_CCU     ES     MetaFrame
                                                           Presentation
Server, Standard Edition|Usuario concurrente
#CITRIXTERM     FEATURE     1.0     MPS_ADV_CCU     ES     MetaFrame
                                                           Presentation
```

```
Server, Advanced Edition|Usuario concurrente
#CITRIXTERM     FEATURE      1.0      MPS_ENT_CCU      ES     MetaFrame
                                                              Presentation
Server, Enterprise Edition|Usuario concurrente
#[Japanese]
#CITRIXTERM     FEATURE      1.0      MPS_STD_CCU      JA     MetaFrame
                                                              Presentation
Server, Standard Edition|\u540c\u6642\u4f7f\u7528\u30e6\u30fc\u30b6\u30fc
#CITRIXTERM     FEATURE      1.0      MPS_ADV_CCU      JA     MetaFrame
                                                              Presentation
Server, Advanced Edition|\u540c\u6642\u4f7f\u7528\u30e6\u30fc\u30b6\u30fc
#CITRIXTERM     FEATURE      1.0      MPS_ENT_CCU      JA     MetaFrame
                                                              Presentation
Server, Enterprise Edition|\u540c\u6642\u4f7f\u7528\u30e6\u30fc\u30b6\u30fc
#
```

4. Force the license server to reread the license file for changes to take effect.

For more information about license files, see the *Getting Started with Citrix Licensing Guide*. This document can be found in the Citrix Support Knowledge Center.

CYCLE BOOTING XENAPP

XenApp servers do not require a regular restart cycle to run effectively. However, if cycle booting is desired, follow these guidelines.

When the IMA service starts after a restart, it establishes a connection to the data store and performs various reads to update the local host cache. These reads can vary from a few hundred kilobytes of data to several megabytes of data, depending on the size and configuration of the server farm.

To reduce the load on the data store and to reduce the IMA service start time, Citrix recommends maintaining cycle boot groups of no more than 100 servers. In large server farms with hundreds of servers, or when the database hardware is insufficient, restart servers in groups of approximately 50, with at least 10 minute intervals between groups.

TIP If the Service Control Manager reports that the IMA service could not be started after a restart of XenApp but the service eventually starts, ignore the Service Control Manager's message. Although the Service Control Manager has a timeout of six minutes, the IMA service can take longer than six minutes to start because the load on the database exceeds the capabilities of the database hardware. To eliminate this message, try restarting fewer servers at the same time.

CHANGING FARM MEMBERSHIP OF SERVERS

XenApp requires the use of the chfarm command to change farm membership. This section discusses the correct use of the chfarm command that ships XenApp.

CAUTION Misuse of chfarm can corrupt the data store. Before running the chfarm command on any server in the farm, back up the data store.

Using chfarm

You can execute chfarm from %ProgramFiles%\Citrix\system32\citrix\ima, the installation CD, or a network image of the CD.

CAUTION If chfarm reports any error, continuing the process can corrupt the data store. Instead, click Cancel and use the process for restoring an unresponsive server. See the section "Recovering an Unresponsive Server" in Chapter 17.

Executing chfarm

When executed, chfarm does the following on the host server:

1. It attempts to remove the server from the farm.
2. It stops the IMA service.
3. It configures the data store.
4. It then restarts the IMA service.

Important chfarm Considerations

Consider the following when using chfarm:

- Running chfarm on a server hosting the data store (such as Microsoft Access or SQL Server 2005 Express Edition SP1) deletes the current data store database. Do not use chfarm on the server hosting the Microsoft Access or SQL Server 2005 Express Edition SP1 database, until all other servers in that farm are moved to a new server farm. Failure to follow this process can result in errors when chfarm is executed on those servers that no longer have a valid data store.
- When creating a Microsoft Access data store on a new server farm, make sure that you do the following:
    - Run chfarm first on the server hosting the new data store
    - Execute chfarm on other servers to be added to the new server farm
    - Run chfarm on any servers that hosted an old data store last

- Close all connections to the Presentation Server Console on the local server before executing the chfarm command.
- Execute chfarm only on a functioning XenApp server. Do not execute chfarm on a server that was removed from a server farm.

NOTE Using chfarm does not migrate published applications or any server settings to the new server farm.

Using chfarm with SQL Server 2005 Express Edition SP1

When using the chfarm utility to change a XenApp's farm membership or create a new farm that will use SQL Server 2005 Express Edition SP1 for the server farm's data store, a named instance must be installed on the server on which you run chfarm. The default named instance that chfarm uses is CITRIX_METAFRAME.

Running chfarm does not automatically install SQL Server 2005 Express Edition SP1; you must install it separately using the SQL Server 2005 Express Edition SP1 Windows Installer installation package included on the XenApp CD.

Chfarm Options When Using SQL Server 2005 Express Edition SP1

Use these options when running chfarm to create a new farm with SQL Server 2005 Express as the data store:

- **/instancename:*name*** This specifies The name of the SQL Server 2005 Express Edition SP1 instance to which you are migrating. The default value is CITRIX_METAFRAME.
- **/database:*name*** This option specifies the name of the SQL Server 2005 Express Edition SP1 database to which you are migrating. The default value is MF20.

NOTE You cannot migrate a database to the same named instance of SQL Server 2005 Express Edition SP1 already in use. If you are already using SQL Server 2005 Express Edition SP1 and you want to migrate to a new farm using SQL Server 2005 Express Edition SP1, you must do one of the following: migrate to another database (Access or a third-party database) and then migrate back to SQL Server 2005 Express Edition SP1, or install another named instance of SQL Server 2005 Express Edition SP1 and then launch chfarm with the /instancename option.

To move a server to a new server farm using SQL Server 2005 Express Edition SP1 as the data store, complete the following steps:

1. Create a named instance of SQL Server 2005 Express Edition SP1 by installing SQL Server 2005 Express Edition SP1 on the first server in the new farm.
2. Run chfarm on the server that you want to use to create the new farm using the /instancename: *name* option, where *name* is the name of the instance of SQL Server 2005 Express Edition SP1 created in step 1.

NOTE If a named instance of SQL Server 2005 Express Edition SP1 CITRIX_METAFRAME already exists, it is unnecessary to use the /instancename option.

BACKING UP AND RESTORING THE SQL SERVER 2005 EXPRESS EDITION SP1 DATABASE

Use DSMAINT BACKUP to back up the SQL Server 2005 Express Edition SP1 database. Specify a local path for the location of the database backup files. Essentially, this command uses a default OSQL script to back up the database. Use DSMAINT RECOVER to restore a previously backed up copy of the SQL Server 2005 Express Edition SP1 database for use as the IMA data store.

If you want to create customized OSQL scripts for backup, refer to the following Microsoft article for further details: http://support.microsoft.com/default.aspx?scid=241397.

NOTE If you are moving the SQL Server 2005 Express Edition SP1 database to a different server in the farm, you need to perform DSMAINT FAILOVER on all indirect servers to point them to the new database server. This action is similar to the "To move or restore an Access data store" description found in the Citrix Knowledge Base article CTX677542.

RENAMING A XENAPP SERVER

The name and Security ID (SID) given to a server when it is installed and added to a server farm generally remains unchanged, but the server can be renamed if necessary. To rename a server in a XenApp farm, complete the following steps:

1. In the Access Management Console, right-click the Administrators node and select New | Add Administrator.
2. Check Add local administrators and click Next, click Next again, and select Full Administration from the list of available privilege settings
3. Use chglogon/disable to prevent users from logging in to the server.
4. Remove the server to be renamed from published applications assigned to that server.
5. Stop the IMA service.
6. Change the name of the server.
7. Restart the server.
8. Log on to Presentation Server Console using the local administrator account.
9. Expand the Servers folder.

10. Remove the old server name from the Presentation Server Console's list of servers.
11. Add the new server name to the list of configured servers for published applications.

UNINSTALLING XENAPP IN INDIRECT MODE

If XenApp is removed from the server with a direct connection to the data store, indirect servers will no longer be able to access the data store. Information such as applications, Citrix administrators, and so on will be lost. Citrix recommends uninstalling the indirect servers first and uninstalling the direct server last. Uninstalling the direct server first prevents any other servers from being uninstalled from the data store.

To force an uninstall of a XenApp when the data store cannot be accessed, use the following command:

```
msiexec /x mps.msi CTX_MF_FORCE_SUBSYSTEM_UNINSTALL=YES
```

Note that mps.msi is the name and location of the MSI package of XenApp. For more on how to pass properties to the Windows Installer, refer to the *Citrix Presentation Administrator's Guide*.

THE CITRIX PRESENTATION SERVER CONSOLE

This section offers recommendations for using the Presentation Server Console in an Enterprise environment.

Performance Considerations

The Presentation Server Console queries the data collector and the member servers for information such as running processes, connected users, and server loads. Depending on the size of the server farm, the Presentation Server Console might affect performance in the server farm. The following are recommendations for managing performance issues with the Presentation Server Console:

- In XenApp deployments with hundreds of servers and thousands of users, connect only one instance of the Presentation Server Console to the farm for each zone.
- Connect the Presentation Server Console to a data collector so that the Presentation Server Console can query data directly rather than through an intermediate XenApp.

- In large farms, the Presentation Server Console can take a long time to refresh. The refresh time depends on the number of servers in the zone, the number of Citrix Clients requesting connections, and the number of Presentation Server Console instances requesting information. If the refresh query takes longer to complete than the specified automatic refresh interval, the data collector becomes overloaded. Set the automatic refresh interval for users and applications as long as is practical. Using the minimum refresh interval of 10 seconds is not recommended. For best performance, disable automatic refresh and manually refresh the data as needed.
- When managing a farm across a congested WAN, run the Presentation Server Console within an Independent Computing Architecture (ICA) session to a remote server, rather than running it locally. Running the Presentation Server Console from within an ICA session reduces the amount of bandwidth consumed across the WAN, and provides better performance from the Presentation Server Console.

Adding a Server to Multiple Published Applications

In customer environments with hundreds or thousands of published applications, adding a new server to all the published applications can be cumbersome. To add multiple applications to a server, you can launch the Presentation Server Console and select the existing published applications that you want to publish to the new server. Drag the selected applications to the server on which you want to publish them to the leftmost side of the console. This automatically adds all the selected applications to the server.

CAUTION Make sure that the new server has access to the user accounts for which the applications are published. If the machine does not have permissions for the existing user accounts, the accounts will be reset and replaced with the built-in user accounts.

Using Server and Application Folders

The Presentation Server Console provides the capability to group servers and applications into folders. No correlation exists between the Presentation Server Console folders and Program Neighborhood folders that appear in application sets.

The Presentation Server Console folders help to manage a large number of servers and applications. They also increase performance because the Presentation Server Console queries for data only for the servers or applications in the current folder view. One way to increase response time is to divide the list of servers into folders based on their zones.

TIP Viewing server details on large groups of servers may result in incomplete information being gathered for all the servers. To reduce this occurrence, group servers in folders under the Servers node of the Presentation Server Console.

ACCESS MANAGEMENT CONSOLE

The Access Management Console extends the capability to manage your deployment by integrating consoles with the Microsoft Management Console (MMC). The Access Management Console provides a central location for managing your Citrix deployment. The following section provides some tips for using the Access Management Console.

Access Management Console is supported on the following platforms:

- Windows 2000 Server, Windows 2000 Professional, Windows XP, and Windows Server 2003.
- Microsoft .NET Framework version 1.1, available in the Support folder of the server CD, is required to install Citrix Access Suite Console.
- The Access Management Console uses "pass-through" authentication. Make sure that you are logged on to the client machine (where the console is installed) as a Citrix administrator for the farm. To avoid issues with credentials, it's advisable to ensure that the console machine belongs to the same domain as the XenApp farm member machines.
- When you are running discovery, only one server name is required for the farm. Once the discovery is run for a certain farm, you can save the discovered objects by saving the .msc (Microsoft Management Console) file. When the .msc file is launched again, it will know about the discovered objects. When launching the console from the ICA toolbar or from the Start menu, the choice to save the .msc file is unavailable because the console is saved automatically every time that you close it.
- The console communicates with the server farm using the MetaFrame COM server service. When troubleshooting, ensure that this service is running on XenApp.

Configuring Data Refresh

By default, automatic refresh of data is disabled in the Access Management Console. Enabling automatic refresh increases CPU utilization by the console and increases TCP traffic on the network. Opening multiple Access Management Console instances in the same farm with automatic refresh enabled increases network congestion.

In some cases, you might want to enable automatic refresh. You can control the frequency of automatic updates to server, server folder, and published application information on the Access Management Console you are running. The auto-refresh settings apply only to the Access Management Console you are running and not other instances of the Access Management Console on your network.

To enable automatic data refresh in the Access Management Console, follow these steps:

In the left pane, select one of the following nodes (depending on what type of user data you want to refresh automatically):

- The farm for which you want to refresh the user data automatically.
- The server for which you want to refresh the user data automatically.
- The application for which you want to refresh the user data automatically.

In the center pane, from the Other Tasks section or the Common Tasks section (depending on the node that you selected), click Refresh user data.

Automatically refresh user data for servers. Selecting this option enables automatic refreshing of each server's configuration and connection information. After selection, the associated Refresh rate field becomes available.

Automatically refresh user data for server folders. Selecting this option enables automatic refreshing of each server's folder organization. After selection, the associated Refresh rate field becomes available.

Automatically refresh user data for applications. Selecting this option enables automatic refreshing of each published application's configuration and connection information. After selection, the associated Refresh rate field becomes available.

In the **Refresh rate (seconds) box**, select the number of seconds between each update (10, 30, 60, or 90).

LOAD MANAGEMENT TIPS

When selecting servers to participate in Load Management or when attaching load evaluators in large farms, a delay of several minutes can occur for population of the Available Servers and Selected Servers lists in the Access Management Console. During this retrieval, the Management Console does not always indicate that it is still retrieving information.

Load-Balancing Published Applications in a Mixed Environment

By default, on XenApp where drive letters are not remapped, most applications on 32-bit servers are installed in C:\Program Files\. On 64-bit servers, however, most 32-bit applications, by default, are installed in C:\Program Files (x86). If you want to load-balance published applications in a mixed environment, you must ensure that the application path for the published application for each server correctly identifies its location.

To edit the path during the publishing process, follow these steps:

1. In the Access Management Console, under the Applications node, right-click the application that you want to load balance.
2. Click Properties.
3. Under Basic, click Location and verify the path.

NOTE If the server is a 32-bit server and the path is correct, all the 32-bit servers in the list will be correct as well. Similarly, the same is true if you select a 64-bit server and the path is correct.

4. After you identify the servers with the incorrect paths, from the Servers node select all the servers with the incorrect paths and click Edit.
5. Select the radio button "Specify custom command line and working directory."
6. In the Command Line field, type the correct location of the published application.
7. Correct the Working Directory, if necessary.
8. Click OK, then OK again to return to the Management Console.

Similarly, the installation paths that you may choose to specify when installing applications may be different on 32-bit and 64-bit servers in your farm. You can use the same procedure as the previous one to specify your applications' customized locations.

Tuning the Load Bias Level

Prior to XenApp 3.0, the data collector temporarily increased the load of a server for each connection by 200 until it received a load update from the server. This increase is known as the *load bias*. In XenApp 3.0, this was changed to calculate the load-bias level based on the load-evaluator settings. For example, if a Server User Load Evaluator was configured to report a full load at 40 users, the new bias level would be 250, not 200. To set the load-bias level manually, you must add the following registry key to the farm's data collectors and potential data collectors:

```
HKLM\Software\Citrix\IMA\LMS\ForceRegLoadBias
```

By default, this value is set to 0 (off). To force the load bias to the one configured in the registry, this value should be set to 1. Although it is not generally recommended or necessary to modify the load bias specified in the registry, you can change this setting by editing the value of the following:

```
HKLM\Software\Citrix\IMA\LMS\LoadBias
```

The default value is 200.

Performance Counters Utilized by Load Management

Some of the Load Evaluator (LE) rules that can be used by Load Management to calculate a server's load, utilize Performance Monitor counters to obtain their values. Table 14-1 outlines these Load Evaluator rules and the associated Performance Monitor counters:

LE Rule	Description	Performance Monitor Value	Task Manager Value
CPU Utilization	Calculates a load based on a moving average of total CPU utilization across all processors in the server.	TSE: System\% Total Processor Time W2K: Processor\(_Total)\% Processor Time	Performance\CPU Utilization
Memory Usage	Calculates a load based on virtual and physical memory currently in use.	Memory\% Committed Bytes In Use	Performance\Memory Usage
Context Switches	Calculates a load based on CPU context switches.	System\Context Switches/sec	A context switch occurs every time the operating system (OS) switches from one executing process to another.
Disk Data I/O	Calculates a load based on the disk I/O throughput in kilobytes.	PhysicalDisk(_Total)\ Disk Bytes/sec	The value used by Disk Data I/O is the total for all disks on the machine.
Disk Operations	Calculates a load based on the number of disk operations per second.	PhysicalDisk(_Total)\ Disk Writes/sec + PhysicalDisk(_Total)\ Disk Reads/sec	The value used by Disk Operations is the total for all disks on the machine.
Page Faults	Calculates a load based on the number of page faults per second.	Memory\Page Faults/sec	A page fault occurs every time the OS accesses physical memory that has been flushed to disk.
Page Swap	Calculates a load based on the number of page swaps per second.	Memory\Pages/sec	A page swap occurs every time the OS swaps physical memory to virtual memory on disk.

Table 14-1. Load Evaluator Rules

NOTE The defaults for these rules are based on a single CPU Pentium 400MHz machine with 192MB of random access memory (RAM), and a Small Computer System Interface (SCSI) Ultra Wide Controller. Servers with multiple processors or disk controllers should change these default values. To determine the best values, use Performance Monitor to track the counters listed in Table 14-1. Use values obtained during idle and full-load conditions to set the appropriate thresholds.

INSTALLATION MANAGEMENT FOR CITRIX XENAPP

This section covers design and architecture topics that you need to understand before using Installation Manager to deploy applications to a XenApp farm in the Enterprise environment. Concepts discussed include data store usage, group size considerations, WAN recommendations, and application deployment recommendations.

Group Size Considerations

Installation Manager permits the installation of applications to predefined groups of servers. A group allows a Citrix administrator to install applications to a specific set of servers quickly and efficiently, so that the administrator does not have to select individual servers with every installation. For example, the administration might restrict an installation to the Accounting Department's servers.

When creating a server group for application deployment, make sure that you consider the following:

- Plan how you want to use and create your server groups.
- Keep your group size reasonable.

Installation Manager deploys applications to servers simultaneously, but it does not use multicasting. Each target server reads the data from the location where the installation package is stored. Large installation packages, such as Microsoft Office XP, copy more than 200MB of data from the package server to the target server. The amount of data transferred across the network is

$$D = I \times N$$

where:

D = the amount of data
I = the size of the installation
N = the number of target servers

Smaller group sizes are needed when installing applications that require a server to restart. Installations occur simultaneously, and XenApp can be forced to restart at nearly the same time. Because of this, a transient load is placed on the data store. The data store server, the internetworking infrastructure, and the performance of the network can be greatly affected during application deployment and server restarting. Table 14-2 provides suggestions based on a 100 Mbps switched Ethernet infrastructure.

	Small	Medium	Large
Application size	<5MB	5–20MB	>20MB
Recommended group size	<100	<80	<50

Table 14-2. Suggested Group Sizes for a 100 Mbps Switched Ethernet Infrastructure

Cluster groups logically. Deployment is more efficient if several logical groups are created that match the schema of the overall enterprise. One group might contain servers that host standard business applications, another group can host engineering applications, and so on.

Network Setup Recommendations

The network setup recommendations for XenApp also apply to Installation Manager. The more efficient and capable the network, the quicker and easier applications are to install. The use of switches, high-speed backbones, and high-speed disk drives greatly enhances the capability of Installation Manager to install applications to large server farms efficiently.

WAN Recommendations

Do not install applications to target servers across a WAN. The amount of bandwidth and time required to install an application over a WAN can congest the network for extended periods of time, which can result in networking timeouts. To avoid this situation, do the following:

- Create a new application package at the remote site where the application is to be deployed.
- If there is more than one remote target server, copy the package and the associated installation files over the WAN once, and then deploy it on that segment.

Installation Manager Application Deployment Recommendations

This section contains application deployment considerations when using Installation Manager with XenApp. Concepts discussed include package server recommendations, deployment server recommendations, the network share account, job scheduling and staggered install, package group deployment, user-specified restart, and recording applications requiring restarts during installation.

Package Server

The package server is used to record an application's installation. The package server can be used to generate packages for applications that do not have MSI installations.

The generated package is then deployed to XenApp. The following package server recommendations help ensure a clean package file:

- Keep the package server as similar in configuration (both hardware and software) as possible to the target server. Make the package server as "clean" as possible. Previously installed applications should be rolled back or uninstalled before recording. For additional information, see the *Installation Manager Administrator's Guide*.
- Do not run other applications while an image is recording.
- You should stop any unnecessary background processes before recording an installation using Packager, including the IMA service, especially if a manual install needs to be performed. Background processes and file changes may be recorded by Packager and could overwrite important files, such as the local access database files used by the IMA service.
- Do not package applications through an ICA session.

Deployment Server

The *deployment server* is the server where the package and installation files reside. All target servers communicate with this server to get the files and information they need to install the application. The following recommendations offer helpful information about deploying packages:

- Put the deployment server on a server grade machine. Each target server requests the same file set from the deployment server. The load on the deployment server can be high. The deployment server must be capable of handling the combined load of the servers connecting and requesting information simultaneously in a deployment group.
- Put the deployment server on a 100 Mbps switched Ethernet port. Running the deployment server in a shared collision domain increases latency. Connections can be refused due to timeout or server overload. This problem increases on a busy network and when many servers are targeted for a single installation.

Network Share Account

The network share account allows the target server to have access rights to the network share point where the package is located. To set up a network share account, complete the following steps:

1. Right-click the Installation Manager node in the Presentation Server Console.
2. Select Properties.
3. Enter the domain account and password to be used to access network shares.

When performing an unattended install, the network share account must have administrator privileges on the target server.

NOTE Installation Manager supports only Window domain authentication models, not workgroups.

Job Scheduling and Staggered Install

The following recommendations can lower bandwidth consumption, allowing the farm to function without a loss of performance:

- Schedule the installation of packages during times of low network usage.
- Avoid installations during scheduled server backups or restorations.

NOTE While an application is being deployed to a server, all ICA connections are terminated until the installation is completed.

Installation Manager supports staggered installations of package groups. Installation window options and multiple dates can be used for package groups to schedule the installation job during a certain time period within specific days. Options include the following:

- Scheduling the installation window during times of low network usage.
- Selecting multiple dates if the installation of the packages in a package group requires multiple dates for installation. The packages that haven't been installed begin installation in the same installation window on the selected dates.

NOTE A staggered installation of a single package is not supported.

Package Group Deployment

Package groups are used to deploy multiple packages to the same target server or server groups in one schedule. The following are recommendations and best practices:

- Create package groups with similar packages to simplify deployment.
- After the package groups have been deployed, do not make changes to the package group (that is, do not add packages to or delete them from the package group) because this causes unnecessary uninstall errors. If you need to deploy new packages, create a new package group and then deploy it.
- If changes are made to a deployed package group, the Job status tab of the Job properties window will not report installation status for the deleted or newly added package.
- After scheduling an installation of a package group, do not make changes to the package group contents, because this may result in temporary inaccurate Job Result information. Refresh the Presentation Server Console to correct this behavior.

User-Specified Reboot

The server restart behavior during package deployment is affected by three options:

- If you set the option "Do not reboot servers if any user sessions are open" before deploying packages, the target server will not restart if it detects a user connection to the target server, even though the package deployment requires a restart. To finish the deployment, the target server will restart after the user logs off. You can override this behavior by selecting the "Force reboot after job" option while scheduling the installation of a package.
- If you deploy a package group and one or more of the applications require a restart at the end of the deployment, you can set the "Delay reboot until the end of Job" option while scheduling the installation to postpone the restart until the end of the entire package group deployment.
- If you set "Force reboot after job," the server will restart after the package has been deployed. Any active user sessions will receive a message from the server, asking the user to log off. The messages will be sent in five minute intervals for 15 minutes (although you can change this default setting). Any active sessions will be terminated and then the server will restart.

Recording Applications Requiring Reboot During Installation

The Installation Manager Packager cannot resume package recording after a reboot during an application's installation. Note the following:

- When recording an application that prompts the user for a restart, cancel the restart and stop the recording on the Packager.
- Installation Manager Packager cannot record an application that forces a restart that the user cannot cancel.
- Installation Manager Packager cannot record an application that requires multiple server restarts during installation.

If an application has an unattended installation program, the Installation Manager Packager will create a package from the unattended installation program only. The Installation Manager Packager will not record the actual installation. When using the Installation Manager Packager to package the application, select "Package an Unattended Program" option to package the unattended install program and any other necessary files. This method allows applications that require one or more restarts during installation to be packaged.

Description of a Package Deployment Process

Table 14-3 describes the details of what happens when a package is deployed to XenApp using Installation Manager. The process of adding a package to the Presentation Server Console has been omitted. For further details about adding packages to the Presentation Server Console, see the *Installation Manager Administrator's Guide*.

Step	Area Involved	Description
1	Presentation Server Console	The administrator chooses to install a package within the Presentation Server Console: Right-click package, Select servers to deploy package to, Select package installation schedule.
2	IMA	Presentation Server Console makes a call to the Installation Manager subsystem to schedule an install.
3	IMA	The Installation Manager subsystem adds entries to the data store based on the administrator's selected options (which servers are to be rebooted and the list of servers to which to be deployed).
4	Presentation Server Console	The Presentation Server Console receives notification that a job has been scheduled and the status of the job changes to Pending.
5	IMA	A notification is sent to all servers of a data store change and the Local Host Cache (LHC) of each server is updated.
6	IMA	The Installation Manager subsystem on each server checks whether the server is a "target server." If so, an installation job is added to the installer queue.
7	Target server	Logons are disabled.
8	IMA	The appropriate installer (MSI, ADF, or MSP) is run.
9	IMA	The Installation Manager subsystem reads the properties from the LHC to see where to get the package.
10	Presentation Server Console	The Presentation Server Console receives notification that the installation has started.
11	IMA	After completing the installation, the Installation Manager subsystem adds a log entry to the data store under InstallationManagement | EventLog. In addition, an entry describing the job status is added to the registry of the server under HKLM\SOFTWARE\Citrix\IMS\2.0\ Jobs*jobid*.
12	Presentation Server Console	The Presentation Server Console receives notification that the installation has completed.
13	IMA	An entry is written to the data store under InstallationManagement | Installations for the newly installed application.
14	Target server	A reboot is performed, if required, or the next package is installed.
15	Target server	Logons are reenabled.

Table 14-3. Package Deployment Sequence of Events

USER POLICIES BEST PRACTICES

With user policies, you can apply select XenApp settings—including shadowing permission settings, printer autocreation settings, and client device mapping settings—to specific users or user groups. Using policies, you can tailor your environment at the user level.

This section contains tips and troubleshooting guidelines for working with user policies in XenApp:

- Assign user policies to user groups rather than individual users. If you assign user policies to user groups, assignments are updated automatically when you add or remove users from the group.
- Disable unused policies. Policies with all the rules set to Not Configured create unnecessary processing.
- Avoid conflicting settings in Citrix Connection Configuration or in the farmwide settings of the Presentation Server Console. Several policy rules can also be set in Citrix Connection Configuration and/or the farmwide settings in the Presentation Server Console. When possible, keep all settings consistent (enabled or disabled) to make troubleshooting easier.
- Use the search functionality to see which policy rules are being applied to users or user groups. Also use the Search function to determine the effective policy being applied to users. The resultant policy returned from a search enables you to determine which rules are in effect for users.
- Use the drag-and-drop feature of user policies to assign the correct priority to a user policy quickly. If you want to move a policy up or down in priority, you can drag the policy above or below the policy that currently has the rank that you want to achieve.

USER-TO-USER SHADOWING BEST PRACTICES

Users can shadow other users without requiring administrator rights. Similar to Citrix Conferencing Manager, multiple users from different locations can view presentations and training sessions, allowing one-to-many, many-to-one, and many-to-many online collaboration.

NOTE Although it is possible for users to shadow each other for collaboration, training, and other tasks, Conferencing Manager or GoToMeeting are more suitable solutions for performing these tasks.

- Do not assume that members of the administrators group have shadow rights by default. Although local administrators may have shadowing rights enabled in Citrix Connection Configuration, they are unable to shadow users who have been assigned to the policy by default. You must add the members of the local administrators group to the list of people with shadow rights in the user policy.

- Although user policies usually take precedence over settings configured in other XenApp utilities, shadowing is an exception to the rule. If shadowing was disabled during XenApp setup or disabled in Citrix Connection Configuration for a particular connection, then user policies with shadowing enabled have no effect.
- Because the most restrictive of the three shadow settings—settings in the Citrix Connection Configuration, settings specified during XenApp installation, and settings in shadow policies—go into effect, avoid unnecessary administration headaches by using shadow policies as the central control to control shadow settings. Exceptions to this rule include the need to adhere to local governmental laws that stipulate certain privacy requirements.

ENHANCED DELEGATED ADMINISTRATION

XenApp delegated administration lets you assign custom roles to individual users or groups to facilitate management of your XenApp environment. In XenApp 3.0, this support was enhanced to include the capability to delegate permissions on Server and Application folders, thus enabling you to delegate administrative abilities at a much more granular level.

It is highly recommended to create Active Directory or NDS groups to which you can assign these custom privileges. When you create your custom Citrix Administrators, simply select the group instead of the user(s). This lets you add and remove users to and from these preconfigured groups without having to reconfigure all the permissions.

One capability of the delegated administration feature is that you can now assign a server to a published application. Thus, without any view or edit permissions to the server and without edit permissions to a published application, a user can still be granted rights to manage the addition and removal of the servers assigned to run this published application.

NOTE For the capability to assign servers to a published application, you must grant the Assign Applications to Servers permission on the server folder that contains the servers that the custom administrator will be allowed to assign. You must also grant at least view permissions on the application folder(s) that contains the application(s) for which the custom administrator is allowed to manage the server list.

NOTE Proper design can be important when dealing with this feature. If an application is published on a server but the custom administrator has not been granted the Assign Applications to Servers permission on the folder containing the server, the administrator will be unable to see these servers in the published application properties. This could potentially lead to confusion for the administrator, as well as to complexities if servers are assigned that have different domain trust relationships.

Another capability is that you can assign permissions to a custom administrator to manage sessions at the application level only. This means that the administrator would only be able to see and manage the users who are using a particular published application but not all the users logged on to the server.

NOTE Multiple published applications may be launched within the same session using the session sharing feature of XenApp. Thus if a custom administrator attempts to use the logoff, disconnect, or reset session management options on a user running a particular published application, that administrator will affect all other session-shared applications running within that session. Again, proper design can be important because if a custom administrator has the rights to reset one published application that a user is running but does not have any rights over another published application, the administrator will still implicitly have rights over the other application if they both run in the same session.

Delegated Administrator Tips

To let a user shadow through the console, enable the following permissions at a minimum:

- **Citrix Administrators** Log on to Presentation Server Console.
- **Servers** View server information.
- **Sessions** View session management.

You must also grant shadowing permissions in the Citrix Connection Configuration tool or configure a XenApp policy to enable shadowing for the user.

CITRIX RESOURCE MANAGEMENT

Resource Manager is a component of XenApp Enterprise or Platinum Editions and is not available in XenApp Advanced Edition.

Resource Manager also includes the Summary Database, which allows historical data to be stored on metrics and servers and reports to be produced on the stored data.

Resource Manager Database and Metric Server

Resource Manager stores all its configurations, settings, thresholds, and metrics in the data store and in the local host cache. Previous versions of Resource Manager contained a local Resource Manager database and a Farm Metric Server. Feature Release 2 introduced a Database Connection Server (DCS) used with Summary Database.

Local Resource Manager Database

Each XenApp with Resource Manager installed has a local database in which it stores the individual server's metric information. It is important to note the following:

- The local Resource Manager database is a Microsoft Access Jet database called RMLocalDatabase.mdb that is located in the %ProgramFiles%\Citrix\Citrix Resource Manager\LocalDB folder by default.

- XenApp accesses the local Resource Manager database when creating real-time graphs, displaying system snapshots, running reports on that specific server, and writing server metrics. You have the capability of real-time graphs, server snapshots, and current reports.
- Server metric and process data are written to the local Resource Manager database.
- The local Resource Manager database holds metric values and application information for the previous 96 hours.
- This database is compacted when the IMA service is started, and once a day while the IMA service is running.

Farm Metric Server

The Farm Metric Server is used for application and server monitoring. The Farm Metric Server gathers its information from the data collector. Because the Farm Metric Server accesses the data collector every 15 seconds to obtain published application counters and every 30 seconds to determine whether machines are offline, configuring data collectors to also perform the role of Farm Metric Servers, and the backup Farm Metric Servers, can improve performance. The Farm Metric Server may also perform the role of the Database Connection Server but this is not recommended in larger farms if the data collector is also the Farm Metric Server. The additional load generated by Database Connection Server activity can affect the performance of your Database Connection Server.

TIP Although Resource Manager can track any Performance Monitor counter as a server metric, Citrix recommends you limit the total number of metrics tracked on a server to fewer than 50.

Alerts

Resource Manager can send alerts to users or groups of users using either e-mail or Short Message Service (SMS). It can also send alerts to a Simple Network Management Protocol (SNMP) management console.

TIP If the e-mail service will not send alerts, the Citrix administrator should confirm that he or she can access the mail server using the configured account. Also, verify that the mail client being used (for example, Microsoft Outlook) is the default mail client for the server and that no additional password is required to connect to the mail server.

TIP To enable Resource Manager to send SNMP traps for application alerts, SNMP must be set up on the primary and backup Farm Metric Servers.

Summary Database

The Summary Database is used for storing historical data from servers in the farm. Citrix administrators can produce reports, such as billing, based on the stored data.

These reports can be based on several criteria, such as CPU usage or application usage.

- Each farm that requires the Summary Database must have a DCS, which writes the metric information from other farm servers to the Summary Database.
- A system Data Source Name (DSN) called RMSummaryDatabase defines the connection between the DCS and the database where the metric information is stored.
- Data are stored on each individual server in summary files. Summary files are updated whenever a session or process terminates or an event occurs and once an hour for metrics.
- Each Resource Manager server in the farm records its own summary data locally for 24 hours and then transmits these data to the DCS at a configurable time of day.
- Reports on data in the summary database can be generated via the Presentation Server Console in a manner similar to those reports made available for the local database for each server.

TIP Report templates for the popular Crystal Reports tool are available from the Citrix web site, http://www.citrix.com.

TIP By default, metrics are stored in the Summary Database. You can change this setting on the Threshold Configuration screen. It is also possible to specify the time of day or week that metrics are recorded in the Summary Database on a per-server basis.

Folders and Zones

XenApp can record which folders and zone a server is in at the time of writing data to the summary file. This information can be used to group servers when creating reports outside of the console. By default, the summary period for server metrics is one hour.

If either the folder or zone has changed for a server, just before writing the next set of server metric records to the summary file, a new Folder and Zone record will be written. All following server metric records are then associated with this new Folder and Zone record. Thus if the folder or zone changes multiple times within the summary period, only the one record will be written prior to writing the new server metric records to the summary file. All other folder and zone changes will go unnoticed.

SDB_Scratch Table

The *sdb_scratch table* is used with the generation of billing reports to store information about the reports currently opened so that the records being displayed in the report can be marked as billed. A record exists in the SDB_Scratch table per open billing report in the farm. When you close a report, the record is deleted from the table.

Data Purging

The Summary Database enables administrators to control how long data are stored by purging the database at set periods. It is also possible to turn off purging, in which case all data are kept for an indefinite period. If a purge is missed—for example, if the DCS is not online at the purge time—a purge is initiated when the DCS next starts up.

NOTE Active sessions, and the processes associated with them, will not be purged from the database whether they are or are not billed.

NOTE Processes are purged only if their "parent" session record is purged (that is, to maintain data integrity, it is not desirable to purge only process records).

Uploads to the Database Connection Server

Uploads to the DCS are initiated by the individual servers in the farm based on the upload time.

The following sequence of events occurs for each XenApp with Resource Manager enabled when the upload time is met each day:

1. XenApp closes the current summary file and begins a new file.
2. XenApp sends a notification to the DCS stating it has a summary file to be uploaded. One notification per summary file is ready to be uploaded.
3. DCS maintains a list of all notifications.
4. DCS requests files to be copied to it. The number of concurrent uploads is limited to reduce congestion.
5. When files are available on the DCS, the import starts. Imports are limited to a maximum concurrent amount.
6. For each file being imported, a new file is uploaded, so 10 files are either being copied or ready to be imported.
7. When the import succeeds, a message is sent to the originating host, informing it that the summary file can be safely deleted. The file is also deleted from the DCS.
8. This continues until there are no further summary files to be uploaded or imported.

Considerations

Consider the following issues regarding resource management:

- Only summary files that are not currently active will be uploaded to the DCS.
- If the DCS receives another request to upload a summary file, it logs a duplicate request and the old request is deleted from the list. Duplicate requests can occur if updates are taking longer than 24 hours.

- The default setting for concurrent uploads is 10. The default setting for concurrent imports is 1. The reason for these default settings is to reduce the requirement on database connection licenses.
- Importing a record into the Summary Database twice will not cause duplicate entries.
- If a summary file takes longer than 30 minutes to transfer, the DCS assumes that it has timed out and deletes any record of requesting it. This file is not retransmitted until the next update period, 24 hours later, unless a manual update is invoked. If the uploaded summary file eventually reaches the DCS after it has timed out, it is ignored and deleted.
- Upload time is compared to the server time. The server's time zone is used to determine whether uploads should begin. For example, a XenApp farm has the majority of the machines in the East Coast of the United States and a smaller zone in the United Kingdom with the upload time set to 1 A.M. The servers in the United States begin to upload files at 1 A.M. EST, whereas machines in the United Kingdom start their uploads at 1 A.M. UK time, which is 8 P.M. EST.
- A "duplicate upload request" message in the DCS server log indicates problems in the system, but it is not an error message. The duplicate request does not cause any invalid or duplicate data in the Summary Database and should be treated as an informational message. An example that could result in a "duplicate upload request" would be a manual upload requested when an upload is already under way—either a timed update or a previously requested manual request—or uploads taking more than 24 hours to complete, resulting in the next daily upload beginning before the previous one has completed.

Summary Files

Summary files are written only when the Summary Database has been enabled in the XenApp farm. Each file is given a random name when it is created. At creation time, a header is written to the file. This header contains the following fields: Schema Version, Server's Name, Server's Domain, and Farm Name.

Additional records are written to the file based on these events:

- When a process terminates, a process record is written to the file.
- Every 60 minutes, a metric record is written for each metric configured to store summary data.
- When a session is started, a session record is written.
- When a session ends, a session record is written.
- When an event is generated, an event record is written.

The following information is stored for each of the record types' metric records: Object Name, Counter Name, Instance Name, Update Time, Server UTC Bias (in minutes),

Sample Period (in seconds), Data Count, Min Value, Max Value, Mean Value, and Std Dev value.

For each of the application metric records, the following information is stored: Application Name, Application Type, Farm Name, Object Name, Update Time, Sample Period (in seconds), Data Count, Min Value, Max Value, Mean Value, and Std Dev value.

The following information is stored for each of the Process records: User Name, Client Name, Client Address Family, Client Address, App Name, App Type, Path Name, Process Name, Version, Product Date, Type, Process ID (PID), Exit Code, Affinity, Start Time, End Time, Total Time, Active Time, Kernel Used, User Used, User Active, Kernel Active, Memory, Memory Active, Working Set, Page File, Page Faults, Paged Pool, Non Paged Pool, Session ID, Server UTC Bias (in minutes), User Domain, and Session Start Time.

For session records, the following information is stored: User Name, Client Name, Client Address Family, Client Address, App Name, App Type, Winstation, Protocol, Session Start, Session End, Duration (in milliseconds), Server UTC bias (in minutes), Session UTC bias (in minutes), Session ID, and User Domain.

The following information is stored for event records: Server Name, NetDomain Name, Farm Name, Event Time, Server UTC Bias (in minutes), and Event Code.

For folder records, the Folder Name is stored, and for zone records, the Zone Name is stored.

NOTE Only Server Up and Server Down events are stored. The Farm Metric Server generates the Server Down event upon detecting that a server can no longer be contacted. The server generates the Server Up event as the IMA service is restarted.

NOTE Summary files can be manually copied to the DCS or other servers before the daily update is started. The header information in the summary file ensures that the records are associated with the correct server.

SDB_Heuristics Table

When there are large amounts of data (for example, of the gigabyte order) in a Summary Database, an administrator generating reports may find that the Management Console cannot display reports that are many megabytes in size. Resource Manager uses the SDB_Heuristics table in the Summary Database to ensure that any Summary Report to be generated can be displayed within the Management Console. By default, the table will contain the entries and values listed in Table 14-4.

When the administrator specifies various report options in the Summary Report generation dialog boxes, Resource Manager does calculations based on these options and the entries in the SDB_Heuristics table to estimate the size of the report to be returned. If this estimated value is greater than MAXIMUM_PRACTICAL_HTML_BYTES in the case of process, user, and server summary reports, and greater than BILL_HTML_MAX in the case of billing reports, a warning message is displayed stating that the report may

HEURISTIC	HEURISTIC VALUE
BILL_HTML_MAX (characters)	72500
MAXIMUM_PRACTICAL_HTML_BYTES (bytes)	1048576
PROCESSES_PER_SESSION	10
SESSIONS_PER_USER_PER_DAY	5
USERSUM_HTML_BYTES_PER_PROCESS	128

Table 14-4. Default Entries and Values for SBD_Heuristics

be too large to display within the Management Console. In such a case, the administrator has the option to cancel the report generation or continue. If the administrator continues and the report is too large to display, an error message is displayed within the report window. The administrator then has the option of saving the report directly to disk for viewing in another application that can display HTML (for example, Internet Explorer).

Depending on the usage of servers in the farm, an administrator may want to configure the values in this table to reflect more accurately the amount of data that may be displayed in reports.

NOTE The capability of the Presentation Server Console to display reports is dependent on the number of report windows currently open. Each time that a report is returned to the Presentation Server Console, a calculation is performed that subtracts the size of the report (in bytes for summary reports and characters for billing reports) from the respective maximum values in the table, producing an "available size" figure for subsequent reports. Accordingly, an administrator is more likely to receive a warning in the report windows that the report cannot be displayed if the system has multiple reports open. Once a report is closed, its "size" is returned to the "available size" figure for future reports.

NOTE If the Summary Database is unavailable, all reports (Current Process, Current User, and Server Snapshot) make use of a hard-coded default value of 1048576 bytes (524,288 characters).

REPORT CENTER IN THE ACCESS MANAGEMENT CONSOLE

The *Report Center* in the Access Management Console extends the reporting capabilities in Resource Manager and lets you easily generate reports from a variety of real-time and historic data sources. A wizard helps you select the type of report, the data to be displayed, and the schedule for running the report. You can view the status of your scheduled reports and adjust the report parameters.

This section provides information about the different reports available, the data sources for these reports, and how to copy reports and report specifications to other servers.

Copying Report Center Reports and Specifications to a Different Console

The Access Management Console provides a Report Center extension that enables Citrix administrators to generate HTML and CSV reports from a variety of real-time and historic data sources. Commands are available to view the reports from within the console and to make the reports more widely available by copying them to other locations or e-mailing them to selected recipients.

Each successful report, along with a copy of the specification used to generate it, is stored locally on the machine running the Access Management Console. For reports that administrators plan to run regularly, they can also generate named specifications recording report formats, farm information, data source details, required time period, and other report parameters. These can then be run manually or scheduled to run when required.

Thus, if an administrator wants to generate reports from an Access Management Console on a different machine, neither previous reports and their associated specifications, nor any named specification will be available from the new console. However, it is possible to copy the necessary files to the machine running the new console and use them from there without editing anything, as long as the second machine has access to the same farm and Resource Manager Summary Database as the first one.

Understanding Where User-Configured Report and Specification Files Are Kept

Report Center stores its user-configurable data on the machine running the Access Management Console. So, a Citrix administrator logged on to a Windows 2003 server can find his or her report and specification files in the directory %APPDATA%\Citrix\ReportCenter.

Specifications are stored as .spec files in appropriately named folders within the directory %APPDATA%\Citrix\ReportCenter\CustomSettings\Specifications.

Generated reports (and their associated unique specifications) are stored under the directory %APPDATA%\Citrix\ReportCenter\DataSets, with each set of related files in a folder with a unique system-generated name (such as 4C7F885E0EF72F30).

NOTE Each report folder's set of files always includes a Results.xml file containing the raw data used to generate the necessary HTML reports, graphs, and CSV files when the user requests them. As the HTML and CSV folders and their contents are generated only when required, they may not be present when you examine the folders within datasets. This is by design, and both types of reports can always be generated when required.

To move previously created specifications and reports to the new console, the administrator should copy all the relevant folders to their corresponding position on the new machine. Once discovery has been run, and the specifications and job displays are refreshed, all the transferred items should be listed as before. Administrators can then view previous reports and generate new ones as required.

Known Issues

In the Jobs display, the Elapsed Time values for the copied reports will be incorrect. (This is because of the way that Report Center calculates elapsed time; it uses the creation time of the files, and this time changes when the reports are copied to the new machine.)

Available Report Center Reports and Their Data Sources

This section illustrates the various Report Center reports that can be created and provides information as to where the data for these reports exists.

Application Availability

Data Source: Summary Database

Table: SDB_APPHISTORY

Purpose: Determining whether applications were always available for clients to connect.

Details: The Application Availability report displays the percentage of time that the application was available in the farm during the reporting time period.

This report determines when the application was available for connection across any of the servers onto which it was published. "Unavailable" is defined as no servers online being able to service the application to clients.

Application

Data Source: MFCOM via servers selected at the time of specification

Purpose: Listing settings for selected applications in the farm. This is a way to get all application settings quickly in one view.

Details: The Application report displays the settings for each published application selected. It details the configured users, servers, application location, working directory, appearance, client options, and current status in the farm—that is, whether it is enabled or disabled.

This report provides information only for applications published to clients, which includes published desktops and published content. It also provides information regarding the unused applications in the farm.

Application Usage

Data Source: Summary Database

Table: SDB_SESSION

Purpose: Viewing the usage of applications across selected servers over a period of time.

Details: The Application Usage report displays the total number of sessions and the maximum concurrent number of sessions for each application selected.

This report displays a table of the most heavily used applications among the list of selected applications. "Heavily used" is defined by the highest values for maximum concurrent users. The total number of applications to display is configurable.

Optionally, the Application Usage report displays a table of unused applications. These are applications that have no sessions during the reporting period.

In addition, the Application Usage report optionally displays a graph of time versus concurrent sessions for each application selected.

Client Type

Data Source: Summary Database

Tables: SDB_SESSION, SDB_CLIENTHISTORY

Purpose: Viewing different types of clients that have connected to the servers.

Details: The Client Type report displays the client type and version for connections made to the selected servers.

This report also includes a graph of the different client types and the percentage of connections made to each.

Disconnected Sessions

Data Source: Summary Database

Table: SDB_CONNECTIONHISTORY

Purpose: Displaying the number of disconnected sessions across a selection of servers over a period of time.

Details: The Disconnected Sessions report shows a graph displaying the number of disconnected sessions across the specified servers over the period of time being reported. It also displays a trend line of these disconnected sessions.

Policy

Data Source: MFCOM

Purpose: Displaying a list of policies in the farm.

Details: The Policy report lists all policies defined in the farm and displays the details of the policies. Policy settings that are not set to either enabled or disabled can be excluded from the report using the Hide Unconfigured Policies check box. Unchecking this box will include all details of the policies, even if they are set to "unconfigured."

Server Availability

Data Source: Summary Database

Table: SDB_EVENTLOG

Purpose: Determining the percentage of time that the selected servers were available to service connections. This report determines the period of time for which servers were down due to scheduled reboots. It also determines the period of time for which servers were down due to unexpected reboots.

Details: The Server Availability report displays a table with the percentages of uptime, unscheduled downtime, and scheduled downtime.

A graph is also displayed with a separate bar for each server selected. The bar is color-coded to show the uptime, the scheduled downtime, and the unscheduled downtime during the reported time period.

Server Performance

Data Source: Summary Database

Tables: SDB_METRICS, SDB_CONNECTIONHISTORY

Purpose: Determining the most heavily used server across a selection of servers based on CPU load, available memory, or maximum concurrent sessions.

Details: The Server Performance report displays load information for all the selected servers.

This report also shows three separate tables detailing the servers that had the highest load. These tables show only servers selected for inclusion in the report.

The number of servers listed in these tables can be configured using the "Number of servers to display" setting.

The tables contain data based on the report period for the following three criteria:

- Highest CPU load
- Lowest available memory
- Highest maximum concurrent sessions

Server Reboot

Data Source: Summary Database

Table: SDB_EVENTLOG

Purpose: Determining when servers have been rebooted. This determines which servers shut down but were not restarted.

Details: The Server Reboot report shows, in table format, the times at which servers started up, the times at which they were available to handle client connections, and the times at which they were rebooted.

Server Utilization (CPU)

Data Source: Summary Database

Tables: SDB_PROCESS, SDB_METRICS

Purpose: Listing processes across servers that take more than a defined average percentage of the CPU. This report displays the average percentage of the server's CPU for the reported time period.

Details: The Server Utilization (CPU) report displays the servers in the selection that have the highest average CPU use during the reported time period. The number of servers to be displayed is configurable, allowing the server selection to be the entire farm, but only allowing the most heavily used servers to be displayed in the table.

A separate table for each server is in the list to show all the processes with high CPU usage during the reported time period. The criterion for "high CPU usage" is configurable.

Server Utilization (Memory)

Data Source: Summary Database

Tables: SDB_PROCESS, SDB_METRICS

Purpose: Displaying the servers with the least available memory. This report displays the processes consuming the most memory on individual servers.

Details: The Server Utilization (Memory) report displays servers that have had the least available memory within the server selection and reported time period. For each server listed, there is a separate table to show the processes that consumed the most memory during the reported time period. The number of servers and processes to be displayed is configurable.

Session Statistics

Data Source: Summary Database

Table: SDB_SESSION

Purpose: Displaying the number of concurrent sessions made to a selection of servers. This report displays the servers that have received the most concurrent sessions.

Details: The Session Statistics report lists, in table format, the servers that have the highest number of concurrent sessions during the reported time period. The number of servers to be included in this table is configurable.

A scatter graph showing the highest number of concurrent sessions across the server selection based on time is also displayed.

CONSIDERATIONS WITH NETWORK MANAGER

Network Manager is a component of XenApp Enterprise edition and is not available in XenApp Advanced Edition. The following are some known issues with Network Manager:

- In Tivoli NetView, sometimes the server icon is green, whereas the subsystem icons are light blue. In this case, highlight the green server icon and perform a status update to update the status of the subsystem icons. This is a Tivoli NetView IP map problem that occurs while running over long periods of time.
- When using Tivoli NetView, if the Trapd.exe process is killed while the Metadis.exe and Metalan.exe services are running, each service acquires 50 percent CPU utilization. The services do not return to normal CPU levels until Trapd.exe is restarted. This is a known issue with Tivoli NetView.
- In HP Network Node Manager, a link-down status is represented by a blue icon. This happens only if the server cannot be contacted by the console when the Status Update is performed. In Tivoli NetView, a link-down status is displayed in red.
- When Network Manager is uninstalled from one of the SNMP management consoles, by default, the Network Management icons stay in the IP map until they are deleted and the nodes are rediscovered. The icons can be deleted prior to uninstalling in NetView, by going to properties under the Edit pull-down menu and selecting the application Network Manager, and then clicking the Properties button. These icons can also be deleted in Openview by selecting properties under the Map pull-down menu, clicking the Application tab, selecting Network Manager, and then pressing the Configure for this map button.
- For Unicenter to be able to reclass Windows servers as XenApp servers, Security Management (secadmin) must be configured and enabled. Otherwise, a message similar to "Security authorization failure. The action has been denied," appears in the Unicenter event log (conlog).

Network Manager SNMP Agent Issues

The following are known issues and recommendations for the SNMP agent:

- For Windows 2003 Server, the SNMP service, by default, accepts SNMP messages only from the local host. Windows 2000 and previous OSs allowed any SNMP messages from any host from the start.

  To address this problem, add more servers to the list of allowed hosts (the recommended solution) or allow messages from any host (this solution is not secure).

- Older versions of Network Manager had the capability to shut down or restart XenApp. To comply with Microsoft SNMP security, these options have been removed in newer versions of the plug-ins. Any attempt to reboot a XenApp with an older version of a Network Manager plug-in is denied.

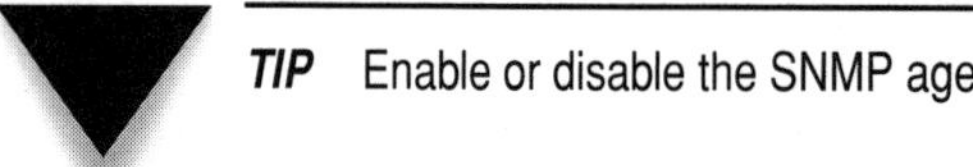

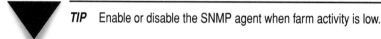

TIP Enable or disable the SNMP agent when farm activity is low.

CHAPTER 15

Password Manager Administration

In this chapter, we explore Password Manager administration. We also look at several security-related topics around the Password Manager agent, Hot Desktop configurations, backing up of the credential store, and managing of multiple domains.

ACCESSING LOGON MANAGER WITH A DISABLED TRAY ICON

In Citrix Password Manager 4.*x*, the administrator can choose whether to display the agent's tray icon on a per-deployment basis. This setting can be deployed as a registry setting or as an agent setting using the Password Manager Console.

The default installation configures the agent to be run with the /background flag, which does not invoke the logon manager on startup, but only starts the background process. Terminal servers start the agent during a logon via the registry entry HKLM\ Software\Microsoft\Windows NT\Current Version\winlogon\appsetup. Desktop operating systems (OSs) start the agent via the Start menu's startup folder. Once the user has logged in and the agent is running, users can invoke Logon Manager by double-clicking the tray icon. If the tray icon is disabled, you can still invoke Logon Manager by running ssoshell.exe without the background flag.

NOTE The shortcut installed in the Start menu contains the /background flag and will not invoke Logon Manager if the tray icon is disabled. In a XenApp environment, you can choose to publish ssoshell.exe with no arguments to allow users to access Logon Manager.

To disable the tray icon, navigate to Shell\Agent Settings in the console, then set ShowTrayIcon to "Do not show the tray icon."

NOTE Changing the tray icon display behavior does not affect the agent until you restart the agent by either logging off or shutting down the agent manually.

AUTOMATIC KEY RECOVERY

This section covers advanced concepts of Citrix Password Manager's Automatic Key Recovery. Topics include the following:

- **Migrating the V4 Secret from one Password Manager Service machine to another** This covers how to migrate the important V4 Secret in case a server is to be decommissioned and replaced by another.
- **A comparison between Automatic Key Recovery feature offered with Citrix Password Manager** This is an overview of how key recovery is handled without Automatic Key Recovery and how Automatic Key Recovery handles this task differently.

Migrating the V4 Secret from One Citrix Password Manager Service Machine to Another

The encryption mechanism uses a master secret named V4. V4 is one of a set of four random numbers used by the Automatic Key Recovery service to generate a key that encrypts and decrypts the primary authentication key. The *V4 Secret* is a cryptographically strong random number that is encrypted using machine-level Data Protection Application Programming Interface (DPAPI) and stored on the local hard drive of the machine running the Citrix Password Manager Service. Only code running on the Citrix Password Manager Service machine can decrypt V4. V4 is the only one of the four random numbers that remains static throughout the course of a deployment. If this number changes and agent users have already registered with Automatic Key Recovery with a previous V4, their credentials are lost.

If multiple instances of the Citrix Password Manager Service are installed in a deployment, and load-balanced using a third-party load-balancing mechanism, it is necessary to copy V4 (as well as the data integrity certificate and private key data) to these other machines.

To facilitate this activity, a command-line tool named CtxMoveKeyRecoveryData is installed with the Citrix Password Manager Service and enables the administrator to copy the secret data from one machine to another. CtxMoveKeyRecoveryData can be found at C:\Program Files\Citrix\MetaFrame Password Manager\Service\Tools>Ctx MoveKeyRecoveryData.

You invoke the tool as follows:

```
CtxMoveKeyRecoveryData [option] [filename]
```

The options include the following:

- **-generation** This option generates new key recovery data for the Automatic Key Recovery function.
- **-export [*filename*]** This option exports the key recovery data, encrypts them with a user-supplied password, and writes them to the specified file.
- **-import [*filename*]** The –import option reads the key recovery data from the specified file, decrypts them with a user-supplied password, and imports them.

On export, the tool creates a 3-DES encrypted file of the V4 secret, using the password to compose the key. After an import, the migrated system uses the password and 3-DES to decrypt the V4 Secret, which is then encrypted automatically using DPAPI.

Comparison between Automatic Key Recovery and Existing Question-Based Key Recovery Methods

Automatic Key Recovery is an alternative to the use of Security Questions (question-based authentication) or Previous Password mechanisms for recovering the authentication key. Automatic Key Recovery, unlike the other methods, does not require any interaction with the user.

Figure 15-1 illustrates the steps when Security Questions or Previous Password is used.

The process works as follows:

1. The user enters primary logon credentials and answers user questions during setup if Security Questions is used.
2. The Crypto API generates a unique Primary Authentication Key during setup (for first-time use).
3. The Primary Authentication Key is encrypted with the password of the primary logon credentials and the resulting key is stored in MS CAPI.
4. If Security Questions is being used, the Primary Authentication Key is encrypted with the user question, and the resulting key is stored in MS CAPI.
5. When subsequent logons occur, successful authentication unlocks MS CAPI, and the Primary Authentication Key is unlocked and becomes available to the Crypto API.
6. Crypto API passes the key to the Shell (agent), which uses it to decrypt user credentials.

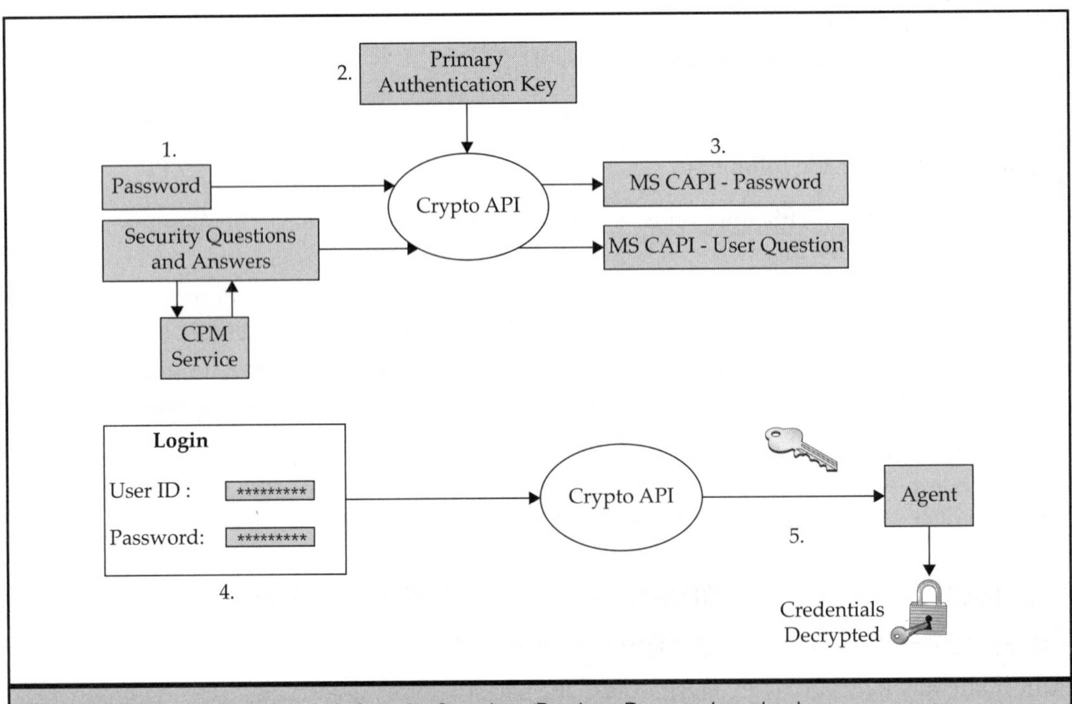

Figure 15-1. Key recovery with Security Questions/Previous Password mechanisms

The main difference between Automatic Key Recovery and other methods is how the authentication key is encrypted. This involves the use of the Citrix Password Manager Service.

Enrollment for Automatic Key Recovery

At a high level, the sequence in Figure 15-2 occurs when a user first uses the Password Manager agent.

The process follows this sequence:

1. The agent executes an algorithm, which results in deriving a 3DES key called the Automatic Key Recovery encryption key (AKRKey). (The agent uses the AKRKey in a similar manner as it ordinarily uses the key derived from the user's Security Questions or Previous Password information.)
2. The agent conceptually breaks the key into two parts. It stores one part of the data in the user's object on the synchronization point. The agent transmits the second part of the data to the Citrix Password Manager Service.
3. The Citrix Password Manager Service encrypts its portion of the key derivation data and stores the resulting encrypted data in the user's folder or under the user's Active Directory (AD) object on the synchronization point.

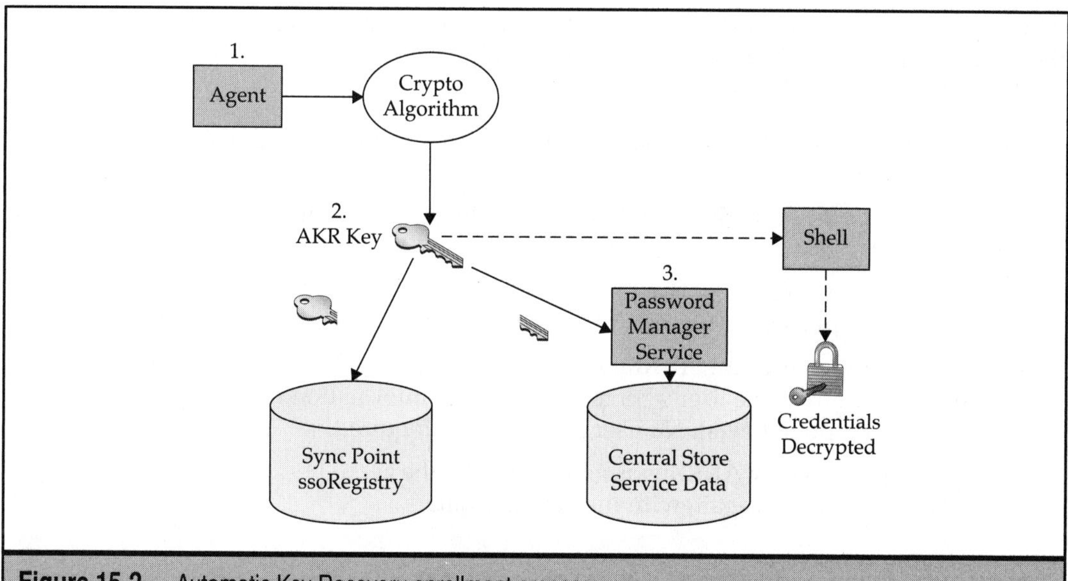

Figure 15-2. Automatic Key Recovery enrollment process

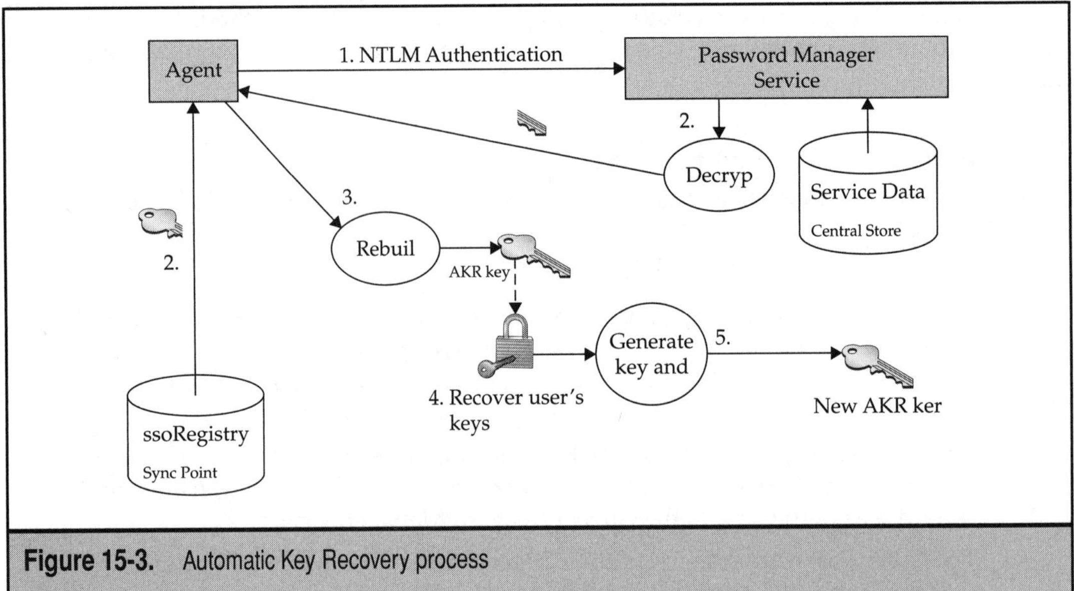

Figure 15-3. Automatic Key Recovery process

Key Recovery

After a password change initiated by the administrator or a self-service password reset, the sequence in Figure 15-3 occurs to recover the key.

The sequence is as follows:

1. The agent authenticates to the Citrix Password Manager Service using NTLM authentication.
2. The service decrypts the data that it originally encrypted and returns them to the agent.
3. The agent retrieves its portion of the key derivation data from the central store and uses both parts of the data to reconstitute the AKRKey.
4. The agent then uses the AKRKey in a similar fashion as it ordinarily uses the key derived from the user's Security Questions information to recover the user's encryption key(s). No user interaction is required.
5. At this point, a new AKRKey is generated and the agent performs the enrollment process again with the new key data.

CONFIGURING AND MANAGING A HOT DESKTOP ENVIRONMENT

The following section covers configuring and managing Hot Desktop.

Bypassing Hot Desktop Mode

All administrative maintenance to a Hot Desktop environment must be performed after bypassing the automatic logon process of the Hot Desktop Shared Account. To bypass the automatic logon process, hold the Shift key during the Windows logon process. For more information on bypassing the automatic logon process, see Microsoft Knowledge Base articles 310584 and 324737.

Hot Desktop Shared Account Automatic Logon

This section lists the Microsoft AutoAdminLogon registry keys used by the Hot Desktop Shared Account automatic logon process. The following describes the registry keys used:

```
[HKEY_LOCAL_MACHINE\SOFTWARE\Microsoft\Windows NT\CurrentVersion\WinLogon]
AutoAdminLogon=dword:00000001
```

AutoAdminLogon is used to enable or disable the automatic logon process used by the Hot Desktop Shared Account. A value of 0 disables the process, whereas a value of 1 enables it. If this key gets altered and the automatic logon process fails, use regedit to re-enable the key to 1. This key is set to 1 to enable the Auto-Admin logon process during the agent installation.

```
[HKEY_LOCAL_MACHINE\SOFTWARE\Microsoft\Windows NT\CurrentVersion\WinLogon]
DefaultUserName="Hot Desktop Shared Account name"
```

DefaultUserName is the account name used in the automatic logon process triggered by the AutoAdminLogon key. If this key gets altered and the automatic logon process fails, use regedit to re-enter your Hot Desktop Shared Account name. This key stores the name of the Hot Desktop Shared Account entered during agent installation.

```
[HKEY_LOCAL_MACHINE\SOFTWARE\Microsoft\Windows NT\CurrentVersion\WinLogon]
DefaultDomainName ="Domain of Hot Desktop Shared Account"
```

DefaultDomainName is the domain to which the HotDesktop Shared Account belongs as specified in DefaultUserName. If this key gets altered and the automatic logon process fails, use regedit to re-enter your Hot Desktop Shared Account name. This key is set to the domain of the Hot Desktop Shared Account entered during agent installation.

```
[HKEY_LOCAL_MACHINE\SOFTWARE\Microsoft\Windows NT\CurrentVersion\WinLogon]
DefaultPassword ="Hot Desktop Shared Account password"
```

This optional key is not recommended for security reasons because it exposes a clear text password in the registry. Normally, the password is stored in an encrypted format inside the NTSecret object. This key enables an administrator to hard-code a password for the Hot Desktop Shared Account to be used in the automatic logon process. This key is not created or set during the agent installation process because the agent stores the password in the NTSecret object.

NOTE If the Hot Desktop Shared Account password is changed or becomes corrupted in the registry, log on to Hot Desktop like a regular Hot Desktop User, but use the Hot Desktop Shared Account. Once logged in interactively, press Ctrl-Alt-Del and perform a normal password change. This process re-encrypts the Hot Desktop Shared Account password and stores it in the NTSecret object used in the automatic logon process.

ShellExecute—Identifying Application Executables

Once you identify the applications that you want to run in the context of the current Hot Desktop user, you must add the executable names to the ShellExecute section of the process.xml file. (This section of the process.xml file is referred to as ShellExecute for the remainder of this chapter.) Consider two variables when adding executables to ShellExecute:

- How will users launch applications (by using Start | Run, a file type association, or a command prompt)?
- What is the correct executable to define in ShellExecute?

Also note the following:

- The following ShellExecute example entries are not case-sensitive.
- The XML syntax is case-sensitive.
- Applications launched with additional parameters are not supported in Shell-Execute.

Using Start | Run If the administrator allows the Run option to be accessible on the Start menu, all forms of the executable should be listed in the ShellExecute section. Executables may require multiple entries in ShellExecute because the Run dialog box does not require file extensions. For example, suppose that the administrator wants calc.exe to run as the current Hot Desktop User each time that it is executed. The following entry is made to the ShellExecute section:

```
process
     namecalc.exe/name
/process
```

If a user entered **calc** (note the missing file extension) in the Run dialog box, it would be run in the context of the Hot Desktop Shared Account, not the Hot Desktop User Account. Specify the executable name without the file extension to allow ShellExecute to launch the application as the Hot Desktop User Account. For example, the following two entries would be required for the calc.exe application to run as the Hot Desktop User Account:

```
process
     nameCalc.exe</name
/process
```

```
process
    nameCalc/name
/process
```

File Type Association Launching an application by file type association provides another situation that ShellExecute must support. In this situation, use wildcards associated with the file type extension in the ShellExecute section to allow ShellExecute to match on the document type and launch the application as the Hot Desktop User Account. For example, the administrator wants notepad.exe, as well as all text (.txt) files opened to be launched as the current Hot Desktop User Account. To complete this requirement, add the following lines to the ShellExecute section:

```
process
    namenotepad.exe/name
process
process
    namenotepad/name
/process
process
    name*.txt/name
/process
```

Command Prompt All applications launched from within a command prompt are launched in the same user account context as the command prompt. By default, the command prompt is launched in the context of the Hot Desktop Shared Account, so any application launched from the command prompt is run as the Hot Desktop Shared Account. To cause all applications launched from the command prompt to run in the context of the Hot Desktop User Account, add **cmd.exe** to the ShellExecute section, as shown here:

```
process
    namecmd.exe/name
/process
process
    namecmd/name
/process
```

Defining the Correct Executable Name Occasionally, the process defined in ShellExecute may have been launched by another executable and, thus, ends up in the context of the user account that launched the calling executable. In this case, tools such as SysInternal's Process Explorer (http://technet.microsoft.com/en-us/sysinternals/default.aspx) allow you to monitor the processes as they launch and determine the correct executable name to place in the ShellExecute section of process.xml.

For example, NetManage Rumba's AS400 display is launched via wddsppag.bin, which is the running process once the AS400 display is started. However, the wddsppag. bin process is launched by rumbawsf.exe, which is the executable that should be defined in ShellExecute, as shown here:

```
process
     nameRumbawsf.exe/name
/process
process
     nameRumbawsf/name
/process
```

To identify the correct executable names, you may use the following steps:

1. In a Hot Desktop environment, log in as a Hot Desktop User Account.
2. Run procxp.exe (SysInternals Process Explorer) as an administrator (administrative permissions are required to see all the process information) by right-clicking (and holding down Shift as well on a Windows 2000 machine) on the procxp. exe and selecting Context | Run as. Enter the administrative credentials.
3. Edit the Process Explorer view to show the user column.
4. Launch the executable in question and use Process Explorer to identify the correct executable to include in the ShellExecute section.

Citrix XenApp Clients—Configuring in Hot Desktop

Using Citrix XenApp clients with Hot Desktop may require some additional configuration. This section is organized by client type and each section details the required configuration changes for that client.

Single Sign-On (SSO) Service (Citrix XenApp Clients) The SSO service provides pass-through authentication to XenApp Clients. In a Hot Desktop environment, the Hot Desktop GINA provides the service with up-to-date user information for the current Hot Desktop User Account. No additional configuration is required.

Program Neighborhood Agent If you are not using the SSO Service, additional configuration is needed for Program Neighborhood Agent to function properly. When Program Neighborhood Agent is installed, a shortcut is placed in the All Users Startup folder and launched automatically at startup. To configure Program Neighborhood Agent to run in the context of the Hot Desktop User account, complete the following steps:

1. Remove the shortcut to Program Neighborhood Agent from the All Users Startup folder to prevent the agent from being launched in the Hot Desktop Shared Account context.

2. Add Program Neighborhood Agent to your HotDesktop startup script to run as the current Hot Desktop User. (For additional instructions, see the following section, "Logon Scripts and Network Shares," as well as the samples provided on the Password Manager CD in the \SUPPORT\HOTDESKTOP folder.)
3. Add PNAgent.exe to the transient process section of the process.xml file. This change causes the Program Neighborhood Agent to be terminated on user logoff or user switch events. The following is an example of a transient process entry for Program Neighborhood Agent. (For additional information, see the *Password Manager Administrator's Guide.*)

```
transient_processes
     process
       namePNAgent.exe/name
     /process
/transient_processes
```

Program Neighborhood Classic Program Neighborhood Classic does not rely on user profiles and can be configured to request authentication from the Hot Desktop User Account, so no special configuration is required. As you will soon note, however, Citrix recommends that all XenApp clients be run in the context of the Hot Desktop User Account for security reasons.

Web Interface When connecting to XenApp via Web Interface, the Internet Explorer (IE) process must be launched in the context of the current Hot Desktop User Account rather than the Hot Desktop Shared Account. Control this behavior by adding the following entry to the ShellExecute section of the process.xml file:

```
process
     nameIExplore.exe/name
/process
process
     nameIExplore/name
/process
process
     name*.html/name
/process
process
     name*.htm/name
/process
```

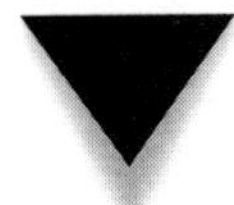

NOTE For security reasons, Citrix recommends that all XenApp clients be run as the current Hot Desktop User rather than the Hot Desktop Shared Account to prevent sensitive data from being left behind in the shared profile.

Profiles When roaming profile users log on to a computer, the user's roaming profile is copied to the local computer and is referred to as the *local profile*. If the user has previously logged on to this computer, the roaming profile is merged with the local profile. Similarly, when the user logs off from this computer, the local copy of the profile, including any changes that the user made, is merged with the server copy of the profile.

If you enable the Microsoft policy setting "Only allow local user profiles," the default roaming profile behavior just describes changes. When the user first logs on, the user receives a new local profile instead of the roaming profile. At logoff, changes are saved to the local profile and not updated to the roaming profile. All subsequent logons use the local profile.

The following registry key controls the profile policy in use on the local machine:

```
[HKEY_LOCAL_MACHINE\SOFTWARE\Policies\Microsoft\Windows\System] LocalProfile=
dword:00000001
```

If this value does not exist, the Hot Desktop GINA creates the value and sets it to 0. Then it is set to 1 during logon, the profile is loaded, and the value is set back to its original value.

You can control the profile-handling behavior further within the Hot Desktop environment. To change the default behavior, the administrator may create the following registry key:

```
[HKEY_LOCAL_MACHINE\SOFTWARE\Citrix\MetaFrame Password Manager\HotDesktop]
LoadLocalUserProfile=dword:00000001
```

- **0** No profile is loaded or unloaded. When using this option, remember that some applications—for example, Program Neighborhood Agent and Web Interface—might require the presence of a user profile to function properly. This setting provides the fastest user-switching time, but at the expense of not supporting some applications requiring access to the Hot Desktop User's user profile.
- **1** A local profile is loaded and unloaded. (This is the default value if the previous registry value is not present.) When this option is used, the local user profile is created, but roaming or mandatory profiles are not loaded. This setting provides compatibility for the widest range of applications (flexibility) while minimizing the profile load time (speed).
- **2** This value ensures that no restrictions are placed on which profile is loaded or unloaded. The standard Windows algorithm is used to locate and load the user's profile. This setting is slower when switching users, but it provides compatibility with all applications using profiles.

Additional information regarding user profiles can be found in the Microsoft article "User Data and Settings Management," located at the URL http://www.microsoft.com/technet/prodtechnol/winxppro/maintain/xpusrdat.mspx.

Logon Scripts and Network Shares

Hot Desktop does not support logon scripts or home folders assigned to a user through AD or NT Domain policies. However, an administrator can use the following alternatives to accomplish the same functionality:

- Logon scripts can be executed through the start script portion of the Session.xml file. Use this section to locate and launch the logon script. Use the account setting to control whether the script is launched as the Hot Desktop User or the Hot Desktop Shared Account. Here is an example of a start script setting in the Session.xml file:

```
startup_scripts
      script
            accountHDU/account
            working_directoryc:\script path/working_directory
            pathc:\script path\scriptname.bat/path
      /script
/startup_scripts
```

- The start script can also be used to access logon scripts on network shares. Before a network share can be accessed, however, you first need to create a logon script that contains the drive letters and network shares that you want to assign to the Hot Desktop User Account. Verify that the script is launched as the Hot Desktop User and not the Hot Desktop Shared Account. In addition, you can also specify that the application run as the Hot Desktop User through settings in the Process.xml file. When the Hot Desktop User launches the application, the user can access the network shares assigned to the user using the start script/logon script solution. Processes that are not running in the context of the Hot Desktop User do not have access to the network shares.
- If logon scripts and network shares are common to all users, they can be assigned to the Hot Desktop Shared Account. In this scenario, the logon script is launched only once during startup of the Hot Desktop environment. The network shares are accessed as the Hot Desktop Shared Account, so access cannot be restricted to a specific user. Also, all Hot Desktop User Accounts have access to all Hot Desktop Shared Account network shares, unlike the previous alternatives.

Because the console allows user configurations to be set at the user level, the administrator can assign different logon scripts and/or network shares to different users via the Session.xml setting in the user configuration. For more information regarding Process.xml and Session.xml, reference the *Password Manager Administrator's Guide*.

Stop Scripts Impact Session Termination Occasionally, a misbehaving session stop script might impact the session termination process and leave the Hot Desktop User's desktop open. As a preventative measure, if the stop script is still running after a 60-second (default) interval, then the Hot Desktop agent terminates the process and allows the session to end. You can control the timeout interval through the following registry key:

```
[HKEY_LOCAL_MACHINE/SOFTWARE/Citrix/MetaFrame Password Manager/GINA/
HotDesktop] ScriptLaunchWaitSecs=dword:0000003C
```

This setting specifies the number of seconds to wait on a session stop script before terminating the script and allowing the session to end. The default is 60 seconds.

Unload User Profile Impacts Session Termination If Windows cannot unload a profile, by default it retries 60 times, at one retry per second. This slows session termination substantially and cannot be controlled using the standard Microsoft Group Policy setting "Maximum retries to unload and update user profile." When Hot Desktop is installed and it cannot unload a profile, it retries 15 times at one retry per second. The Hot Desktop setting can be configured through the following registry key:

```
[HKEY_LOCAL_MACHINE\Software\Citrix\HotDesktop]
UnloadUserProfileRetries=dword:000000F
```

This setting specifies the number of retry attempts to unload a user profile before ending the session without unloading the profile. Each attempt occurs at 1-second intervals. This setting impacts user switching if the user profile cannot be unloaded.

Storage Location for User Profile Data and HKCU Normally, the user's local data is stored and protected by the user's profile. All the files are located in the user profile's application data folder (C:\Documents and Settings\ *username*\Application Data\Citrix\ MetaFrame Password Manager) and access to this folder is controlled by access rights inherited from the user profile. Similarly, the HKEY_CURRENT_USER (HKCU) hive is loaded from, and protected by, the user profile.

In a Hot Desktop environment, the agent runs in a shell that has the Hot Desktop Shared Account as the interactive user. In some user cases, the profile of the currently logged-on Hot Desktop User Account does not exist on the workstation. So, the user's profile folder (C:\Documents and Settings*username*\Application Data\Citrix\ MetaFrame Password Manager) is unavailable for the agents to access.

To work around these restrictions, the Hot Desktop installer creates the Citrix\ MetaFrame Password Manager subfolder under the All Users\Application Data folder. It adjusts the ACLs on the Citrix\MetaFrame Password Manager folder, so the agent can create a subfolder for a user when executing as that user. The ACLs match those of the People folder created by the File Share Synchronization Point Preparation tool, CtxFileSyncPrep.exe.

The user's Password Manager registry data reside in the [HKEY_CURRENT_USER] portion of the registry. During normal agent operation, these data are duplicated on the central store's synchronization point and updated in the registry at each synchronization event.

In the Hot Desktop environment, the [HKEY_CURRENT_USER] hive belongs to the Hot Desktop Shared Account, so the Hot Desktop User account does not typically have access to this registry hive. With a Hot Desktop installation, the user's Password Manager registry data instead reside in a new file—Registry.MMF—that is located in the same folder as the user's local data.

CONFIGURING AND MANAGING SELF-SERVICE PROCESSES (PASSWORD RESET AND ACCOUNT UNLOCK)

This section covers the following topics:

- The sequence flow of the Security Questions (question-based authentication) registration process. This covers the various stages that take place during Security Questions registration.
- A sequence flow of the self-service process. This covers the various stages that take place during Password Reset and Account Unlock.
- Special privileges required to restrict the self-service account. This includes the requirements to limit the domain user to an account with the minimum privileges to carry out this sensitive function. It also covers factors influencing registration and reregistration—what causes a user or users to be forced to reregister.
- Lockout policies and how they affect authentication for self-service and the capability to do Account Unlocks.

A Sequence Flow of the Security Questions Registration Process

The registration process involves the use of the Password Manager Service. Figure 15-4 illustrates the sequence of steps that occur when the user is enrolled for self-service Password Reset, which follow:

1. The administrator configures self-service Password Reset and/or Account Unlock for a user configuration.
2. On Initial Credential Setup (for a first-time user), the agent reads the user's self-service configuration status from the central store.
3. The user is prompted to register for self-service and initiates a registration request.
4. The service reads the set of questions from the central store and forwards them to the agent.
5. The user responds to the set of questions.
6. The service saves the user responses on the central store.

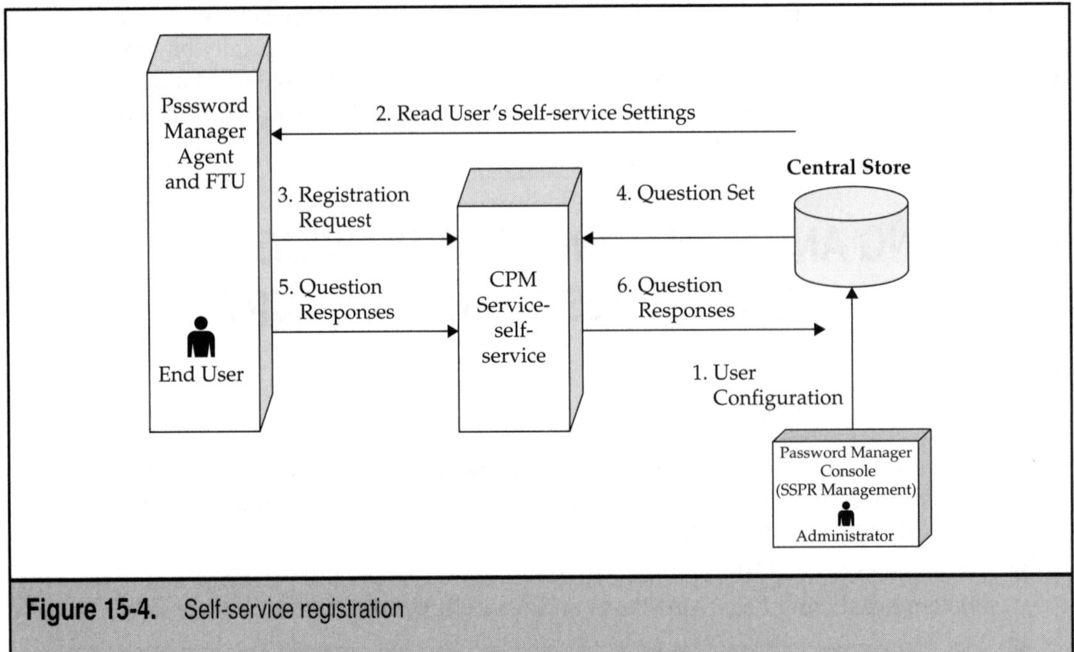

Figure 15-4. Self-service registration

A Sequence Flow of the Self-Service Process

The reset/unlock process, shown in Figure 15-5, also involves the use of the Password Manager Service. The user seeks to be authenticated by supplying the answers given to the questions during the time of enrollment.

The process works as follows:

1. To do a reset, the user first must be authenticated by submitting his or her user name.
2. The service does a proxy read to determine whether the user has registered.
3. The service sends a series of questions to the user.
4. The user supplies the response, which is compared to what the service reads from the central store. If a match occurs, the user is presented with the next question.
5. Once all questions are answered correctly, the user is allowed to proceed with account self-service.
6. The service attempts a Password Reset or Account Unlock on the Authentication Authority.
7. The user is informed of the result: success or failure.

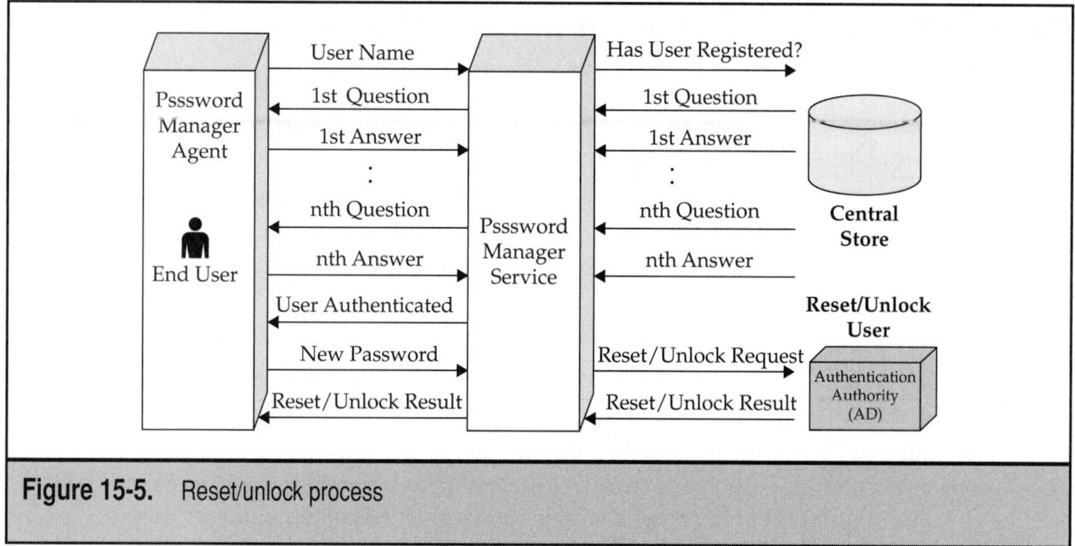

Figure 15-5. Reset/unlock process

Special Privileges Required to Restrict the Self-Service Account

To maximize security, the self-service account should be a domain user with the minimum privileges required to carry out this sensitive function:

- The self-service account must be a local administrator on the Password Manager Service machine.
- The self-service account must have the following Active Directory permissions on the Organizational Unit (OU) where the Password Manager users are located:

Reset Password	User Objects
Read pwdLastSet	User Objects
Write PwdLastSet	User Objects
Read LockoutTime	User Objects
Write LockoutTime	User Objects
Read ntPwdHistory	User Objects
Write ntPwdHistory	User Objects

Using the Active Directory Service Interface (ADSI) EDIT utility, apply the permissions by choosing the self-service account and select the respective check boxes for the remaining privileges.

Factors Influencing Registration and Reregistration

Users are required to register in the following situations:

- ▼ The administrator has enabled self-service by checking Password Reset and/or Account Unlock in the user configuration.
- ▲ Security Questions is chosen for key recovery. This alone does not allow self-service actions, however, unless one of the previous two options is selected. For more details on question-based key recovery, see the *Password Manager Administrator's Guide*.

  Users are required to reregister in any of the following circumstances:

  - ■ The administrator has changed the set of selected questions in the questionnaire and has decided to force reregistration for all users.
  - ■ The user's questions have been revoked by the administrator. Administrators can choose individual users to have their questions revoked and require them to reregister. (See the *Password Manager Administrator's Guide,* available in the console, for details on this task.)
  - ■ The administrator has decided to force reregistration for all users, using the task of this name in the console.

Lockout Policies

The following section details lockout policies and their effect on users' sessions.

Authentication

This lockout policy affects the user's capability to do self-service. If a user exceeds the number of chances given to respond to any question, that user is locked out for a period of *Y* minutes from using the self-service features. The policy enforces the following rules:

- ▼ The number of valid chances available to be authenticated to do self-service is allocated on a per-question basis: The user gets *X* chances (a default of four chances on install) to answer each question, after which the user gets locked out.
- ■ Once locked out, the user must wait *Y* minutes (a default of 60 minutes on install) before again attempting to do self-service.
- ▲ The count for attempts on a question is reset to the full amount after *Z* minutes. That is, the user gets *X* chances renewed for that question *Z* minutes (a default of 60 minutes on install) after the last attempt to answer that question.

  The policy variables are thus summarized as follows:

  - ■ *X* is the Lockout Threshold.
  - ■ *Y* is the Lockout Duration.
  - ■ *Z* is the ResetAttemptsDuration.

The administrator can edit these variables in the QBAuthConfig section of the C:\Program Files\ Citrix\Citrix Password Manager\Service\WebService\web.config file on the Service machine.

The following example indicates the number of chances available to the user for each question prior to that attempt. The example assumes a default of four chances, with just four Security Questions (as in a new installation).

Remaining Chances before Each Answer

	4	3	2	1
Question 1	Wrong	Wrong	Wrong	Correct
Question 2	Correct	-	-	-
Question 3	Wrong	Wrong	Correct	-
Question 4	Wrong	Correct	-	-

Whenever the user answers a question correctly, the number of chances is reset to the original amount of *X* and the user is presented with the next question. If the user successfully answers the final question, the user is informed that all the answers were correct and is prompted to enter a new password or has his or her account unlocked.

Account Unlock

This affects the frequency with which Account Unlocks can occur. If a user exceeds the number of times to do an Account Unlock, that user is disallowed for a period of *Y* minutes from doing Account Unlocks with Password Manager. This policy enforces the following rules:

- The number of valid chances available to do an Account Unlock is set as a variable on the service machine. The user gets *X* chances (a default of four chances on install) to do Account Unlocks, after which the user can no longer unlock this function with Password Manager.
- Once the user is barred from doing Account Unlocks, the user must wait *Y* minutes (a default of 60 minutes on install) before again attempting to do Account Unlocks.
- The count for attempts on a question is reset to the full amount after *Z* minutes. That is, the user gets his or her original *X* chances renewed for that question, *Z* minutes (a default of 60 minutes on install) after the last time that an Account Unlock was attempted.

The following table summarizes the policy variables:

	CPM Service Variable	Default	Range
X	Lockout Threshold	4 chances	1–999
Y	Lockout Duration	60 minutes	1–99,999
Z	ResetAttemptsDuration	60 minutes	1–99,999

These variables are editable in the SSAULockOut section of the C:\Program Files\Citrix\Metaframe Password Manager\Service\WebService\web.config file on the service machine.

CITRIX PASSWORD MANAGER—HOW TO MIGRATE USER CONFIGURATIONS FROM A CHILD DOMAIN TO A PARENT DOMAIN IN AN AD FOREST

This section describes the steps and the tools available to migrate Citrix Password Manager from a child to a parent domain. These steps can be followed to move Password Manager from a pilot into production or from a parent to a child domain.

Assumptions

This section discusses assumptions about the forests and the procedure for the migration. The procedure assumes that the schema in the forest has been upgraded with the CtxSchema-Prep.exe utility from Citrix. This utility is available on the Password Manager CD in the Tools directory or from the Autorun in the Prerequisites, Create Your Central Store Active Directory.

To use Autorun to create the central store, you must execute the process using an account that is part of the Schema Admin Group.

NOTE For more information about Flexible Single Master Operation (FSMO) roles in Active Directory and how to determine which Domain Controller in the Active Directory forest is the owner of the Schema master role, refer to Microsoft Knowledge Base article 324801, "How to View and Transfer FSMO Roles in Windows Server 2003," available at http://support.microsoft.com/default.aspx?scid=kb;en-us;324801.

Warnings

Migrating a user configuration from a child domain to a parent domain or vice versa uses the Memory Mapped File (MMF) saved locally on the computer where the agent is installed. During the procedure, "Delete user's data folder and registry keys"

(Delete-OnShutdown) is disabled and Password Manager uses the data saved in the local profile to point the users to the new synchronization point. During the procedure, a Microsoft tool provided in the Microsoft Windows 2003 distribution media is used. The Active Directory Migration tool must initiate the move on the Domain Controller acting as the Relative Identifier (RID) master of the domain that currently contains the object.

Procedure

Follow this procedure to migrate user configurations from a child domain to a parent domain in an Active Directory forest.

Step 1: Create a Synchronization Point on the Child Domain

In a typical migration scenario, the synchronization point is created on a child domain:

1. Create the synchronization point. The Password Manager CtxDomainPrep.exe utility prepares the domain, creating the required objects and attributes and applying the necessary permissions. The Citrix utility is available on the Password Manager CD in the \Tools folder.
2. Verify the synchronization point. In the Active Directory Users and Computers, a new object is created under the domain \Program Data. The object can be seen interactively by using specialized tools, such as ADSIEDIT (available in the Windows 2003 distribution media as SUPPORT\TOOLS\SUPPORT.CAB), or by selecting View | Advanced Features in the Active Directory Users and Computers Management Console.

Step 2: Create a User Configuration on the Child Domain

Deploy the Citrix Access Suite Console on a workstation that is part of the child domain. You must have administrative rights to the domain to be able to perform a successful discovery. To migrate the user configuration successfully, you should disable the Data Integrity and Retrieve Key Automatically settings. You can enable these settings after migration.

1. Using the Password Manager distribution media, choose Installation | Install Citrix Password Manager Console.
2. Create a new user configuration for the child domain by launching the Access Suite Console from Programs | Citrix | Management Consoles.
3. Configure and run Discovery. Click Next.
4. In the Identify Central Store Screen, select Active Directory, and then click Next. In the following screen, do not select Data Integrity. If Data Integrity is part of the pilot or proof of concept, you must deactivate it before the migration. After the migration is completed, you can reactivate it.

5. Click Next and complete the discovery process.
6. Create or import applications and policies, then create a new user configuration.
7. In the new user configuration, do not use Retrieve Key Automatically for the identity verification method. You need to disable this setting before the migration.

Step 3: Deploy Citrix Password Manager Agent on a Workstation in the Child Domain

After the creation of the new user configuration, at least one workstation should have the Password Manager agent installed:

1. Using the Password Manager distribution media, choose Installation Menu | Install MetaFrame Password Manager Agent—Confirm the EULA.
2. Do not choose Data Integrity. If Data Integrity is a requirement, you can reactivate it afterward.
3. Specify Active Directory as the synchronization point.
4. Reboot the workstation and log on.
5. The agent either asks for the Identity Verification Question or uses the current password as the Identity Verification Question, depending on how the user configuration has been created.

Step 4: Create a Synchronization Point in the Parent Domain

Each Password Manager synchronization point contains specific information relating to the domain in which it was originally created. In the case of multiple domains within the same forest, each of those domains needs to run the CtxDomainPrep utility.

Step 5: Export Administrative Data Using Access Console on the Child Domain

Export the applications, application templates, user verification questions, and password policies:

1. Using Access Suite Console, launch the Citrix Access Suite Console from Programs | Citrix | Management Consoles.
2. Select the Password Manager node by right-clicking or pressing Tab until you get to the Export Administrative Data task.
3. Export the administrative data and save the XML file to a disk or to a secured network location accessible from the parent domain.

Step 6: Import Administrative Data Using the Access Console on the Parent Domain

Deploy the Access Management Console in a workstation that is part of the parent domain. To perform a successful discovery, you must have administrative rights to the domain.

1. Using the Password Manager CD, choose Installation | Install Citrix Password Manager Console.
2. Configure and run Discovery. Click Next.
3. In the Identify Central Store screen, select Active Directory and then click Next.
4. Click Next and complete the discovery process.
5. Launch the Access Management Console from Programs | Citrix | Management Consoles.
6. Select the Password Manager node by right-clicking or pressing Tab until you get to the Import Administrative Data task.
7. Import the administrative data from the XML file saved in "Step 5: Export Administrative Data Using Access Console on the Child Domain."

Step 7: Create a User Configuration on the Parent Domain

Create a new user configuration for the parent domain by launching the Access Suite Console from Programs | Citrix | Management Consoles.

Step 8: Redirect User Configuration on the Child Domain

Follow these steps:

1. Select the Password Manager node.
2. Select the user configuration that you need to migrate.
3. Right-click and select Redirect Users.
4. On the Redirect Users page, leave Active Directory selected.

NOTE The *Password Manager Administrator's Guide* explains in detail what happens when the user configuration is redirected.

Step 9: Use the Active Directory Migration Tool to Move the Users from Child Domain to Parent Domain

Use the Active Directory Migration tool to move users from child to the parent domain in an Active Directory forest.

NOTE The tool is included in the Windows 2003 distribution CD or is available for download from the Microsoft web site for the Windows 2000 distribution at http://www.microsoft.com/windows2000/downloads/tools/admt/default.asp. The tool needs to be executed pointing to the RID masters of each domain.

Step 10: Move Workstations from Child to Parent Domain

Follow these steps:

1. Disjoin all user workstations from the child domain.
2. Restart the user workstation.
3. Rejoin all user workstations to the parent domain.
4. The first time that the user logs on after migration, the verification of the last password or Identity Verification Question is prompted to verify the user.

HOW TO USE A SINGLE SYNCHRONIZATION POINT FOR MULTIPLE DOMAINS THAT HAVE AN ESTABLISHED TRUST BETWEEN THEM

As enterprises expand, companies often create multiple trusted domains within their forests, yet administrators require centralized administration of products, such as Citrix Password Manager. This section addresses a solution for administrators who have more than one domain for their users to authenticate to, but who do not want to administer multiple synchronization points. This is achieved through the creation of shortcuts and permissions. The following example is the best way to explain the process.

In this example, Robert logs in to three domains within his enterprise: Domain *A*, Domain *B*, and Domain *C*. Robert has three separate user IDs for each of these domains: DomainA\Robert, DomainB\Bob, and DomainC\RobertK.

Robert is a domain administrator in Domain *A* and already has a file synchronization point located there. He would like to have his credentials stored at the same file synchronization point when he logs in to Domain *B* and Domain *C*.

These are the steps Robert can use to solve his problem:

1. Open the synchronization point in Domain *A* and go into the People folder.
2. Create a new shortcut to identify Robert in Domain *B* (DomainB\Bob) and Domain *C* (DomainC\RobertK). Have these new shortcuts point to the DomainA\ Robert folder.
3. Add permissions to the DomainA\Robert folder for his two other accounts in the other domains (see the section in the *Password Manager Administrator's Guide* that details the required security settings).

After completing the previous steps, Robert can log in from any of the three domains and still maintain his credentials from a single synchronization point.

PREVENTING USERS FROM DISABLING THE CITRIX PASSWORD MANAGER AGENT

As a Citrix administrator, you may want to force all users to use the Citrix Password Manager agent. To accomplish this, you must prevent users from disabling the agent by all possible means. The following is a list of steps to accomplish your goal:

1. Prevent the user from being a member of the computer's administrative groups.

   The user should not have administrative privileges and should not be part of the Administrators, Power Users, Server Operators, Domain Administrators, or any other group that gives the user administrative rights. Without these privileges, the user cannot alter any program files, system files, or registry keys that may affect the behavior of the agent.

2. Disable access to the Add/Remove Control Panel applet, the command prompt, Task Manager, the Run command, and the ability to create and modify shortcuts.

   It would be efficient to create a Group Policy with the following settings and apply it to the OU or group that contains the user accounts:

   - **Add/Remove Control Panel** Disabling access to this applet prevents the user from being able to remove the agent or other components that the agent may rely on to operate. To apply this setting, open the Group Policy and enable the following policy:

     ```
     User Configuration|Administrative Templates|Control
     Panel|Add/Remove Programs|Disable Add/Remove Programs
     ```

   - **Command prompt** Prohibiting a user from accessing the command prompt prevents the execution of any commands that may delete or alter files, shut down programs, or cause other results that would disable the agent. To apply this setting, open the Group Policy and enable the following policy:

     ```
     User Configuration|Administrative Templates|System|Disable
     the command prompt
     ```

     The previous policy, however, only disables the CMD.exe file. In the WINNT\ System32 folder, there is another command-line utility—command.com— that a user can still run and disable the agent. To avoid this, you must restrict the user from running the command.com file. To do this, enable and edit the following policy:

     ```
     User Configuration|Administrative Templates|System|Don't run
     specified Windows applications.
     ```

     Then click the Show button and add command.com.

Alternatively, enable the following policy:

```
Computer Configuration|Windows Settings|Security
Settings|Software Restriction Policies|Additional Rules
```

Then create a new Hash Policy to prohibit the execution of command.com.

- **Run** Similar to the command prompt, removing the Run command prevents the execution of any commands that may delete or alter files, shut down programs, or cause other results that would disable the agent. To apply this setting, open the group policy and enable the following policy:

  ```
  User Configuration|Administrative Templates|Start Menu &
  Taskbar|Remove Run menu from Start Menu
  ```

- **Task Manager** If a user can access the Task Manager, he or she can end processes and tasks relevant to the agent, thus causing the agent to stop. You can enforce a policy that prohibits the user from accessing the task manager. To apply this setting, open the Group Policy and enable the following policy:

  ```
  User Configuration|Administrative Templates|System|Logon/
  Logoff|Disable Task Manager
  ```

- **Ability to create and modify shortcuts** Although we have restricted the user from being able to execute any command-line commands, he or she can still create a shortcut and modify the properties of that shortcut to add the switch /shutdown, which would disable the agent. To prevent this, you should disable the user's ability to create and modify shortcuts. To make this secure, you must modify two policies. To apply these settings, open the Group Policy and enable the following policies:

  ```
  User Configuration|Administrative Templates | Windows Components |
  Windows Explorer | Disable Windows Explorer's default Context menu.
  ```

  ```
  User Configuration | Start Menu & Taskbar | Disable drag-and-drop
  Context menus on the Start Menu.
  ```

- **Citrix Password Manager Agent tray icon** If the user has access to the Password Manager Agent tray icon, he or she can easily right-click the icon and choose to shut down the agent. As a Password Manager administrator, you can configure the agent to hide the tray icon while the agent still functions normally. To configure this setting, edit your user configuration, and under Agent User Interface, disable the setting "Show notification icon."
- **Credential storage settings** By default, if a user opens an application requiring authentication, the agent asks whether the user would like to store his or her credentials in Logon Manager. The user could simply click No without storing his or her credentials in Logon Manager.

When the dialog box is disabled, users are not prompted with the question of whether to store credentials but instead are directly prompted to store their credentials in Logon Manager. To configure this behavior, edit your user configuration and, under Client-side Interaction, disable the setting "Enable users to cancel credential storage when a new application is detected."

SETTING THE CITRIX PASSWORD MANAGER AGENT LAUNCHER DELAY

Occasionally, the Citrix Password Manager agent may not recognize or submit credentials to web applications. This issue stems from Password Manager initializing before the web page is ready for input. To alleviate this issue, Password Manager now has incorporated an "agent launcher delay." This section discusses how you can manually set this delay by using the registry on a per-agent basis.

Technical Background

When launching published applications, occasionally the SSOLauncher will prematurely determine that SSOShell and SSOBHO are ready. The SSOLauncher makes this determination using the FindWindow() function on SZ_WND_TRAY + SZ_WND_BHO_HOOK. In some cases, this prevents the Password Manager agent from submitting credentials to the published web applications launched by the user.

Configuring the Citrix Password Manager Agent Launcher Delay

To alleviate this issue, Password Manger has incorporated a registry setting that can be implemented manually. After setting the registry entry, the SSOLauncher sleeps a predetermined amount of time after detecting SZ_WND_TRAY and SZ_WND_BHO_HOOK. The default setting for this sleep interval is 0, but the interval can be customized with a new registry value, LauncherDelay. This value is a DWORD expressed in milliseconds.

To add LauncherDelay to the registry manually, follow these steps:

1. As an administrator, launch regedit.exe and browse to HKEY_LOCAL_MACHINE\SOFTWARE\Citrix\MetaFrame Password Manager\Shell\.
2. If the entry LauncherDelay does not exist, create a new DWORD value named LauncherDelay and set it to 1 or higher.

NOTE You will need to experiment a bit to find the proper timing.

CHAPTER 16

Tuning and Optimizations

This section suggests optimizations that can increase the performance of XenApp. Many of the recommendations are from Microsoft Knowledge Base articles. Make sure that you read the articles from Microsoft to better understand ramifications and expected results from any tuning you perform on the systems.

DISK OPTIMIZATIONS

Several registry settings can be modified to increase disk performance and throughput. Enhancements include disabling disk caching, increasing input/output (I/O) locks, and disabling last file access updates.

I/O Locks

The registry setting *IoPageLockLimit* specifies the limit of the number of bytes that can be locked for I/O operations. Because random access memory (RAM) is being sacrificed for increased disk performance, determine the optimal setting for this value through pilot tests. Changing this setting from the default can speed file system activity. Use Table 16-1 as a guide for changing the registry setting.

Modify the registry setting as follows:

```
HKEY_LOCAL_MACHINE\SYSTEM\CurrentControlSet\Control\Session Manager\
Memory Management
Value: IoPageLockLimit (REG_DWORD): 0 (512KB is used)
```

For additional information on the IoPageLockLimit registry setting, see Microsoft Knowledge Base articles 121965 and 102985.

Last Access Update

The NTFS file system stores the last time that a file was accessed, whether it is viewed in a directory listing, searched, or opened. In a multiuser environment, this updating can

Server RAM (MB)	IoPageLockLimit (Decimal)	IoPageLockLimit (Hex)
64–128	4,096	1,000
256	8,192	2,000
512	16,384	4,000
1,024+	65,536	10,000

Table 16-1. IoPageLockLimit Settings

cause a small performance decrease. Modifying the following registry setting and adding the following value disables this feature:

```
HKEY_LOCAL_MACHINE\SYSTEM\CurrentControlSet\Control\FileSystem
Value: NtfsDisableLastAccessUpdate (REG_DWORD): 1
```

MEMORY OPTIMIZATIONS

This section describes configurations for the direct-mapped level 2 (L2) cache, the system paging file, and system page table entries.

Level 2 Cache

For processors that use a direct-mapped L2 cache, configuring the value manually can yield a performance improvement. Direct-mapped L2 cache does not provide performance gains on Pentium II and later processors. For more information, see Microsoft Knowledge Base support articles 228766 and 183063. The following registry setting can be used to modify the direct-mapped L2 cache:

```
HKEY_LOCAL_MACHINE\SYSTEM\CurrentControlSet\Control\Session Manager\
Memory Management
Value: SecondLevelDataCache (REG_DWORD): x, where x is the L2 size in
decimal (default: 0, which sets the cache to 256KB)
```

For example, if the CPU has a 512KB cache, you would set the entry to 512 (in decimal).

Paging File

The paging file is temporary storage used by the operating system (OS) to hold program data that do not fit into the physical RAM of the server. The ratio of physical memory to paged memory is the most important factor when determining the size of a paging file. When configuring the paging file, follow these guidelines:

- A proper balance between physical memory and paged memory prevents thrashing. Verify that more memory is in physical RAM than paged to disk. For optimal performance, this ratio should be approximately 3:1.
- Place the paging file on its own disk controller or on a partition that is separate from the OS, application, and user data files. If the paging file must share a partition or disk, place it on the partition or disk with the least amount of activity.

- To prevent disk fragmentation of the paging file, always set the paging file initial size as the same as the maximum size.
- The optimal size of a paging file is best determined by monitoring the server under a peak load. Set the paging file as three to five times the size of the physical RAM, and then stress the server while observing the size of the paging file. To conserve resources, set the paging file to a value slightly larger than the maximum utilized while under stress.
- If the server is short on physical RAM, use the paging file to provide additional memory at the expense of performance.

NOTE For debugging purposes, create a paging file on the root partition that is slightly larger than the amount of RAM installed.

NETWORK OPTIMIZATIONS

Some simple changes to network settings can often improve network performance. This section covers a few common issues that you can remedy by adjusting the default Windows network configuration.

Network Cards

Previous versions of the Advanced Concepts Guide suggested manually configuring NICs and switch ports to support full duplex and the highest speed available on both devices. New evidence suggests that NICs and switch ports should be configured to auto for both speed and duplex. See Cisco tech note 10561 for additional information.

Verify that only the necessary protocols are installed and the binding order of those protocols to the network interface card (NIC) lists the most commonly used protocol first.

Refused Connections

The server can refuse connections due to self-imposed limits specified by the MaxMpxCt and MaxWorkItem registry values. If this happens, users see the following errors:

```
System could not log you on because domain domainname is not available.
You do not have access to logon to this session.
```

Before adding these values, read the Microsoft Knowledge Base article 232476. When modifying these registry settings, be sure that the MaxWorkItems value is always four times the MaxMpxCt value. Suggested new values for MaxMpxCt and MaxWorkItems are 1024 and 4096, respectively.

```
HKEY_LOCAL_MACHINE\SYSTEM\CurrentControlSet\Services\LanmanServer\Parameters
Value: MaxMpxCt (REG_DWORD): 1024
Value: MaxWorkItems (REG_DWORD): 4096
```

SERVER OPTIMIZATIONS

Correctly configuring Windows services and applications for use in a multiuser environment improves performance and prevents system problems.

Auto-End Tasks

If an application does not properly exit when closed or on server shutdown, the OS can be configured to terminate the application using Auto-End Tasks. *Auto-End Tasks* terminates any task that does not respond to a shutdown notice within the default timeout period.

Enabling Auto-End Tasks affects all applications on the server and can cause issues with some applications that require a shutdown time period that is longer than the default timeout period. Therefore, the default timeout period must be greater than the time required for the longest successful shutdown for any server application. To enable Auto-End Tasks and set the default timeout period, modify the following registry settings:

```
HKEY_USERS\.DEFAULT\Control Panel\Desktop
Value: AutoEndTasks (REG_SZ): 1
Value: WaitToKillAppTimeout (REG_SZ): x, where x is the interval in
milliseconds (default is 20000)
```

For more information, see the Microsoft Knowledge Base articles 123058 and 191805.

Processes Preventing a Graceful Logoff

When a process does not terminate within a XenApp session, it may prevent the session from logging off gracefully, and the session still appears active in the Presentation Server Console. In the Presentation Server Console, you can see the processes running in the session. Killing the responsible process allows the logoff to complete. One example of such a process is Wisptis.exe. *Wisptis* is an acronym for Windows Ink Services Platform Tablet Input Subsystem. This is a pen-input device tool for the Microsoft Tablet PC platform. Sometimes Wisptis.exe can be observed in a session running Windows Office 2003. You can modify the registry to allow the logoff process to ignore such processes and successfully complete a graceful logoff. To add a process to the ignore list, follow these steps:

1. Open the registry and navigate to HKEY_LOCAL_MACHINE\SYSTEM\CurrentControlSet\Control\Citrix\wfshell\TWI.
2. Choose Edit | Add Value if no LogoffCheckSysModules value exists.
3. Type **LogoffCheckSysModules** in the Value Name box.
4. Select REG_SZ in the Data Type box. Click OK.
5. Type the name of the processes' executable in the Data box. Click OK.
6. Enter the list of executable names with a comma and no spaces between them.

For more information about LogOffCheckSysModules, see Citrix Knowledge Base article CTX891671.

System Hard Error Messages

Messages generated by system hard errors appear on the server console. If left unanswered on an unattended console, messages can cause ICA sessions to hang. You can configure system hard errors to create an entry in the system log instead of displaying a message on the console.

Disabling the display of messages to the console decreases the likelihood of hung ICA sessions, but it increases the need to monitor the event log for these types of errors. For more information, see Microsoft Knowledge Base articles 124873 and 229012.

The following registry change disables system hard error messages on the console:

```
HKEY_LOCAL_MACHINE\SYSTEM\CurrentControlSet\Control\Windows
Value: ErrorMode (REG_DWORD): 00000002
```

Dr. Watson

If you are using Dr. Watson, run the Dr. Watson Application Compatibility script to prevent stability problems. Citrix recommends you disable the Visual Notification option, available on the main screen of Drwtsn32.exe.

You can disable Dr. Watson completely by clearing the following registry key value:

```
HKEY_LOCAL_MACHINE\SOFTWARE\Microsoft\Windows NT\CurrentVersion\AeDebug
Value: Debugger REG_SZ: (blank)
```

You can restore Dr. Watson as the default debugger by executing this command: drwtsn32.exe –i.

Configuring the Event Log

Change the default event log configuration to prevent log files from running out of space, which generates errors, as follows:

1. Launch Event Viewer.
2. Right-click system log and choose Properties.
3. Set the Maximum Log Size to at least 1,024KB.
4. Choose Overwrite events as needed.
5. Click OK to save the settings.
6. Repeat steps 3–5 for the application log.

Configuring Print Job Logging

By default, each print job logs two informational messages to the system log. On servers running XenApp with many users, this feature generates numerous events and fills the log faster. If these messages are not wanted, disable them by changing the following registry setting:

```
HKEY_LOCAL_MACHINE\SYSTEM\CurrentControlSet\Control\Print\Providers
Value: EventLog (REG_DWORD): 0
```

Removing the EventLog value from the registry and restarting the server re-enables the logging of all print events.

RPC Services

When opening Remote Procedure Call (RPC)–aware applications, such as Windows Explorer and Control Panel, delays of several minutes can be the result of incorrect service startup settings. Verify the RPC service Startup type is set to Automatic and that the RPC Locator service Startup type is set to Manual.

USER OPTIMIZATIONS

Correctly setting up users can provide additional performance gains. Where possible, modify the default user profile to include the following recommendations.

TIP When making changes to the default user profile, you may need to restart the server before the changes can take effect because the Ntuser.dat file is in use and unavailable to new users.

Windows Policies

Use system and Group Policies where possible, especially in an Active Directory environment. For more information about configuring policies, see Microsoft Knowledge Base article 260370.

Profiles

Users require an initial setup when logging on for the first time. You can minimize the setup time by using roaming profiles. For more information about configuring roaming profiles, see Microsoft Knowledge Base article 324749.

Observe the following when you set up roaming profiles:

- Configure a dedicated server to host the profiles. If placing the profiles on a dedicated server is impossible, place them on an isolated disk or partition.
- When using a server or drive dedicated to profiles and temp files, change the users' profile and temp directories to point to the dedicated location.

Cached Profiles

Disable locally cached profiles by changing the access of the following registry key and all subkeys to read-only access for everyone except SYSTEM (which should have Full Control):

```
HKEY_LOCAL_MACHINE\SOFTWARE\Microsoft\WindowsNT\CurrentVersion\ProfileList
```

Menu Refresh

You can change the menu refresh rate to expedite menu response time by modifying the following registry key:

```
HKEY_USERS\.DEFAULT\Control Panel\Desktop
Value: MenuShowDelay (REG_SZ): 10
```

REMOVAL OF UNNECESSARY FEATURES

To conserve ICA bandwidth, remove any unnecessary drive mappings, printers, or ports. Unless any of the following features are needed for specific applications, disable them:

- Active Desktop (disable Active Desktop through the Terminal Services configuration)
- Desktop wallpaper (in addition, remove any .bmp files found in the %system-root% directory to prevent users from selecting them)
- Screen savers
- Microsoft Office FindFast
- Microsoft Office Assistants

Smooth Scrolling

Many applications have smooth scrolling or other features that increase the frequency of updates sent to the client workstation. If applications exhibit poor performance, disable these features to improve performance. Two common settings are in Microsoft Excel and Microsoft Internet Explorer:

- Microsoft Excel 97/2000/2003:
  1. Choose Tools | Options.
  2. Select the Edit tab.
  3. Clear the Provide feedback with Animation option.

NOTE In Excel 2007 this setting is located under Excel Options | Advanced | General.

- Microsoft Internet Explorer 5 and later:
  1. Choose Tools | Internet Options.
  2. Select the Advanced tab.
  3. Clear the Use Smooth Scrolling option in the Browsing section.

TIP While the server is in install mode (change user /install), changes to the application settings will apply to all future users. When you are finished, place the server back into execute mode (change user/execute).

Microsoft Internet Explorer Wizard

On the first launch of Microsoft Internet Explorer, the Internet Connection Wizard requests the connection type. If the connection type is a local area network (LAN) connection, you can bypass this dialog box requesting the connection type by editing the default user's registry settings as follows:

```
HKEY_USERS\.DEFAULT\Software\Microsoft\Internet Connection Wizard
Value: Completed (REG_DWORD): 0x1
```

Explorer Tips

Modifying the following registry settings disables the tips displayed at server startup:

```
HKEY_CURRENT_USER\Software\Microsoft\Windows\CurrentVersion
\Explorer\Tips
Value: DisplayInitialTipWindow (REG_DWORD): 0x0
Value: Next (REG_DWORD): 0x100
Value: ShowIE4 (REG_DWORD): 0x0
```

Reduce ICA Traffic by Disabling the Windows Network Status Icon

In Windows 2003 Server, an available option shows the network icon in the system tray. When this option is selected, a network icon is displayed in the system tray within the session, and this network icon blinks each time that network traffic occurs. Because the network icon blinks for each update, an infinite feedback loop occurs. When the network icon in the system tray blinks, it causes the ICA session to update and, because the ICA session is being updated, network traffic occurs that causes the network icon to blink, thus causing the infinite loop. To disable the Windows network status icon, follow these steps:

1. Go to Start | Settings | Control Panel | Network and Dial-up Connections | Local Area Connection.
2. Right-click Local Area Connection and select Properties.

3. Uncheck "Show Icon in notification area when connected."
4. Repeat these steps for each network adapter or connection on every server in your farm.

ICA PRIORITY PACKET TAGGING

The Citrix ICA protocol includes a feature that identifies and tags ICA data based on the virtual channel from which the data originated. This feature, referred to as ICA Priority Packet Tagging, lays the foundation for a more granular quality of service (QoS) solution by providing the capability to prioritize ICA sessions, based on the virtual channel data being transmitted. This section describes virtual channel priorities and how ICA data are tagged with these priorities when sent over an Ethernet network using TCP/IP. We also discuss important considerations to be addressed by QoS solutions when implementing ICA Priority Packet Tagging.

This section assumes that you are generally familiar with ICA virtual channels, the TCP/IP protocol, and QoS solutions.

Virtual Channel Priorities

ICA Priority Packet Tagging provides the capability to prioritize ICA sessions based on the virtual channel data being transmitted. TCP/IP must be the protocol used. You accomplish this tagging by associating each virtual channel with a two-bit priority. This two-bit priority is included as part of each ICA framing header (the ICA framing header is described in more detail in the section "Quality of Service Solutions"). The two priority bits combine to form four priority values:

- 00 (0)—high priority
- 01 (1) —medium priority
- 10 (2)—low priority
- 11 (3)—background priority

Each virtual channel is assigned one of these priority values. The default virtual channel priorities are described in Table 16-2.

The priority settings for all virtual channels are stored in the following registry key:

```
[HKLM\System\CurrentControlSet\Control\Terminal Server\Wds\icawd\Priority]
(REG_MULTI_SZ)
```

This key contains one line for each virtual channel in the format:

```
VirtualChannelName,Priority
```

`VirtualChannelName` is the standard virtual channel abbreviation as specified in Table 16-2.

Virtual Channel	Default Priority	Description
CTXTW	0	Remote windows screen update data (ThinWire)
CTXTWI	0	Seamless windows screen update data (ThinWire)
CTXCLIP	1	Clipboard
CTXCAM	1	Client audio mapping
CTXLIC	1	License management
CTXVFM	1	Video server video (that is, not ThinWire video)
CTXPN	1	Program Neighborhood
CTXCCM	2	Client COM port mapping
CTXCDM	2	Client drive mapping
CTXCM	3	Client management (Auto Client Update)
CTXLPT1	3	Printer mapping for nonspooling clients (that is, WinTerms)
CTXLPT2	3	Printer mapping for nonspooling clients (that is, WinTerms)
CTXCOM1	3	Printer mapping for nonspooling clients (that is, WinTerms)
CTXCOM2	3	Printer mapping for nonspooling clients (that is, WinTerms)
CTXCPM	3	Printer mapping for spooling clients
OEMOEM	3	Used by original equipment manufacturers (OEMs)
OEMOEM2	3	Used by OEMs

Table 16-2. Virtual Channel Descriptions and Priorities

`VirtualChannelName` must be seven characters, so trailing spaces must be added before the comma when necessary. Priority is one of the following numeric priority: values: 0, 1, 2, 3.

The ThinWire virtual channels (CTXTW and CTXTWI) are the only high-priority virtual channels by default, thus ensuring that time-sensitive user interface data are sent ahead of all other data.

ICA Data Transmission

You can more easily understand the implementation details of ICA Priority Packet Tagging by examining the different layers of the ICA protocol and how the ICA protocol interacts with TCP/IP to send ICA data over an Ethernet network. The priority bits used for ICA Priority Packet Tagging are determined and set within this data transmission process.

Figure 16-1 depicts the flow of ICA data through each protocol layer as they are generated by the client application (or server) and packaged for delivery to a server (or client application) over a TCP/IP network.

ICA data, travel through the same protocol layers but in the reverse direction when received at the destination (client or server). All ICA protocol layers reside at the Presentation layer of the OSI networking model. The ICA protocol layers depicted in Figure 16-1 are described further in the following sections.

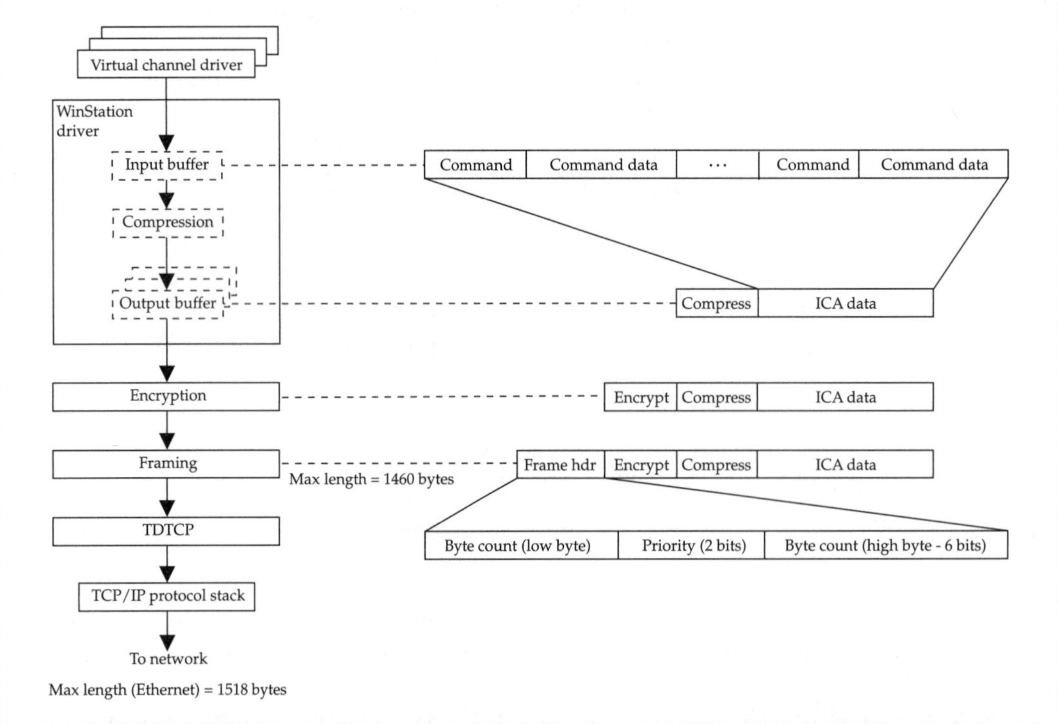

Figure 16-1. ICA data flow through the stack

Virtual Channel Drivers

Each virtual channel has its own virtual channel driver that sends virtual channel data to the WinStation driver (described in the following subsection). The format of the virtual channel data is not standardized as it depends completely on the virtual channel implementation.

WinStation Driver The WinStation driver receives ICA virtual channel data from multiple virtual channel drivers, and packages the data for receipt by lower network layers. The WinStation driver works at the Application, Presentation, and Session layers of the OSI networking model. The WinStation driver performs the following functions:

- It establishes the ICA session between the client and the server and maintains session information, such as whether compression and encryption are turned on and whether ICA Priority Packet Tagging are to be used.
- The driver encodes ICA command information and transforms input virtual channel data into ICA packets, which are placed in the WinStation driver's input buffer. An ICA packet consists of a single command byte followed by optional command data, as shown here:

Command	Command data

An ICA packet is not required to contain command data and therefore may contain only a single command byte. An ICA packet contains data from only one virtual channel. The maximum length of a single ICA packet cannot exceed 2,048 bytes (2KB).

- It compresses the ICA packets (when compression is turned on).
- WinStation combines or separates compressed ICA packets (or uncompressed ICA packets if compression is not being used) into an available output buffer. The WinStation driver determines the amount of data to include in each output buffer so that the length of the ICA data when leaving the framing protocol driver does not exceed 1,460 bytes (to keep ICA data from being broken up when transmitted by TCP/IP).
- It appends a compression header to the beginning of the output buffer (when compression is turned on).
- The WinStation driver determines the priority of each output buffer based on the virtual channel from where the data originated and passes this information to the framing protocol driver. When multiple ICA packets are combined into one output buffer, the WinStation driver determines the priority of the output buffer based on the highest-priority ICA packet included. For example, if the output buffer contains ThinWire (priority 0) and printing (priority 3) ICA packets, the output buffer is given a priority of 0 based on the included ThinWire data.
- It forwards the output buffer to the encryption protocol driver (when encryption is turned on).

Encryption Protocol Driver When encryption is turned on, the encryption protocol driver adds an encryption header to the output buffer data passed from the WinStation driver. All data after the encryption header are encrypted, including the compression header (if it is included).

Framing Protocol Driver The framing protocol driver calculates the byte count of the output buffer and adds a framing header. In addition to the byte count, the framing header includes a two-bit priority value, as determined by the WinStation driver. For example, if the total byte count of the output buffer is 1,320 bytes and the packet is high priority, the binary value of the framing header is as follows:

00101000	00	000101
Low order byte count	Priority bits	High order byte count

The low-order and high-order bytes are reversed for network transmission, and the framing header is created as follows:

00	000101	00101000
Priority bits	High order byte count	Low order byte count

TCP Transport Driver (TDTCP) The ICA protocol transfers control to the TCP/IP protocol stack through TDTCP, the TCP transport driver. TDTCP is the interface of ICA (and Remote Desktop Protocol [RDP]) to the TCP/IP protocol stack. TDTCP does not append any additional header or trailer information to the ICA data.

TCP/IP

Once TDTCP transfers control to the TCP/IP protocol stack, the TCP/IP protocol drivers prepare the ICA data for network transmission. Detailed information on the TCP/IP standards and how TCP/IP encapsulates data for network transmission can be found in the Request for Comments (RFC) and Standards (STD) documents available on the Internet (http://www.faqs.org/).

Quality of Service Solutions

QoS solutions are designed to prioritize ICA traffic against all other traffic on the network. These solutions are able to identify network traffic as ICA traffic either based on the TCP port (1494 by default) or by identifying the ICA initialization handshake that occurs when a new session is established (this is safer than using the TCP port because the TCP port number is configurable). Some QoS solutions can also identify ICA traffic based on other information, such as published application or source IP address. This identification allows ICA sessions to be prioritized against each other across the entire network. For example, all ICA sessions where users are running a business-critical application, such as

PeopleSoft, can be given a higher priority than sessions performing functions that are not as business critical.

ICA Priority Packet Tagging provides QoS solutions with the opportunity to identify virtual channel priorities within an ICA session, so that ICA sessions transmitting higher priority data are delivered first. ICA Priority Packet Tagging requires that the following considerations be addressed when used in combination with a QoS solution:

- TCP and IP are stream-oriented protocols. When ICA data are received by TCP and then by IP, they may be combined or broken up differently than how they were packaged by the ICA protocol drivers. The ICA output buffers are specifically limited to 1,460 bytes, so they remain intact when delivered to the TCP/IP protocol stack. However, the output buffers are not guaranteed to remain intact. Therefore, the priority bits in the ICA framing header may not always be in the same place in the TCP segment or IP packet. This prevents QoS solutions from relying on a data offset to identify the priority bits at the TCP or IP layers. To circumvent this potential issue, QoS solutions must verify that the byte count in the header information of the TCP and IP layers matches the byte count in the first two bytes of the ICA data (when aligned correctly, these first two bytes include the priority bits and the byte count of the ICA framing header). When the byte counts do not match, the ICA output buffers are most likely not intact within the TCP segments, so the first two bits of ICA data in the IP packet should not be interpreted as priority bits.
- ICA Priority Packet Tagging is implemented at the Presentation layer (the sixth layer of the OSI networking model). Most routers read data at lower layers (layers two through four). Therefore, routers don't have access to the ICA Priority Packet Tagging information. When IP packets are sent through a router, the packets may be fragmented. If this is the case, the first packet contains the framing header, including the priority bits and a now incorrect byte count (because the packet has been fragmented). Subsequent packet fragments do not have a framing header and thus do not include the priority bits (or a byte count). Therefore, if QoS solutions receive the ICA traffic after fragmentation by a router, not all IP packets will have the priority bits. Verifying the byte counts between the IP layer and the ICA framing header as previously described ensures that the priority bits are interpreted correctly.
- TCP requires an acknowledgment of receipt for each TCP segment in the TCP buffer before it sends additional segments. This prevents QoS solutions from being able to implement functionality that holds back printing ICA data and forward on ThinWire ICA data within a single ICA stream (which is also a single TCP stream). TCP would report a failure of receipt for the TCP segments being held because they were not received by the destination in a timely manner. QoS solutions must implement ICA Priority Packet Tagging in such a way that the transmission speed of each TCP stream is dynamically altered based on the priority bits of the ICA data being transmitted, instead of attempting to hold back individual pieces of data within the stream.

SUMMARY

ICA Priority Packet Tagging provides a mechanism for prioritizing ICA sessions based on the virtual channel from which the data originated. The implementation of ICA Priority Packet Tagging is best understood after examining how ICA data are packaged for transmission across an Ethernet network using TCP/IP. QoS solutions that take advantage of ICA Priority Packet Tagging provide QoS benefits that are more granular than prioritizing ICA traffic based only on application name or user name.

CHAPTER 17

XenApp Troubleshooting

This chapter describes XenApp troubleshooting techniques. It includes sections on troubleshooting the Independent Management Architecture (IMA) service, collecting Citrix technical support information, handling frequently encountered obstacles, troubleshooting dropped sessions, and understanding known issues.

TROUBLESHOOTING IMA

The IMA service is the core of XenApp and runs on all farm servers. The solutions presented in this section can help resolve many production IMA issues.

IMA Service Fails to Start

The following guidelines and hints can be useful when the IMA service fails to start:

- If the Service Control Manager reports that the IMA service could not be started, but the service eventually starts, ignore the message. The Service Control Manager has a timeout of 6 minutes. The IMA service can take longer than 6 minutes to start because the load on the database exceeds the capabilities of the database hardware or because the network has high latency.
    1. Go to HKEY_LOCAL_MACHINE\SYSTEM\CurrentControlSet\Control and, if it does not already exist, create a new DWORD value, ServicesPipe-Timeout.
    2. Right-click the ServicesPipeTimeout DWORD value and then click Modify.
    3. Click Decimal and type a value of **600000**, and then click OK. This value is in milliseconds and is equivalent to 10 minutes. This change will not take effect until the server is restarted. You can adjust the value to suit your needs.

NOTE You can increase the default timeout value for the Service Control Manager in the registry.

- Examine the following registry setting: HKEY_LOCAL_MACHINE\SOFTWARE\Citrix\IMA\Runtime\CurrentlyLoadingPlugin.
- If the IMA service fails to start and this value is blank, the IMA service could not connect to the data store or the local host cache is missing or corrupt.
- If a value exists, the IMA service made a connection to the data store. The value displayed is the name of the subsystem that failed to load.

NOTE During the normal startup process of the IMA service, this value cycles through the names of the subsystems as the subsystems are loaded. Once the IMA service has started successfully, the value will be blank.

- If a direct connection to the data store is being used, verify that Open Database Connectivity (ODBC) exists. For more information, see the section "ODBC Connection Fails," later in this chapter.
- If an indirect connection to the data store is being used, verify that the IMA service is running on the direct server.
- Review the entries in the event log for the IMA service error code that is returned. See "IMA Error Codes" in Appendix A for more information on why the IMA service fails to start.
- Verify that the Spooler service is started in the context of system rather than a user.
- If you get an "IMA Service Failed" message when restarting a server, with error code 2147483649, the local system account might be missing a temp directory. Change the IMA service startup account to the local administrator. If the IMA service starts under the local administrator's account, check for a missing temp directory.

  Switch the service back to the local system account and try to create the temp directory %systemroot%\temp manually. Verify that both the TMP and TEMP environment variables point to this directory. For more information, see Microsoft article 251254.

IMA Service Fails to Stop

The System Management Server (SMS) NetMon2 client utility is not supported on XenApp. The IMA service fails to stop when running on a server with this utility installed. Uninstall the NetMon2 client when installing XenApp on servers that already have this utility installed.

ODBC Connection Fails

If you are using direct mode connections to the data store, ODBC connectivity is required for proper operation of the IMA service. If you suspect ODBC issues, try the following:

- Verify that the database server is online.
- Verify the name of the DSN file that the IMA service is using by looking in the registry at HKEY_LOCAL_MACHINE\SOFTWARE\Citrix\IMA\DataSourceName.
- Attempt to connect to the database using the DSN file with an ODBC test utility (such as Oracle ODBC Test, DB2 Client Configuration Assistant Test, or SQL Server ODBC Test).
- Verify that the correct user name and password are being used for database connectivity. You can change the user name and password using the dsmaint config command. For more information, see the *Citrix Presentation Server Administrator's Guide*.

- Reinstall MDAC 2.6 SP1 or later to verify that the correct ODBC files are installed.
- Enable ODBC tracing for further troubleshooting. For more information, see the section "ODBC Tracing."

XenApp Fails to Connect to the Data Store

This error can indicate a corrupt local host cache (LHC). Before attempting these steps, verify ODBC connectivity to the database, as in the previous section.

- Copy imalhc.mdb to another directory for backup purposes.
- Stop the IMA service. You can do so from the Services control panel or from a command prompt by typing **net stop imaservice**.
- From the command prompt, re-create the local host cache using the dsmaint recreatelhc command.
- Start the IMA service. You can accomplish this from the Services control panel or from a command prompt by typing **net start imaservice**.

Failed to Initialize Permanent Storage During Installation

This error usually indicates that the IMA service is unable to create objects in the data store. Before attempting these steps, verify ODBC connectivity to the database.

- Verify that the user account for the database has permissions to create tables, stored procedures, and index objects. For Microsoft SQL Server, the permission is db_owner. For Oracle, the permission is resource. For DB2, the permission is database administrator authority or the list of permissions set in the *Citrix Presentation Server Administrator's Guide*.
- Verify that the system tablespace is not full on the Oracle server.

RECOVERING FROM A FAILED INSTALLATION

If installation fails, there is a possibility that the data collector will continually attempt to contact the failed server that was uninstalled.

After a failed installation, you should compare the list of servers in the Management Console to the list of servers returned by queryhr. Use the command queryhr -d *hostID* to remove any servers listed in the queryhr results that are not listed in the Management Console.

CAUTION Do not use the –d switch on farm servers that are functioning properly. This switch removes the server from the farm. You must reinstall the server into the farm to regain functionality.

RECOVERING AN UNRESPONSIVE SERVER

If a member server is no longer responding to IMA requests and the IMA service cannot be started, the server is considered unresponsive. The chfarm command cannot be used with an unresponsive server because the command requires connectivity to the data store.

CAUTION The original state of the server cannot be recovered after performing the next procedure. Before using this technique, first attempt all other solutions presented in the previous section, "Troubleshooting IMA."

To rejoin an unresponsive server to the farm, perform the following steps:

1. Uninstall XenApp on the unresponsive server.
2. Remove the unresponsive server from the farm using the Citrix Management Console.
3. Reinstall XenApp on the unresponsive server and rejoin the farm during installation.

RESOURCE MANAGER TROUBLESHOOTING QUESTIONS AND ANSWERS

The following apply to Resource Manager for XenApp regarding the Database Data Source Name, alerts for high-context switches, the zone elections counter, certain error messages that are sent when using Oracle, and multiple duplicate import request messages.

Resource Manager Summary Database Data Source Name

The *RMSummaRyDataBASE* Data Source Name (DSN) is *not* case-sensitive; any case can be used for the Summary Database DSN.

Resource Manager Node Still Shows in Management Console after Being Uninstalled

If Resource Manager is uninstalled from all farm servers and the Resource Manager node is still visible in the Presentation Server Console you can remove the Resource Manager node from a Presentation Server Console by removing or renaming C:\Program Files\Citrix\Administration\Plugins\ResourceManager.jar and restarting the console.

Alerts Regarding High-Context Switches/Second

The default metric threshold values are a *baseline configuration* for an administrator to tune. The default metric threshold values are determined for a minimal server configuration and, although most metric defaults will be suitable as a "one size fits all" solution, such as Processor–%Processor Time defaults, some metrics such as System–Context Switches/Sec need to be tuned for the environment for which they are intended.

Administrators can achieve more realistic threshold values for their environment by utilizing the Visual Threshold Configuration graph in a test-bed or production environment. Here, an administrator can see where the peaks and troughs exist for up to 96 hours worth of sampled data and estimate based on this real data what the threshold value should be for the environment.

Zone Elections Counter

Data collectors store dynamic data about the Zone. This can be a considerable amount of data if you have many active connections, users, published applications, servers, and so on.

Monitoring this metric can be useful to determine whether excessive data collector elections are taking place, because of intermittent networking, IMA service restarts, data collector failures, or requests from another XenApp for an election. This can happen when a communication failure occurs between any XenApp servers in any Zone.

Proactive monitoring can help prevent excessive amounts of data from transmitting between Zones as elections are won. This can also be tracked with the Citrix MetaFrame Presentation Server–Zone Elections Won metric.

Resource Manager Error Message: "[Oracle][ODBC][Ora]ORA-02074: Cannot ROLLBACK in a Distributed Transaction"

When you are using Resource Manager with Oracle, the system may continually generate messages about rollback of distributed transactions. This can occur if the Disable Microsoft Transaction Server (MTS) support in the Oracle ODBC driver workarounds configuration is set.

If the workaround is not enabled (by default on most Oracle ODBC configurations), this leads to a unique key violation that terminates the SQL transaction and the following Resource Manager server log entry: "[Oracle][ODBC][Ora]ORA-02074: cannot ROLLBACK in a distributed transaction."

Resource Manager Error Message: "Must Reparse Cursor to Change Bind Variable Datatype"

After you reboot the Resource Manager Database Connection Server, the system may generate an Oracle ODBC error in the Resource Manager server log, such as this:

```
14 June 2007 11:32:26 - System - [Oracle][ODBC][Ora]ORA-01475: must
reparse cursor to change bind variable datatype
```

To resolve this, set the Oracle ODBC workaround for Enable Closing.

Resource Manager Error Message: "Failed to Create Summary Database"

If Summary Database (SDB) creation fails, the system may generate an error indicating schema deployment problems for the Summary Database. Here's a typical "Failed to create summary database" error in the Resource Manager server log:

```
July 2007 12:26:02 - System - Failed to create summary database.
```

The following are the most common causes for Resource Manager to produce this error:

- A database problem has been creating the SDB schema initially. For example, an Oracle database configuration, such as the rollback segment, is too small and non-autoextending. This can prevent successful deployment of the Resource Manager schema when Resource Manager is creating some of the packages.
- The database user has insufficient privileges to create the schema. For example, Resource Manager may be unable to insert data into tables or create packages.

Possible solutions to this error include the following:

- Check the Oracle or SQL Server configuration settings to ensure that enough space is in the database to create the schema. Several megabytes should be enough space to create the schema.
- Check that all rollback segments are autoextending. These can be tuned after the database is created.
- Ensure that the user has rights to the database and can successfully communicate with the database server.

Resource Manager Error Message: Multiple Duplicate Import Request Messages

The resource manager server log is showing multiple duplicate import request messages. These informational messages appear in the Resource Manager server log when multiple duplicate import requests occur. A message such as the following is usually observed many times in the server log file:

```
22 November 1978 00:02:10 - System - Ignoring duplicate import request for
file "C:\Program Files\Citrix Resource Manager\SummaryFiles\1C2865FABC926CA"
from host "XXXXXXX".
```

This usually occurs because a user has activated the Update Now button multiple times or spurious network conditions are causing the server to request an import more than once. In these conditions, this message is quite normal and summary file imports will complete unaffected.

TROUBLESHOOTING NOVELL DIRECTORY SERVICES INTEGRATION

This section lists troubleshooting tips and known issues that can arise when you are using XenApp in a Novell Directory Services (NDS) environment.

Novell Troubleshooting Tips

If you are unable to log on or to assign rights to published applications using NDS credentials, try the following troubleshooting tips to correct the problem:

- Verify that NDS is enabled for the farm. Launch the Access Management Console Right-click the farm node in the left pane of the console and choose Properties. In the Properties dialog box expand the Farm-wide node if necessary, expand the Presentation Server node if necessary, and highlight General. Verify that the Novell Directory Services Preferred Tree is set correctly.
- Verify that you are using a valid user name, password, context, and tree name during logon by logging on from another computer using the same information.
- Verify that the Novell Client is configured correctly by browsing the tree and logging on from the console of the server.
- If the ZENworks Dynamic Local User (DLU) policies are not being applied on some servers running XenApp, check the Novell Workstation Manager component of the Novell Client and verify the following settings:
  - Workstation Manager is enabled.
  - The tree name is set to the tree that has the DLU policies applied.
  - All other options have the default settings applied.

If you set the Dynamic Local User policy in NDS to delete users after they log out (Volatile User option) and the volatile user accounts are not being deleted, make sure that the Enable Volatile User Caching option is disabled.

If you are experiencing autologon problems with or without the ZENworks DLU feature as the Windows authentication method, try the following:

1. Make a desktop connection using an ICA Custom Connection with the Autologon feature enabled.
2. Specify the following user credentials:
   - **Username** A valid Distinguished Name, such as .SampleUser.company
   - **Password** A valid password
   - **Domain** The NDS tree name is contained

NOTE The following "if" statements are not always true if the custom connection is not created exactly like the above description.

3. Launch the connection and, based on the result, troubleshoot using these guidelines:
   - If Novell Client displays an error message about an invalid user name, server, or tree:

     Action: Log on to the console as the same user. If the logon is not successful, then the Novell Client is not configured properly.
   - If Microsoft Client prompts you to reenter your credentials or displays an error message:

     Action: Click Cancel to return to the Novell logon dialog box. On the NT/2000 tab, view the user information.
   - If the User name field in the NT/2000 tab field contains a Distinguished Name (.username.context.):

     Action: Upgrade to Novell Client 4.81 or later. (Older Novell Clients do not parse the user name from the Distinguished Name.)
   - If the Domain name is blank or set to the local machine name and the ZENworks DLU feature is being used:

     Action: Troubleshoot DLU policies. (DLU is not functioning properly.)
   - If the Domain name is blank or is set to the local machine name and the ZENworks DLU feature is not being used:

     Action: Locate or create the the registry key HKEY_LOCAL_MACHINE\Software\Citrix\ NDS\SyncedDomainName and set the registry key value to the name of the NT domain that is synchronized with the NDS tree.
   - If the Domain field contains the name of the NDS tree:

     Action: Enable NDS integration.
   - If the Domain field contains the name of an NT domain and you are not using the ZENworks DLU functionality for Windows authentication:

     Action: Verify the server has a valid trust relationship between the server's domain and the user's domain.

Known Issues and Workarounds

Logging on to XenApp can fail if you uninstall the Novell Client from the server after XenApp is installed. If this occurs, do not restart XenApp until you follow these instructions.

- To add the registry keys after uninstalling the Novell Client on XenApp, you need to reapply the proper settings to the registry after removing the Novell Client. The following registry key contains the GINA values:

  ```
  HKEY_LOCAL_MACHINE\Software\Microsoft\Windows NT\CurrentVersion\
  Winlogon
  ```

  The registry values for the default XenApp logon screen (without the Novell Client) are as follows:

  ```
  GinaDLL Data: Ctxgina.dll
  ```

  ```
  CtxGinaDLL Data: Msgina.dll
  ```

- The session-sharing feature is not supported for Win32 Client custom ICA connections that are configured for NDS user credentials.

  Workaround: To use session sharing for custom ICA connections in Program Neighborhood, do not specify user credentials on the Login Information tab in the Properties dialog box.

NOTE The Novell Client does not set the APPDATA environment variables.

COLLECTING CITRIX TECHNICAL SUPPORT INFORMATION

This section discusses methods for collecting information that Citrix Technical Support can use for debugging purposes. Before contacting Citrix Technical Support, try the solutions in the previous section "Troubleshooting IMA."

Obtaining Installation/Uninstallation Logs

If the XenApp installation fails to complete, Citrix Technical Support requires an installation log file to troubleshoot the problem. Because the XenApp installation is a Windows Installer package (.msi file), the Windows Installer must be invoked with the /l command line option to create an installation log file. Citrix recommends that if the installation fails, a second installation be attempted, using the following command line to create a log file:

Msiexec /i CD\ MF\MPS.msi /l*v %SystemDrive%\msi.log

Replace *CD* with the CD drive letter (for example, D:) containing the installation CD. If the installation CD was copied to a hard drive or network share, you could also replace *CD* with the full path to the installation CD image. This command line creates a log file named msi.log in the root of the system drive.

For additional information about the Windows Installer, visit http://technet2.microsoft.com/windowsserver/en/library/708db7ad-6e8a-4171-a5ef-57e3344d2aea1033.mspx?mfr=true.

Capturing Presentation Server Console Debug Output

To capture debug output from the Presentation Server Console, the Presentation Server Console must be launched with the –debugFile command-line option. The recommendation is that you create a shortcut using the following process:

1. Right-click on the desktop and select New | Shortcut from the context menu.
2. The Create Shortcut Wizard starts. In the "Type the location of the item" field, enter **%SystemRoot%\system32\java.exe**. When prompted to "Type a name for this shortcut," enter descriptive text, such as Console Debugging. The shortcut is then created.
3. Right-click the new shortcut and select Properties from the context menu.
4. In the Shortcut tab, enter the following text in the Target field (the following text is word-wrapped, but it must be entered as one line):

   java.exe -Djava.ext.dirs="ext;%ProgramFiles%\Java\jre1.4.1\lib\ext" -jar Tool .jar -debugFile:output.log
5. Change the Start in field to **%ProgramFiles%\Citrix\Administration**.
6. Click the Change Icon button and enter **%ProgramFiles%\Citrix\Administration\ctxload.exe**.
7. In the Layout tab, configure the Screen buffer size properties to 9,999 lines.
8. Click OK to save the shortcut.

When the shortcut is launched, two windows are displayed. The first is a command window containing the debug messages output by java.exe. The second is the Presentation Server Console user interface. If the Presentation Server Console hangs or otherwise fails, press Ctrl-Break in the command window to view the stack trace.

NOTE This may fail if another Java application is installed that loads the Java Access Bridge screen reader. If this software is installed, you may need to modify the path before launching the Presentation Server Console in this manner. Before launching the Java command, strip the path down to only the essentials, similar to the following: \path=c:\winnt\system32; c:\winnt\java -Djava.ext.dirs=Ext -jar tool.jar.

Obtaining System Information

Citrix Technical Support may also request information about the state of the system when troubleshooting an issue. The easiest way to obtain such information is to execute winmsd, which launches the System Information tool on Windows Server 2003. From the MMC Action menu, select Save as System Information File. The file may then be sent to Citrix Technical support, if necessary.

ODBC Tracing

Citrix Technical Support or the database vendor support team may request additional ODBC tracing information. The procedure to enable ODBC tracing depends on the database server software being used.

To activate Microsoft SQL Server ODBC tracing, follow these steps:

1. Launch the ODBC Data Source Administrator.
2. Select the Tracing tab.
3. Enter a path for the log file in the Log File Path box.
4. Click Start Tracing Now to begin tracing. Click Stop Tracing Now to end tracing.

To activate Oracle ODBC tracing, follow these steps:

1. Launch the Net8 Assistant.
2. Select Configuration | Local | Profile.
3. Select General from the drop-down box on the right pane.
4. Use the Tracing and Logging tabs to configure ODBC tracing as needed.

To activate IBM DB2 ODBC tracing, follow these steps:

1. Launch the DB2 Client Configuration Assistant.
2. Select Client Settings | Diagnostics.
3. Set the Diagnostic error capture level to 4 (all errors, warnings, and information messages).

Installation Manager Debug Files

Obtain the relevant Installation Manager files before calling Citrix Technical Support for Installation Manager troubleshooting questions:

- wfs (the package script)
- ael (the recorder log file)
- aep (the packager project file)
- log (the windows installer log file)

TROUBLESHOOTING FREQUENTLY ENCOUNTERED OBSTACLES

This section covers frequently encountered obstacles that are a result of misconfiguration or misconception.

Program Neighborhood Agent Cannot Connect through Secure Gateway for Citrix XenApp

If a client receives the popup message "Cannot connect to the Citrix server: Protocol driver error" when attempting to connect to Secure Gateway from Program Neighborhood Agent, the cause is most likely that the client machine does not have the proper encryption level installed. The client needs to have 128-bit encryption installed.

Cannot Launch Secure Web Interface for Citrix XenApp Application through Internet Explorer

If you have users connecting through a secure Web Interface site (HTTPS) and they receive an error message of "ICA file not found," ensure that the security settings within Internet Explorer are not set to "Do not save encrypted pages to disk." To check security settings in Internet Explorer:

1. Open Internet Explorer.
2. Click on Tools | Internet Options.
3. Click the Advanced tab.
4. Scroll down to Security.
5. Ensure that there is no check in the box next to "Do not save encrypted pages to disk."
6. Click OK to close this process.

Folders Do Not Appear in Program Neighborhood

Folders that you create to organize applications in the Management Console are not related to application folders that appear in Program Neighborhood. To specify application folders for Program Neighborhood, use the Program Neighborhood Settings tab in the Properties dialog box for the published application:

1. Right-click the published application in the Presentation Server Console and then choose Properties.
2. On the Program Neighborhood Settings tab, type the folder name in the Program Neighborhood Folder box.

Importing Network Printers from Other Domains

Printers cannot be imported from a Network Print Server under the following circumstances:

- The print server resides in a workgroup.
- The printer is in a different domain from any servers in the server farm.

To enable the printer to be imported, follow these steps:

1. Do one of the following:
   - Add the Network Print Server to the same domain as the servers running XenApp.
   - Add one of the servers running XenApp to the same domain as the Network Print Server.
2. Assign the printers to the Everyone group instead of to groups or users. Authenticate without credentials to receive the list of printers assigned to everyone.
3. To let Novell users access Microsoft Print Servers, you must enable the Guest account and assign Everyone or Guest access.

Windows Server 2003 Issues, Recommendations, and Workarounds

This section illustrates the most common issues, recommendations, and workarounds for forest trusts and multidomain environments.

Forest Trusts

With Windows Server 2003 Active Directory forests, you can create a two-way forest trust that allows a transitive trust between all child domains in the trusted forests. The Presentation Server Console does not support the use of this type of trust between child domains and will be unable to browse a child domain from a trusted forest. If you require a trust between two child domains in separate forests, then creating an explicit trust between domains is necessary.

Another workaround for trusts is to place all servers running XenApp in the same domain. Create a local group in this domain, then populate this domain local group with global groups from other domains.

User Access to Terminal Servers

By default, on Windows Server 2003, members of the Administrators and Remote Desktop Users groups can connect via Terminal Services. The Remote Desktop Users group contains no users when it is initially created. You must manually add any users or groups that require Terminal Services access. If the users are not already members of the computer's local group, it is also necessary to add them. Unlike Windows 2000 Server policies, the Computer Local Policy under User Rights, "Allow log on locally," no longer provides access to Terminal Services connections. For additional information, please refer to the Windows Server 2003 online documentation.

TROUBLESHOOTING TIPS, ERROR MESSAGES, AND CONDITIONS

This section will help troubleshoot issues with Presentation Server Console launch failures, PDA synchronization, the Citrix XTE service, and disconnected sessions.

Presentation Server Console Fails to Launch

If the Sun Java Runtime Environment (JRE) 1_5_0_02 is installed prior to installing the Presentation Server Console, logins to the console may fail. When JRE 1.5 is already present, the JRE 1.4.2_06 installer doesn't add a registry key that is needed by the console. This is resolved by manually adding one key and one value to the registry:

1. Create the following registry key:

   ```
   HKEY_LOCAL_MACHINE\Software\JavaSoft\Java Runtime Environment\1.4
   ```

2. Create a string value "JavaHome."
3. Locate the following key in the registry:

   ```
   HKEY_LOCAL_MACHINE\Software\JavaSoft\Java Runtime Environment\1.4.2_06
   ```

4. Copy the data from the "JavaHome" value in that key to the "JavaHome" value in the key that you created.

PDA Synchronization Potential Issues and Workarounds

The following is a list of issues encountered during the testing of the PDA synchronization feature:

- **PDA synchronization/ActivSync does not function properly within a Conferencing Manager session.** This is as designed.
- **Launching a published instance of ActivSync opens, but then closes before you can insert the PDA into the USB cradle.** Check the command line for the published application. To make ActivSync available as a published application properly, it is important to specify WCESMGR.EXE as the application to be launched, not WCESCOMM.EXE. WCESCOMM.EXE is the system tray process. Although both executables can start each other once a PDA is detected,

if WCESCOMM.EXE is the only application in a session and no PDA is present at ICA session startup, the ICA session may log off before a user can insert a PDA. This is as designed.

- **Nonseamless ICA sessions to ActivSync as a published application do not log off completely.** When you are running ActivSync as a nonseamless published application, you do not see the ActivSync connection icon in the system tray. If you close the main ActivSync window, you are unable to log off the ICA session completely until the PDA is removed. Because the PDA remains in the universal serial bus (USB) cradle, the WCESCOMM.EXE process is still active and, although you may not see the system tray icon, you cannot close the session until this process is closed.
- **Using the default ActivSync driver that ships with Windows XP can cause issues.** For example, the PDA may not disconnect when the ICA session closes. The next ICA session attempting to connect to the PDA will be unable to do so unless the PDA is removed and replaced in the USB cradle. For optimal performance, install the most recent version of ActivSync. You can download the latest version of ActivSync from Microsoft's web site.
- **ActivSync fails when installed in application isolation environments.** ActivSync does not require an application isolation environment for Terminal Services compatibility. Because Activeync installs a service and isolation environments do not isolate services, if you install ActivSync in an isolation environment, it will fail. You can configure isolation environments on XenApp to isolate other applications without impacting ActivSync.
- **Allowing COM port connections within ActivSync can result in problems.** If you modify the connection settings within ActivSync to allow COM port connections, and then disconnect and reconnect the PDA in rapid succession, the PDA connects but you cannot start WCESMGR.EXE until the currently running WCESMGR.EXE is killed or a one-minute timeout occurs. This is a third-party issue with ActivSync and can occur on a console outside of an ICA session as well. The easiest way to avoid this issue is to disable COM port connections through ActivSync. If you manually disable COM port connections in the GUI, you must log off and log back on to resolve the issue. To disable COM port connections for all users, modify the following registry key:

```
Key: HKLM\Software\Microsoft\Windows CE Services
Value: REG_DWORD:ConnectTypesAllowed

Settings:
Allow serial cable or infrared connection to a COM port:
0x00000002

Allow network (Ethernet) and Remote Access Service (RAS) server
connection with the desktop computer:
0x00000004
```

```
Allow USB connection with the desktop computer:
0x00000008
```

The per-user key is created the first time that the user uses ActivSync, at which point all key values are populated using the defaults in HKLM.

NOTE Users can reenable ActivSync COM port connections by modifying the options in Connection Settings.

Citrix XTE Service MaxThreads and Session Reliability

When Session Reliability is enabled for client connections, the number of connections is limited to 150 users on a server powerful enough to accept more. This is due to the ThreadsPerChild value of 150 in the httpd.conf configuration file located in the %Program Files%\Citrix\XTE\conf folder. The value is persistent, but you can change it by editing the registry. In HKLM\Software\Citrix\XTEConfig, add a DWord Value called MaxThreads. Modify the value of MaxThreads to be a decimal value equal to or greater than the number of users that you expect to get on the machine. After the value is set, stop and restart the IMA service or reboot the machine so that your changes take effect.

Troubleshooting Disconnected Sessions

XenApp can log Transport Driver (TD) errors to a log file. This log can track any kind of Winsock errors that the client receives. This capability is useful in troubleshooting why sessions may be getting disconnected. To enable the logging, you must add the following parameters when launching the ICA connection via wfcrun32. The command is

```
Wfcrun32 /c:0x00000040 /e:0x00100000 /logfile:log file path connection name
```

The 0x00000040 tells the server to log in Transport Driver. The 0x00100000 tells the server to log any Auto Client Reconnect–related information.

If an error is encountered, it is contained within the log file along with an error code. The error code may be a Winsock error code. Check the Microsoft Developers Network (MSDN) site for the code: http://msdn.microsoft.com/library/default.asp?url=/library/en-us/winsock/winsock/windows_sockets_error_codes_2.asp.

CHAPTER 18

Troubleshooting the Other Platinum Edition Components

This chapter presents an overview of Citrix policies, tips for using GoToMeeting, and Troubleshooting Access Gateway with Advanced Access Control. Additionally, we review troubleshooting and issue resolution scenarios for Password Manager.

CITRIX POLICIES OVERVIEW

This section provides information regarding the Citrix policies available in the Presentation Server Console. Although the policies are configured in the Presentation Server Console, the MetaFrame Component Object Model Software Development Kit (MFCOM SDK) can also be used to facilitate the process. Utilizing the MFCOM SDK is beyond the scope of this chapter. For information about using the MFCOM SDK, see the Citrix Developer Network: http://community.citrix.com/cdn.

Citrix policies are not the same as the Microsoft policies. They are applied on a per-ICA session, not tied to a specific user account, and can be prioritized to customize which configured policies take precedence when applying configured settings.

XenApp contains 44 specific Citrix policy rules that govern the user experience in the following areas:

- Bandwidth
- Client devices
- Printing
- User workspace
- Security

To determine the scenario under which a policy is applied, you can choose a filter from the following options:

- **Access Control** The policy is applied based on connections made through MetaFrame Secure Access Manager or Access Gateway.
- **Client IP Address** The policy is applied based on the actual client IP address or range of addresses.
- **Client Name** A policy can be applied to the name of a client device.
- **Servers** A policy can be applied to a specified XenApp.
- **Users** A policy can be applied to specified local server accounts, Windows NT Domain accounts, Active Directory accounts, and Novell NDS trees.

NOTE The name of the client device is a string value that can be manually configured on the client host. As the client device name can be set to an arbitrary value by the client, it may not always be appropriate to base-policy filtering decisions on this value. In cases where the client should not be permitted to influence the policy filtering, then it may not be appropriate to make use of the client device name. See CTX107705 for more information.

Architecture Details

The Policy subsystem receives requests from the IMA Policy Subsystem SAL and returns responses. The Policy subsystem SAL makes calls to the local host cache (LHC), which in turn makes calls to the data store. When an ICA connection is established and a Citrix policy is applied to the session, policy information is stored in the registry under HKLM\Software\Citrix\ Policies\LogonID. This information is deleted at session logoff.

Citrix policies are IMA-related and information regarding Citrix policies is also stored in the farm's data store. Figure 18-1 outlines the Citrix policies architecture.

Hierarchy

Citrix policies override settings contained in Citrix Connection Configuration, MFCFG.exe, or TSCC.msc. They also override Microsoft policies, those related to typical Remote Desktop Protocol (RDP) client connection settings, such as the following:

- Desktop wallpaper
- Menu animations
- Windows contents while dragging

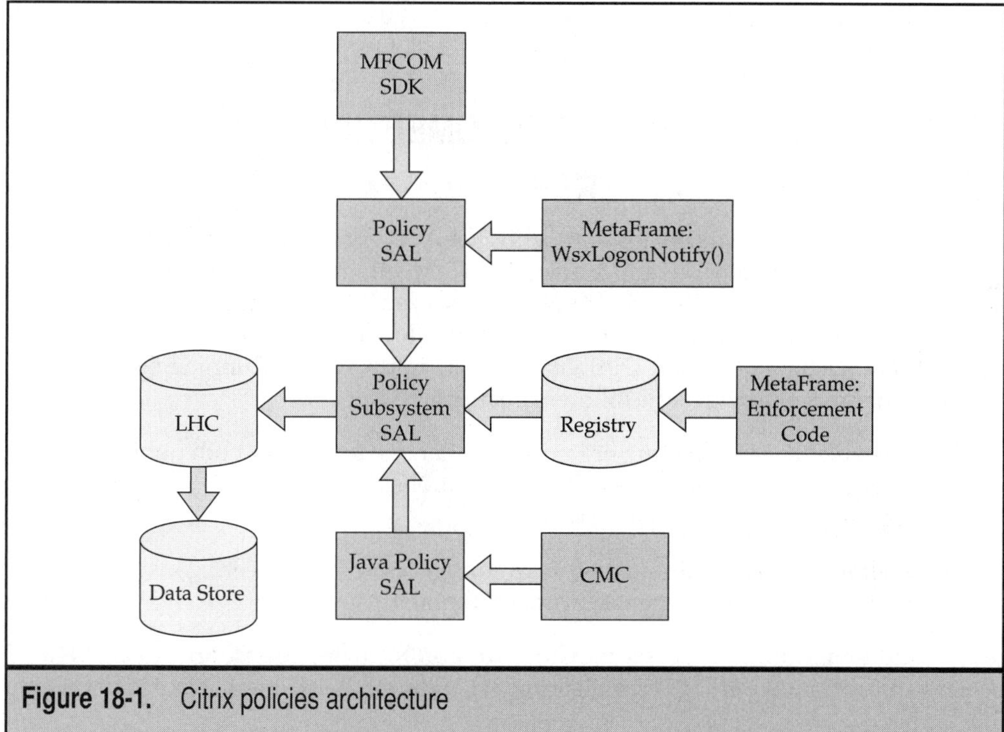

Figure 18-1. Citrix policies architecture

Scalability

Scalability may be impacted by an increase in logon time. The increase is proportional to the number of policies and the complexity of the policies used (that is, the number of filters, number of rules, and so forth). When policies are not used, there should be no impact to logon time. If logon time performance is a concern for your environment, perform tests to determine an acceptable level of performance for your environment and adjust the Citrix policies accordingly.

Troubleshooting Policies

If policies are not being applied or not working properly, you can perform tracing to troubleshoot all Citrix policies. Using Common Diagnostics Facility(CDF) tracing, specify the following modules:

- IMA_Library_ImaRpc
- IMA_Sals_ImaRpcClient
- IMA_Subsystems_Policy
- IMA_Subsystems_PolicyApi
- MF_DLL_Wsxica (the WsxLogonNotify MetaFrame function in wsxica.dll)
- MF_Session_Wfshell

DISABLE THE INSTALLATION OF GOTOMEETING INTO A USER PROFILE ON XENAPP

GoToMeeting provides for integration with XenApp for 32-bit Windows. Using the GoToMeeting Installation Wizard to install GoToMeeting on XenApp allows XenApp administrators to install GoToMeeting on the server. GoToMeeting also redirects all meetings to the local client desktop while still allowing integration with published applications, such as Microsoft Outlook and IBM Lotus Notes. Running GoToMeeting on the client device provides the following benefits:

- It enables a GoToMeeting organizer or attendee to present both published applications and locally installed applications.
- It avoids any impact to the XenApp resources.
- It allows XenApp administrators to configure the GoToMeeting installment to best suit the specific client-server environment.

For additional information, see the Citrix Support Knowledge Base article "CTX110967—Citrix Presentation Server Administrator's Guide for Installing Citrix GoToMeeting 3.0."

To prevent users from being able to install GoToMeeting into their profile during a session on either a 32-bit or 64-bit XenApp, a registry key can be created:

```
HKLM\Software\Citrix
Under this key add DWORD: AdminBlockGoToMeeting
Set the value to 1.
```

This blocks users from installing GoToMeeting into their local profile on the XenApp. This is especially important on XenApp for 64-bit Windows, as GoToMeeting is not currently supported on a 64-bit XenApp platform.

When the previous key is added to the server's registry, if a user attempts to run either the ActiveX or a downloaded installation of GoToMeeting, he or she receives an error message and the local client machine's browser is redirected to https://www.gotomeeting.com/.

TROUBLESHOOTING ACCESS GATEWAY WITH ADVANCED ACCESS CONTROL

This section provides troubleshooting information for Access Gateway with Advanced Access Control. Topics covered are how to enable verbose scan results for the Citrix Advanced Access Control 4.5 End Point Analysis scans, and registering .NET Framework if Internet Information Server (IIS) is not installed first.

Registering .NET Framework If IIS Is Not Installed First

If you have a problem accessing the Authentication Service test page, it may be because the .asmx, .aspx, or .config extensions are not correctly registered in Internet Information Server (IIS). This may happen if the .NET Framework was installed before IIS. You can either uninstall and reinstall the .NET Framework or register the appropriate extensions in IIS, by following these steps:

1. Open the IIS Manager (Windows 2003).
2. Right-click the AuthService virtual directory (located underneath the Access Center virtual directory) and select Properties.
3. On the Virtual Directory tab, select the Configuration button.
4. Under Application Mappings, select Add.
5. For the executable, enter the location of the .NET Framework aspnet_isapi.dll. This is usually located under WINNT\Microsoft.NET\FrameWork\v1.1.*xxx*.
6. For the extension, enter **.asmx.**
7. Limit verbs to GET,HEAD,POST,DEBUG.
8. Check the box for the script engine.
9. Repeat this sequence, adding the same entry for the .aspx and .config extensions.

NOTE Lack of proper registration may cause problems with other file extensions.

Verbose Scan Results for Citrix Advanced Access Control 4.5

When using Citrix Advanced Access Control 4.5 in an environment with multiple End Point Analysis scans applied to a logon point, troubleshooting client access issues may be confusing for administrators. Using this diagnostic procedure can be helpful in identifying denied client criteria as configured in the admin console.

To use this troubleshooting capability, find the following file on the Advanced Access Control server:

- **Path** C:\inetpub\wwwroot\citrixlogonpoint\samplelogonpoint (or the appropriate logon point directory)
- **File** disallowed.ascx

Open this file with a text editor. Toward the bottom of the file, you see the following section commented out with apostrophes. Uncomment this section and save the file.

```
if(hash.Count > count)
          scanFailure2.InnerHtml = "<table border=2><tr><th>" &
          Citrix.LogonAgent
.Util.Localization.ResourceManager.GetString( "EPARULE" )
          scanFailure2.InnerHtml = scanFailure2.InnerHtml & "</th><th>" &
Citrix.LogonAgent.Util.Localization.ResourceManager.GetString("EPAVALUE")
          scanFailure2.InnerHtml = scanFailure2.InnerHtml & "</th></tr>"
          Dim keys(hash.Count) as String
          hash.keys.CopyTo(keys, 0)
          Dim n as Integer
    n = 0
    Do
            if(keys(n) <> "EPAReferenceID")
            ' This adds one line of text for each EPA output variable
giving its
            ' name and value; but other HTML could be added as desired
            ' such as making it a table
            Dim line as String
            line = "<tr><td>"&keys(n)&"</td><td>"& hash.item(keys(n))&
"</td></tr>"
            scanFailure2.InnerHtml = scanFailure2.InnerHtml + line
          end if
          n = n+1
    Loop Until n = hash.Count
          scanFailure2.InnerHtml = scanFailure2.InnerHtml + "</table>"
    else
```

```
                scanFailure2.InnerText =
Citrix.LogonAgent.UserInterface.DisallowedPage.GetEmptyResultString()
    end if '(hash.Count > count)
        end if
```

Doing so enables verbose results, which do not pass all End Point Analysis scans as configured in the console, to be displayed to clients attempting to connect to the logon point. Table 18-1 shows an example of the output shown to the client.

NOTE Once the administrator has finished troubleshooting, it is highly recommended that the previously mentioned section of code in disallowed.ascx be commented out.

TROUBLESHOOTING THE CITRIX PASSWORD MANAGER SERVICE

The best troubleshooting resources for Citrix Password Manager Service are the error messages encountered in the console, agent, and XTE Service Error logs. The most common error messages have been included in this chapter to help you quickly locate and resolve the issues that prompt the messages. This section is organized into seven parts to provide easy access to the most common errors encountered:

- **Password Manager Service Frequently Asked Questions**
  - What is the XTE Service?
  - Are the signing and validation certificates related to the Secure Sockets Layer (SSL) certificate?
  - Do I have to use CtxCreateSigningCert?
  - How do I enable Data Integrity on an environment that already has been established as a "non–Data Integrity" deployment?

Rule	Output Value
Citrix Scans for Internet Explorer. IE Scan. Verified-Internet-Explorer-Installed.	True
Citrix Scans for Windows Service Pack. Windows Service Pack Scan. Verified-Windows-Service-Pack.	True
Citrix Scans for Domain Membership. Domain Scan. Verified-Domain.	False
Citrix Scans for Internet Explorer. IE Scan. Verified-Internet-Explorer-Connecting.	True

Table 18-1. Verbose Scan Results for Citrix Advanced Access Control 4.5

- **Issues and Errors Encountered on the Service Machine**
  - Service Configuration tool does not start
  - Service Configuration tool does not complete its configuration
  - Shutting down/restarting the Citrix XTE Service
  - Using the Data Signing tool
- **Issues and Errors Encountered on the Console Machine**
  - Configure and run discovery (Data Integrity)
  - Console error messages (Data Integrity)
  - Console error messages (Provisioning)
- **Issues and Errors Encountered on the Agent Machine**
  - Data Integrity–related errors
  - Automatic Key Recovery authentication failed, module could not be contacted
  - Automatic Key Recovery post-password change
  - Self-Service Password Reset registration failed
  - Provisioning: Failure to consume queued commands
- **Troubleshooting the Connection**
  - Testing the connection
  - Repairing the connection
- **Data Integrity—Recovering from Data Corruption**
- **XTE Service Error Log**
  - SSL certificate/machine name mismatch
  - SSL handshake failure
  - User not authorized to access the page
  - Require user/group line is invalid
  - File not found or unable to start
  - Attempt to serve directory

Password Manager Service Frequently Asked Questions

What is the XTE Service? Is it the same as the Access Suite's XTE Service?

XTE stands for eXtensible Transformation Engine. XTE is a common infrastructure component used in multiple Citrix products. The XTE Service hosts the Password Manager web services.

This service is the same XTE Service that Citrix Access Suite uses; however, it uses added modules with a different configuration. The added modules and configurations prevent the Password Manager Service from being installed on a machine with other Citrix applications that use the XTE Service. In addition, the security model recommends that the Password Manager Service server be placed in a physically secure location with limited access.

Are the signing/validation certificates related to the SSL certificate?

No, the SSL certificate (supplied from your certificate authority) is a totally separate entity from the signing/validation certificates created by the Password Manager Service.

What is the purpose of the SSL certificate?

An SSL certificate is necessary to ensure encrypted communication from the Service to the agents and console, and to guarantee that the agent and console are talking to the correct Service machine. The SSL certificate name must exactly match the fully qualified name of the Password Manager Service machine to verify that the Password Manager Service machine is, indeed, the correct machine.

What is the purpose of the signing/validation certificates?

The signing and validation certificates are created by the Password Manager Service and have no relation to the SSL certificate. They are used by the Data Integrity Service to authenticate the information stored in the central store. Automatic Key Recovery and Self-Service Password Request also use the signing certificate to verify the user identity token. The signing certificate absolutely does not encrypt any data. It takes the data from the console and generates a cryptographic signature, which is appended to the data. If the data are changed without using the signing service to append a new signature, the agent displays a validation error when attempting to use the data and discards the data.

Do I have to use CtxCreateSigningCert to create the signing/validation certificates?

In most cases, no. After a successful configuration of the Password Manager Service using the Service Configuration tool, the signing and validation certificates are created automatically. You would only create a new signing/validation certificate pair when you want to sign the data using a new certificate pair. You would need a new certificate pair if the certificate expires or is compromised.

How do I enable Data Integrity on an environment that already has been established as a "non–Data Integrity" deployment?

Follow these steps:

1. Sign the data with the Signing tool from the Password Manager Service machine. More information on using the Signing tool can be found in the *Password Manager Administrator's Guide.*

2. Configure and run discovery on the console. The console should automatically recognize that the data on the central store are signed and prompts the user to enter the Password Manager Service uniform resource identifier (URI).
3. Modify the installation of the agent to enable Data Integrity by selecting the Data Integrity feature and entering the URI of the Password Manager Service machine.

Service-Side Issues and Resolutions

The following section can be used to help troubleshoot service-related issues.

Service Configuration Tool Will Not Start

Here are the two most common reasons for the Service Configuration tool not starting:

- **The Service cannot find a valid SSL Web Server Certificate installed on the Password Manager Service machine.** An SSL web server certificate from your certificate authority (CA) is required. Also, the root CA must be trusted on every machine that contacts the Service: the agent, console, and Service.
- **The user running the Service Configuration tool must be a member of the domain and a member of the local machine administrators group.**

Service Configuration Tool Does Not Complete Its Configuration

Depending on where it stops, the Applying [Configuration] Settings status dialog window can give clues as to what function of the Service Configuration failed.

A. **Failure to configure the Data Proxy account:**

   Error: The account credentials provided for the application are invalid.

   Issue: This usually occurs because the user credentials configured to run the Data Proxy were entered incorrectly. Go back to the "Configure data proxy" page of the Service Configuration tool and re-enter the credentials.

B. **Failure to configure the Self-Service Password Reset account:**

   Error: The account credentials provided for the application are invalid.

   Issue: This usually occurs because the user credentials configured to run the Self-Service Password Reset account were entered incorrectly. Go back to the "Provide password reset credentials" page of the Service Configuration tool and re-enter the credentials.

C. **Failure to start the XTE Service:**
   Several issues can cause this failure:

   a. **The SSL certificate name does not exactly match the fully qualified domain name (FQDN) of the Password Manager Service machine.**

      Error: The server process could not be started. Make sure that the port is not in use. Refer to the Windows event log and Citrix XTE Server error log for more information.

Issue: The only way to verify this is the problem is to look at the Citrix XTE Service error logs. Refer to the "XTE Service Error Log" section later in this chapter for more details on a resolution to an SSL server certificate/machine name mismatch.

b. **The Port is in use by another service (that is, IIS Admin Service).**

Error: The server process could not be started. Make sure that the port is not in use. Refer to the Windows event log and Citrix XTE Server error log for more information.

Issue: If you are unsure which program is occupying the Password Manager Service default port 443, run port monitoring software to determine what is running on the port. The typical culprit is IIS. Uninstall the IIS Service (or other web service running on 443) or choose to run the Password Manager Service on a different port.

c. **Credentials are incorrect.**

Error: The server process could not be started because the account name is invalid or does not exist, or the password is invalid for the account name specified.

Issue: Go back to the "Configure service" page of the Service Configuration tool and re-enter the account credentials for the Citrix XTE Service.

Shutting Down and Restarting the Citrix XTE Service

Refer to "Resolution 3: Restart the XTE Service and COM+ Objects" below for steps to shut down and start the Citrix XTE Service.

Using the Data Signing Tool

The *Data Signing tool* is a command-line utility located on the Password Manager Service machine at C:\Program Files\Citrix\MetaFrame Password Manager\Service\SigningTool\. The Data Signing tool (CtxSignData.exe) should be used in the following situations:

- When enabling or disabling Data Integrity in an existing deployment of Password Manager
- When verifying all the signatures on a central store that has Data Integrity enabled
- When re-signing all the data on the central store with a newly created signing certificate after data corruption or after signing/validation certificate expiration.

Details and examples on using the Data Signing tool are located in the *Password Manager Administrator's Guide.*

Console-Side Issues and Resolutions

This section deals with console-related issues and troubleshooting.

Impact of Data Integrity on Configure and Run Discovery

When running "Configure and run discovery" on the console with a central store that has never been configured, the administrator is provided a choice to enable Data Integrity. When "Configure and run discovery" is activated on a central store that has previously been configured—either with Data Integrity on or off—the administrator is not allowed to change the Data Integrity setting from the console. See the *Password Manager Administrator's Guide* for more on disabling or enabling Data Integrity in an existing deployment.

When running "Configure and run discovery," if Data Integrity is enabled, the user must fill in the Service URI and port number for the Citrix Password Manager Service machine. The following issues may be encountered:

- The Service URI is typed incorrectly or the console is unable to contact the Service.
- The Service port is typed incorrectly.
- SSL certificate trust failed.
- An unexpected error occurred.

Each of the specific errors is explained here:

- **Service URI Error: The underlying connection was closed: The remote host-name could not be resolved.**

  The Service URI is typed incorrectly or the console is unable to contact the Password Manager Service machine.

- **Service Port Error: The remote service point could not be contacted at the transport level.**

  The Password Manager Service port is typed incorrectly or the Citrix XTE Service is not running on the Password Manager Service machine.

- **SSL Trust Error: SSL server certificate could not be validated. The SSL server certificate is not trusted and a connection will not be made.**

  The XTE Service error log also prints the following if the SSL handshake failed (that is, when the SSL certificate is not trusted): "SSL handshake from client failed." See the "XTE Service Error Log" section for more details on how to avoid this error.

- **An exception of unknown type has occurred during connection to the service host. Service may have encountered internal error or misconfiguration.**

  Issue: This error typically appears when an unauthorized user is trying to configure and run discovery on a central store that has Data Integrity enabled. Not only will the console user require read-write access to the central store, but in the case of Data Integrity, the console user also needs access to the PrivateKeyCert.cert file on the Password Manager Service machine. If you are not activating the "Configure and run discovery" feature as a domain administrator, special access must be granted to the user or group of users that use the signing certificate (PrivateKeyCert.cert) on the Password Manager Service machine.

NOTE This error can also occur when you are trying to configure Data Integrity with a Password Manager Service machine that does not have the Data Integrity Service component installed. You can only enable Data Integrity on a console with a Password Manager Service that is running the Data Integrity Service.

Resolution: Read the Citrix XTE Service error log in C:\Program Files\ Common Files\Citrix\XTE\logs\ to verify that the issue is a "user not authorized" error. Proceed to the "XTE Service Error Log" section for more information to resolve this issue.

- **Console error message: One or more <CentralStoreRoot objects> could not be read from the central store. Your Windows Event Log contains additional error information.**

Resolution: Check which object has been corrupted using the Event viewer. Refer to the *Password Manager Administrator's Guide* and the "Data Integrity—Recovering from Data Corruption" section later in this chapter for more information.

- **Console error message: Provisioning is disabled. Enable provisioning and provide the address to the Citrix Password Manager Service.**

Resolution: You will receive this error message after selecting a user configuration and attempting to run either Generate Provisioning Template or Run Provisioning tasks from the console. This is because the selected user configuration does not have the provisioning module enabled or configured. Edit the user configuration and, on the provisioning module, enable the feature by checking the Use Provisioning option and then enter the service URL and port.

Error: "Batch, Failure, The name resolver service could not resolve the host name."

Issue: You will receive this error when running the Run Provision task from the console. This is because the service URL specified in the selected user configuration cannot be resolved.

Resolution: Edit the user configuration and, on the provisioning module, use the validate button to verify the service URL and port. Refer to the "Troubleshooting the Connection" section later in this chapter for more information on how to resolve this issue.

Error: "Data Integrity Status Mismatch."

Issue: You will receive this error message when running the Run Provision task from the console. If Data Integrity is enabled or disabled, it must have the same on/off setting throughout the Password Manager environment.

Resolution: Verify that Data Integrity is consistently enabled or disabled in the following places:

- **The central store** The data must be signed or unsigned.
- **The Service Configuration tool** Data Integrity must be on or off.
- **The agent** Data Integrity must be on or off.

Agent-Side Issues and Resolutions

This section addresses the most common agent-related issues for Password Manager.

Data Integrity Errors

The agent's most common Data Integrity error, "Data integrity failed...1," occurs on agent startup. When you are using the agent, if a Data Integrity failure occurs, the agent is unable to grab any settings applied with the console. On first-time use of the agent, you will be unable to get a license. When you receive this error, verify the following:

- The root CA is trusted on the certificate *physical store* of the agent machine.
- The Password Manager Service URI and port have been typed correctly on the agent installation. The registry key that holds this information is HKLM\Software\Citrix\Citrix Password Manager\Extensions\Server\BaseURL.
- Connect via Internet Explorer (IE) to the Password Manager Service machine from the agent machine. Refer to the "Troubleshooting the Connection" section for details on contacting the Password Manager Service via IE.

All the necessary checks can be performed by following the instructions in the "Troubleshooting the Connection" section.

Automatic Key Recovery: Authentication Failed or Key Management Module Could Not Be Contacted

The following errors may occur if authentication fails or the key management module cannot be contacted:

Error: "Password Manager authentication failed."

Error: "The Password Manager Service Key Management Module could not be contacted. Contact your administrator. Password Manager agent will now shut down."

Issue: The most common Automatic Key Recovery error, "Password Manager authentication failed...," occurs on agent startup. When using the agent for the first time, the Automatic Key Recovery Service is called immediately to generate a key used to decrypt credentials in case of a future password change.

Several possible issues can cause these errors:

- The Central Store Proxy account does not have adequate permissions. To verify that this is not the case, try making the Central Store Proxy account a domain administrator. Also, the Central Store Proxy account must have access to AuthenticatedWS web service—refer to the "XTE Service Error Log" section for more information. Regarding Central Store Proxy account permissions, see the section "Configuring Citrix Password Manager Administrative Access without Being a Domain Administrator" in Chapter 10.
- There is a Data Integrity status mismatch: If Data Integrity is enabled or disabled, it must have the same on/off setting throughout the Password Manager environment. If Data Integrity is disabled, this setting must be present in three places:
  - The administrator must verify that the central store remains unsigned.
  - The Service Configuration tool must have Data Integrity disabled.
  - The agent must have Data Integrity disabled.

The console must also remain consistent and the console administrator is automatically prompted to configure and run discovery if the central store Data Integrity setting has changed.

Automatic Key Recovery: Post-Password Change

The following error may occur after a password change occurs:

Error: "The Password Manager Service Key Management Module could not locate your keys. Contact your administrator. Password Manager agent will now shut down."

Issue: Three possible causes for this error exist:

- The Central Store Proxy account does not have adequate permissions. To verify this is not the case, try making the Central Store Proxy account a domain administrator. Also, the Central Store Proxy account must have access to AuthenticatedWS web service—refer to the "XTE Service Error Log" section for more information. Regarding Central Store Proxy account permissions, see the section "Configuring Citrix Password Manager Administrative Access without Being a Domain Administrator" in Chapter 10.
- The AKR.dat Service key (V4) has changed on the Password Manager Service machine. This can occur if someone moves the Password Manager Service machine without exporting AKR.dat using the CtxMoveKeyRecoveryData tool. The V4 (AKR.dat) must remain static throughout a deployment when users have configured application credentials. For more information on migrating AKR.dat, see the section "Advanced Concepts in Automatic Key Recovery" in Chapter 15.
- The user's data have not replicated across multiple domain controllers.

First-Time Use: Self-Service Password Reset Registration Failed

The following errors may occur during first time use of the Self-Service Password Reset:

Error: "You cannot register for the password reset feature. Please contact your administrator."

Issue: This error can appear both before and after a user encounters any Self-Service Password Reset questions.

The following lists reasons why the error appears both before and after Self-Service Password Reset questions are encountered:

- Check that the Password Manager Service URI is correctly configured on the agent machine. The registry key that holds this information is HKLM\Software\ Citrix\Citrix Password Manager\Extensions\Server\BaseURL. Copy this URI from the key and paste it into IE and then add the required .asmx filename to the end of it. The .asmx files associated with this error are NTLMAuthSvc.asmx, EnrollmentSvc.asmx, and AuthSvc.asmx, in the order they are called. Refer to the "Troubleshooting the Connection" section for more information on testing the connection to these component service pages.
- If you are using a central store proxy account that is not a Domain Administrator, check that the account has adequate permissions on the central store. Also, the central store proxy user, when not in the Domain Administrators group, must be added to the "require group" line of the XTE Service httpd.conf file. Refer to the "XTE Service Error Log" section for more information to resolve this issue. Also, to verify this is indeed a permissions issue, try configuring the Password Manager Service with a Domain Administrator as the central store proxy account (using the Service Configuration tool).
- Check that the root CA is trusted in the certificates' *physical store* of the agent machine. Refer to the "Troubleshooting the Connection" section for more information on how to resolve this issue.
- There is a Data Integrity status mismatch: if Data Integrity is enabled or disabled, it must have the same on/off setting throughout the Password Manager environment. If Data Integrity is disabled, this setting must be present in three places:
  - The administrator must verify that the central store remains unsigned.
  - The Service Configuration tool must have Data Integrity disabled.
  - The agent must have Data Integrity disabled.

The console must also remain consistent and the console administrator is automatically prompted to configure and run discovery if the central store Data Integrity setting has changed.

Provisioning: Failure to Consume Queued Commands

The following error may occur during provisioning:

Error: The agent does not consume a provisioning command for a user that has a provisioning command in his or her queue.

Issue: If the agent fails during the provisioning operation that occurs each time that the agent is launched (when provisioning is enabled), the user does not receive an error, but the agent silently fails and continues with normal operations. To determine what is causing the provisioning operation to fail, you should enable the agent's advanced logging capabilities. Once the logging has been enabled, restart the agent to reproduce the failure. In the generated agent log, find the following line:

```
ProvisionAgent(), GetProvisioned() returned: X
```

In this example, the *X* at the end of the line refers to the failure status code that can be determined from most commonly found codes in the following list. Once you determine the reason for the failure, refer to the "Troubleshooting the Connection" and "XTE Service Error Log" sections for more information on how to resolve this issue.

1. Not Authorized
2. Deprovisioned
3. Refused Auth
4. Failure
5. Auth Failure
6. Success
7. Completed
8. Nothing To Do
9. Timed Out

Troubleshooting the Connection

The two most common issues related to Password Manager Service configurations are SSL certificate and Domain Name System (DNS) issues. In the situation where the console or agent is unable to connect or interact with the Password Manager Service, the following series of steps may help determine whether the issue is related to DNS configuration, SSL certificates, or both.

Testing the Connection

This section describes the process for testing the connection for the Password Manager Service.

Check 1: Contact the Password Manager Service through Internet Explorer

With a failure to connect to the Password Manager Service, the first and most important step is to check whether it is accessible through the network. The Password Manager

Service is a web service, so each of the web services is accessible through IE. Seven component service pages are associated with the Automatic Key Recovery, Self-Service Password Request, and Data Integrity modules of the Password Manager Service. Listed next to each component service are the services that use the component service. You should test any service that fails by visiting its corresponding component pages.

- **/MPMService/AuthenticatedWS.asmx** Data Integrity, Automatic Key Recovery, Self-Service Password Reset (accessible only to users in the "require group" line in httpd.conf)
- **/MPMService/AuthSvc.asmx** Self-Service Password Request
- **/MPMService/DataIntegritySvc.asmx** Data Integrity
- **/MPMService/EnrollmentSvc.asmx** Automatic Key Recovery, Self-Service Password Request
- **/MPMService/KeyRecoverySvc.asmx** Automatic Key Recovery
- **/MPMService/NTLMAuthSvc.asmx** Automatic Key Recovery, Self-Service Password Request
- **/MPMService/PwdResetSvc.asmx** Self-Service Password Request
- **/MPMService/ProvisionSvc.asmx** Provisioning Request
- **/MPMService/ProvisionAgentSVC.asmx** Provisioning Agent consumption

Each of these individual web services is accessible as a web page through IE. The format to view these pages when the Password Manager Service is running is https://*FQDN of Service Machine*:*Port*/MPMService/*webservice*.asmx. For example, to test that the Data Integrity Service is running, go to https://*FQDN of Service Machine*:*port*/MPMService/DataIntegritySvc.asmx. Based on the possible results listed here, proceed to the next check or resolution indicated:

- **Result 1.1: You were unable to reach the Password Manager Service page through IE:**
  (Proceed to Check 2)
  If you are unable to connect to the Password Manager Service through IE, check that you typed the correct web address, including HTTPS and the port. Proceed to Check 2.
- **Result 1.2: You were able to reach the Password Manager Service page, but IE asked you whether you trust the SSL certificate:**
  (Proceed to Resolution 1)
  If you were able to view the Password Manager Service page, but only after you answered yes to trust the SSL certificate, proceed to Resolution 1.
- **Result 1.3: The Password Manager Service page reports an "Error in Application":**

  (Proceed to Resolution 3)
  If an "Error in Application" page is displayed when you contact one of the Password Manager Service component pages in IE, go to Resolution 3.

Check 2: Ping the FQDN of the Password Manager Service Machine

If you were unable to view the Password Manager Service page, the next step is to see whether you can ping the FQDN of the service. Ping the fully qualified name (as opposed to the NetBIOS name) of the Password Manager Service machine from the client machine.

▼ **Result 2.1: The FQDN ping request fails:**

Now, ping the NetBIOS name of the service from the client machine. If you receive a reply, then do an NSLOOKUP of the service machine from the client machine. If you receive a different FQDN than expected, check that the Password Manager Service machine and the client machine have the DNS settings set up correctly. The Password Manager Service machine name should exactly match NSLOOKUP's reply of the fully qualified name of the Password Manager Service machine. If a mismatch exists between the NSLOOKUP reply and the actual FQDN of the Password Manager Service machine, proceed to Resolution 2.

▲ **Result 2.2: The FQDN ping succeeds:**

Go to the service machine and check that the Citrix XTE Service is running. On the service machine, use IE to contact the web services (the previous Check 1). Verify that you tried contacting the service machine on the correct port.

Repairing the Connection

The following resolutions describe how to repair the connection for the Password Manager Service.

Resolution 1: Add the Certificate to the Trusted Root Certificates

You take this step when you are able to view the Password Manager Service page but cannot proceed without first trusting the SSL certificate. If your CA is located within the same domain that uses the Password Manager Service, then you should automatically have trust established. To check that your root CA is trusted, you must open the certificates component of the Windows Management console (choose Run from the Start menu and enter **mmc**). Choose the certificates (Local Computer) snap-in and view Trusted Root Certificates. The root CA must be trusted on the physical store of each of the client machines (not the registry per user).

Resolution 2: Fix the DNS Settings of the Password Manager Environment DNS settings can cause some machines to "resolve" differently within different places in an environment. DNS must be set up consistently throughout an environment. The DNS configuration is especially important in regard to connections to the Password Manager Service. This is because of the SSL security involved in verifying the identity of the Password Manager Service machine.

Resolution 3: Restart the XTE Service and COM+ Objects The Citrix XTE Service runs in the Services Console in Windows. To shut down the XTE Service, go to Administrative Tools | Services (or choose Run from the Start menu and enter **Services.msc**) and look for Citrix XTE Server. Use the Services Console GUI to restart the service.

NOTE When changes are applied with the Service Configuration tool, the XTE Service and COM+ objects are restarted.

If you go to the Properties page for the Citrix XTE Server, you see the user who was entered in the Service Configuration tool.

CAUTION Do not manually change users here! Use the Service Configuration tool, because several directories are in the Password Manager Service machine, where permissions are set for the XTE Service user account in addition to the various other hidden configurations made by the Service Configuration tool.

Data Integrity—Recovering from Data Corruption

If the Data Integrity Service detects an inconsistency between data on the central store and their associated signature, an error is thrown in the console when trying to make changes to the central store. These errors prevent the console administrator from making changes to a central store deployment. To recover, unsign the data on the central store and then sign the data with a new signing certificate (for maximum security). The re-sign option from the signing tool cannot be used because the re-sign operation verifies the data first and, if it encounters corrupted data, fails.

Because you want to ensure that you do not sign bad data, you should first get an idea of which data are corrupted. Five basic areas exist where data corruption could occur: CentralStoreRoot, ADMINOVERRIDES, ENTLIST, FTULIST, and SYNCSTATE. If data corruption occurs on an object within the CentralStoreRoot, the console administrator is notified of it when a change is attempted on the object. The exact object can be manually deleted using Explorer or ADSIEdit on the central store. If data corruption occurs on one of the ADMINOVERRIDES, ENTLIST, FTULIST, or SYNCSTATE objects, you must perform the following steps to ensure proper security:

1. For maximum security, close access to the central store.
2. Using the signing tool, unsign all the data on the central store.
3. Use the signing certificate creation tool CtxCreateSigningCert.exe to create a new signing certificate.
4. Sign the central store with the new signing certificate.
5. Open the console.
6. At this point, all settings in ADMINOVERRIDES, ENTLIST, FTULIST, and SYNCSTATE must be reset for all deployments. The only way to guarantee an update of these four objects is to make changes to the CentralStoreRoot that will force the objects to be redeployed to all user configurations:
   - **ADMINOVERRIDES** A change in client settings, such as "show computer name," forces an update of ADMINOVERRIDES on a "per user configuration" basis.

- **ENTLIST** A change in policies, applications, and sharing groups forces an update of ENTLIST on a "per user configuration" basis.
- **FTULIST** A change in Identity Verification Questions, initial credential setup applications, or key recovery type forces an update of FTULIST on a "per user configuration" basis.
- **SYNCSTATE** This object is updated for all deployments when any change is made to the CentralStoreRoot.

7. Reopen access to the central store.

All future agent logins following these changes receive the new settings and verify the integrity of the information on the central store using the new validation certificate (PublicKeyCert.cert).

XTE Service Error Log

This section lists possible errors encountered in the Citrix XTE Service error logs, ranked from the most common to the least common. The XTE Service error log is located at C:\Program Files\Common Files\Citrix\XTE\logs\error.log.

SSL Certificate/Machine Name Mismatch

The following error may occur if a mismatch exists between the SSL certificate and the machine name:

Error: "The certificate with identifier *ID* for virtual server *FQDN of Service Machine*: *Port* has subject common name (CN) *Not FQDN*. The subject common name must match the server name of the virtual host."

Issue: Although the Service Configuration tool starts when it finds an SSL server certificate, the XTE Service is later unable to start unless the name on the SSL server certificate exactly matches the name of the service machine.

Resolution: The service machine name must be referred to by its FQDN; therefore, when creating the SSL server certificate, the name on the certificate must be the FQDN of the service machine.

SSL Handshake Failure

The following error may occur if an SSL handshake fails:

Error: "SSL handshake from client failed."

Issue: Handshake errors usually occur when the client does not have the root CA in the Trusted Root Certificates bin in its physical computer certificate store (as opposed to registry store).

Resolution: The root CA must be trusted in the physical certificate store of the service machine and all clients (agent and console).

User Not Authorized to Access the Page

The following error may occur if a user is not authorized to access the page:

Error: "[client *x.x.x.x*] Overlapped I/O operation is in progress. : mod_auth_ntlm: User is not authorized to access the page."

Issue: The user on machine with IP address *x.x.x.x* was unable to use the AuthenticatedWS web service. This issue typically occurs when using Data Integrity with a Password Manager Console administrator account that has not been added to the Citrix XTE Service configuration file (httpd.conf). Also, it can occur if the central store proxy account has not been added to the XTE configuration file.

The AuthenticatedWS web service provides access to the PrivateKeyCert.cert file, which the console needs in order to sign and verify data (it is also used by the C.S. proxy to encrypt the AKR data on the central store). This error is received when a user tries to access this web service but is not permitted to use the key. Typically, a Password Manager administrator running the console receives this error because the user has not been added to the group that is allowed to use the PrivateKeyCert.cert file to sign data. This error also occurs when the C.S. proxy account has not been added to the group. By default, the group permitted to use this signing service is the Domain Admins group.

Resolution: To remedy this issue and add a user or group of users to those permitted to use the signing certificate, you must modify the XTE Service configuration file, httpd.conf. The configuration file is found at C:\Program Files\Common Files\Citrix\XTE\conf\. Open it in a text editor and add the following lines for each user or group within the AuthenticatedWS tag:

```
require user "Domain\\User"
require group "Domain\\Group"
```

The following line has been added inside the AuthenticatedWS tag and can be used as an example for syntax:

```
require group "Domain\\Domain Admins,"
```

The Required User or Group Line (in httpd.conf file) Is Invalid

The following error may occur if the user or group line in the httpd.conf file is invalid:

Error: "No mapping between account names and security IDs was done: mod_auth_ntlm: Failed to lookup for a group name - *BadDomain**Group* or *Domain**BadGroupName*."

Issue: This error occurs on more rare occasions, but it occurs when the Password Manager administrator modifies the httpd.conf file by adding an invalid "require user/group" line.

Resolution: To remedy this issue, open the httpd.conf file and modify the required user or group line that was in the error log: *BadDomain**Group* [or *Domain**BadGroupName*].

File Not Found or Unable to Start

The following error may occur if a file is not found or is unable to start:

Error: "Mod_aspdotnet: File not found or unable to start: .../Service/ WebService/ DataIntegritySvc.asmx."

Issue: If you are running "Configure and run discovery" on the console and you point to a Password Manager Service machine that does not have Data Integrity installed, this error message is received.

NOTE You will also receive this error message when you are trying to contact the Password Manager Service via IE and type the filename incorrectly.

Resolution: Install Data Integrity on the service machine to which you are pointing, or point to a Password Manager Service machine that has the Data Integrity Service installed.

Attempt to Serve Directory

The following error may occur if the index file cannot be found:

Error: "Attempt to serve directory .../Service/WebService/."

Issue: When you try to connect to the Password Manager Service machine using the following address, the index file will not be found:

`https://`*`FQDNofServiceMachine`*`:`*`Port`*`/MPMService/`

Resolution: There is not an index page for the Password Manager web services. To contact each individual web service, refer to Check 1 in the "Troubleshooting the Connection" section.

ADFS Account Mapping or ADFS Shadow Accounts cannot unlock their ADFS Session

When ADFS Shadow Accounts are unable to unlock their ADFS Session it may be because Shadow account users do not know their Resource shadow account password, so if their session locks, they will not be able to provide a password to unlock it.

When implementing Active Directory Federated authentication, users may be authenticated in one forest domain in order to access resources located in another forest domain. When deploying Active Directory Federated Services organizations are identified as:

- **Account**: the organization that authenticates a user
- **Resource**: provides resources for a user that has been authenticated by **Account**

ADFS uses account mapping to map user accounts in the account organization to a shadow account located in the Resource organization. Shadow accounts are created in Active Directory in the Resource organization, and mirror user accounts existing in the account organization. The following options are possible for account mapping:

- **Map many *Account* users to one *Resource* account** This minimizes the number of *Resource* accounts, but Password Manager is unable to determine the identity of the user and therefore is not supported in this option.
- **Map one *Account* user to one *Resource* account** This offers full scalability as each *Account* user has a dedicated shadow account at *Resource*

The *Resource* organization trusts the *Account* organization to authenticate its own users without the need for any domain trust relationships. It is also not necessary to enable shadow accounts for interactive logon, since they are never used for that purpose, and shadow account passwords are not known to the *Account* user.

To prevent Password Manager from auto locking the shadow account, applications should not be flagged for forced re-authentication. Also, the re-authentication timeout should be left at the default 8 hour value and not made too small to prevent the agent from locking the session.

PART III

Appendices

APPENDIX A

Error Messages

This appendix provides a listing of Independent Management Architecture (IMA) error codes and event log (imamsgs.dll) error messages intended to help in troubleshooting and resolving problems with Presentation Server.

IMA ERROR CODES

Table A-1 lists the IMA service error codes that might appear in the Event viewer.

Hex Value	Signed Value	Unsigned Value	Mnemonic
00000000h	0	0	IMA_RESULT_SUCCESS
00000001h	1	1	IMA_RESULT_OPERATION_INCOMPLETE
00000002h	2	2	IMA_RESULT_CALL_NEXT_HOOK
00000003h	3	3	IMA_RESULT_DISCARD_MESSAGE
00000004h	4	4	IMA_RESULT_CREATED_NEW
00000005h	5	5	IMA_RESULT_FOUND_EXISTING
00000009h	9	9	IMA_RESULT_CONNECTION_IDLE
00130001h	1245185	1245185	IMA_RESULT_DS_NOT_INSTALLED
00130002h	1245186	1245186	IMA_RESULT_SECURITY_INFO_INCOMPLETE
002D0001h	2949121	2949121	IMA_RESULT_ALREADY_MASTER
80000001h	–2147483647	2147483649	IMA_RESULT_FAILURE
80000002h	–2147483646	2147483650	IMA_RESULT_NO_MEMORY
80000003h	–2147483645	2147483651	IMA_RESULT_INVALID_ARG
80000004h	–2147483644	2147483652	IMA_RESULT_UNKNOWN_MESSAGE
80000005h	–2147483643	2147483653	IMA_RESULT_DESTINATION_UNREACHABLE
80000006h	–2147483642	2147483654	IMA_RESULT_REFERENCE_COUNT_NOT_ZERO
80000007h	–2147483641	2147483655	IMA_RESULT_ENTRY_NOT_FOUND
80000008h	–2147483640	2147483656	IMA_RESULT_NETWORK_FAILURE
80000009h	–2147483639	2147483657	MA_RESULT_NOT_IMPLEMENTED
8000000Ah	–2147483638	2147483658	IMA_RESULT_INVALID_MESSAGE
8000000Bh	–2147483637	2147483659	IMA_RESULT_TIMEOUT

Table A-1 IMA Error Codes

Hex Value	Signed Value	Unsigned Value	Mnemonic
8000000Ch	–2147483636	2147483660	IMA_RESULT_POINTER_IS_NULL
8000000Dh	–2147483635	2147483661	IMA_RESULT_UNINITIALIZED
8000000Eh	–2147483634	2147483662	IMA_RESULT_FINDITEM_FAILURE
8000000Fh	–2147483633	2147483663	IMA_RESULT_CREATEPOOL_FAILURE
80000010h	–2147483632	2147483664	IMA_RESULT_SUBSYS_NOT_FOUND
80000013h	–2147483629	2147483667	IMA_RESULT_PS_UNINITIALIZED
80000014h	–2147483628	2147483668	IMA_RESULT_REGMAPFAIL
80000015h	–2147483627	2147483669	IMA_RESULT_DEST_TOO_SMALL
80000016h	–2147483626	2147483670	IMA_RESULT_ACCESS_DENIED
80000017h	–2147483625	2147483671	IMA_RESULT_NOT_SHUTTING_DOWN
80000018h	–2147483624	2147483672	IMA_RESULT_MUSTLOAD_FAILURE
80000019h	–2147483623	2147483673	IMA_RESULT_CREATELOCK_FAILURE
8000001Ah	–2147483622	2147483674	IMA_RESULT_SHUTDOWN_FAILURE
8000001Ch	–2147483620	2147483676	IMA_RESULT_SENDWAIT_FAILURE
8000001Dh	–2147483619	2147483677	IMA_RESULT_NO_COLLECTORS
8000001Eh	–2147483618	2147483678	IMA_RESULT_UPDATED
8000001Fh	–2147483617	2147483679	IMA_RESULT_NO_CHANGE
80000020h	–2147483616	2147483680	IMA_RESULT_LEGACY_NOT_ENABLED
80000021h	–2147483615	2147483681	IMA_RESULT_VALUE_ALREADY_CREATED
80000022h	–2147483614	2147483682	IMA_RESULT_UID_EXCEEDED_BOUNDS
80000023h	–2147483613	2147483683	IMA_RESULT_NO_EVENTS
80000024h	–2147483612	2147483684	IMA_RESULT_NOT_FOUND
80000025h	–2147483611	2147483685	IMA_RESULT_ALREADY_EXISTS
80000026h	–2147483610	2147483686	IMA_RESULT_GROUP_ALREADY_EXISTS
80000027h	–2147483609	2147483687	IMA_RESULT_NOT_A_GROUP
80000028h	–2147483608	2147483688	IMA_RESULT_GROUP_DIR_ACCESS_FAILURE
80000029h	–2147483607	2147483689	IMA_RESULT_EOF
8000002Ah	–2147483606	2147483690	IMA_RESULT_REGISTRY_ERROR
8000002Bh	–2147483605	2147483691	IMA_RESULT_DSN_OPEN_FAILURE
8000002Ch	–2147483604	2147483692	IMA_RESULT_REMOVING_PSSERVER
8000002Dh	–2147483603	2147483693	IMA_RESULT_NO_REPLY_SENT

Table A-1 IMA Error Codes (*continued*)

Hex Value	Signed Value	Unsigned Value	Mnemonic
8000002Eh	–2147483602	2147483694	IMA_RESULT_PLUGIN_FAILED_VERIFY
8000002Fh	–2147483601	2147483695	IMA_RESULT_FILE_NOT_FOUND
80000030h	–2147483600	2147483696	IMA_RESULT_PLUGIN_ENTRY_NOT_FOUND
80000031h	–2147483599	2147483697	IMA_RESULT_CLOSED
80000032h	–2147483598	2147483698	IMA_RESULT_PATH_NAME_TOO_LONG
80000033h	–2147483597	2147483699	IMA_RESULT_CREATEMESSAGEPORT_FAILED
80000034h	–2147483596	2147483700	IMA_RESULT_ALTADDRESS_NOT_DEFINED
80000035h	–2147483595	2147483701	IMA_RESULT_WOULD_BLOCK
80000036h	–2147483594	2147483702	IMA_RESULT_ALREADY_CLOSED
80000037h	–2147483593	2147483703	IMA_RESULT_TOO_BUSY
80000038h	–2147483592	2147483704	IMA_RESULT_HOST_SHUTTING_DOWN
80000039h	–2147483591	2147483705	IMA_RESULT_PORT_IN_USE
8000003Ah	–2147483590	2147483706	IMA_RESULT_NOT_SUPPORTED
80040001h	–2147221503	2147745793	IMA_RESULT_FILE_OPEN_FAILURE
80040002h	–2147221502	2147745794	IMA_RESULT_SESSION_REQUEST_DENIED
80040003h	–2147221501	2147745795	IMA_RESULT_JOB_NOT_FOUND
80040004h	–2147221500	2147745796	IMA_RESULT_SESSION_NOT_FOUND
80040005h	–2147221499	2147745797	IMA_RESULT_FILE_SEEK_FAILURE
80040006h	–2147221498	2147745798	IMA_RESULT_FILE_READ_FAILURE
80040007h	–2147221497	2147745799	IMA_RESULT_FILE_WRITE_FAILURE
80040008h	–2147221496	2147745800	IMA_RESULT_JOB_CANNOT_BE_UPDATED
80040009h	–2147221495	2147745801	IMA_RESULT_NO_TARGET_HOSTS
8004000Ah	–2147221494	2147745802	IMA_RESULT_NO_SOURCE_FILES
80060001h	–2147090431	2147876865	IMA_RESULT_ATTR_NOT_FOUND
80060002h	–2147090430	2147876866	IMA_RESULT_CONTEXT_NOT_FOUND
80060003h	–2147090429	2147876867	IMA_RESULT_VALUE_NOT_FOUND
80060004h	–2147090428	2147876868	IMA_RESULT_DATA_NOT_FOUND
80060005h	–2147090427	2147876869	IMA_RESULT_ENTRY_LOCKED
80060006h	–2147090426	2147876870	IMA_RESULT_SEARCH_HASMORE
80060007h	–2147090425	2147876871	IMA_RESULT_INCOMPLETE

Table A-1 IMA Error Codes (*continued*)

Hex Value	Signed Value	Unsigned Value	Mnemonic
80060008h	–2147090424	2147876872	IMA_RESULT_READEXCEPTION
80060009h	–2147090423	2147876873	IMA_RESULT_WRITEEXCEPTION
8006000Ah	–2147090422	2147876874	IMA_RESULT_LDAP_PARTIALINSTALL
8006000Bh	–2147090421	2147876875	IMA_RESULT_LDAP_NOTREADY
8006000Ch	–2147090420	2147876876	IMA_RESULT_BUFFER_TOO_SMALL
8006000Dh	–2147090419	2147876877	IMA_RESULT_CONTAINER_NOT_EMPTY
8006000Eh	–2147090418	2147876878	IMA_RESULT_CONFIGURATION_ERROR
8006000Fh	–2147090417	2147876879	IMA_RESULT_GET_BASEOBJECT
80060010h	–2147090416	2147876880	IMA_RESULT_GET_DERIVEDOBJECT
80060011h	–2147090415	2147876881	IMA_RESULT_OBJECTCLASS_NOTMATCH
80060012h	–2147090414	2147876882	IMA_RESULT_ATTRIBUTE_NOTINDEXED
80060013h	–2147090413	2147876883	IMA_RESULT_OBJECTCLASS_VIOLATION
80060014h	–2147090412	2147876884	IMA_RESULT_ENUMFAIL
80060015h	–2147090411	2147876885	IMA_RESULT_ENUMNODATA
80060016h	–2147090410	2147876886	IMA_RESULT_DBCONNECT_FAILURE
80060017h	–2147090409	2147876887	IMA_RESULT_TRUNCATE
80060018h	–2147090408	2147876888	IMA_RESULT_DUPLICATE
80060019h	–2147090407	2147876889	IMA_RESULT_PS_NOTINITIALIZED
8006001Ah	–2147090406	2147876890	IMA_RESULT_USING_ORACLE_7
8006001Bh	–2147090405	2147876891	IMA_RESULT_USING_ORACLE_8
8006001Ch	–2147090404	2147876892	IMA_RESULT_USING_ORACLE_UNKNOWN
8006001Dh	–2147090403	2147876893	IMA_RESULT_LOAD_DAO_ENGINE_FAILED
8006001Eh	–2147090402	2147876894	IMA_RESULT_COMPACT_DB_FAILED
80060033h	–2147090381	2147876915	IMA_RESULT_ODBC_NO_CONNECTIONS_ AVAILABLE
80060034h	–2147090380	2147876916	IMA_RESULT_CREATE_SQL_ENVIRONMENT_ FAILED
80060035h	–2147090379	2147876917	IMA_RESULT_SQL_EXECUTE_FAILED
80060036h	–2147090378	2147876918	IMA_RESULT_SQL_FETCH_FAILED
80060037h	–2147090377	2147876919	IMA_RESULT_SQL_BIND_PARAM_FAILED

Table A-1 IMA Error Codes (*continued*)

Hex Value	Signed Value	Unsigned Value	Mnemonic
80060038h	–2147090376	2147876920	IMA_RESULT_SQL_GET_COLUMN_DATA_FAILED
80060039h	–2147090375	2147876921	IMA_RESULT_REPLICATED_DATA_CONTENTION
8006003Ah	–2147090374	2147876922	IMA_RESULT_DB_TABLE_NOT_FOUND
8006003Bh	–2147090373	2147876923	IMA_RESULT_CONNECTION_EXIST
8006003Ch	–2147090372	2147876924	IMA_RESULT_QUERY_MAX_NODEID_FAILED
8006003Dh	–2147090371	2147876925	IMA_RESULT_SQL_FUNCTION_SEQUENCE_ERROR
8006003Eh	–2147090370	2147876926	IMA_RESULT_DB_CONNECTION_TIMEOUT
8006003Fh	–2147090369	2147876927	IMA_RESULT_SQL_INVALID_TRANSACTION_STATE
80060040h	–2147090368	2147876928	IMA_RESULT_DB_NO_DISK_SPACE
80110104h	–2146369276	2148598020	LMS_RESULT_NO_SERVER_AVAILABLE
80110105h	–2146369024	2148598272	IMA_RESULT_FULL_SERVER_OR_APP_LOAD_REACHED
80130001h	–2146238463	2148728833	IMA_RESULT_MORE_ITEMS
80130002h	–2146238462	2148728834	IMA_RESULT_INVALID_ACCOUNT
80130003h	–2146238461	2148728835	IMA_RESULT_INVALID_PASSWORD
80130004h	–2146238460	2148728836	IMA_RESULT_EXPIRED_PASSWORD
80130005h	–2146238459	2148728837	IMA_RESULT_GROUP_IGNORED
80130006h	–2146238458	2148728838	IMA_RESULT_BUILTIN_GROUP
80130007h	–2146238457	2148728839	IMA_RESULT_DC_NOT_AVAILABLE
80130008h	–2146238456	2148728840	IMA_RESULT_NW_CLIENT_NOT_INSTALLED
80130009h	–2146238455	2148728841	IMA_RESULT_ACCOUNT_LOCKED_OUT
8013000Ah	–2146238454	2148728842	IMA_RESULT_INVALID_LOGON_HOURS
8013000Bh	–2146238453	2148728843	IMA_RESULT_ACCOUNT_DISABLED
8013000Ch	–2146238452	2148728844	IMA_RESULT_PREFERRED_TREE_NOT_SET
80160001h	–2146041855	2148925441	IMA_RESULT_NODE_NOT_FOUND
80160002h	–2146041854	2148925442	IMA_RESULT_NODE_NAME_INVALID
80160003h	–2146041853	2148925443	IMA_RESULT_NODE_NOT_EMPTY

Table A-1 IMA Error Codes (*continued*)

Hex Value	Signed Value	Unsigned Value	Mnemonic
80160004h	–2146041852	2148925444	IMA_RESULT_NODE_MOVE_DENIED
80160005h	–2146041851	2148925445	IMA_RESULT_NODE_NAME_NOT_UNIQUE
80160006h	–2146041850	2148925446	IMA_RESULT_NODE_RENAME_DENIED
80160007h	–2146041849	2148925447	IMA_RESULT_CONSTRAINT_VIOLATION
80160008h	–2146041848	2148925448	IMA_RESULT_LDAP_PROTOCOL_ERROR
80160009h	–2146041847	2148925449	IMA_RESULT_LDAP_SERVER_DOWN
8016000Ch	–2146041844	2148925452	IMA_RESULT_NODE_DELETE_DENIED
8016000Fh	–2146041841	2148925455	IMA_RESULT_CANNOTCHANGE_PASSWORD
80160010h	–2146041840	2148925456	IMA_RESULT_CANNOTCHANGE_LAST_RW
80160011h	–2146041839	2148925457	IMA_RESULT_LOGON_USER_DISABLED
80160012h	–2146041838	2148925458	IMA_RESULT_CMC_CONNECTION_DISABLED
80160013h	–2146041837	2148925459	IMA_RESULT_INSUFFICIENT_SERVER_SEC_ FOR_USER
80160014h	–2146041836	2148925460	IMA_RESULT_FEATURE_LICENSE_NOT_FOUND
80160015h	–2146041835	2148925461	IMA_RESULT_DISALLOW_CMC_LOGON
80260001h	–2144993279	2149974017	IMA_RESULT_NW_PRINT_SERVER_ALREADY_ PRESENT
80260002h	–2144993278	2149974018	IMA_RESULT_SERVER_ALREADY_PRESENT
802D0001h	–2144534527	2150432769	IMA_RESULT_TABLE_NOT_FOUND
802D0002h	–2144534526	2150432770	IMA_RESULT_NOT_TABLE_OWNER
802D0003h	–2144534525	2150432771	IMA_RESULT_INVALID_QUERY
802D0004h	–2144534524	2150432772	IMA_RESULT_TABLE_OWNER_HAS_CHANGED
802D0005h	–2144534523	2150432773	IMA_RESULT_SERVICE_NOT_AVAILABLE
802D0006h	–2144534522	2150432774	IMA_RESULT_ZONE_MASTER_UNKNOWN
802D0007h	–2144534521	2150432775	IMA_RESULT_NON_UNIQUE_HOSTID
802D0008h	–2144534520	2150432776	IMA_RESULT_REG_VALUE_NOT_FOUND
802D0009h	–2144534519	2150432777	IMA_RESULT_PARTIAL_LOAD
802D000Ah	–2144534518	2150432778	IMA_RESULT_GATEWAY_NOT_ESTABLISHED
802D000Bh	–2144534517	2150432779	IMA_RESULT_INVALID_GATEWAY
802D000Ch	–2144534516	2150432780	IMA_RESULT_SERVER_NOT_AVAILABLE

Table A-1 IMA Error Codes (*continued*)

Hex Value	Signed Value	Unsigned Value	Mnemonic
80300001h	–2144337919	2150629377	IMA_RESULT_SERVICE_NOT_SUPPORTED
80300002h	–2144337920	2150629378	IMA_RESULT_BUILD_SD_FAILED
80300003h	–2144337921	2150629379	IMA_RESULT_RPC_USE_ENDPOINT_FAILED
80300004h	–2144337922	2150629380	IMA_RESULT_RPC_REG_INTERFACE_FAILED
80300005h	–2144337923	2150629381	IMA_RESULT_RPC_LISTEN_FAILED
80300006h	–2144337924	2150629382	IMA_RESULT_BUILD_FILTER_FAILED
80300007h	–2144337925	2150629383	IMA_RESULT_RPC_BUFFER_TOO_SMALL
80300008h	–2144337926	2150629384	IMA_RESULT_REQUEST_TICKET_FAILED
80300009h	–2144337927	2150629385	IMA_RESULT_INVALID_TICKET
8030000Ah	–2144337928	2150629386	IMA_RESULT_LOAD_TICKETDLL_FAILED

Table A-1 IMA Error Codes (*continued*)

XENAPP SERVER EVENT LOG ERROR MESSAGES

Table A-2 lists the event log error messages created in the Windows 2003 Server Event viewer by XenApp.

Message ID	Message Text
3584	Failed to open system registry key with error %1
3585	Failed to initialize registrar component with error %1
3586	Failed to prepare the transport system for operation with error %1
3587	Incompatible Winsock version
3588	Failed to prepare the messaging system for operation with error %1
3589	Invalid FailedComponentId (%1)
3590	Failed to prepare the plugin system with error %1
3591	Failed to initialize all components with error %1

Table A-2 Event Log Error Messages

Message ID	Message Text
3592	Failed to start transport with error %1
3593	Failed to create a new message port with error %1
3600	Failed to create an event queue with error %1
3601	Failed to load initial plugins with error %1
3602	Failed to unload initial plugin with error %1
3603	Failed to unload subsystems with error %2
3604	Failed to destroy system event queue with error %1
3605	Failed to stop transport with error %1
3606	Failed to stop system with error %1
3607	Failed to uninitialize system with error %1
3608	Failed to start system with error %1
3609	Failed to load plugin %1 with error %2
3610	Failed to initiate RPC for Remote Access Subsystem with error %1
3611	Failed to connect to the database. Error - %1 Increase the number of processes available to the database. See MetaFrame XP documentation for details.
3612	The server running MetaFrame Presentation Server failed to connect to the data store %1. Invalid database user name or password. Please Make sure they are correct. If not, use DSMAINT CONFIG to change them.
3613	Failed to connect to the database with error. Error - %1. The ACCESS. mdb file is missing.
3614	The server running MetaFrame Presentation Server failed to connect to the data store. Error - %1. The database is down or a network failure occurred.
3615	The server running MetaFrame Presentation Server failed to connect to the data store. Error - %1. An unknown failure occurred while connecting to the database.
3616	Configuration error: Failed to read the farm name out of the registry on a server configured to access the data store directly.

Table A-2 Event Log Error Messages (*continued*)

Message ID	Message Text
3617	Configuration error: Failed to get the farm name from the data store proxy server with Error - %1. This server is configured to access the data store indirectly. The server specified as the data store proxy is unavailable. Verify that the data store proxy server is accessible and the IMA service is started on it.
3618	Configuration error: Failed to open IMA registry key.
3619	Since last successful connection to the data store, 96 hours have passed. This server will no longer accept connections until successful connection to the data store is established.
3840	Unable to bind to group context in data store. Group consistency check will not run. (Result: %1.)
3841	Unable to locate groups in data store at DN %1. Group consistency check will not run. (Result: %2.)
3842	Group consistency check: Group at DN %1 is missing the GroupMember attribute.
3843	Group consistency check: Group at DN %1 contains reference to an unknown object with type %3 and UID %2.
3844	Group consistency check: Group at DN %3 contains an object with UID %1 and type %2. This object is missing the %4 attribute.
3845	Group consistency check: Group at DN %3 contains an object with UID %1 and type %2. This object is missing the value for the %4 attribute.
3872	Unable to bind to server contexts in data store. Server consistency check will not run. (Result: %1.)
3873	Server consistency check: Unable to locate host records in data store. The server host record consistency check will not run. (Result: %1.)
3874	Server consistency check: Unable to locate common server records in data store. The common server consistency check will not run. (Result: %1.)
3875	Server consistency check: Unable to locate MetaFrame Server records in data store. The MetaFrame server consistency check will not run. (Result: %1.)

Table A-2 Event Log Error Messages (*continued*)

Message ID	Message Text
3876	Server consistency check: Host record for HostName %2 at DN %1 references a common server record that cannot be found in the data store.
3877	Server consistency check: Host record for HostName %2 at DN %1 references a common server record that has a HostName of %3. This mismatch is an error.
3878	Server consistency check: Host record for HostName %2 at DN %1 references a common server record that cannot be found in the data store. (Result: %3.)
3879	Server consistency check: Common server record for HostName %2 at DN %1 references a host record that cannot be found in the data store.
3880	Server consistency check: Common server record for HostName %2 at DN %1 has a HostID of %3. The corresponding host record has a HostID of %4. This mismatch is an error.
3881	Server consistency check: Common server record for HostName %2 at DN %1 references a host record that cannot be found in the data store. (Result: %3.)
3882	Server consistency check: The common server record with HostName %1 at DN %2 is invalid. There is no registered server product for this record.
3883	Server consistency check: The common server record with HostName %1 at DN %2 is invalid. The corresponding MetaFrame Server record cannot be accessed.
3884	Server consistency check: The MetaFrame Server record with HostName %1 at DN %2 is invalid. The associated common server UID is not set.
3885	Server consistency check: The MetaFrame Server record with HostName %1 at DN %2 is invalid. The associated common server record cannot be accessed.
3886	Server consistency check: The MetaFrame Server record with HostName %1 at DN %2 may be invalid. The MetaFrame Server record HostID of %3 does not match the common server record HostID of %4.

Table A-2 Event Log Error Messages (*continued*)

Message ID	Message Text
3887	Server consistency check: The MetaFrame Server record with HostName %1 at DN %2 is invalid. The associated common server record has a different HostName (%3).
3888	Server consistency check: Unable to locate Load Manager for MetaFrame XP server entry for HostName %1. (Result: %2.)
3889	Server consistency check: The MetaFrame Server record with HostName %1 at DN %2 may be invalid. The Load Manager for MetaFrame XP server entry was not found.
3890	Server consistency check: The MetaFrame Server record with HostName %1 at DN %2 is invalid. The associated Account Authority Server record was not found.
3904	Unable to bind to application contexts in data store. Application consistency check will not run. (Result: %1.)
3905	Application consistency check: Unable to locate common application records in the data store. Common application consistency check will not run. (Result: %1.)
3906	Application consistency check: Unable to locate MetaFrame application records in the data store. MetaFrame application consistency check will not run. (Result: %1.)
3907	Application consistency check: The common application record at DN %1 does not have a Friendly Name. (Result: %2.)
3908	Application consistency check: The common application record at DN %1 does not have a Browser Name. (Result: %2.)
3909	Application consistency check: The common application record with Friendly Name %1 at DN %2 does not have a specialized application UID. (Result: %3.)
3910	Application consistency check: The common application record with Friendly Name %1 at DN %2 references a MetaFrame application record that cannot be accessed. (Result: %3.)
3911	Application consistency check: The common application record with Friendly Name %1 at DN %2 references a MetaFrame application record. This record does not have a Friendly Name. (Result: %3.)
3912	Application consistency check: The common application record with Friendly Name %1 at DN %2 references a MetaFrame application record. This record does not have a Browser Name. (Result: %3.)

Table A-2 Event Log Error Messages (*continued*)

Message ID	Message Text
3913	Application consistency check: The common application record at DN %2 has a Friendly Name of %1. The corresponding MetaFrame application record has a Friendly Name of %3. This mismatch is an error.
3914	Application consistency check: The common application record at DN %2 has a Browser Name of %1. The corresponding MetaFrame application record has a Browser Name of %3. This mismatch is an error.
3915	Application consistency check: The MetaFrame application record at DN %1 does not have a Friendly Name. (Result: %2.)
3916	Application consistency check: The MetaFrame application record at DN %1 does not have a Browser Name. (Result: %2.)
3917	Application consistency check: The MetaFrame application record with Friendly Name %1 at DN %2 does not have a common application UID. (Result: %3.)
3918	Application consistency check: The MetaFrame application record with Friendly Name %1 at DN %2 references a common application record (UID %3) that cannot be accessed. (Result: %4.)
3919	Application consistency check: The MetaFrame application record with Friendly Name %1 at DN %2 references a common application record. This record does not have a Friendly Name. (Result: %3.)
3920	Application consistency check: The MetaFrame application record with Friendly Name %1 at DN %2 references a common application record. This record does not have a Browser Name. (Result: %3.)
3921	Application consistency check: The MetaFrame application record at DN %2 has a Friendly Name of %1. The corresponding common application record has a Friendly Name of %3. This mismatch is an error.
3922	Application consistency check: The MetaFrame application record at DN %2 has a Browser Name of %1. The corresponding common application record has a Browser Name of %3. This mismatch is an error.
3936	Common application cleanup, deleting record at DN <%1>.
3937	MetaFrame application cleanup, deleting record at DN <%1>.
3938	MetaFrame server cleanup, deleting record at DN <%1>.

Table A-2 Event Log Error Messages (*continued*)

Message ID	Message Text
3939	Common server cleanup, deleting record at DN <%1>.
3940	Server host record cleanup, deleting record at DN <%1>.
3952	Unable to open Citrix Runtime registry key. Application terminated. (Status: %1.)
3953	Unable to read Neighborhood name from registry. Application terminated. (Status: %1.)
3954	Unable to initialize data store connection. This server must have a direct connection to the data store. Application terminated. (Result: %1.)
3956	Data store validation utility. Version: %1.
3957	Unable to initialize event log. Messages will be displayed on console only.
3958	%1 [/Clean] Perform validation checks on a MetaFrame farm's data store. Results will be displayed on the console and also entered into the event log. The /Clean option will delete records that are inconsistent. The data store should be backed up prior to using the /Clean option.
3959	All consistency checks were successful.
3960	Some consistency checks were unsuccessful. The following results indicate the number of errors or –1 for test not run: Server errors = %1, application errors = %2, group errors = %3.
3961	The data collector is out of memory, and the Dynamic Store data might be out of sync. Please elect a new data collector and make sure you have enough memory on the new data collector.
3968	Buffer overrun detected.
3969	Error occurred during uninstall. Some objects may not have been removed from the data store properly. Subsystem id = %1, error = %2. Please verify data store consistency.

Table A-2 Event Log Error Messages (*continued*)

APPENDIX B

Registered Citrix Ports

Table B-1 provides a complete listing of the various registered ports and private enterprise numbers (SNMP MIB) for XenApp. For detailed illustrations of ports used in cross-component connections and communications see the Citrix Knowledge Center article CTX109929.

NOTE The Access Management Console uses MSRPC on port 135 for communications.

Name	Number	Protocol	Description
ica	1494	TCP	ICA
ica	1494	UDP	Not used
ica	0x85BB	IPX	ICA
ica	0x9010	SPX	ICA
icabrowser	1604	TCP	Not used
icabrowser	1604	UDP	ICA Browser
icabrowser	0x85BA	IPX	ICA Browser
citrixima	2512	TCP	IMA (server to server)
citrixima	2512	UDP	Not used
citrixadmin	2513	TCP	IMA (Presentation Server Console to server)
citrixadmin	2513	UDP	Not used
citriximaclient	2598	TCP	Session Reliability
citriximaclient	2598	UDP	Not used
citrix-rtmp	2897	TCP	RTMP (Control) Video Frame
citrix-rtmp	2897	UDP	RTMP (Streaming Data) Video Frame
Citrix Systems	3845	MIB	Private Enterprise Number. Used for Simple Network Management Protocol (SNMP) MIB object ID and Active Directory Schema Object IDs (OID).

Table B-1. Registered Citrix Ports

APPENDIX C

Tested Hardware

The following hardware was used in the Citrix eLabs for testing XenApp Platinum Edition.

SERVERS

Dell OptiPlex GX1	Dell OptiPlex Gxa	Dell PowerEdge 1400	Dell PowerEdge 1600SC
Dell PowerEdge 1655MC	Dell PowerEdge 1650	Dell PowerEdge 1750	Dell PowerEdge 1800
Dell PowerEdge 1850	Dell PowerEdge 1855	Dell PowerEdge 2650	Dell PowerEdge 2850
Dell PowerEdge 6650	Dell Precision 220 machines	Dell Precision 340	Dell Precision 360
Hewlett Packard (HP) NetServer E60	HP NetServer LXe Pro	HP TC4100	HP Aero
HP Deskpro DPENM	HP Deskpro DPEND	HP Deskpro EN SFF	HP Proliant DL320
HP Proliant DL360	HP Proliant DL380	HP Proliant DL580	HP EVO T20
HP Proliant 1850R	HP Proliant 800	HP Proliant 8500R	HP Proliant ML330
HP Proliant ML350	HP Proliant BL20p	HP Proliant BL25p	HP Proliant BL30p
HP Proliant BL35p	HP Proliant BL40p	HP Proliant ML150	HP Proliant DL360
HP Proliant DL585	HP XW 4400	IBM BladeCenter HS20	IBM IntelliStation APro
IBM IntelliStation EPro	IBM IntelliStation MPro	IBM NetFinity 3000	IBM NetFinity 3500 M10
IBM NetFinity 3500 M20	IBM NetFinity 5500	IBM xSeries 226	IBM xSeries 325
IBM xSeries 335	IBM xSeries 336	IBM xSeries 440	

CLIENT MACHINES

Acer Power Sd—PIV	Acer TravelMate C100	Acer TravelMate C110	Apple iMac
Apple Power MAC G4	Apple PowerBook G4	Fujitsu LifeBook P Series	Fujitsu Stylist IC 4100
Fujitsu Stylistic ST4000 tablet PC	HP Jornada	HP TabletPC	IBM IntelliStation M-Series
IBM IntelliStation E-Series	IBM ThinkPad R32	Sun Blade 150	Sun Ultra 5
Toshiba Portege 3500	ViewSonic Airpanel 100	Wyse Winterms WT9450, WT1200LE	

TWAIN TESTING

Canon CanonScan 3200F	Epson Perfection 3170 Photo—USB	Hewlett Packard OfficeJet 7130 All-in-One
HP ScanJet 8290	Microtek ScanMaker 5950—USB	QuickCam Messenger Logitech
Visioneer OneTouch 9320	Xerox DocuMate 510	

CLIENT PERIPHERAL DEVICE

HHP USB Barcode Scanner

FOR PDA SYNCHRONIZATION

Dell AXIM X5	HP iPAQ h4350	HP iPAQ h4150

NOTE The devices used to test the PDA Synchronization feature are not the only devices supported for this feature. See Citrix Knowledge Center articles CTX114161 and CTX821115 for more information.

STRONG AUTHENTICATION

Axalto: Reflex 72 Reader, Reflex USB Reader, Reflex Reader V3
all with Cyberflex Access Card 64K (V2c)

GemPlus: GemPlus Serial GemPC410, GemPC 430 USB, GemPC USB SL
all with GemSafe Logon Card

Identix Biometric Login USB devices (fingerprint)

Panasonic PrivateID iris-scan

Precise Biometrics 100MC fingerprint readers (USB)

Startek fingerprint reader (USB)

Xyloc XC-2 with Xyloc [Ensure Technology] Proximity Badge

BIDIRECTIONAL AUDIO DEVICES

Philips SpeechMike 6174

Philips SpeechMike 6184

Philips SpeechMike Classic 6164

Philips SpeechMike Pro 6284

WIRELESS NETWORK INTERFACE CARDS

Cisco Aircards (802.11b)

DLink DWL-650+ Wireless Card (22MB)

Sierra Wireless PCMCIA cards

PRINTERS

Dell Laser 1700n	Dell Laser 3100cn	Dell Workgroup Laser M5200	Dell Workgroup Laser W5300
Dell Laser 5100cn	HP Color LaserJet 4550DN	HP DesignJet 5000	HP DeskJet 5550
HP DeskJet 5700	HP DeskJet 5740	HP DeskJet 6540	HP DeskJet 5650
HP DeskJet 6122	HP LaserJet 4600	HP LaserJet 4200	HP Business InkJet 1100
HP Business InkJet 2300	Lexmark All-in-One X6170 Inkjet	Ricoh Afficio CL-7100 with two-tray finisher and duplex unit	

NETWORKING DEVICES

Alteon 2424 Load Balancer	Checkpoint Firewall-1 Firewall	Cisco Wireless WAP
Cisco LocalDirector 416	Cisco PIX 515 Firewall Appliance	EMC Celerra SE
F5 BigIP 540 Load Balancer	Gateway ALR 7200	HP ProCurve Switches
HP StorageWorks FC-AL Switch	HP StorageWorks RA4100	HP StorageWorks MSA1000
HP StorageWorks MSA1500	HP TaskSmart N2400	Lucent NavisRadius
Lucent Pipeline ISDN Router	NCipher nForce SSL Accelerator Card	Net6 SSL VPN
Nortel Networks Alteon 184 hardware load balancer	Nortel Networks Alteon Application Switch 2424 load balancing device	Packeteer AppVantage ASM-70
Packeteer PacketShaper 2500	Packeteer Packetshaper 4500	Rainbow CryptoSwift 200 SSL Accelerator Cards
Rainbow CryptoSwift 600 SSL Accelerator Cards	RSA SecurID	Secure Computing Gauntlet G2 Firewall
Secure Computing SafeWord	Shunra Storm	

INDEX

B

C

D

E

F

G

H

I

J

K

L

M

N

O

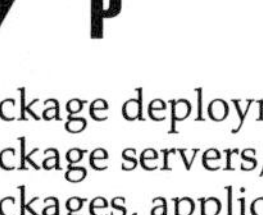

P

Q

R

S

T

 U

V

W

X

Y

Z